Drag-Free Drifts

Fifty Years of Fly Fishing Trips

Hal W. Gordon

To Jean, Bethany and Grady

And to all the fish I've become attached too

Table of Contents

Acknowledgements

This work would never have been possible without the contributions of family and friends who have blessed my life. A special thanks to Don Nelson at the River City Fly Shop, who tested my fly tying skills and provided an endless supply of tying material; the guys at Washington County Fly Fishers who provided lively discussion and fishing; Bob Kloskowski, founder of the International Fly Fishing Association who provided opportunities to meet and fish with fine people throughout the world; Steve Stevenson who graciously invited me deer hunting over a decade (which over time turned into fishing trips); The many fly tyers at the Oregon Council Federation of Fly Fishers - Fly Tyers Expo; Wayne Bell who taught me to tie my first fly at age twelve; Bethany Gordon my editor and publisher; my children Bethany and Grady who helped me understand the true meaning of life; and finally my gracious wife Jean who lovingly allows me to pursue my passion.

Preface

At the end of life one should not arrive at the grave with an un-scathed body, but rather slide in sideways, worn out, roughed-up, and screaming "what a ride!" I've fished from Alaska to New Zealand and from Samoa to South Carolina. It's been my passion to fish often and everywhere. I may not spend as much time on the water as others, but when the opportunity arises I rarely turn down an invitation. Years ago I was challenged by Art Nelson, my high school science teacher, to keep a detailed account of my fishing exploits. This is not a book of essays or short stories. This text is a compilation of a lifetime's worth of hand-written notes and photographs. It is a journal of lifelong experiences written to instruct, entertain, enlighten, and hopefully be of historical interest in the distant future. Many entries were letters to fishing partners, family, and friends. My intentions are not to brag about my fishing prowess, I am just an average fisherman. Hopefully you will find portions entertaining and, at minimum, gain empathy for the obsessed and irrational behavior of many fly fishermen. There are a few non-fishing stories I found amusing, but most entries are about fishing my home waters in Oregon. At the request of a few fishing partners who have shared their favorite waters with me, I have kept some information vague with the hope of not advertizing their special locations. However, lake and river conditions change so rapidly than any specific fishing locations are relatively meaningless in the long run. Most of my fishing is on well known public waters with adequate access and room to spread around and find solitude. This journal is not intended to be a guide on where or how to catch fish - you need to discover your own water and develop your own techniques. I share my fishing locations and methods with you having faith that you will have success and in turn develop a deeper appreciation of our precious fisheries and renew your efforts to improve and protect them. My intention was to document my experiences for posterity and re-live memorable fishing trips when I'm confined to a rocking chair in my senior years.

Hal Gordon
Aloha, Oregon

Drag-Free Drifts

Fifty Years of Fly Fishing Trips

1961 – 1979

Spring, 1961
I was born in Salt Lake City, Utah and grew up in Bountiful, Utah. I was the second of five children and had three brothers and one sister. My father grew up in the city and my mother was raised on a ranch. My parents compromised by living on the edge of town, but within walking distance of farms and the national forest.

May 1967
I've always been drawn to moving water and caught my first fish when I was six years old. My family had a picnic up Mueller Canyon east of Bountiful, Utah. I begged a few hooks, leader and a couple of feet of kite string from my dad and tied it all to a long willow stick and headed to the creek. I turned over a few rocks, found a small worm, threaded it on the hook and threw it into a small pool. A few seconds later I flipped a fat little trout onto the stream bank but he slipped off the hook and flipped back into the water. I desperately tried to grab him but failed. I was very disappointed and did not catch another fish the rest of the day.

July, 1969
My grandfather Nebeker took my brother Jay and me camping at our old family ranch up Conner Basin near Flaming Gorge, Utah. We slept in an ancient canvas tent and warmed by an old sheep herders wood-stove my grandfather had been using since the depression. We spent several days searching for arrowheads and fishing for trout in Sheep Creek. The small creek was easily waded and meandered through pine forest and meadow. There were deep pools on the outside corners that were full of eager trout. My grandfather taught us to cast with old rusted steel telescopic fly rods and brown braided fly line. At first we used live grasshoppers but later graduated to flies. We literally caught "gunny sacks" full of skinny trout

with large heads. It was obvious the stream was overstocked and not healthy. My grandfather explained that the growth of fish was stunted because there were too many fish and not enough food. He insisted we keep a few fish for dinner to keep things in balance.

Fish Camp, Sheep Creek, Utah

We cooked them over a fire in tin foil. This was one of the trips in which my grandfather taught me about the outdoors, self-sufficiency and how to "make do or do without."

June 1970
My first fishing rod was a four foot green fiberglass casting rod with a Zebco reel. I picked it out of a barrel in the back of Scotty's Grocery-Hardware store in Bountiful, Utah. I practiced casting on my front lawn for hours. A few months later my grandfather gave me an old sheet-metal aluminum fly reel. I turned my fishing pole into a fly rod by cutting off the handle and thumb-rest with a hacksaw and sliding the cork handle down the rod. It worked pretty well for ten foot casts in

brush over grown small creeks near home. I caught a lot of trout, over the years, with that rod.

July 1970

The nearest fishing was two miles from our home on Centerville Creek in the Wasatch National Forest. My mother would drop me off at the base of the canyon for a day's worth of hiking and fishing. I mostly fished alone, but sometimes I took my younger brother Keith or a friend. If I was lucky my mother would pick me up at the end of the day, but most of the time I walked home. I spent three or four days a month during the summer up Centerville Canyon until I graduated from high school. I grew to know the canyon fairly well. On a good day I caught three trout, other days only one. On occasion we were "skunked." We had to work hard for our fish. Grasshoppers made the best bait, unless we found fishing flies along the creek. The trout were all wild rainbows, six inches to a foot long. During thunder storms we took cover in several small caves or an old mine tunnel a mile or so up the canyon. About two miles up the canyon grew an old apple tree where we built a fire and cooked trout in tin foil with wild garlic picked from the south slope of the canyon. We ate green apples, salmon berries, choke cherries and Oregon grape until we were sick. We read all the Field and Stream and Outdoor Life magazine articles about wilderness survival and prided ourselves in "living off the land." These were good times even though I was sunburnt and itchy from poison ivy most of the summer.

October 1970

I attended J. A. Taylor Elementary School, a three-quarter mile walk from home. When I was in fourth grade my friend Mark Whitney and I found a dead skunk in the middle of the road. Mark offered me a quarter if I'd kick the skunk. I was wearing my brother's shoes because mine were wet from the day before. I gave the skunk a good swift kick. Mark paid up, I got my quarter and we continued off to school. Miss Gillespie, my class, the rest of the school and the principal could not figure out where the smell was coming from. They checked all the vents, duct-work and crawl space under the school and found nothing. Just before lunch the school janitor discovered the source of the smell and hauled me to the principal's office. The principal tried to give me a

stern lecture while holding back a smile. He called my mom on the phone and she told him to keep me barefoot at school and that I should walk home as usual at the end of the day. Later I helped the janitor bury my shoes (my brother's shoes) near the flagpole in front of the school.

April 1971

I didn't spend all my free time fishing. I played left field and third base on our city league baseball team from age ten to fourteen. My parents also made each kid in our family take piano lessons for five years. I hated every minute of it. In later years I took up the harmonica but only for playing alone around campfires.

July 1971

My mother and I discovered a small bluegill pond hidden in a grove of trees on the frontage road a few miles from our house. My mother would drop my younger brother and me off for an afternoon of fishing. We caught dozens of small bluegills, the biggest fish was five inches long. We used small wet flies and short lengths of fly line and caught the most fish in the shadows of cottonwood trees. Much of the water filling the pond came from a broken irrigation pipeline that bubbled up through a small pocket of white sand.

May 1972

At age eleven, I was introduced to fly tying by one of my Webelos scout leaders. He was a beginner himself, but his enthusiasm was contagious. I earned enough money mowing lawns to buy my first fly tying kit, mail ordered from Herters Catalog. My grandfather raised pheasants and chickens and was also a hunter, so he provided fur and feathers for my first flies. I also made a deal with the neighbors down the road. I killed, skinned and cleaned their chickens in exchange for the feathers. I had a dozen rooster skins by the end of the summer.

July 1972

Our family was vacationing at a ranch near Mt. Pleasant, Utah. At breakfast the owner introduced us to Grandpa Jukes, the voice of God in the Charlton Hesston movie The Ten Commandments. We spoke for a few minutes, then in his low, very deep voice he re-enacted his most famous lines from the movie: "Take thy shoes from off thy feet, for the ground on which thou standist is holy ground". It really impressed me and I think of it often.

August 1972

Scott Johansen, a neighbor friend my age, and I tried to hike to the summit of Centerville Canyon where we heard there were several beaver ponds. The trail petered out about halfway up the canyon so we forged our own trail about a mile along the creek. The creek was difficult to fish, the fast cold water and steep gradient limited each pool to one fish. We discovered a twenty yard run that was unusually full of trout and gave up our quest for the summit. We spent the rest of the day drifting worm, beetles and caddis larva in front of nervous rainbows. We saw them, they saw us but there was no place for them to go but sulk in the undercut willow bank. We caught a few fish and spooked twice as many more. We soon discovered that if we were going to find the beaver ponds, it was not by hiking up the canyon. We'd have to hike from the road at the ridge top down.

May 1973

I survived elementary school after enduring a hippy-chick from San Francisco who tried to teach us macramé in third grade and a part-time potato farmer who had permission from our parents to slap our knuckles with a ruler if we misbehaved in sixth grade. We had to walk a mile to school and often cut through Mr. Session's fields to save time. Mr. Sessions did not appreciate our trails and when he did catch us he threatened to tell our parents (which he never did). He sported a shotgun during pheasant season that shook us up a little.

May 1973

I signed up for the Boy Scout fishing merit badge and made an appointment with Wayne Bell to complete the requirements. He volunteered to teach me to tie flies and we met the following week in his basement workshop to tie. He tied simple, basic flies to catch fish and was a patient instructor. He was "old school" and stored all his tying materials in canning jars with mothballs. He heavily waxed the tying thread, did not use a bobbin and tied a knot after each piece of material was lashed onto a fly. He was not interested in tying "pretty" flys but tyed flys to catch fish. His favorite fly was a #14 Renegade, and we tied a half dozen that evening and I was hooked (pun

intended). We tied a few more times over the summer and I really appreciated his time and patience as he opened up the world of fly tying.

June 1973

My friends and I finally made it to the beaver ponds at the summit of Centerville Canyon by convincing my mother to drive us there via Highland Drive, which ran from Bountiful to Farmington. There were still a few scattered snow banks along the road but nothing to worry about. I jumped out of the car, ran to the edge of the beaver dam and cast my fly and bubble toward the deepest part of the pond. Several casts later I hooked the first fish.

Beaver Ponds, Centerville Creek, Utah

He seemed to get bigger as I reeled him in. There were two fish on the line. The first trout took my fly and the second got hooked on the open brass swivel. Next trip I decided I needed to tie a fly with all brass wire.

July 1973

My family took a vacation to Yellowstone National Park and we rented a cabin near Fishing Bridge. We fished the south shore of West Thumb, on Yellowstone Lake. The beach was sandy and sloped off to about four feet deep fifty yards out into the lake. We began spin casting #10 Wooly Worms behind egg bubbles half filled with water for casting weight. We did not catch any fish. Next I tied on a #8 Muddler Minnow six feet below the bubble and filled the bubble completely with water so it would sink. I heaved the rig as far as the eight pound line would handle and let the bubble sink to the sandy bottom. I hoped the deer hair muddler would float a foot or so above the bottom of the lake and not snag. It worked. I caught a monster eighteen inch Yellowstone Cutthroat who put up a real fight. I beached him on the sandy shore and was ready for another one. We caught and released another dozen trout ranging from two to five pounds that morning, all great fish. We only fished one day and spent the rest of the week sightseeing the geysers, mud pots, waterfalls and wildlife.

July 1973
Most of my lake fishing was with a four piece Eagle Claw backpacking rod and a Mitchell 300 spinning reel. The technique was simple and very effective. I would slip a plastic egg float (the kind with the center pin that pops out and is filled half full with water) on eight pound line so it would slide up and down the line. Next, I would attach a barrel swivel to the line to keep the float from sliding off the line. Then I would attach six feet of five pound leader to the swivel, and finally tied on a wet fly. The weight of the egg float allows casts of over 100 feet. Because the float slides up the line when a fish takes the fly deep into the water, and creates no drag, the fish fight hard and the technique is sporting. The best retrieve is slow, barely creating a wake on the lake surface, and while reeling a little lop sided to give the fly a pulsating action. In calm water I would reel slower, and in windy water with ripples reel a little faster. My favorite flys were a #12 Wooly Worm and a #14 Renegade.

August 1973
I participated in my local Scout Troop 569 and never missed an opportunity to camp and fish. We had great scout leaders and almost two dozen scouts in out troop. Most of our gear came from the Army Surplus store including my five pound steel and canvas pack. We spent a week hiking and fishing the small alpine lakes in the Uinta Mountains in northeastern Utah. Early Monday morning we drove to the trailhead at Spirit Lake and hiked into Tamarack, Fish and Burnt Fork Lakes. Every day we would each catch over a hundred rainbow or cutthroat trout. We usually kept two or three fish for dinner, and released the rest. We started out fishing with spinning rods and an egg slip bubble, swivel and six feet of leader, and graduated to fly rods when we could get close enough to see fish. The best flies were #12

Renegades and #12 Wooly Worms. We worked especially hard to catch the recently planted grayling in Spirit Lake but were not successful.

September 1973
There was a large apple orchard just west of my home where we would spend hours climbing trees and eating green apples. My first paid job was picking apples for J.C. Bangerter, who paid fifty cents a bushel. I could pick about ten bushels per day. We also pruned, irrigated and sprayed the orchard and picked onions, beans and radishes. Later, J.C. offered me a job working in the potato warehouse, cleaning, sorting and packaging. In the summer and fall I started work at 5am in the warehouse and after school in the orchard. Many of the other employees were ex-convicts. It was an interesting and educational job for a teenager.

September 1973
I was fascinated with bugs and fish. My junior high school science fair project was to identify what small stream trout ate. I went fishing up Centerville Creek for three months and collected the stomach contents of several trout each week. I preserved the samples in alcohol, identified the insects and wrote a report. That same summer I found and brought a praying mantis egg cluster (that looked like foam insulation) into my bedroom for observation. After the eggs warmed up over a week the little creatures thought it was spring and hatched. About a thousand quarter inch mantises began crawling around my room and eventually the whole house. They were very difficult to capture, but took care of themselves in a few days by cannibalizing each other. My family was not impressed.

May 1974
I'd asked for a fly rod for my birthday and my parents gave me a nine foot, two piece, seven weight fiberglass rod. I added a floating line to my grandfather's old fly reel and begged them to take me to some real fly water. The family packed a lunch and we headed up Provo Canyon to the Provo River. I headed to some likely looking water and tied on a #12 Dry Renegade. After an hour of frothing the water I finally saw a fish poke up and take a look at my fly. A couple of casts later I hooked a 11 inch rainbow, my first dry fly fish on a real fly rod (not counting my grandfathers steel telescopic fly rod). I let the fish

go and started planning my next trip to the Provo River.

June 1974
I spent part of three summers working for my uncle Glen Nebeker in the national parks of southern Utah, collecting lichens, moss and plants. We spent the most time in Arches, Capitol Reef and Zion National Parks, hiking into remote areas, to measure lichen growth and collecting plant and rock samples.

Zion National Park, Utah

Glen was working on his Masters degree and was measuring the accumulation of pollutants in lichens over decades. He was also collecting plant samples and weather data for other projects. My job was to backpack the plant materials to the truck. My pay was meals, a tent and a promise of unlimited fishing. My uncle made good on that last promise and most nights we caught fish. We'd play the game "I bet ya can't catch a fish there…", and then pulled trout out of the smallest puddle of water in the desert. We also hiked into many Indian cliff ruins and found several arrowheads.

June 1974
My uncle Glen and I found a small lake just south of Shay Mountain in the Abajo Mountains, east of Monticello, Utah. We camped there for a week. The lake was swampy and surrounded by cattails. Each evening, bats appeared by the dozens and fed on insects flying over the lake. We caught a few fat rainbows on #12 Woolley Worms, and almost hooked a few bats. Glen slept in the back of his truck and I pitched a small tent and enjoyed the cool air, stars and night sounds.

July 1974
Uncle Glen and I spent several days tromping through the foothills around Panguitch, Utah collecting lichens for Glen's graduate work. Several hundred acres of juniper had been recently chained and were lying on the ground, roots up. Porcupines were everywhere and we chased a few down to see what they would do. They just stared at us. I found an arrowhead and a few obsidian flakes. Each evening after work we fished Panguitch Lake and caught several dozen two and three pound rainbows on #12 Renegades near the boat ramp. Fish were rising all over the lake and fishing was easy. We kept a couple of trout for dinner each night. They were large enough to fill a large frying pan.

Rainbow Trout Dinner, Panguitch, Utah

After eating corned beef hash the last few days fresh trout was a welcome change. My mother was fearful that we would starve so before each trip she would fill a box with canned food and day old bakery goods (the kind with so many preservatives they never go bad). We never went hungry, but we also never ate well. We were so broke that is was a real treat was getting a half pound bag of salted sunflower seeds at the grocery store and spitting the seeds out the window of Glen's pick-up.

July 1974
Glen and I were working in southern Utah near Bryce Canyon National Park when we crossed the Hatch River for the first time. At 60 mph the water looked good so Glen pulled off the highway and we rigged up our fly rods. The river came out of a canyon, entered a culvert under the highway and dumped into a large deep hole. We parked on the side of the road. The land was not posted so we jumped the barbed wire fence and fished. On

the first cast I caught a nice brook trout. My uncle took his fly rod and headed downstream to fish the undercut banks in an overgrazed meadow. The cows that used to be in the pasture had left behind very little grass, lots of thistles and stream banks that were eroded and sloughed off into the river.

Brown Trout, Hatch River, Utah

The water did not look promising for trout but several minutes later my uncle whistled and I ran down river just in time to see him land a three pound brown trout. I caught several smaller browns and a few more brookies before we went back on the road.

August 1974
My scout troop spent a week at Camp Steiner near Bald Mountain in the Uinta Mountains. We made several hikes above timberline and one night heard a cougar screaming across the canyon. We fished Scout Lake every evening and watched hundreds of trout dimple the water chasing emerging midges. At the closing camp campfire, I won a trophy for the largest trout caught that week, a sixteen inch brute.

September 1974
My friend Brent Israelson and I spent many weekends riding our bikes and hiking the canyons of the Watach Range between Salt Lake City and Farmington. Brent was raised like an only child because his next nearest sibling was ten years older. His parents always invited me on their camping trips so he had someone his own age to be with. They liked to camp in Utah's Uinta Mountains, mostly at Trial Lake. We hiked and fished all the surrounding lakes and streams, leaving before sun up and getting back to camp after dark. During the morning and evening hours

the trout went nuts chasing midge pupa to the surface of the lake. The creeks were also full of trout, but it seemed no one fished the moving waters in the high mountains. We caught dozens of rainbow, cutthroat and brook trout on wet #12 Renegades. Occasionally the Fish and Game Department stocked albino rainbows in the lakes. We could see the pink-orange fish hundreds of feet away. But try as we might, never caught one.

Trial Lake, Uinta Mountains, Utah

October 1974
Our family took several sightseeing vacations, but never specifically for fishing. I can remember my dad taking me on a camping-fishing trip twice, once to Yellowstone and another time to Strawberry Reservoir, Utah. Early one Saturday morning my dad and I drove with a neighbor to fish East Portal Bay on Strawberry Reservoir. We rigged up #6 Double Renegades and cast them from shore along the thick aquatic weeds. We caught several three to five pound rainbows and cutthroat trout. It was tough keeping them out of the weeds but we managed. In the morning it was easy to walk the frozen mud flats along the shoreline, but the return trip in the late afternoon was more difficult when everything turned to mud. We had mud up to our knees.

November 1974
I hunted deer and pheasant with my father and grandfather Gordon a few times, but did not get my first pheasant until I was thirteen. I was walking home early one morning through the orchard from work at the potato warehouse and saw a cock pheasant hiding at the base of an apple tree. I took my shirt off and used it as a net to

catch him. After ringing his neck I took him home where my mom cooked him for dinner. Luckily, it was the first Saturday of pheasant season so my parents did not chew me out. A few days later my dad took my brother and I to the Farmington Bay Bird Refuge, where I shot another pheasant. After that friends and I began hunting the refuge, working the ditches for pheasants and the open water for ducks. At best we shot a few green wing teal each trip and a couple of pheasants.

April 1975

At age fourteen I went into the fly business. My mother cut a deal with our auto mechanic to let me sell my flies in his repair shop. I made a small wooden box and filled it with wooly worms, double renegades and wet flies. Most of my customers fished Strawberry Reservoir and wanted streamers. I gave away more flies than I sold.

May 1975

My uncle Glen and I camped a few days at a small lake in the shadow of Mt. Thomasaki in the Manti La Sal National Forest east of Moab, Utah. The lake sat in a bowl surrounded by tall pine and was sheltered from the wind. The first evening we caught so many stocked rainbows our arms hurt. The second evening the lake looked like boiling water because there were so many fish, we figured that they must have stocked the fish the previous weekend. Several bait fishermen appeared in the late afternoon and set up rods across the small lake. After an hour of catching nothing they were clearly getting frustrated watching us catch all the fish. Finally they came over and borrowed a few flies and began catching fish. I thought we'd made friends for life the way they were thanking us on their way home.

May 1975

Glen and I got totally lost along the Utah-Colorado border in the Manti La Sal National Forest and finally wandered into an old mining camp. Decades ago, miners had built a two acre pond to store water for the gold sluices. I had a few minutes to fish while Glen asked the camp caretaker for directions back to the main road. Small clumps of floating algae covered the pond making it difficult to drag a fly though the water. The pond was calm and a few large trout were eating insects on the surface. My first couple of

casts were worthless; my fly was covered with a fistful of green slime. I finally put on a dry fly, cast it into relatively open water and let it sit. A fish rose about twenty feet away and I slowly twitched the fly. A minute later he gulped my fly and headed to the bottom, luckily avoiding most of the floating algae. The water was relatively warm and the large brown tired easily. I beached him and was surprised by his age and size. He had a beautifully hooked jaw, weighed about three pounds and must have been at least four years old. I don't think a fish in the entire pond had been caught before. I took a photo, but a few days later dropped my camera in a creek and ruined the film. Glen was in a hurry to get back to civilization so I didn't get another cast into the lake, but I wish we could have stayed and fished.

June 1975

We collected plant samples for several days at Capitol Reef National Park and my uncle Glen picked a campsite near the park on the Aquarius Plateau, near Loa, Utah. There were several high elevation lakes on Boulder Mountain that were rumored to host large brook trout. We were unsuccessful at every single lake. We made up for it on a small creek that ran down the mountain into Bicknell Bottoms that was loaded with small brook trout. Any dry fly worked and we caught a fish on at least every other cast. There were so many trout they were becoming stunted. We threw a few into the brush for the mink and otter. This was Indian country and on a small island in the creek that was covered with sedges I found a very nice six inch stone knife blade, made of red jasper. Southern Utah is known for its pre-historic Indian art.

Petroglyphs, Southern Utah

Working in the southern Utah national parks we found numerous petroglyphs, Indian ruins and artifacts. Water was widespread but not difficult to find and we took advantage of it for swimming and drinking during our long hikes.

July 1975

Glen and I fished the Fremont River, west of Capitol Reef National Park, and caught a few ten inch rainbows. The locals fish this stretch of river heavily and cattle had overgrazed much of the stream bank. Glen could not find the plants he was looking for and we didn't spend much time on the river. It just wasn't right. The cattle should be kept out of the creek. We were headed down the highway when a rancher's stray dog suddenly ran onto the road and we hit him at sixty mph. We pulled over and felt bad, until we saw the dog's owner a half mile away running toward us and we took off. I felt bad, but it was an accident and we did not want to face the dog's owner. We wanted to spend the next few days at Fish Lake, east of Koosharem, Utah, but it was hot and the fishing was poor. We really needed a boat to fish this lake and we did not have one. I caught two small fish and we decided to camp elsewhere.

July 1975

Glen and I spent a few days working near Cedar Breaks National Park. Late one afternoon we were heading back to Cedar City, Utah, when we noticed a small pond a short distance from the road. I talked Glen into pulling over. He took some target shots with his .22 pistol while I rigged up my fly rod. It was not really a pond, more like a small spring that ranchers developed a generation ago for livestock water. It was round, about fifty feet across and appeared to be at least ten feet deep. The moss was thick and trout could be hiding anywhere in the pockets and submerged crevices. There were plenty of bugs to feed a few fish. I hoped that someone planted a few trout in the pond, because there was no other way for them to get there. I crept up to the water with the sun to my back to avoid spooking fish in the bright afternoon sun. Nothing happened after a few casts. I walked a few more feet around the pond for a better casting position and found a large broken white agate Indian spear-point. My luck was going to change. On the next cast a very large trout came slowly out of the depths and snapped at my lure, turned and took a second

look, then sank back into the deep moss. I was disappointed and a little frustrated. This fish was huge, at least twenty inches, and hooked-jawed. He's probably still there enjoying his desert solitude.

August 1975

I spent a week backpacking in the Uinta Mountains in north eastern Utah with my scout troop. We hiked and fished throughout the East Fork of the Bear River basin, and each caught over fifty cutthroat and rainbow trout per day. Our gear was low tech and we were lucky to cast farther than twenty or thirty feet. We hung around stream inlets of lakes and pools in small creeks and always found willing fish. I fished with a #14 Renegade exclusively.

Renegade

May 1976

I graduated from Junior High School, which was an adolescent blur. Most of my education took place during lunch breaks in the library where a couple of buddies and I read *Outdoor Life* and *Field and Stream* magazines. We got into trouble catching seagulls on the football field by putting a piece of bread crust on a large dull barbless hook, attached to twenty feet of fishing line that was tied to a pencil stick in the ground. The poor birds would get hooked in the beak, fly in circles while anchored to the ground, until the hook flipped out of their beaks. The show disrupted our first period class as we watched from our classroom window. Mr. Hires our vice principal finally caught onto what we were doing and we had to look for other ways to disrupt class.

May 1976
My uncle Glen and I worked the canyon lands south of Cedar Breaks National Monument. We had a few days off and were looking for a nice place to camp. We fished Navajo Lake with little success. There were too many tourists and too few fish. After spending so much time in the wilderness it became difficult to deal with people and we decided to camp elsewhere.

June 1976
Glen and I camped a few days at Johnson Reservoir, west of Capitol Reef National Park. We fished where the creek entered the lake. We caught a few trout but fishing was slow. While my uncle was fixing breakfast one morning, I took my fly rod and walked up the creek several hundred yards. I had been practicing casting a fly line and was getting better. The sun was on the hill above the creek but not yet on the water. The smell of sage and rabbit brush filled the air. That morning everything came together. I noticed a nice run along the stream bank below a clump of willows. There had to be a nice fat rainbow in the small slot in the undercut bank. I stood about thirty feet downstream, straightened my leader and put on a dry #12 Renegade. On the first cast I hit the target and a large rainbow took my fly from the surface and made a strong run. I was surprised and excited at the same time, first large river trout on an upstream cast with a dry fly. We had trout for breakfast. I'll always remember that fish.

July 1976
We found excellent fishing in Meadow Creek about twelve miles above Johnson Reservoir, west of Capitol Reef National Park. Glen was collecting grasses and the area was open range with beef cows, sagebrush and no fisherman. We did not have to worry about losing flies on back casts because there were no trees in the open meadow. Dozens of wild brook and a few rainbow trout readily took our deer hair grasshoppers. Glen and I wasted a lot of time on this creek because the fishing was so good.

August 1976
We spent several days working in the Henry Mountains in southeastern Utah, about as far

from civilization as you can get in Utah. Glen collected a number of lichens and mosses and I packed them back to the truck. We looked for fish as we traveled between research sites, but most of the creeks were dry and the rest were just trickles.

Navajo Mountain, Utah

From the top of the mountain we spotted a herd of buffalo in the distance and followed them around for a few hours. We had lunch and sodas in the 100 degree weather of Hanksville, Utah better known for its cowboy outlaws than fishing.

September 1976
Glen and I had been working north-east of Salt Lake City on the Weber River near Devil's Slide collecting plants, when we took a break to fish. For an hour I threw a Muddler Minnow into the fast pocket water with no luck. At a particularly deep hole I put a lead split shot a foot above the fly and threw it upstream into an undercut rock ledge and worked the fly back to my feet. I felt a light tug, set the hook and pulled in the biggest trout I'd ever hooked. He must have been at least five pounds and twenty five inches long, but his head was covered with fungus and apparently he could not see very well. Luckily he broke off next to shore so I did not have to unhook him. It was exciting and disappointing at the same time to see such a large fish where there were few trophy fish.

November 1976
My friends and I hunted birds at Farmington Bay Bird Refuge. We walked the ditches for pheasants and hunted the open water for ducks. At best we shot a couple of green wing teal and a few pheasants. Most of the time we just walked the refuge dikes, enjoying the open fields and marsh land, shooting whatever moved or was a

challenging target. The game warden always kept an eye on us and regularly checked our licenses and gear. We were always legal.

May 1977

I spent the summer working for the Boy Scouts at Bear Lake Aquatics Camp, near Laketown, Utah. I was the trading post manager and had my tent pitched a short cast from the lake. I fished every morning, noon, and evening. About a dozen boys would hang around the trading post in the evening and I taught them how to rig their rods, tie knots and cast. By the end of the week each boy could catch fish on a fly. I was also able to get the camp director to purchase several fly tying kits. We taught an evening fly tying class in the lodge.

Bear Lake Aquatics Camp, Laketown, Utah

There were tons of crayfish in Bear Lake and the staff paid the younger scouts to collect crayfish, a nickel a dozen, so we could have fresh water "lobsters" each Saturday night. The younger scouts had no common sense. One morning a group of boys gathered around a young scout who had caught a small rattlesnake and was playing with it. I ran to rescue the snake. Luckily the boy was not bitten. We caught several rattlers during the summer, some up to four feet long. The best way to find them was to sit in the outhouse in the morning and watch them crawl onto the warm concrete pad at your feet. I quickly discovered it's difficult to run with your pants around your ankles. We also discovered that when you cut their heads off, they would still try to bite several hours later. I would often keep a head in a shoebox at the trading post to show boys this interesting fact. I was the merit badge counselor for wilderness survival and one of the requirements was to eat

ten wild foods. Each boy was required to collect and prepare ten foods. It was easy to catch crayfish, trout, cactus, grass seed, sego lily, and other foods. We were always one item short. The best that I could do was ants, of which there were plenty. After a few phone calls from parents, we had to discontinue this practice. There was a Girl Scout Camp and the Sweetwater Resort twenty miles around the lake and we occasionally thumbed rides to attend the resort dances. I made a friend with one of the resort dishwashers and when it was too late to thumb a ride home he would let me sleep on the floor of his shack. I guess he was not a great friend because he would not lend me a blanket or pillow, but we got along.

June 1977

Early one morning I noticed several large fish working the shallows of Bear Lake about a quarter mile south of camp. I grabbed a fly rod and a couple of scouts and headed down the beach to investigate. We assumed they were carp until we hooked a large sucker fish. They came close to shore and we had no problem putting a fly in front of them. They were slowly cruising and circling in groups of a half dozen fish. They were probably spawning on the sandy flats but it was hard to tell. We had good sport for several days, catching three to five pound fish on light tackle, until they disappeared.

July 1977

We volunteered to help the Pickleville, Utah, Playhouse dig their new septic line trench one Saturday afternoon. They had a live melodrama theater Friday and Saturday nights for the locals and tourists. We were volunteered because our senior staff leader liked the owner's daughter, who was also one of the lead actresses. After digging and installing the pipeline, we received season tickets as long as we wore our scout uniforms and participated in the play. We were required to stand up and cheer for the hero and boo for the villain. The audience thought it was funny. We had a great time and met some fun girls.

August 1977

Bear Lake was large enough that when a thunder storm blew through it created three foot waves on the beach. We would go out "dock riding" by tying a rope to the end of the floating dock and ride out the storm. During one memorable storm, two fancy waterskiing boats broke loose from Sweetwater Resort and drifted across the lake. We set out to rescue the drifting boats from grounding on the rocky shore. Two staff members took out the motor boat, our boss took five of us in the war canoe. He would not let us take out the other motor boat, and said "you'll see" when we asked him why. We tied ropes to the drifting boats and pulled them away from the rocky shore. There was no place to anchor the drifting boats because of the sandy bottom and the buoys had washed onto shore. The motor boat pulled their boat easily while we worked hard in the war canoe keeping our boat safe. During the worst of the storm, the motor boat could not keep up and drifted to shore and damaged the boat on the rocks. We in the war canoe, working together, were able to give just a little more physical energy to save our boat. Sweetwater Resort gave us free weekend passes for saving the boats. We ate at the restaurant, attended a concert, swam in the pool and slept that night on the floor in the dishwasher's cabin. In the morning we began walking the twenty miles back to camp, when our boss picked us up along the highway. We received a mild scolding for not making arrangements for the trip home.

September 1977
In the fall, I discovered Farmington Creek, a secluded small trout fishery. Farmington Canyon was about five miles north of our house and on a bus route (which made mom a little less necessary). The creek was similar to Centerville Creek above our house, but was a little more open. The road up the first mile of the canyon was paved, and then became a rocky, washed out dirt road the rest of the way up to the summit. The locals bait fished the holes along the road but rarely bush wacked the more remote areas. I wet waded every inch of the first three miles of canyon and caught three dozen fish in a day's trip. Granted, the fish were only eight to ten inches long, but they were plentiful, wild and readily took dry flys. My favorite fly was a yellow #14 Muddler Minnow fished dry to imitate grasshoppers. The fish just attacked the fly.

October 1977
I attended Viewmont high school in Bountiful, Utah and worked part time at Dicks Market, in Centerville, as a bagger, stocker and checker. I enjoyed the work and being out of the house as much as possible. The store was a short half mile walk across the farm field behind our house. There were always a few girls my age to hang out with at the store. We worked hard and had fun. I was able to put a lot of money away for college working thirty hours a week. My homework suffered a little but I didn't worry about it.

January 1978
Scott Johansen, a friend of mine since elementary school, had an uncle who was the track coach at our high school and an avid fly fisherman. We talked him into sponsoring a high school Fly Fishing Club and developing a half-credit physical education class that we called "Fly Fishing 101".

Viewmont High School Fly Club, Utah

To keep the administration happy, he made us run a few laps on the track before we practiced casting, tying knots, tying flys and studying entomology. We started out our sophomore year with a dozen students and had over twenty students our junior year. I was responsible for scheduling field trips for the club (which we were allowed one per semester) and fetched the "excused absence" passes from the attendance clerk for our group. Every time I submitted the paperwork for our trips the secretary gave me a funny look, but it was all official. We made a couple of trips to the Ogden River to practice casting and study bugs. The school district caught onto what we were doing and cancelled the class our senior year. Good things can't last forever.

February 1978
One winter day I decided to hike alone up the Wasatch Mountain foothills and see Morgan County. I started at the trailhead just north of Centerville Canyon and hiked up the ridge. Near the first summit I ran into snow three feet deep, but plowed through to the next ridge. Below me, several hundred deer had concentrated in a small valley. Since so many homes were built on the Wasatch Front, most of their winter habitat had disappeared. Finally I made it to Skyline Drive, a gravel road on the ridge. I was disappointed to see snowmobile tracks in the snow. I never did make it to the summit and got home well after dark.

May 1978
During my second year at Bear Lake Aquatics Camp I was the Waterfront Director and counselor for the sailing, rowing, fishing and canoeing merit badges. Having procured several vises and materials the year before from *Herters Catalog*, I taught a fly tying class to about a dozen kids each week.

Cutthroat Trout, Bear Lake, Utah

I was always sunburned due to my fair skin, so I used zinc oxide to protect my nose against blisters in the hot sun. One morning a particular group of scouts gave me a hard time so I told them that the white stuff on my nose was seagull poop and that it was the natural way to prevent sunburn. They believed me and quickly located some poop on the dock and liberally smeared it on their faces. I didn't have the heart to tell them I was joking but had a good laugh with the other staff members. Later, calls came to the boss from angry parents. He chewed me out royally. There were always a few porcupines in camp and we'd scare scouts by advising them to check their sleeping bag before crawling in each night. Everyone knows porcupines love to curl up at the bottom of sleeping bags. We would sneak pine boughs into particularly obnoxious boy's sleeping bags when they weren't watching. We could hear the yells and screams a half mile away when the boys crawled into their bags. It worked a few times each week until they figured it out. The amenities at camp were sparse. We had open roof showers with wood panel walls. One late afternoon a few of us were showering when a thunder storm dumped marble sized hail on us for about ten minutes. A few guys made a run for their tents, but I stayed put holding my towel over my head. It really hurt. We had the opportunity to fish every morning and evening and we caught a lot of nice fish. The fish were mostly twelve to fourteen inches long and readily took a #12 Grizzly Wooly Worm with a red tail. My biggest fish of the summer was 19 inches long, bright silver with a blue back and very few spots. My guess he was a Bear Lake Cutthroat, unique only to Bear Lake.

July 1978
While working at Bear Lake I had weekends to myself and one Friday evening hitchhiked to the top of Logan Canyon and hiked into Tony Grove Lake. The brook trout were thick in the lake and readily took my fly in the evening. The next day I fished the creek back down the canyon and caught dozens of stunted brook trout. On the hike out I heard something big crashing through the brush and quickly stepped off the trail. A big bull moose limbered past me on the trail. He was being chased by two cowboys who were trying to rope him. Luckily they were unsuccessful. I can't imagine what a lassoed moose would do to a couple of guys on horseback. That night I camped under the highway bridge near the top of Logan Canyon. The next morning I walked about five miles before hitching a ride to Garden City with

an old rancher and his wife. I was limping along and I guess they felt sorry for me. I caught another ride back to the scout camp on the eastside of Bear Lake with a hippy couple from California. They asked for a tour of camp and we took a sailboat out on the lake.

August 1978

My friend Brent Israelson picked me up at Bear Lake for a weeklong backpacking and fishing trip to the Wind River Mountains in western Wyoming. We drove to Big Sandy and hiked to the Cirque of Towers past Arrowhead Lake. Not only was fishing poor, but on the third day we got slammed by an early snowstorm. For most of the next three days we were stuck in our two man backing tent. I read an old copy of Field and Stream from cover-to-cover several times. With the storm worsening, we decided to clear out before getting stuck there for the winter. After hiking twenty miles to the trailhead in foot-deep snow, we were relieved to make it back to our car.

September 1978

I started taking girl friends fishing on Farmington Creek. On the second date my rule was to always take them on a fishing trip, and if they did not enjoy the trip there was no third date. We would wet wade in the hot afternoon, taking turns with the fly rod, have dinner over a small campfire and get home at dusk. Sometimes we took a few fish home to cook so I would not have to buy dinner. One girl, Ann, lived at the base of Farmington Canyon so we headed up the canyon every couple of weeks. She was a good sport and not afraid of poison ivy or rattle snakes. She was in a hurry to "get serious" so things did not work out. I became pals with her father and talked fishing with him long after I quit seeing her. Then, I met Julie at work and invited her fishing in the canyon on a first date. It was a disaster. It was the Fourth of July holiday. After a long day's fishing we hiked up the mountain, made a small camp fire, cooked hotdogs and watched the fireworks from a distance at the Lagoon Resort. The next morning the mountain we hiked up had a wildfire and burned a couple hundred acres. Julie called me on the phone in a panic, she was sure the cops were going to track us down and throw us in jail. After a week she calmed down and lost interest in me and fishing. We never did find out the cause of the fire.

February 1979

Brent Israelson set things in motion for the worst date in high school history. Since he was shy, he had his older sister line him up with her neighbor's daughter, who had a twin sister. He asked her out, and not wanting to leave her twin sister out, invited her to go along and he'd find her a date (or so he thought). He begged me to go with him. I should have never promised to go. We got all decked out, flowers, reservations and tank of gas - the works. Then we knocked on the door… I'll never let a "friend" line me up again! I was to go out with one twin and him the other. How was I to know that the twin he talked to on the phone thought that only she was being asked out, and not both of them. Their parents graciously invited us in, we sat down, flowers in hand waiting for the customary belated entrance of the young ladies. The first twin showed up, we exchanged a few jokes, and then she said "let's go" and started walking toward the door. Her parents came back into the room. We explained the situation, they laughed. I wanted out fast. Her mother had the bright idea of lining me up with the neighbor girl, and had her on the phone before I realized what was going on. Suddenly I heard her say, "and they'll pick you up in half an hour." I choked. They smiled and told us not to worry about anything (where had I heard that before?) Her parents had to go to a company party, so they left us watching *Love Boat* on TV. Just as they left, the second twin showed up with her boyfriend. She smiled as the first twin introduced us, and her boyfriend laughed when she got to the part about the mix up. It was then and there I decided never to date again. Our half hour was finally up and we were off to the neighbor's house. The neighbor girl turned out to be cute. Maybe this whole deal wasn't so bad after all. Wrong. Because we were running late our restaurant reservations were canceled so we went to the nearest restaurant, waited another half hour for seats, and finally the waitress seated us. It was like pulling teeth trying to get those two girls to talk, they would just look at us and smile. Things started to lighten up when we got our orders. Funny thing is they both seem to have been vegetarians. The conversation seemed to evolve around our latest fishing trip and their state champion football team, we didn't play football and they didn't fish, so not much was said. As we were having dessert, Brent's date dropped her fork on the floor and went beet red. I couldn't believe it, but her parents were walking across the restaurant toward the door. What else could go wrong? She tried to hide, thinking that her parents were following us, but her folks spotted us and came over. This is where their company party was. I was all for sending the girls home with them, but they were gone before I could suggest it. We made it to the dance with an hour left, our lucky break. We danced a few dances, which was fine, but my biggest problem was avoiding school friends because for the life of me I couldn't remember my date's name. At midnight the dance was over. We piled into the car, both girls in the back seat. Not one word was said on the forty five minute drive home. I didn't even dare to look in the back seat. Finally we got to the girl's homes, walked them to the door (the neighbor girl insisted on going to the twin's house) said the usual, thanks a lot, we had a good time and good bye. As we were walking back to the car, we heard them laughing behind the door. We stopped at a truck stop on the way home for something to eat and a long talk. If there was anything I learned from the experience it is this: Only go to formal dances when a girl asks you out.

April 1979
A couple of my friends and I were exploring and hiking around Antelope Island in the Great Salt Lake. We were surprised to find several large trout washed up on the salty shore. Near as we could tell the fish washed into the salt water from a nearby creek and pickled in the salty brine. The fish were months, if not years old. I've heard that the Piute Indians traveled the shores of the Great Salt Lake gathering baskets full of salted grasshoppers and crickets for winter feasts. Maybe they also had a few trout.

May 1979
Bill Grey, a friend from school, and I fished Farmington Creek just after the spring snowmelt. We wet-waded and caught and released a bunch of wild trout. We were surprised to find a pot plantation hidden in the willows on a small island in a remote section of the canyon. Someone had diverted water from the creek, through the thick willows, to irrigate the plants. I snipped a few leaves to show my uncle the botanist. Bill kept a few buds for his father's pipe. We went back a few weeks later to fish again and found the plants up-

rooted and gone. Hopefully they were confiscated by the county sheriff.

June 1979
I graduated from high school where my favorite classes were in natural sciences. My best teacher was Art Nielson, who wore a three piece suit to his biology class every day. He treated us like adults. For the most part, high school was a game I did not play well, too many social and status rules to follow. I just wanted to start college. During the summer I worked part time at Dick's grocery store and full time for a construction company in Salt Lake City.

July 1979
I spent my free time fishing Farmington Creek. I got to know the river pretty well and could easily catch a half dozen fish an hour. I found a couple of copper mine tunnels at the base of the canyon and found small raw copper nuggets in the creek. I had plenty of time to figure out what I was going to do with the rest of my life.

August 1979
I attended Ricks College at the foot of the Teton Mountains in Rexburg, Idaho, studied Ecology and Natural Resources, and had a part-time job at the local grocery store where I delivered groceries to customer's homes. On sunny (not necessarily warm) days in the fall my roommates and I would fish and swim at Beaver Dick State Park on the Henry's Fork of the Snake River. The fishing was poor. We caught small brown trout and an occasional whitefish and sucker. One afternoon we pulled a large log into the river and floated down river holding our fly rods, looking for better places to fish. We also had a great time jumping off the highway bridge into the river. Classes went well and I dated a few girls. There were four girls to every guy on campus, it was almost impossible to go a weekend without a date or a good meal.

September 1979
My old high school friend, Bill Grey, picked me up in Rexburg and we headed to Yellowstone for a fishing weekend. We had no idea where we were going and looked for adventure. We did not want to pay campground fees, seeing as we were totally broke. We took a service personnel only access road and camped near the West Thumb of Yellowstone Lake for a couple of days. We had

the place to ourselves, except for the black bears and a few noisy Ospreys. It was hot and sunny and the fishing was poor. We only caught a few small Cutthroat trout and cooked them in tin-foil for dinner. Bill stayed at my place for a few days before going back to Utah. We were bored and picked up a few girls for a day out on the sand dunes near St. Anthony, Idaho. It started to snow and on the way back to town Bill slid off the slick road and into a dry irrigation canal. Never stopping his car he gunned the engine and jumped back over the top of the ditch, through the sagebrush and back onto the road. The girls were screaming, crying and yelling at Bill. We had a great time.

1980 – 1989

May 1980
I did voluntary church work in Missouri, Kansas, Oklahoma, and Arkansas for two years. I enjoyed doing service for others and meeting people from all sorts of backgrounds. I traveled throughout the area and grew to know and love the culture of the backwoods people of the Ozarks.

December 1980
One frosty morning in a Cassville, Missouri Cameron Sidwell and I stopped at a donut shop to warm up and have breakfast. We started a conversation with an older gentleman whom we later found out owned and managed a fish hatchery near Roaring River, Missouri. We quickly became good friends and he let us fish the brood-stock pond on Christmas Eve:

Rainbow Trout, Spring Creek, Missouri

the best Christmas gift I'd ever received. We caught and released fat, lazy brood fish all morning. It was not very sporting but we had a great time. A few weeks later he plowed a field on his property for the first time and he invited us back to hunt for arrowheads. I filled a pint jar with bird points and broken pieces of knife blades.

June, 1981
Larry Croizer, Guy Teagle, and I found a small farm pond hidden away in the wheat fields west of Pittsburg, Kansas. From the gravel road it looked fishy. We couldn't see any "no trespassing" signs

as we scouted the area. A week later we arrived a little after six in the morning and began casting for largemouth bass. Larry caught and lost the first fish, a very large bass. This was going to be good. It looked like no one had fished here in years. The next cast Larry hooked another bass and landed a nice five pounder. I hooked the next largemouth, he was about four pounds. Over the next hour we caught another dozen largemouth, keeping a half dozen over three pounds. In the distance a diesel truck engine broke the silence; the nearest farm house was less than a mile away. We jumped the fence and had the bass in the car trunk just as the farmer drove up behind us. The land owner was friendly enough, but refused our request to fish his pond when he saw our rods lying on the hood of the car. He used to let friends and family fish the pond, but did not think there were fish in the pond anymore.

Largemouth Bass, Pittsburg, Kansas

He told us about a good pond a few miles down the road. We thanked him and wished him a good day. We probably should not have fished his pond, but the thrill of the hunt and the possibility of lots of big fish were too much to resist. We found other small ponds to fish, but the bass were smaller and less plentiful.

August, 1981

Guy Teagle and I received permission to fish a small farm pond on the outskirts of Pittsburg, Kansas, as long as we released all the fish. The owner stocked the pond every few years with bluegill, crappie, largemouth bass and sunfish. We were asked to release all fish. We were able to cover the entire pond from shore. The fish would hang out in the murky water just a few feet off-shore in debris piles or under overhanging tree limbs. We caught dozens of crappie and bluegill on lead-head feather jigs. The color of our lures did not matter, they took anything that moved. The domesticated geese wandering around were annoying and I picked up a bad case of chigger bites, but for the most part it was great sport on a hot, humid afternoon.

Crappie, Pittsburg, Kansas

June 1982

I took evening math and statistic classes at the University of Utah, worked at the grocery store and spent much of the summer hiking and fishing the small creeks in the Wasatch and Uinta Mountains. A lady at work, Kathy, insisted that I date her daughter Nancy, which was fine by me because she was cute and worked at Baskin Robbins Ice Cream. How could I go wrong? After we were introduced I invited her up Farmington Canyon for a day of hiking and wet wading for small trout. After the third fish Nancy realized I was serious about my fishing and kept up pretty well, wading though deep holes and thick willows. At dusk we sat and talked on a rock ledge where the creek ran though a rock chute and watched the sun set. Her folks barbecued the two trout we took home and seemed surprised we caught fish.

July 1982

Brent Israelson and I fished the Weber River near Coalville, Utah. We cast for an hour to a pod of rising rainbows with no luck. We did not have the skill or equipment to catch these finicky fish. I switched to a #14 Latex Caddis Nymph and began catching whitefish. They were a lot of fun in the hot weather and we easily caught a dozen of the schooling fish in each hole.

August 1982

I attended my second year at Ricks College working towards an Associate in Science Degree in Ecology and Natural Resources. Several professors and students talked a lot about fishing, but we were too busy to spend much time on the river. I worked as a resident assistant at the men's dorm and evenings at the Rexburg grocery store.

October 1982

My roommate Ivan Lamaro was from Saudi Arabia. I was also dating a girl named Amy who was from Louisiana, she was a lot of fun but bad luck. Every time we borrowed our friend Joe's truck we got stuck in the woods. The first time was in a snow drift while trying to see the elk herd in Jackson Hole, Wyoming. The second time we were fishing the Snake River, luckily some good-old-boys pulled us out of a mud-hole well after midnight. I had to take the truck to the car wash at 3am to get the mud off, and Joe wondered why the truck doors were frozen shut the next morning. One weekend Joe, Linda, Amy and I went camping at Beaver Dick County Park on the Henry's Fork of the Snake River, not far from Rexburg, Idaho. It was a cool, crisp, clear day. We gave up fishing in the late afternoon when the wind kicked up. We had a large campfire that evening and spent most of the night laughing and having a good time. The next Monday Dr. Moss, my economics professor, asked me in front of the whole class if I had a good weekend. I assured him that I did and asked why he was asking? He and his family were in the campsite next to us over the weekend and they did not appreciate our behavior. After that I paid a little more attention to my economics studies and was grateful for a B in his class. Amy swore she would never live anywhere but Louisiana, so after graduation she got a job training race horses back home in Bossier City. We wrote a few letters, but lost interest over time. A few years later I heard she married a guy in Germany.

January 1983
During winter break, I thumbed a ride several times to fish the South Fork of Snake River. The "snow fly" chronomid hatch was the best fishing of the year. During one afternoon blizzard near St. Anthony, Idaho, I caught a dozen rainbow trout and whitefish up to eighteen inches. The fish ignored all flies larger than a size #22 Griffiths Gnat. The big, slow pools held most of trout, and a long cast and drag-free drift was required to catch fish.

March 1983
My ecology-biology class went on a field trip to the Idaho pan-handle to float the Middle Fork of the Salmon River. We saw two dozen Bighorn Sheep, several mountain goats and a dead horse that a bear was eating. We didn't stay long or have much time to fish. Something about a bear-kill takes the fun out of everything.

April 1983
I received an Associate in Science in Ecology and Natural Resources from Ricks College and was the only student to receive that degree in the last several years. I enjoyed my studies and was determined to follow my interests. I lived at home for the summer, worked at the grocery store, and took a few math and statistic classes at the University of Utah. I fished Farmington Canyon every chance I got. Not so much for the fish, but to find solitude and enjoy the outdoors.

August 1983
I attended Utah State University, and started working towards a B.S. degree in Range Science. I was interested in botany and ecology, but wanted to work in the field rather than at a desk job. Range Science seemed like a good fit because we studied soils, plants, wildlife, livestock, forestry, planning and economics. During student orientation I specifically selected my major professor, Dr. Neil West, based on his credentials as the selecting official for student scholarships. I worked hard my first year, got good grades and with the help of my major professor won an academic scholarship which paid full tuition. I worked three jobs each semester. I did paste-up and lay-out for the college newspaper three nights

a week from 10pm to 1am. I was a dish washer and short order cook for an on-campus restaurant from 5 to 9am weekdays. I also worked for the range science department identifying seeds under a microscope. I rarely bought groceries and ate breakfast and dinner at the restaurant because for every three hours we worked we got a free meal. My grandmother thought I was a poor starving college student and sent me a three pound brick of cheese every month, which I made into sandwiches for lunch. I did not have much time to fish or tie flies, but did take a lot of botany field trips near some great looking water.

January 1984
I met Jean Munns while working at Carousel Square, an on-campus restaurant. I was a dishwasher and she was the salad lady and a party girl for the catering service. She asked me out to a girl's choice dance and we started dating, but only Friday and Saturday nights because we were so busy at school and work.

June 1984
I worked in the Payette National Forest for the U.S. Forest Service as a Range Technician. I knew every creek and lake in the area. I worked four ten-hour days per week and had three-day weekends. I saved my pay check and had fish for dinner regularly. I caught some nice catfish in Brownlee Reservoir.

Catfish, Brownlee Reservoir, Idaho

When I grew tired of catching catfish, there were always trout in the mountain streams. I found a cheap, rundown apartment in town next to the Mexican movie theater and across the street from three bars. It was a rough neighborhood so I always kept a loaded .22 rifle in the closet. Soon after moving in, the railroad unloaded several tons of onions in the stockyards across the street. For several weeks I had teary eyes from the strong odor. During the Old Time Fiddler Festival, which was very entertaining, the Hells Angels motorcycle gang came to Weiser, Idaho from California. They liked to frequent the bars across the street and revved their bikes all hours of the night. The police could not control them and many locals came down to the "strip" to watch the action. I met several bikers and discovered that many were doctors and lawyers who financed the rest of the gang, in exchange for riding with them. On the job we spent a lot of time spraying thistle, repairing fence and checking woodcutting permits. We made friends with a couple of Basque sheep herders who barely spoke English. Their cabin was at the dead end of a thirty mile dirt road on the shore of Brownlee Reservoir. Once a week they would fill a gunny sack with catfish from the lake and dump them into the stock water trough. They had no electricity or plumbing but they always had fresh fish to eat.

July 1984
I went from Range to Fire Technician and became a member of a two-man initial attack fire crew. I moved out of town to Brownlee Guard Station on the east side of Hells Canyon. After several weeks my partner Rex got drunk the afternoon before we were called on a late evening fire. The fire boss fired him on the spot and I spent the rest of the summer at the guard station alone. I had a pumper fire truck, trail motorbike, and an old horse named Alpo. I spent days on the motorbike doing trail maintenance. Alpo liked to wander and several times I had to track him down after he jumped the fence. He'd go miles before I'd find him. He wasn't much to ride. I suppose that's why they named him after dog food. A small stream full of trout ran about a hundred feet outside the main cabin and provided a meal once or twice a week. The nearest town was Cambridge, Idaho, about an hour east, where I did my laundry and picked up groceries. At the guard station we had an old gas powered electrical generator the service let me run for one hour each evening, but most of the time I didn't use it. We had five forest fires during the summer. Typically, I would get a radio call from the fire lookout tower with map coordinates and

take the pumper truck to the fire, report to the fire boss and then begin fighting the fire. Several hours later other firefighters would show up to assist. Most fires were brush fires and were contained in two or three days. We focused on protecting cabins and structures from wildfire. In our free time we cleaned public campgrounds and fenced miles of streams and springs from livestock. I was detailed to one large project fire in Montana. On the way I picked up several other firefighters in McCall, Idaho, and drove to the Rocky Boy Indian Reservation, south of Havre, Montana. We joined 500 other firefighters for a week-long adventure. I was assigned to night shift: I drove the back roads, located hot spots and put them out. One evening we noticed flames at the top of the ridge and loaded our piss pump backpacks and headed up the mountain. We surprised a band of Indians who were having a ceremony, around a bonfire, on top of a ridge. After causing a commotion we quickly excused ourselves and ran down the mountain. The next day the tribe filed a complaint with my boss about our behavior. The tribe was not upset for very long and asked our team to stay several days after the fire was contained to train the local Indian fire crew.

July 4, 1984
I attended the Independence Day festivities in the small ranching community of Cambridge, Idaho. The most popular event was the porcupine races. A dozen or so contestants captured porcupines in the woods days before the race and trained them to run using a straw broom and plastic garbage can. On the day of the event people came from miles around and lined up around the high school football field. The first porcupine to run goal-to-goal won the event. A few porcupines caused a stampede by running into the crowd, but most behaved, ran well and were later released back into the woods. The parade down Main Street only took a few minutes and was limited to a few floats and the high school marching band. The most memorable float commemorated a deer hunting trip taken by two Californians a few years earlier. The hunters rented horses in town and headed up the hills for the day. The weather turned nasty and they got lost in a blizzard. One guy had the bright idea to shoot the horses, gut them and crawl inside to keep from freezing. The next morning they awoke to the sound of a semi-truck heading

down the highway not 100 yards from where they were camped. They thumbed a ride back to town, paid for the horses and were never seen again in town. The parade float had a paper-mache horse with two blaze-orange deer hunters sitting inside. The crowd cheered as the float passed by, everyone had a good laugh.

August, 1984

Wildhorse Canyon met all the requirements for the perfect trout stream. Located near Hell's Canyon Dam in the "Grand Canyon of the Snake River," it had vertical rock walls choked with poison ivy. Rattlesnakes could be found on the south facing slopes and made a lot of noise when approached. I had the creek to myself. Wading up the middle of the creek was the only safe access to good fishing. Wildhorse Creek had a nice run of rainbow trout and an occasional kokanee salmon. One afternoon I waded several miles up the creek and caught several rainbows on a #8 Muddler Minnow, which fished like a grasshopper. I caught and released three dozen trout before sundown.

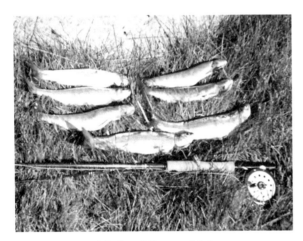

Trout, Payette National Forest, Idaho

On the way back to my car, I noticed bear tracks in the mud overlaying my own tracks. A bear had been following me upstream while I was fishing. I do not know how we passed each other within the canyon's sheer rock walls. I suppose the bear hid in the willow trees and watched me pass on my way downstream. I got back to the road well after dark to find a game warden leaning against my car. "Son, let me see your fishing license" he said, pointing to the Utah license plates on my car. I smiled and showed him my non-resident Idaho fishing license. He was not happy, having waited

several hours for me to return, probably missing his dinner. He counted the fin-rays on the trout I had kept for dinner to see if they were salmon. I returned back to Brownlee Guard Station lucky to have dodged a hungry bear and foiled a determined warden.

August 1984

A few weeks before college started, a classmate of mine Paul Kelly and I took the rough dirt road to Paddock Reservoir in southwest Idaho. We wanted to fill our freezers with crappie for the winter. The crappie took everything we threw at them. I cast a #10 Wooly Worm into the deep water along shore and got a hook-up on almost every other cast. At the end of the day it took two hours to fillet our fish and we each left with a five gallon bucket filled with fillets. On the way home we got a flat tire in Paul's old pick-up and put on his bald semi-inflated spare tire, hoping we would make it back to town. We did make it back and put the fish in the freezer a little after midnight.

September 1984

I fished the Logan and Blacksmiths Fork Rivers and caught many brown trout. It always upset my California roommate Dave when I came home with my limit. He had new and expensive gear, but rarely caught fish. I had a cheap rod and my shirt pocket held all my tackle. I did not enjoy fishing with him. He was too competitive and how he looked was more important than catching fish.

April 1985

During Easter break from college, a co-worker Ben Hatch, his brother Bob and I took a trip to Lake Powell, Utah. We borrowed my grandmother's old beat-up Toyota station wagon for the trip. At the reservoir we took our backpacks and caught a tourist sightseeing boat to Rainbow Bridge. We didn't fit in with the typical tourists; they asked a lot of silly questions. At Rainbow Bridge we took a short swim to cool off, and noticed schools of fish swimming in the shadows of the sandstone cliffs. We rigged up hand lines and caught a bunch of largemouth bass and bluegill for dinner. Up the canyon from Rainbow Bridge we found an old tourist camp from the early 1900s with several old brass beds, outhouses and lots of trash. We spent the next five days backpacking all over Navajo Mountain.

Rainbow Bridge, Utah

Luckily it was a good water year and all the springs had water. We found several old abandoned Indian hogans and many petroglyphs. We had read many stories about skinwalkers and other Navajo legends that made us skittish. Mid-week we tried to hike to the top of Navajo Mountain which is a sacred Indian site and the center of the Navajo world. Near the top of the mountain we enjoyed a wonderful view of the surrounding canyon lands and watched the sun set. It was dark on the return hike back to camp. Bob ran into a large porcupine on the trail, screamed and scared us. Our camp that night was in the bottom of a steep canyon in the black-brush. As the moon suddenly appeared over the canyon wall around midnight we all awoke, startled by the light. It was as if someone had turned a spotlight on us. We swore that we could see skinwalkers on the canyon rim above camp. The next day we hiked out to another spring, as we were getting short on water. We spent the next day relaxing, bathing and looking for cliff dwellings. On our last day we hiked back to Rainbow Bridge and caught the tour boat back to the car. That night we slept on the lawn at a church, in Page Arizona. The cops showed up after midnight shining flashlights in our eyes, but they did not bother us because we were on private property. On the drive back to Logan we lost the car muffler somewhere near Kanab, Utah, and enjoyed the endless irritating drones of un-muffled combustion for 300 miles.

June 1985
I wrote a research proposal and received funding from the National Science Foundation and USU to perform research on a coal strip mine near

Kemmerer, Wyoming - the hometown of J.C. Penney stores. Several of us lived in an old trailer, across the road from the golf course. We knew everything about everyone in the trailer court, but never met any of them. We heard all the conversations through the walls in a tightly packed trailer park. I also worked for several weeks researching and collecting plant data in Tintic, Utah. I spent several days riding a horse in circles, broadcasting seed and measuring hoof print density after trampling the seed into the soil, to determine how well hoofs improved seeding success. I'm sure the old horse we borrowed from a nearby ranch thought I was crazy. I stayed in the Tintic motel (which was really a double wide trailer) which had a sign in the front window that read: "We change the sheets weekly". We tried to get a room the first part of the week.

July 4, 1985
My girlfriend, Jean Munns, and I fished the Logan River, Utah, just below the old power plant. We arrived early to beat the Forth-of-July holiday crowd. Within two hours I caught a dozen brown trout without moving from under the shade of a large maple tree.

Brown Trout, Logan River, Utah

The fish were piling up below a small island where the outflow from the hydropower plant dumped into the main river. Fish were taking caddis flys that were emerging off the concrete wing-walls and screens of the weir. Jean was being polite all morning, sitting on a log, relaxing and carrying on casual conversation. She finally broke down, took my rod and caught another half dozen trout. I could not get the rod away from her the rest of the morning. The fact that she did not have a fishing license did not discourage her at all. By late morning the river was crowded but we were the only ones catching fish. By noon we had our limit and laughed as we walked back to our car and watched several other fishermen run to take our vacated spot on the river.

August 1985
Jean Munns and I planned a hike to Tony Grove Lake. After looking at the topography maps we decided to take a shortcut and bush-wacked up the canyon from the Logan River. We soon learned we had hiked into the wrong canyon. I explained to Jean that "they must have moved the lake." Several hours later after finding the right canyon, and after herding several moose off the trail, we arrived at White Pine Lake. We caught two brook trout in the lake. On the hike back to the highway along White Pine Creek we caught dozens of small brook trout.

September 1985
I did not own a vehicle until age 25, but rode a bicycle. I did borrow my grandmother's Toyota for several months each summer. I was able to get around pretty good. I didn't buy many groceries because I worked at a restaurant, didn't have much time for recreation because I was carrying a full class load and working one to three part-time jobs. I always dated girls or had fishing buddies that had cars and could go anywhere I wanted by buying a tank of gas. The last couple of years I had five roommates and shared a three room apartment. We came from all corners of the world: An Asian from China, two black guys from France and Africa, a marine from Idaho and two of us from Utah.

February 14, 1986
I attended the Society for Range Management meetings in Orlando, Florida, where I presented a professional paper and interviewed for graduate schools. When I got home Jean and I got engaged and we picked a wedding day in June. Four days later Jean borrowed my car, which I was

borrowing from my parents. An older gentleman ran a stop sign and totaled the car. Jean was fine but a little shaken-up. After the accident she came up to my office and handed me the engagement ring and sobbed "we can't get married now" and headed down the hall. I had to hold back my laughter. My boss threatened to fire me if I did not find Jean and give the ring back to her.

June 8, 1986
I received a Bachelors of Science degree in Range Science from Utah State University, and graduated Cum Laude at the top of my class in the College of Natural Resources. I had no debt, no student loans, borrowed nothing from my parents and had $5,000 in the bank. Of course I did without a lot of luxuries, like not owning a car. I prided myself on being cheap. Life was good focusing on school work and a couple of part-time jobs.

June 12, 1986
Jean and I got married in Salt Lake City, Utah. My parents gave us the insurance money for the totaled car Jean was driving as a wedding gift (about $1,000). Jean and I collected Indian Rice Grass for our wedding reception table decorations and my brother's girl friend Cara made our wedding cake. My old roommate Bruce Crane lent us his cabin at Mink Creek, Idaho for our honeymoon. He stocked the cabin with groceries and asked all the neighbors to bring us meals each evening. Sometimes you just want to be left alone. We hiked and fished a little but I don't remember catching many fish.

July 1986
Jean and I toured several National Parks in Southern Utah and Colorado on the way to begin graduate school at New Mexico State University and study agricultural economics. We were happily surprised when we arrived at my major professor's house in Las Cruces. Alan Torell welcomed us, handed me the keys to his house and said "See you in a month we're going on vacation. Eat all the food, feed the horse, read this book and learn how to write spreadsheets." And then they walked out the door.

June 1987
I took some time off from collecting sagebrush data for my theses in northern New Mexico to fish. We visited the San Juan River, but had poor

luck as the river was running high and off-color. We fished the Chama River where I caught a twenty inch rainbow in fast pocket water. A few days later we headed toward Taos and spotted a small lake off the highway. I hooked a skinny rainbow on my second cast on a #12 Wooly Worm, and released him. We caught no fish the rest of the trip.

July 1987

As a graduate research assistant at New Mexico State University in agricultural economics I spent most of the field season clipping sagebrush plots, interviewing ranchers for cow-calf budgets and writing my thesis. I also worked for the Extension Service as an economic development coordinator. I spent a lot of time with ranchers who had financial problems, developing strategies to keep them in business. I spent many stressful days with families at their kitchen tables pouring over financial records trying to help them keep the ranch in the family. I was also hired as an expert witness for several lawyers who were settling a water dispute between Texas and New Mexico. Las Cruces was very hot, averaging about 105 degrees in the summer and 80 degrees in the winter. On very hot days we drove to Carlsbad Caverns to cool off in the caves. My wife Jean and I took several hikes on weekends to see Indian petroglyphs and photograph desert flowers. At Christmas we drove to White Sands Missile Range and hiked the white sand (gypsum) dunes because it looked like snow. We also liked to attend the Mexican festivals and eat Mexican food.

February 1988

Several graduate students and I borrowed a New Mexico State University van and headed across Texas to Corpus Christi to attend the Society for Range Management meetings. We arrived a day early and decided to charter a fishing boat for the day on the Gulf of Mexico. That was a big mistake. Put a couple of cowboys on a small sea-going boat, throw in diesel smoke and rotting cut-bait, mix up the weather with six foot swales and you have a real party. I was seasick before we past the harbor bar. We were dry-heaving off the stern within an hour. The captain smiled, he was not turning back with a ship full of paying customers. Two hours out we tied up to an oil derrick and fished. I was determined to catch something, and when I did the captain told me to throw it back.

He said "You caught a mother-in-law fish", what the heck is that I asked? He replied "It's ugly and has a big mouth." Back into the drink it went. Most of the afternoon I lay on my back in the center of the boat to calm my stomach (along with most of my fellow passengers). Bill seemed to be the only person not affected and really ticked us off by eating a tuna fish sandwich, smoking a cigarette and asking "What's up with you guys?" A couple of the guys caught rockfish, small sharks and one stingray. Back at the dock I got my land legs back ten minutes off the boat. I was hungry and had a large burger and fries for dinner. It was a long time before I hit the deep ocean again.

May 1988

I spent most of the last year clipping grass and collecting data on sagebrush sites all over New Mexico. A couple of times I camped in slick-rock and juniper to save money and travel time. The university gave me a brand new white Trans Am sports car to drive, one of the universities repossessed drug cars. Ranchers were really confused when they saw me driving up to the ranch in a hot rod with an Extension Service logo on the car door.

July 1988

I graduated with a Master of Science degree in agricultural economics and a minor in statistics. My thesis was *The Economics of Sagebrush Control on the Colorado Plateau*. The most important lesson I learned at graduate school was to learn the rules, play the game and work within the system rather than fight the system. Jean worked full-time at an arts and craft store and took a few evening classes. We had no debt, no student loans and $10,000 in the bank. Luckily, Jean believed in thrift as much as I did. I took a job working for the New Mexico Extension Service, until my major professor told me about a better job.

July 4, 1988

I began work as an agricultural economist in Portland, Oregon for the Soil Conservation Service at the west regional office. Because it was a federal holiday, my first day on the job was a paid holiday. I worked with private landowners and evaluated the economics of implementing conservation practices on their farms and ranches. I was able to use both my Range Science and Economics degrees.

August 20, 1988

My boss, Bob Caldwell, told me about a hot spot for sea-run cutthroat trout on the Nehalem River. Jean and I fished below the bridge on the road toward Mist and Jewel, just off Sunset Highway. I tied on a #10 Spruce Fly and on the second cast caught a nice sea-run cutthroat trout. Over the next two hours we caught and released two dozen cutthroat ranging from eight to fourteen inches. We headed home after breaking the hook point off my last fly on a rock.

September 1988

Mike Wahl, a neighbor in our apartment complex, invited me fishing on the Deschutes River. He told a good fishing story so I agreed to go with him. We left at 4am and headed toward the Cascades. I had no idea where we were going, apparently neither did he. We crossed the Deschutes River at Warm Springs without knowing it. We were in Madras, Oregon before he admitted he was lost. We asked for directions, and finally found the Deschutes River at Maupin, Oregon. We cast flys the rest of the day. Neither of us knew how to fish the river. I finally caught a six inch rainbow at the base of a big boulder at Box Car Rapids on a #12 Renegade.

December 10, 1988

I was invited on my first steelhead trip. Bill Daley from work picked me up at 4am and we headed to the Wilson River. We unloaded his drift boat in the pre-dawn fog and rigged up corkies, yarn, and lead slinkies. Not being familiar with steelhead, I used my trout rod and eight pound line unbeknownst to my fishing partner. We began drift fishing when it was light enough to avoid the snags. We caught no fish the first two miles. Just past Mills Bridge I cast into a deep, fast channel along the willow lined bank. The line stopped. I set the hook. A bright steelhead leaped clear out of the water, attached to my line. Bill dropped anchor in the backwater above a broad hole and I cranked on my reel. The fish jumped a half dozen times, each time pulling out line and testing the limits of my drag. I leaned against the front of the boat. Finally after ten minutes we netted a seven pounder. This was my first steelhead and the only fish of the day. Bill asked if I wanted to take the fish home. What was he thinking? This was the biggest fish I'd ever caught, and a hatchery fish to boot.

Steelhead, Wilson River, Oregon

At the take-out Bill had a few beers so I drove home through the rain with Bill sleeping in the back of his camper van.

February 24, 1989

It had been raining the last few days and the Wilson River was the right color for steelhead fishing, a light shade of olive green. The water was high this year and eroded the far bank above the Rock Garden hole. I tied on a red-orange corkie, looped a knot of chartreuse yarn above the hook and attached a piece of slinky lead weight two feet up from the hook and began working the drift downstream. I tried to keep my slinky bouncing on the bottom of the river - about one bounce every five feet. I had the hole to myself.

Steelhead, Wilson River, Oregon

After a half hour a steelhead rolled as my lure rose to the surface at the end of the swing. A couple of casts later the same fish took my lure and the fight was on. He almost broke off after looping around a large submerged boulder in the middle of the river. Five minutes later I beached a twenty seven inch, seven pound, hatchery steelhead. I took him home and we had fresh steelhead for Sunday dinner.

March 1989
My wife worked Saturdays managing a craft store leaving me the day to wander, tie flies and fish. Bill Daley and I fished the coastal rivers, always stopping for advice and gear at the Guide Shop, an old shack where the Wilson River enters the Tillamook Valley. The hired help slept in the back room but always let us in when we knocked on the door, even at 4am. The sign said open twenty-four hours and they meant it. Sometimes Bill worked there as a guide when the shop was overbooked. Bill always knew where the fish were and kept a graph of fish-counts in his desk at work. He also kept meticulous records of each fishing trip, recording water, weather and fishing techniques. We floated the Trask and Wilson Rivers often and averaged two or three fish each trip.

Steelhead, Wilson River, Oregon

Occasionally we had fish that ripped out line and broke off. They were probably early spring Chinook but could have been twenty pound steelhead. We'll never know. Most of our steelhead were in the seven to twelve pound range.

March 11, 1989
We took Bill Daley's drift boat down the Wilson River from Vanderzanden put-in to Sollie Smith Bridge. We did not have much luck drifting corkies until we got below the RV park near the mouth of the canyon. Bill hooked a very nice steelhead, which took him all over the river. A mink on the far bank was as excited as we were and kept running up and down the river bank following us around. He knew a good meal when he saw one. Finally, I slipped a net under a bright twelve pound steelhead, which could have not been fresher from the ocean. It still had sea lice crawling on its belly. That was the only fish of the day, and well worth it.

March 14, 1989
We fished the Deschutes River at Warm Springs after work one evening. I only had hip waders and could not get too far out into the river. Bill Daley had chest waders and caught a half dozen Redside Rainbow Trout on #6 Black Stonefly Nymphs. No one else was fishing. Over dinner that evening we thought that perhaps that section of river might have been closed until spring. We were lucky not to have received a ticket.

March 18, 1989
I fished the Wilson River for most of the morning, dredging every inch of the Rock Gardens hole with a corkie and yarn, and caught no fish. I've been told that the color of the corkie should be based on the color of the water. In murky water use red or orange, in slightly off-color water try bright green and in clear water use a pink corkie. The color of yarn is less important, I usually use chartreuse or orange.

March 24, 1989
I fished the Wilson River again. The Rock Garden hole was clear and the water level was dropping. I put on a pink corkie and chartreuse yarn and ran it deep thought several likely looking ruins. Mid-morning I hooked a nice nine pound steelhead. He took my lure behind a submerged boulder the size of a car, raced around the river and did flips in the air trying to shake the hook. I was alone and wished I have invited a friend along with a camera. I fell in the river landing him on a gravel bar. I was cold and wet but I went home early and happy.

April 7, 1989
Having read about surf fishing I had always wanted to try it. I took Jean to Seaside, Oregon, to a sandy beach near the golf course.

Seaside, Oregon

I tied a three ounce pyramid sinker to a swivel at the end of my line. Two feet up the line from the sinker I tied a #8 Chartreuse Wooly Worm on a dropper and a second fly another two feet up the line. I ran down the beach with the receding surf and cast beyond the breaking waves, then ran up the beach hoping not to get hit by a returning wave. I kept the line tight and waited for something to happen. At high tide I caught one small pink-fin perch.

May 6, 1989
I fished the Deschutes River, nine miles south of Maupin. I hiked beyond the locked gate and cast #8 Black Stonefly Nymphs. I was surprised at how good the fishing was and caught a dozen Redside trout, ranging from ten to twelve inches.

May 1989
I had such good luck fishing Oregon I figured that all water had fish. I'd driven Highway twenty six over Mt. Hood several times and noticed a deep canyon with what appeared to be a fishable creek, a couple of miles southwest from Government Camp, Oregon. I headed up the mountain early one foggy morning, the day after several days of rain. The area had been burned over a decade earlier and the hillside was covered with alders and a few scattered firs. The creek was choked with willows and had a fair amount of silt and debris. I

hiked down a talus slope that was really too steep and dangerous for a lone hiker and began fishing. About fifty yards upstream I found some bear scat that was half as long as my arm and so fresh it was still steaming in the cold damp air. It was time to go. I headed straight up the hill back to the car. Fish or not, I was not prepared to share the water with an ornery spring black bear.

June 10, 1989
I fished the Trask River with Bill Daley. We walked into the Hog Farm Hole first thing in the morning and cast #6 Black Marabou Wooly Buggers. There were a few other plunkers throwing eggs in the deep water. None of us caught fish. The rest of the day we floated down to the Highway 101 takeout in Bill's drift boat. We fished hard but caught no fish. I drove home while Bill slept in the back of his van.

June 17, 1989
We floated the Trask River again for Spring Chinook and steelhead. This time we went further up the river and had a longer drift. Bill caught and released one steelhead.

June 30, 1989
After working in Anchorage, Alaska for several days, Bill Daley and I took several days off to fish. We hired a boat to take us up the Talkeetna River to Clear Creek at the base of Mt. McKinley. We had over twenty hours of day light. As we hiked up Clear Creek a young man came down the trail with a forty pound Chinook salmon. He walked right up and said "Hi Hal." I said, "How ya doing Rob?" This stunned Bill, how did we know each other miles out in the Alaska bush? Rob and I had gone to college together in New Mexico several years earlier. The army had transferred Rob to Alaska. What were the odds of two friends meeting in the wilderness four thousand miles from where we knew each other? It's a small world. We had a good talk. I was pleased to hear that Rob had won a big fish contest with a fly I had tied for him in New Mexico. During this trip we caught grayling, char, and Chinook salmon. I hooked fourteen Chinook in twenty-four hours and had a hard time landing each one. We caught all the fish on flies. I kept one salmon and a very large char to smoke and take home. We stayed at our friend's Doug Whit's cabin near Palmer, Alaska. I borrowed his canoe and trekked up Jim

Creek to several small lakes every evening after work. The mosquitoes were fierce. I caught several silver salmon smolt. One evening I hiked around a lake and fished off a tall pile of brush where it was easy to cast. I smelled something dead, but didn't worry about it. When I climbed off the brush pile I noticed a small sign and a bear trapping permit. I had been fishing off of a trapper's bear bait. In the future I'll be more careful. While canoeing home, I passed within yards of several moose and worried about getting between a moose and her calf. We fished a small lake near the University of Alaska's experimental dairy and caught many small rainbow trout.

August 5, 1989
I was invited to go camping and fish at Olallie Lake on a fathers and sons outing with a group from church. It was sunny and hot and I caught several small stocked trout on #12 Woolly Worms. We saw no fish rising in the evening or morning; we must have been on the wrong side of the lake.

August 25, 1989
The staff from work fished the Deschutes River. We camped near the locked gate in the back of pick-up trucks. I started fishing with my boss Bob Caldwell and we picked up a couple of fourteen to sixteen inch rainbows along the grass banks on a #14 Grey Hare's Ear.

Redside Trout, Deschutes River, Oregon

About noon we found Dave Hoodenpile sleeping under a tree. He hadn't caught any fish. Another co-worker, Ken Krug, did not catch any fish either. He was chain-smoking and I suppose the nicotine spooked the fish. Dave and I fished

together in the afternoon. It was very hot and the fishing was tough. I noticed several fish in a calm back eddy, taking midges. I was showing off when I showed Dave a #24 Midge and said watch this. A nice trout took the fly, jumped and spun line through my drag. A few minutes later we landed a nice sixteen inch trout on two pound tippet. It is amazing how much fish a small hook can hold.

September 1989
I went salmon fishing on the Trask River near Tillamook, Oregon. At 4am, I paid my three dollars for access to the dairy farm and was surprised to find another dozen fishermen at the same spot I wanted to fish. Before sun up and high tide several Chinook salmon were on the bank. Beautiful twenty five pound fish, even if a bit on the dark side. Finally I hooked a nice fish, fought it for about twenty minutes and with the help of another fisherman netted it. She was a native hen, full of eggs and a bit on the dark side. She had been in fresh water for some time. I released the fish back into the water. What happened next shocked me. Several other fishermen yelled at me: "Why'd ya let it go?", "Should have given it to me!" and other insults. I couldn't believe it. These were not sportsmen. I only increased their odds of catching more fish. I didn't feel like fishing anymore and went home disappointed.

September 13, 1989
Bill Daley, Howard Thomas and I were working on a small watershed project near Neola, Utah and fished each night after work. We each caught several dozen eight to ten inch cutthroat trout from the Uinta River and nearby beaver ponds. The trout took every small fly we cast to them. Most fish were stunted and we should have kept a few to reduce the population. The Ute tribe had taken over the management of this area a few years ago and was trying to improve fish and wildlife.

October 7, 1989
I fished the Hospital Hole on the Trask River, near Tillamook, Oregon. I was greeted by a dozen other fishermen who had also paid their three dollars to fish on the dairy farm. Just after sun up I hooked a strong Chinook salmon on a corkie and yarn. It took me about a minute to lose him around a tree root wad that was lodged in the

main channel. I spent the rest of the day watching others catch fish.

October 14, 1989

I went back to the Trask River a week later with Mike Wahl. I really did not want to go because of my bad experience a few weeks ago, but Mike talked me into going. At sun up people were two deep along the riverbank. Good thing we arrived early and staked out our territory, even though it was only ten feet of bank. We caught a couple of fish that morning. Mike hooked and landed a twenty five pound Chinook salmon, which he took home to smoke. It was a dark fish. On the way back we surprised two Japanese tourists behind their car sneaking an early lunch of fresh salmon eggs, squeezed out of their recently caught salmon.

December 6, 1989

I took my first solitary steelheading trip, pulling out of the driveway at 4am in a downpour. By the time I got to the Coast Range it started to snow and dumped about three inches on the highway. The snow turned to rain again on the Necanicum River just east of Seaside, Oregon. I rigged up a corkie and yarn and began fishing a nice long hole and riffle beneath a grove of alders. Within two hours I hooked and landed a bright five pound steelhead, so fresh it still had sea lice on its belly. By the time I rigged up again, another fisherman had taken my place. I headed home.

1990 – 1999

March 19, 1990
My wife and I spent a day on the beach and surf fished at Cape Meares, west of Tillamook, Oregon. It was a rare sunny day and a little chilly with the wind. There were two other fishermen within sight. The guy next to me caught a nice sole and the other guy caught several small rockfish. I did not catch any fish.

May 1990
Our daughter Bethany was born. I was a little nervous but Jean had everything under control.

June 9, 1990
I took a group of 11 year old scouts to the St. Louis Ponds, off of Highway 101 between Woodburn and Salem, Oregon. The small ponds were dug to get gravel to build the highway. We fished the deep water for two hours with no luck. We noticed small bluegills in the shade below overhanging brush. I rigged each scout with a short line and small fly. The rest of the day was history. Each scout caught a dozen bluegills, for some it was their first fish. Several boys wanted to keep their fish, but quickly changed their minds when they began catching more fish. I think they now understand the concept of "catch and release".

July 4, 1990
We took our daughter Bethany on her first fishing trip. We found a nice shady spot next to a small creek near the Hood River on Mt. Hood.

Coastal Cutthroat, Mt. Hood, Oregon

We caught and released several very small cutthroats and enjoyed lunch in the shade of the forest.

July 21, 1990
Bill Daley and I fished the Sandy River, near the confluence of the Salmon River on Mt. Hood, Oregon. We were swinging streamers and wooly buggers in the early morning. I hooked and lost a summer steelhead at the tail-out of a large pool. A short time later Bill caught a small summer steelhead a bit further downstream.

September 29, 1990
Allen Torell, my advisor from New Mexico State University, was in Portland for a meeting, so we invited him to stay the night and fish the next day. I took him to the Hospital Hole on the Trask River. Alan was a big guy, when he hooked his first salmon people were scrambling to get out of the way. He chased the Chinook up and down the bank for about five minutes, slipping on the mud several times. He finally lost the fish when the line got tangled on a root wad. When the twenty pound line snapped it sounded like a shot from a .22 rifle. Later in the day I foul hooked a fish and let it go.

February 8, 1991
Bill Daley and I fished the Wilson River for steelhead and caught no fish. The river was high and off-color. Making the best of a bad fishing day we headed past Tillamook to Nehalem Bay (at the end of Tohl Road) and collected two limits of soft shell clams in the rain.

March 22, 1991
It was a sunny and warm day. Jean and I made a trip to Sauvie Island just to wander around. We fished the Gilbert River for catfish, crappie, carp and whatever else was there. We caught no fish.

April 20, 1991
We gave Sauvie Island another try. We fished small jigs in the Gilbert River and Sturgeon Lake and still caught no fish.

June 1992
I made a trip to American Samoa to work on a watershed project. All land is communally owned in Samoa and I needed permission from the chief

to visit or work in various parts of the island. We had opening ceremonies with the governor of Samoa when we first arrived. I later saw him on TV casting one delegate vote in the 1992 presidential election. The island was small. We could drive the length of the island in about an hour.

American Samoa

Along the road we bought octopus from a fisherman, and the motel cooked it for us. The motel owners prepared all the meals for our group. Star-Kist Tuna had a fish processing plant in Pago Pago that really smelled when the wind blew our way. We fished several evenings and caught several bottom fish from shore. I only had my lightweight pack-rod so I had difficulty landing fish. The last night of our trip the local community prepared a dinner for us. They served roast pig, baked fish, local fruits and sushi. As we were leaving I asked one of our field technicians from work if she could help me find some local colorful cloth for my wife to make a quilt. She took me to the market and picked out some material for me. She did not give me a choice, I guess in their culture men don't get a choice. She then told the clerk to put it on her bill. The chief's daughter has privileges.

July 25, 1992

We attended my wife Jean's family reunion at a campground near Mantua, Utah. My brothers-in-law Mike, Wes and Sheldon and I were bored so we headed to Box Elder Creek east of Brigham City, Utah. It was a hot day and we enjoyed the cool shade of the cottonwoods and wading in the shallow cold water. We did not think there were

fish in the creek, but cast #12 Deer Hair Grasshoppers into the larger pools and were surprised to catch half a dozen ten inch trout.

July 30, 1992

We had a family picnic at Wildwood Park on the Sandy River near Mt. Hood. It was cool and quite in the dense forest and we caught several small stocked rainbows. The water was cold and clear and felt good in the hot afternoon.

October 10, 1992

I spent the week deer hunting with Steve Stephenson. We dry camped near a slash pile in a clear cut on the east slope of Mt. Hood. Steve goes to extremes with camp meals. One night he was deveining shrimp at 10pm for shrimp cocktails. I prefer the simpler menu out of a can or freeze dried. I don't want to be tied to an ice chest. During the week we saw only does and did not get a shot off. We drove into Badger Lake one afternoon and found the last mile of road extremely rough. We should have walked in. I caught a half dozen ten to twelve inch rainbows on a #14 Wooly Worm in half hour. We quit early because Steve wanted to get back to hunting. I was disappointed to leave behind such good fishing.

October 12, 1992

I fished the Deschutes River with Jim Morris. We worked the stretch below Box Car Rapids, Jim had a bad back and could not walk very far. We caught several small trout on #14 Renegades. The fishing was not that great.

May 1993

Our son Grady was born. This time we knew what to expect. Everything went well, until Jean looked at my shoes in the delivery room and was not happy about the duct tape holding them together.

October 2, 1993

I spent the week deer hunting with Steve Stephenson. He may be coming around. We fished for a few hours each day. Maybe he thinks I'll quit coming with him if we don't fish more. We fished Boulder Creek on the east slope of Mt Hood, near an irrigation diversion. The creek was shallow, cold and completely over shadowed by large fir trees. We still managed to catch a dozen small native cutthroat trout. They took #16 Elk

Hair Caddis in the slow pools. On a whim we fished the White River, which was very silty and turbid from a glacier on Mt Hood. I was surprised to hook and land a skinny thirteen inch rainbow in the chalky water.

October 4, 1993
We deer hunted the rough road into Clear Creek, a tributary to the White River on Mt. Hood. At Keeps Mill we bush-whacked through the thick forest underbrush to reach fishable water. The river was wadeable, but very cold and fast. We caught a dozen small, colorful native trout in the pocket water on #16 Elk Hair Caddis.

June, 18, 1994
After teaching a class at the College of Eastern Oregon for a week, a few of us from work fished the Imnaha River. We drove the road between Troy and Elgin, Oregon and hiked into the wilderness area on the Cross Creek Trail. The trail was very steep and dropped several hundred feet. We caught a few small rainbows and saw several spawned out Chinook salmon. I spent an hour casting to a large Bull Trout, but he was not interested. It was a tough hike out with wet waders and the rest of our gear. We were a bit concerned about the black bear foraging in a meadow, a ridge away, but we all made it out safely.

October 1, 1994
Another deer hunting trip with Steve Stephenson was uneventful. No venison was hanging in our camp. One cold windy afternoon we fished Paulina Lake near Little Crater Campground. I caught a dozen rainbows on a #12 Wooly Worm. We saw several pods of five to ten pound brown trout rolling near the shore. I suppose they were trying to spawn, there were no rivers running into the lake. I threw every type of fly I had at them from #22 Midges to #4 Rabbit Leeches. They would not even look at a fly, even when I bumped them on the nose.

March 25, 1995
The closest place to fish from our house was Dorman's Pond, a small pond next to Gales Creek, near Glenwood, Oregon. I'd take our kids Bethany and Grady fishing every chance I could get, especially when Jean wanted a break. This was kid fishing with a spinning rod, six feet of leader, a swivel tied to the leader and an egg bubble that slid up the line from the swivel. After I cast the kids reeled the fly in. It was here that Bethany caught her first trout. We usually kept two or three fish for dinner and released the rest. I taught them catch and release, trying to instill in them the concept that you don't have to keep everything you catch. The trout were all stocked, and we caught at least a dozen twelve to fourteen inch fish.

June 17, 1995
We took our 11 year old scouts on a camping-fishing trip up the Columbia Gorge to Eagle Creek. We hiked up to punch bowl and wet waded and swam a little. The trail was crowded and the fishing poor so we decided to visit the fish hatchery on the way home and take the boys on a short tour of the facilities. We noticed several people fishing in the brood stock pond at the hatchery and asked the warden what was going on. He said they needed to clean out the ponds to stock new fish, and invited us to help fish out the pond. We gladly obliged and filled our limit. The boys had great fun casting and catching large fish on flies. We left after dark and rushed the boys home. That night several concerned parents called to ask me "What the heck are you doing taking my kid fishing at the trout hatchery after dark?" I explained, but still got stern looks from parents every time I take their boys on an outing.

July 18, 1995
We worked on the Warm Springs Indian Reservation for a week, and camped on the shores of Lake Billy Chinook where the Metolius River enters the lake. The tribe set up long houses and teepees for us to sleep in. We fished after work each evening. We caught several dozen Brown and Rainbow Trout in the lake that were rising to midges and mayflies. I cast and swung a #6 Black Marabou Leech through the deep pool at the confluence and caught an eight pound bull trout. An Indian woman immediately ran down the hill and asked for my fish, which I gave to her. The next morning a tribal elder gave a talk about "not playing with our food". I wondered if he was talking to me about releasing so many fish. The last evening the Warm Springs Tribe had a traditional meal prepared for us. We had salmon, elk, eel, huckleberries and various other roots and berries.

October 4, 1995

I fished the Deschutes River with our regional biologist, Ken Krug. We camped in the back of his truck at the locked gate south of Maupin. We fished heavily weighted #8 Black Stonefly Nymphs and I caught a dozen thirteen to fifteen inch Redside Rainbows. On the way out of the canyon we pulled off to the side of the road at a nice looking pool, seconds before another fisherman drove up and asked if we were going to fish there. This must be a good spot. I offered Ken the pool because, I'm embarrassed to say, he had not caught any fish on this trip. He refused, and headed around the bend to the next riffle. I rigged up a gray #14 Hares Ear, weighted with a split-shot, and cast it into the white water at the head of the run. On my third cast I hooked a fish. I knew it was a steelhead after he jumped and rolled on the surface. For fear of disappointment, I struck hard on the line, twice, just to make sure he was well hooked and that the four pound tippet would hold. He screamed across the hole taking all my fly line and a couple of turns of backing, then turned and headed right at me. I could not keep him on the spool, but frantically stripped line onto my boots. He surged upstream past the boulders at the head of the pool and I was able to get the line tight and back on my reel. Once again he headed downstream. Passing within a rod's length of where I was standing. For the next five minutes he circled the tail end of the pool, until I beached him on the sand. Before I could grab him by the tail, the barbless hook fell out and he thrashed in the shallow water. I was shaking as I tailed a bright eight pound steelhead buck! This was my first Deschutes steelhead. I yelled to Ken to come take a picture. He apparently did not understand me as he yelled back "just a minute". When he finally did come around the willows he was surprised. I felt bad about out-fishing our fisheries biologist.

October 5, 1995

On the way home from the Deschutes Ken Krug and I fished two lakes on Mt. Hood. Trillium Lake was a bust because it was cold and the wind silted up the shallow lake. Lost Lake was a little warmer but by then it started to snow. I promised Ken we would not leave until he caught fish. Two hours later Ken finally caught a small trout and we went home cold.

April 13, 1996

Grady and I fished Dorman's Pond, near Highway 8 and Gales Creek. We only caught two trout. Towards the end of the day I caught a particularly nice fish, decided to keep it for dinner, and went back to casting. Grady noticed the fish, ran over and threw it back into the water before I could catch him. This mildly irritated me until an old gentleman laughed and asked, "Is your kid an environmentalist?"

May 25, 1996

I took Grady on his first camping trip to Fort Stevens, on the Oregon coast. We fished Coffenbury Lake in the evening and caught one trout from the dock. We watched another kid hook a stocked steelhead on a single salmon egg. He was one excited kid.

July 20, 1996

My son and I fished Hagg Lake, near Forest Grove, Oregon. We caught several stocked trout near the dam. There were too many people casting to the only accessible pool, so we headed south to the picnic-boat ramp area. We slid down the steep shoreline and waded through several inches of slick mud to cast wet flies through the weed beds. We caught several dozen very small crappie and perch.

August 1996

We took a group of Boy Scouts to Camp Cooper near Willimina on the Oregon Coast Range. We fished Lake Hurl, which was named after several boys who had a hard time keeping camp food down. The first night at camp several boys caught their first fish. It's sad their fathers or older brothers missed teaching and watching them catch their first fish. The second night a few boys from another troop joined us, and we caught a few more fish. I had encouraged the boys to release all their fish. Only two boys kept fish. The third night fish were rising all over the lake, but we caught no fish. I suppose we educated the fish the previous two days.

February 22, 1997

Skip Gaudreau and I took our Boy Scouts surf fishing at Cape Meares, Oregon. At high tide we spin-casted orange and red wooly buggers tied eighteen and thirty six inches above a three ounce pyramid sinker. We did well, filling a five gallon bucket with a dozen fish in less than an hour. The pink-finned perch were as shinny as new silver dollars and almost as round. We had several doubles and the boys had a great time taking turns reeling them in. On the way home we stopped at the Oyster House on Tillamook Bay and enjoyed watching the boys try their first raw oysters. A few oysters did not stay down and returned to see the light of day.

June 2, 1997
I fished Meacham Creek with Jay Gibbs and Kevin Conroy near where it dumps into the Umatilla River on the Umatilla Indian Reservation. We fished #16 Pheasant Tails and caught two dozen small trout. Kevin and I purchased tribal fishing permits. Jay did not and received a stern warning from the tribal game warden who threatened to take his truck. Lesson learned.

June 5, 1997
I fished McKay Reservoir, near Pendleton, Oregon, with several guys from work. This was my first experience in a float tube. The cool water felt good in the hot afternoon, and the compressed water pressure on my waders and feeling of weightlessness was a new experience. I caught six crappies on #10 Marabou Buggers near the submerged willows on the south shore.

June 20, 1997
I fished Lost Lake in the coast range in Clatsop County, Oregon. Casting was difficult from the steep wooded shoreline. There was no trail around the lake and wind-blown timber littered the ground making it impossible to fish except a few isolated spots. A boat is really needed to fish this small lake. The water was deep, very clean and pure. I caught three stocked trout on #16 Wet Renegades.

June 27, 1997
I took Grady on his first hike-in fishing trip with one of my scouts Zack Watson. After driving past Trillium Lake on Mt. Hood, Oregon on a very rough road, we hiked a mile into Veda Lake. The fishing was slow in the middle of the day, but we still managed to catch three fat brook trout on #16 Wooly Worms.

Brook Trout, Veda Lake, Oregon

I cast the fly and Grady reeled it in. He was able to land one trout and was very excited. He was a little tired on the steep hike out and slept all the way home. We had an enjoyable day.

July 8, 1997
Grady and I spent the day at Vernonia Pond kid fishing. I rigged up a spinning rod with a #12 Wooly Worm, five foot leader tied to a swivel and an egg bubble (filled three-fourths with water) sliding on the line above the swivel. I'd cast and Grady would reel the line in. We caught several dozen small bluegill and perch.

July 24, 1997
Grady and I fished Lost Lake on Mt. Hood. It was a hot, sunny day and the fish were not biting. We only caught one trout. On top of that, there were too many people boating, jogging, biking and walking around the lake. We left the crowds for the deep woods and picked a gallon of huckleberries. On the way home we stopped at Cascade Locks and watched several fisherman catch squawfish in the Columbia River, where a bounty is paid for each squawfish caught and killed. Several guys were also catching shad on streamers in the spill-way. The Sturgeon fisherman had no luck.

August 23, 1997
On a family road trip we stopped at Elk Lake on the Cascade Lakes Highway for a picnic. A few small fish were rising to termites that the wind was blowing into the water, I only had a few minutes and quickly rigged up a rod and caught one small trout on a #14 Wooly Worm.

September 13, 1997
Grady, Bethany and I spent the day at Vernonia Pond. We caught over a hundred small bluegill, crappie and perch on #14 Olive Damsel Nymphs. The fish were so plentiful they would have taken almost any fly. I caught a two pound largemouth bass on a small bluegill that I'd hooked seconds before.

October 3, 1997
I hunted deer with Steve Stephenson at Magone Lake, north of John Day, Oregon. We set up camp late and did not have time to fish the first evening. The next morning Steve and his son David set out early up the ridge east of the lake. I left camp at sun up and caught two brook trout before I heard several shots echoing up the hill. I kept on fishing, catching a few more brookies and one rainbow trout on #14 Scuds and #12 Damselfly nymphs. Most of the fish were in the weedy shallows. I noticed Steve walking down the hill, blood up to his elbows. He got his deer. While hiking around the lake back to camp, my knee-high boot got stuck in the muck and slipped off. I was surprised to find a large dragon fly nymph, the size of my thumb, inside my boot. I spent the rest of the day helping clean, quarter and haul venison off the hill.

October 11, 1997
I wanted to get one more fishing trip in before it started to rain for the winter. My wife Jean needed a break so I took our daughter Bethany for a long drive. We ended up at Lost Lake, in Clatsop County, Oregon. It was a cold, calm day and the fish were not biting. We stretched our legs by walking part way around the lake on an old logging road.

Lost Lake, Clatsop County, Oregon

On the way back to the car we noticed a small ring from a rising fish not far from shore. We quickly headed in the fish's direction and I tied on a small wet fly. I cast for twenty minutes without any luck. My daughter protested as I prepared to take one more cast. The fish rose again about fifty feet from the first rise and I cast another ten feet in the direction the fish was heading. A sixteen inch rainbow took my fly and headed towards a sunken tree. I turned and landed him in the gravel shallows. Bethany was not impressed, but we took the fish home for dinner anyway.

November 8, 1997
I was invited elk hunting with Steve Stephenson. We hiked into Bloom Lake, less than a mile off August Fire Road, in Clatsop County, Oregon. We saw several small native cutthroats taking mosquito larva on the surface of the shallow lake. I spooked almost every fish I cast towards. They were very leader shy. I finally hooked a fish but did not land it. We did not see any elk and left when the mosquitoes got worse.

November 11, 1997
I took Bethany and Grady fishing at Faraday Reservoir near Estacada, Oregon. Beth can cast her own fly and does a pretty good job. While I helped Grady she walked down the shore to a small point threw out a fly and then started screaming "I got one, I got one!" This was Bethany's first trout all by herself. Of course she released it. We also fished Small Fry pond at Promontory Park, which was kid only fishing, and caught several rainbows.

December 26, 1997
Grady and I took a hike on the Oregon coast the day after Christmas. It was nice weather, partly sunny and about 60 degrees. We walked the beach from Cape Meares to the South Jetty, about four miles. We fished the surf until we reached the jetty. On our return trip we trekked back through the forest trail. We explored Oceanside, an old town on the sand spit that washed away in a big storm thirty or more years ago. Half way home Grady tired out. He did well for a four year old. I made a travois and dragged him two miles to the car. We caught no fish but had a great time.

December 30, 1997
I fished the North Jetty, near Barview, Oregon. I met and fished with a guy who was a corrections officer for Tillamook County. I never did get his name. He had the perfect job. He was able to fish every high and low tide because he set his own schedule at the jail. His clients were not going anywhere. We fished rubber jigs deep along the rock rip-rap. The local scuba divers had marked the good holes by painting small diving flags on the rocks. We fished at high tide. My friend caught a toothy three foot long ling cod. This type of fishing is new to me. I did not get a hit.

March 5, 1998
I had been thinking all winter about Lost Lake, on the Coast Range and was going stir crazy at home. I drove my car around windblown timber on the logging road to be the first to fish the lake this year. It was snowing, so no fish were rising and I caught nothing.

March 7, 1998
I took a solo fishing trip to the coast and arrived at Cape Meares just before high tide. I tied on two #10 yellow marabou streamers, above a three ounce pyramid sinker, and caught a couple of Surf Perch as the tide was receding. After lunch I headed to the North Jetty, near Barview, to fish the low tide. I cast a five-eighth ounce white rubber jig with twelve pound line and twenty pound tippet. I cast, let the jig sink for five seconds, and then slowly retrieved the lure. The tide kept my line taunt and gave the lure a pulsating action. Having little experience with tides or saltwater, I was surprised how strong the tides were. I repeated the process in five second intervals until I hit the rocks on the bottom at thirty seconds. I caught a nice five pound Black Rock Bass on the outgoing low tide. He put up a fight for a few minutes but went lifeless when he got close to the rocks. I had no problems lifting him out of the water over the large jetty boulders. An hour later on the incoming low tide I caught a twenty four inch Ling Cod, just barely legal to keep. Both fish did not fight like freshwater fish, but they made up for it in size and teeth. I tried for steelhead in the Wilson River on the drive home, but had no luck. A lot of guys think that March is the best time for Wilson River steelhead because they are bigger and mostly native, and

because there are fewer people to contend with. I'll have to give it another shot next year.

Ling Cod, Barview, Oregon

March 13, 1998
I fished the Deschutes River black stonefly hatch with Treg Owings. We parked at Lower Bridge, just west of Terrebonne, Oregon and fished the first mile up from the bridge. I tied on a #16 Black Parachute Stonefly with a tent wing. The river was at flood stage all winter because there were no irrigation withdraws. Most of the trout were next to shore where the current was not as strong. I walked up a flooded pasture and fished several runs through the semi-submerged willows. I caught my first brown trout in two feet of water on a flooded cow trail. I waded through an acre of cattails and muck to fish several small back eddies along the main channel. I was rewarded with several two pound brown trout. Most fish were fourteen to sixteen inches long and feisty. The fishing was good, but it was difficult to maneuver in the mud and muck.

March 19, 1998
I fished the Wallowa River in Oregon, near Big Canyon, with several guys after work. We were told that several steelhead were caught there the week before. We swung streamers and indicator nymphed #10 Glo-Bugs. We caught no fish.

March 28, 1998
Grady and I fished Vernonia Pond. It was fairly cold and cloudy. We caught a dozen stocked trout

and a few small crappie and bluegill. While hiking around the lake we found a foul-hooked ten pound largemouth bass floating in the weeds.

April 11, 1998
We took the Boy Scouts camping at Fort Stevens State Park on the coast, and explored the old fort in the evening. We spent the next day at Whisky Springs Fish Hatchery, a privately owned hatchery managed by local sport fishermen. We helped fin-clip over 100,000 fall Chinook smolts and had a great time meeting and working with other fishermen.

May 11, 1998
I took a road trip with Jay Gibbs and Kevin Conroy from work. We spent the first night at Dave Franzen's house on the Snake River near Homedale, Idaho, fishing for carp. The next day we drove through West Yellowstone and camped at Bear Trap Canyon, on the Madison River. We missed the Mother's Day caddis fly hatch by a few weeks. After a tough morning of fishing I caught one whitefish on a nymph. We spent the next four days camping near Craig, Montana, fishing the Missouri River. We shuttled pontoon boats up to the bridge below Halter Dam each morning and floated down to the campground just south of town.

Rainbow Trout, Missouri River, Montana

Many fish were rising to midges and blue wing olives and we caught quite a few on #18 BWO Parachutes and #20 Griffiths Gnats. Most of the rising fish were close to shore out of the current. There were hundreds of spent mayflys and midges in the back-eddies. We preferred to fish drys but could only do so when fish were rising. Most fish were caught sub-surface on #16 San Juan Worms, #16 Pink Scuds, and #18 Pheasant Tails. We each averaged a half dozen two to three pound rainbow trout each day. These were strong, wild, smart fish who were very aware of fishermen trying to do them harm. For a change of pace towards the end of the week we hiked up and fished the Dearborn River. The fishing was slow, but we caught a few small trout. The Missouri River was fishing better.

Dearborn River, Montana

On the trip home we stayed at Bob Dunagon's cabin near Sand Point, Idaho. We shot clay pigeons from the porch and split wood in their barn. Bob had an ancient rusting pot-belly stove in the barn that I traded for forty eight dozen flies. We polished the nickel and re-blacked the cast iron and the stove is now sitting in our living room.

June 8, 1998
Grady and I took his Grandmother Gordon fishing at Vernonia Pond. We caught a bunch of small crappie and bluegill. It was hot and humid so we spend most of the day in the shade of the big ash and maple trees. We chased a few carp in the Nehalem River, but had no luck with the big fish.

June 27, 1998
Grady and I fished Lawrence Lake, near Parkdale, Oregon. We caught several small stocked trout from the steep bank west of the boat ramp. The fish were jumping everywhere and we sight cast to most of the fish. They were taking damsel nymphs.

July 5, 1998
We had a family picnic with Mark and Dixie Larson and their family at Vernonia Pond. The lake had a light green algae bloom, but we managed to catch two dozen crappie and bluegill. It was hot and humid and we tried to fish under the large maples on the far side of the lake.

August 15, 1998
I took ten boy scouts on a fifty mile, six day hike around Mt. Hood, Oregon. We began at Lolo Pass, hiked through Cloud Cap, Timberline Lodge, and down Zig Zag Mountain to meet our ride out. Each day we hiked about twelve miles. We spent one day relaxing at Dumbbell Lake, swimming, fishing and enjoying a crayfish lunch. The huckleberries were ripe and plentiful. We saw numerous bear scrapings on the fir trees.

August 29, 1998
I took our scout troop on a stream inventory down the Wilson River, Oregon. We floated on inner-tubes and saw one steelhead and a few small trout. There were few fishermen on the river.

September 26, 1998
I surf fished the spit north of Cape Meares, Oregon. I caught no fish, but hooked and landed a large Dungeness crab on a #8 Orange Marabou Shrimp. There was an unusual amount of debris in the water and I had to clean my lure off after each cast.

January 1999
Treg Owings, a fishing fanatic I worked with, invited me to join a new internet computer fly fishing group called the International Fly Fishing Association. The founder, Bob Kloskowski, was a retired engineer living in Bozeman, Montana. Bob had done well in his career on the east coast and retired at a young age. He and his wife Judi moved out west to fish full time. The purpose of the IFFA group is to share information about fly fishing and develop worldwide friendships. The unwritten goal was to have a member in every country of the world who could host fishing trips for association members. Each member gets at least a dozen emails each day from the group. We spend a lot of time discussing where in the world to have our next association fishing conclave. Over time many of us have become family and

I've made some good friends and learned a lot more about fly fishing from the group.

February 26, 1999
I fished the Deschutes River, northwest of Redmond, Oregon, about a mile upstream from Odin Falls. There were cold, scattered showers, and it was a bit windy. I fished the back eddies along the flooded stream channel. By the end of the day I had landed a dozen browns and one rainbow trout. My best fly was a #16 Black Parachute Stonefly, but I did pick-up a few fish on a #18 BWO Parachute.

March 20, 1999
My son Grady and I took the neighbor kids fishing at Vernonia Pond. We caught two stocked trout with a spinning rod, bubble and fly. We left because we were soaked after a downpour.

April 19, 1999
I was in Clyde Scott's carpool for several years, he drove every day to work and never charged me for gas. He only asked for my fly box every spring, to which he helped himself to several dozen flies. As our biologist he taught me much about habitat management and had given me several entomology books on aquatic insects. He had been retired for a several years when he called me to go fishing. I took him to Lost Lake on the coast range. We pumped up our pontoon boats and entered the lake amidst dozens of rising fish. By noon we each had caught three or four dozen stocked rainbows. This was too easy. They must have stocked the trout the previous week. I was fishing a #12 Carey Special with a sink-tip line, and caught the most fish in the middle of the small lake. Clyde was having a great time, but a little stiff getting around. By the time we went home in the late afternoon, we had caught over a hundred fish. This was my last trip with Clyde. He died of cancer six months later.

April 30, 1999
I returned to Lost Lake on the coast range and was blessed with a Callibaetis mayfly hatch. I sight-cast to rising fish and caught two dozen rainbows on a #16 Elk Hair Caddis. After the hatch I picked up a few more stocked rainbows on #12 Carey Specials. It was another good day on a peacefully quite lake.

May 31, 1999
We fished Vernonia Pond with fly rods for the first time. Grady and I got a lot of casting practice and caught a dozen bluegill and crappie on #14 Damselfly Nymphs.

June 1999
I fished with the International Fly Fishing Association on the Green River, Utah. We camped at Dripping Springs Campground. We each averaged two dozen fish a day, mostly browns but occasional a rainbow.

Brown Trout, Green River, Utah

Most fish were sixteen to eighteen inches, but we did catch a few twenty inch fish. Most of us fished nymphs. The set-up was a yarn strike indicator a few inches down the leader from the fly line, nine feet of leader, a small lead split shot ten inches above the upper fly, ten inches of tippet tied to the hook bend and the lower fly. The upper fly was a #10 San Juan worm, #12 pink bead head scud or a #14 pheasant tail nymph. Most fish were caught on the lower fly which was a #18 or #20 bead head pheasant tail, brassy, tan-green scud or red annelid. Because the water was so high, three times the average at 10,000 cfs, the majority of the fish were hooked within ten feet of the bank. Most casts were less than thirty feet. We tried to get a slow drag-free drift that occasionally bumped the bottom. I did take a break from nymphs one afternoon and cast dry flies. Fish rose to Griffith Gnats, foam beetles, ants and a deer hair cicada. The cicada was the most exciting. I watched a large brown trout follow my fly for ten feet, rise slowly, open her mouth slowly and gulp down my fly. I tried to set the hook and pulled the fly right out of her mouth. A few moments later

another large brown jumped completely out of the water and tried to hit the cicada on the way down. I never hooked either fish, but it was terrific sport. The total cost of the seven day 1,800 mile trip was: Shared transportation: $200, Meals: $150, Campground $50, Miscellaneous Expenses: $100. The total cost was $500.

July 23, 1999
Todd Wilson and our boys fished the Salmon River, near Mt. Hood, Oregon. We caught three dozen, six to ten inch, native cutthroat and wild rainbow trout. The best fly was a #16 Renegade and #16 Elk Hair Caddis.

August 20, 1999
Our scout troop spent a week backpacking and fishing on the Salmon River on Mt. Hood, Oregon. We had the whole river to ourselves and caught native cutthroats and wild rainbows. Beautiful fish, not too big, most in the ten to twelve inch range. All were caught on dry flies. The best flies were #12 Yellow Madam X and #14 Elk Hair Caddis. We didn't catch any steelhead, but spooked a few. All six boy scouts caught and released their first trout on dry flies. We each averaged about two dozen fish per day. I really enjoy helping someone catch their first fish on a fly, especially a dry fly. My assistant scout leader could not make the trip so we took Rob, who was on our scout troop committee. He had little outdoor experience and I was leery about taking him, but we could not get another adult to go so he came. The second day he stood on a yellow jacket hornet's nest. He got stung about a dozen times before he figured out what was happening. Though not allergic to bee stings, he panicked, ran to find me and stood on a rock in the middle of the river waving and screaming. As I approached, he passed out. One of my scouts and I held him on the rock so he would not fall into the river. Finally, he came to and we carried him to shore where he fainted again. Then he went into shock (very white and sweating). I sent two boys to the main trail to look for help, but no one was within miles. Finally Rob calmed down and pulled out of it. We helped him back to the trail and back to camp. With the help of some aspirin, he slept the rest of the day and felt fine the rest of the week. It was a learning experience for the scouts. Two days later we saw several hikers with horses packing kayaks up the trail. We didn't think

much of it until they floated past where we were camping. They told us they were looking for a hiker who had been missing for three weeks. They suspected he had drowned in the river. We were a bit concerned as we had been drinking water out of the same small creek where they were looking for the body! At times like this you really hope your water purifier works. Besides the usual pranks and behavior of boy scouts, and raccoons visiting our camp at night, it was a good trip.

August 27, 1999
Grady and I went camping at Silver Falls State Park, near Silverton, Oregon. We fished about a half mile of Silver Creek, a pristine small stream in old-growth forest, and caught a few native cutthroats. It is amazing under what conditions a trout can survive. There was a 250 foot waterfall upstream and an eighty five foot waterfall downstream. I don't know how fish, over hundreds of years, could maintain an existence through such obstacles. The area had never been stocked and the fish were very wild.

August 30, 1999
Grady and I went surf fishing at Cape Meares, Oregon. We got sun burned, which is difficult to do in the Pacific Northwest. We caught one pink-fin surfperch on a #8 Grey Ghost. Surfperch will strike at almost everything, we've even caught them on stonefly nymphs. It was relaxing to fish in a cool breeze and watch the waves break onto beautiful sandy beaches. On the way home we stopped at the Guide Shop on the Wilson River. They said that the steelhead fishermen could not keep the sea-run cutthroat trout off the line long enough to hook steelhead. We timed it just right and caught three dozen sea-run cutthroats on elk hair caddis and wooly worms. They were in every hole in the lower river.

October 9, 1999
I camped with my hunting partner Steve Stephenson and his son David. They hunted deer, I fished. We ate more fish than venison. In six days we fished six Cascade lakes west of Bend, Oregon. I took the Oregon grand slam by catching rainbow, brown, brook trout and small mouth bass on the same trip. We camped at Wickiup Reservoir and caught brown trout at sun up and sun down; it was very slow during the day. We should have caught rainbows at Davis Lake,

but only landed a few small bass. It was cold and rainy in my float tube. North and South Twin Lakes produced a few small rainbows, but they had a lot of fishing pressure. Crane Prairie Reservoir was excellent and we caught many large fat rainbows, in the three pound range, in warm and sunny weather. The best lake was Lava Lake. I caught two fat brook trout and a couple dozen rainbows. The three largest rainbows were eighteen inches, hooked jawed, and they really jumped. The only fly that worked was a #8 Black Bead Head Wooly bugger.

October 23, 1999
A neighbor Jerry Mailing and our boys surf fished at Tunnel Beach, near Oceanside, Oregon. It was raining, windy and a very high surf. We caught one Pink Finned Surf Perch. I cast a spinning rod with a three ounce pyramid sinker and a #8 Chartreuse Marabou Leech. We barely made it through the tunnel and safely back to the parking lot before high tide.

December 22, 1999
I picked up Aaron Widen at 5:30am and met Treg Owings in The Dalles, Oregon two hours later. We fished the Deschutes River where it emptied into the Columbia River. The day began slowly. It was cloudy, about 40 degrees, with a slight wind. The lower part of the river was a little off-color but fishable. I was fishing a seven weight, sink tip with four feet of ten pound leader and a weighted #6 Red and Black Marabou Leech. The Deschutes River where we were fishing was about 100 yards across, relatively shallow and swift. We waded out to the slower water up to our chests, cast across the river and slowly swing our flys downstream. After several casts, we would step downstream several feet and repeat the process. Three otters surfaced as they floated by, laughing at me because they had fish and I didn't. I caught one thirteen inch trout before noon. Just before dark and after a mile hike up and back down the river, I cast across a long drift and felt a small tug and saw a flash of silver tail. A nice steelhead took a long run downstream, jumped completely out of the water several times and headed upstream. She fought back and forth across the river before finally tiring out. I slowly waded towards shore and beached her on the sandy bank. She was a beautiful steelhead of about seven pounds, twenty four inches long, fat and chrome silver.

Steelhead, Deschutes River, Oregon

She was a fin-clipped hatchery fish so I kept her for Christmas dinner. We fished until it was pitch black and our fingers and feet were numb. That steelhead was one of the best gifts I have ever received for Christmas.

2000

February 3, 2000
I tie a lot of flies, which I enjoy. I even made a deal with my children. My nine year old daughter had a school homework assignment to read to a parent for half-hour every night. She reads to me while I tie. My six year old son likes to watch me tie and rummage through my dead animals, asking a lot of questions. So we talk. My wife knows what I'm doing and can keep an eye on me. I also listen to talk radio and have all but given up on television. I usually tie a dozen flies every night and a couple dozen each weekend during the winter. It's no problem getting rid of flies, I like to barter. I've got the neighbor's kids trained. They trade all sorts of fur and feathers for flies. Last month alone I received squirrel tails, a woodpecker, and deer and elk hides. A secretary at work even traded an old mink coat for a framed classic salmon fly. I've got several of my Boy Scouts who chop and stack wood, mow our lawn, and rake leaves in exchange for flies. I also fish with several guys who take me fishing in exchange for flies. For every hour they drive, I tie. It was a good deal for me. It's nice when your hobby can pay for itself.

February 21, 2000
We took our scouts surf fishing at Tunnel Beach near Oceanside, Oregon. It was cloudy and windy. We caught three Pink Finned Surf Perch.

March 4, 2000
I met a few friends on Mt. Hood for our annual winter snow camp at Nanitch Lodge, below Timberline Lodge. It snowed most of the night, but was a relatively warm 30 degrees with very little wind. The next morning I headed to Terrebonne, Oregon and turned west to the Deschutes River. Two varieties of little black stoneflys and midges were all over the water. Brown trout were dimpling the surface along the flooded cattails and willows. It was time for small black parachute dry stoneflys. I hooked six and landed four brown trout, between twelve to sixteen inches. The sun never did come out, but luckily I avoided the rain for most of the afternoon. It was a good day to be alone on the river. I stopped at the fly shop in Welches on my way home and almost bought a pontoon boat I'd been looking at the last few months.

April 6, 2000
I tie flies as a hobby and have the goal of making my hobby pay for itself. I don't have the fanciest rods or reels, but I am able to purchase all my tying materials, equipment, and pay for travel from my profits selling flies. I tie for friends and always keep several dozen in my day pack to trade or sell to people I meet fishing. I've sold flies at a neighbor's Christmas bazaar, and last year made about $300. I sold several framed salmon flies over the Internet for $50 each. I am still developing my classic salmon skills and hope to be able to charge more as I become more proficient. I also barter for goods and services. I traded several dozen flies to a carpenter to replace our entire kitchen's wood trim and traded forty eight dozen flies for a $2,000 wood stove.

April 17, 2000
I worked on the island of Saipan in the South Pacific, halfway between Japan and New Guinea. The first evening on the island we went fishing. We hired a boat for $70 and caught grouper, triggerfish and several kinds of snapper. I also caught a large shark but we couldn't get it to the boat, it broke the twenty pound monofilament line. We also brought several dolphin fish (mahi mahi) to the boat, but we couldn't hook them. We took the fish to the hotel restaurant and they cleaned and cooked them for us in exchange for several of the fish.

Saipan, Northern Mariana Islands, Pacific

The next evening I made friends with a local fisherman who had a boat. I bought gas and we trolled for sailfish and marlin. We caught neither, but did see a barracuda chase a whole flock of flying fish out of the water near our boat. We fished together after work the rest of the week. This time my friend didn't charge for gas, but I bought the ice and drinks. We lured several fish to the surface but didn't get anything in the boat. Several flying fish jumped near the boat and almost fell into our laps. Barracuda swam up next to our boat, but we could not get our lures out fast enough to cast to them. We got lost trying to find the harbor after dark, but safely arrived after several attempts. The coral reefs were dangerous in the area. At the end of the week we exchanged gifts with several people we worked with. My favorite gift was several necklaces with reef fish carved out of an ivory nut. I also received a large fish carved out of two pieces of water buffalo horn. The last evening we sat on the beach while my fishing partner, Gibson, told stories he heard as a child from his fisherman grandfather. He told us the Mangrove Snapper will stick its tail out of the water on the roots of the mangrove. After a while, flies will smell the fish and buzz around trying to lay their eggs on the fish. The flies attracted rats that thought the fish had washed ashore and was an easy meal. As the rat bites the Mangrove Snapper's tail, the fish flips the rat into the water and eats the rat. Gibson says that the Mangrove Snapper is a very smart fish because rats were not native to South Pacific islands, and were introduced only within the last 150 years. For a fish to figure this out is quite amazing. He also told us that many years ago all the fish called a meeting to decide how to fight the birds that were attacking them. All the fish came to the meeting except the sole, flounder, and halibut. After the meeting the fish began to battle the birds, and many fish died. After the battle the fish were angry at the sole, flounder, and the halibut for not helping, so they trapped them and beat them. That is why both their eyes were on the same side of their heads.

April 29, 2000
I fished Lost Lake, in the coast range up the logging road from the Spruce-Run Campground on the Nehalem River. I caught three dozen stocked rainbows on a #12 Bead Head Carey Special. There were several dozen planted

steelhead swimming the margins of the lake. Oregon Fish and Wildlife must have had a few fish left over from their fish hatchery program and released them into the lake.

June 8, 2000
I fished the Deschutes River with Treg and Sue Owings in our pontoon boats. We drifted from Warm Springs to Trout Creek, about eight miles. The river was slightly off-color. We had sunshine, a few clouds, 70 degrees and occasional strong wind gusts. The conditions were perfect for fishing. The first week of June usually brings large stoneflys in great abundance to the Deschutes - this year was no exception. There were thousands of three-inch black stoneflys and slightly smaller golden stoneflys on the river. Several stoneflys will feed a large trout for a day. The fishing was not that great. The fish must have been stuffed, or at least that was my excuse. I did manage to hook a dozen and land three large rainbows that were about sixteen inches long. In addition to stoneflys, there were caddis, mayflies, and midges on the water making it difficult to choose the right fly. Many fish were rising to mayflies and midges in the back eddies and ignoring the larger insects. Stonefly imitations worked best in the deeper runs below trees and shrubs, but occasionally fish would rise in shallow water. I had the most success wading next to the deep undercut banks and casting beneath tree limbs next to the shore. The riparian grasses were three feet tall and prime habitat for mating stoneflys because livestock grazing is not allowed along the river.

Mecca Flat, Deschutes River, Oregon

The best dry fly was an orange or black foam stonefly, with dark deer hair wing, badger hackle, and rubber legs. Stoneflys were easy to cast: just slam the fly on the surface to get the trout's attention. Real stoneflys hit the surface hard and cause a lot of commotion. I did catch a couple of trout on stonefly nymphs, but only switched to wet flies when the wind was blowing strong enough to make dry fly casting difficult. All the trout I caught attacked the fly, jumped a half dozen times, ran thirty feet of line off my reel, and reluctantly came in. Once released, they still had enough energy to dart off into the depths. These were tough fish. A large trout could put up a strong five minute fight. The Deschutes River is in good condition and managed as a native rainbow fishery. There were an estimated 1,700 mature Redside trout per river mile. The native steelhead were relatively abundant, and hatchery steelhead were plentiful. We saw several steelhead redds in the shallow riffles. This year had the best Chinook salmon return in the last fifty years. The Warm Springs Tribe had the best fishing holes locked up around Sherar's Falls.

June 24, 2000

To offset our son's hunting trips in the fall, my deer hunting partners Steve Stephenson, Doug Healy, and I took our daughters fishing. Our daddy-daughter trip was to Little Lava Lake, where we spent four days camping and fishing ten high Cascade lakes and the upper Deschutes River in central Oregon. Fishing with three ten year old girls is quite an experience. They brought their dolls and make-up and kept us up half the night giggling. My daughter Bethany is a pretty good fly fisher and she insists on catch-and-release so she doesn't have to eat fish. One morning before breakfast we had been fishing for half an hour with no luck. Bethany came down to the river after sleeping in and hooked a brook trout on her first cast, landed and released the fish and promptly set the rod down and hiked back to camp laughing. At Wickiup Reservoir, we fished for half an hour with no luck until Bethany decided to fish and she caught two fish in two casts. The girls fly fish with spinning reels, using a slip egg float behind a swivel, six feet of leader, and a wet fly. They were all good casters, flinging the four pound test line and fly over fifty feet into the lake. They laughed when trout jumped out of the water. We caught Brown Trout at Wickiup Reservoir, Brook Trout at Little Lava Lake, and Rainbow Trout at the other lakes. Our largest

trout was seventeen inches, but most of the fish were in the eight to twelve inch range.

Brown Trout, Wickiup Reservoir, Oregon

Doug lost a bet with his daughter and she painted his fingernails red. The poor guy had to put his hands in his pockets every time we ran into other people. On the way home he forgot about the nail polish as he was paying for dinner at a restaurant. The cashier gave him a strange look and then scowled. He smiled and was very embarrassed. We were already planning our trip for next year.

July 10, 2000

I fished with the International Fly Fishing Association at Roche Lake near Kamloops, British Columbia. It was a 500 mile, nine hour drive from home. We each caught about a dozen fish each day, with at least two over twenty inches. The fishing was relatively slow for this area and the weather was unseasonably cold. The damselfly and caddis hatch was late. My best fly was a #12 Olive Hackle Brown Bead Head Wooly Bugger, fished close to the bottom with short slow strips. I used twenty feet of 4X leader on a floating line. We fished each day from 6am until 10am. I took a short nap mid-afternoon after a quick meal of crackers and smoked oysters. I hooked the fabled thirty inch trout in Monster Bay. It took my fly and headed at a forty five degree angle away while still pulling line out of my reel. The line was stripping through the water like a water skier towrope. The fish jumped three times and broke off. It was big and strong. Each night we had a pot-luck dinner around the campfire and told stories. It went well the first two nights, but on the third night Raven Wing shared a few stories that gave us the creeps. She's an Indian who claims to be a Wicken. She sat directly across the campfire from me and her eyes glowed as she spoke of the fish gods and spirit of the mother earth. I didn't sleep well that night. And to make matters worse, we saw a bear cub in camp the following evening. Call me paranoid but I was sure mother bear and Raven were looking for trouble that night as I lay trying to sleep in my tent.

Rainbow, Roche Lake, British Columbia

The last day of the trip I got caught out in the lake during a rain, hail, thunder, and lightning storm. It's interesting how all the water around you turns white during such a storm. I made it to shore before the lightning started and watched the show under a dry fir tree. After the storm the traveling caddis were out and with the encouragement of the BC fly fishers in our group, I tried a #14 Tom Thumb dry fly. Who would believe that pulling around a dry fly on the surface, creating a wake would bring big fish to the surface? The trip cost: Transportation: $100, Car: 1,700 Miles, Meals: $100, Campground $20, Miscellaneous Expenses: $50, six Days, Total Cost: $270

July 22, 2000
Grady and I fished Faraday Reservoir, near Estacada Oregon. Fish and Game stock the lake every few weeks so there were always a lot of fish, and fishermen. We caught and released a dozen stocked rainbows. I cast a fly with a spinning rod and Grady reeled in the fish. We had Taco Bell burritos on the way home, it was becoming our fishing trip tradition.

July 29, 2000
My family spent the day on the beach sightseeing and collecting shells. On the way home we fished the lower Wilson River. Above the Rock Gardens we caught and released two dozen small trout and a few steelhead smolts on #18 barbless dry flies.

July 31, 2000
Don Welch, my fellow scout leader, and I took our Varsity Scouts on a Cascade Lake canoe trek for six days. We set up base camp at Link Lake near Santiam Pass in central Oregon. There were a dozen lakes within five miles of our base camp. Most lakes were about thirty acres across and ten feet deep. All the lakes had native cutthroat trout and a few stocked brook and rainbow trout. We had the lakes all to ourselves for four days, until other campers starting showing up for the weekend. We had some unwelcome visitors the first afternoon. Three older gentlemen visited our camp Monday evening and asked if we were planning to camp at the lake all week, to which we responded yes. They were planning on bring 120 young women from a church group to "our" lake and camp Thursday and Friday night. Our fifteen year old scouts went ballistic with anticipation. It was a dream come true for the boys - a nightmare for me. We convinced the gentlemen to camp at the next lake a half mile away, to which they reluctantly agreed. Our scouts were disappointed but immediately began planning night raids to the girl's camp. Luckily, we avoided any disasters and the boys were well behaved. However, they stewed around our campfire every night as they heard the girl's campfire programs a half mile away. The fishing was slow during mid-day but picked up during the evenings. It was a hot 80 degrees, sunny, and dry the whole week. We caught many small eight to ten inch cutthroats on small wet flies, mostly #16 Renegades. The brook and rainbow trout must have been sulking at the bottom of the lake as none were caught. We took afternoon swims, which were refreshing as long as you floated in the top layer of water (about 70 degrees). Below three feet deep it got cold, especially near the underwater springs. We took a side trip to Clear Lake. The McKenzie River flows beneath several miles of lava rock and emerges at springs at the upper end of the lake. The lake is so clean and sterile you can see thirty feet deep into its depths. There were a few naturally reproducing fish in the lake, and I managed to catch a fourteen

inch cutthroat. Continuing to follow the McKenzie River downstream, we took another side trip to Trail Bridge Reservoir and were unfortunate to arrive one hour after the state hatchery truck released 5,000 rainbow trout into the lake. Our scouts were catching and releasing trout about every third cast. I'm afraid we spoiled them for good fishing. I gave them a lecture on fishing ethics and the pros and cons of artificial stocking. We ate wild huckleberry pancakes each morning, nuts, dried fruit, and chocolate for lunch and a dutch-oven meal over the campfire each evening.

August 28, 2000

I fished the Rogue River, in southwest Oregon, with Roy Mann, a retired friend from work. We drifted several miles from Dodge Bridge to the White City area. We put in at four in the afternoon and fished until dark. We fished sink tip and floating lines and streamers, trailing them behind the boat while rowing to slow us down in the current. The best patterns were the Irish Hilton and Red Ant. We drift-fished through the fast water and anchored up and cast along good pools. We caught several native cutthroat trout while the sun was on the water. As soon as the river was in the shadows of the tall pines the steelhead began to hit. The first steely smacked my fly, stripped line out and broke the leader. At the next riffle I hooked another bright steelhead. She zipped upstream right at the boat, saw us and headed downstream pulling out the drag. The next few minutes were spent chasing her back and forth across the river until we finally netted her. She was about twenty inches but full of fight. She was a nice hatchery fish. I took her home for the barbecue. After several more cutthroats it was dark and we headed for the take-out. We spooked several deer as we shuttled the trucks to pick up the boat and headed to town. The Rogue River was one of the first rivers in the United States to be designated as a "Wild and Scenic River" in the 1960's, and receives special watershed protection from development. It is a beautiful river with pristine habitat and clear, cold, water full of insects.

September 16, 2000

I took Todd Wilson and our boys fishing at Vernonia Pond. The water was shallow and warm which makes for poor fishing. We caught one

small bass then walked down to the Nehalem River to cool off in the shade. We saw several large carp jumping and took a few casts. Later we fished a nice riffle and caught a dozen small rainbows, six to eight inches, on #18 Pheasant Tail Nymphs.

September 23, 2000

Grady and I fished Harriet Reservoir, on the Upper Clackamas River. It was a hot and clear day. The fished were stocked the week before. We caught a half dozen trout on wet flies.

October 2, 2000

Our deer hunting group camped at Olallie Lake for the week. Steve Stephenson and the boys hunted while Doug Healy and I fished. What a fantastic week: I caught eleven Rainbow trout over six pounds. The largest rainbow was ten and three-quarter pounds and thirty inches long. The best area to fish was the shallow shoals east of the lodge. Pods of large trout cruised the area looking for food throughout the day. Mid-afternoon was the best. We sight cast to fish from pontoons when the water was calm.

Rainbow, Olallie Lake, Oregon

The best set-up was a seven weight rod to cast in the wind and a four pound twelve foot leader. The most effective fly was a #10 Black Bead Head Leech with sparkle, about two inches long. The large trout would gently grab the fly, slowly swim away, and then react violently when hooked. The fish would strip off line for at least thirty seconds before tiring out. Often they would tail-walk across the water trying to break off, and several times they did. It's really something to see a seven to ten pound trout leap out of the water and flip in the air. When we did bring a large trout in, they would strip off another thirty yards of line when they saw us. This happened several times until they were tired out and ready to be beached on the sandy shore.

Rainbow, Olallie Lake, Oregon

I let all my fish go except the ten pounder which the lodge manager wanted to keep. The resort manager introduced me to the lodge owner and asked if I was interested in tying flies for the lodge. Their fly tier had quit the previous season. He gave me an order for sixty dozen flies on the spot and we set up a meeting in Bend this winter to work out the rest of the details. At the campground one night we had a black bear tear the garbage cans apart. I'm glad my small Kelty tent offered adequate protection from the beast. We hiked a half mile into Lower Lake and caught several beautiful cutthroat trout and a dozen rainbows. The lake was pristine with shoals and a small campground at the north end. We stopped at Trillium Lake on the way home and caught one small rainbow trout.

November 11, 2000
Aaron Widen, one of my former boy scouts, told us he had caught fish in the Tualatin River below Roud Bridge, not far from Hillsboro High School. Being so close to home, I took Grady and his friend to the river and saw several crappie taking midges below the waste water treatment plant overflow pipe. There was a strong chlorine smell. We could not reach the rising fish.

December 6, 2000
My brother David flew to Oregon for a business meeting and we headed for the coast. At sun up we fished the lower Wilson River. We paid a Dairy farmer $3 for access to fish his property. The river was unusually low with only six inches of rain in November. A guy just upstream from us caught a nice steelhead. By mid-morning it was sunny and 60 degrees so we headed for the beach. At Tillamook's North Jetty, we caught a hefty Black Rockfish. It was nice to fish in the winter sunshine, which was very unusual in the Pacific Northwest. On the way home we purchased five fresh Albacore Tuna for $1.25 per pound. Each fish weighted about twelve pounds. We fished the Wilson River as the sun was going down and spooked several steelhead in the low water, but hooked nothing. There were several thirty plus pound Chinook salmon carcasses along the riverbank. This was a good sign for the next few years.

December 19, 2000
I fished with Mike Wahl on the Wilson River. One steelhead was caught in the Donaldson Hole in the morning. In the afternoon we took Mike's drift boat to the Nestucca River and floated from Three Rivers to Cloverdale. We caught no fish. Where there was an easy access road, there were more fisherman. We could not compete.

2001

April 7, 2001
After work I fished the Deschutes River behind the Riverhouse Motel, in Bend Oregon. I caught half a dozen rainbows on #20 Griffiths Gnats and #16 Dry Renegades.

April 12, 2001
I took our scout troop and my son Grady camping on the Oregon Coast at Cape Lookout State Park. The next day we volunteered to work at the Whiskey Creek Fish Hatchery, a private not-for-profit hatchery owned and operated by the Tillamook Anglers.

Tillamook, Oregon

We clipped the adipose fin off of spring Chinook smolts to identify them as hatchery fish (because native fish must be released). All the volunteers clipped about 70,000 four to six inch fish. In several weeks they will be released in the nearby rivers to migrate to the Pacific Ocean. Hopefully they will return in three to four years to provide sport fishing.

April 13, 2001
Grady and I fished Dorman's Pond off of Highway 6 towards the Oregon coast. We caught a half dozen stocked rainbows with spinning rods, egg bubbles, and small wet flies.

April 30, 2001
I sold fifteen dozen flies to two guys from California who were fishing Alaska this summer, and another ten dozen to the owner of the Olallie Lake Resort. The price was $.75 to $1 per fly.

May 19, 2001
I fished with Todd Wilson and our sons for the day. We made an exploratory trip and fished five different lakes. We drove up to Mt. Hood, Oregon early Saturday morning and checked in at the Welches Fly Shop to see which lakes were fishing well. After purchasing a few fly tying feathers we headed to the south side of Mt. Hood. Our plan was to fish several lakes as we worked our way home. We chose the Clackamas River watershed as our path down the mountain. We began at Trillium Lake and caught several small rainbows as the sun was coming up. The road to the lake had just opened at the beginning of the week so we had most of the lake to ourselves. Our next stop was Timothy Lake, where we hiked around the west side of the lake to get away from the crowd, and fished several small coves. We picked up about two dozen rainbows in the ten to fifteen inch range. They were hitting #12 Wooly Worms. After a quick lunch we headed down Oak Grove Fork to Harriet Reservoir. We fished Harriet for a few minutes, it was getting pretty hot, at 70 degrees, and the fish were not cooperating. Our next stop was Frog Lake, a hydroelectric power plant impoundment of about five acres. The water was very clear and cold, but no fish were rising. Later we learned the power company had emptied the reservoir the year before to repair the outlet and spillway. It would take a year or two before the fish could be planted again. We headed further down the Clackamas River to the last lake, Faraday Reservoir. We caught two dozen small rainbows from shore until the sun went down. Most fish were less than ten inches but we did see a large rainbow, maybe a lost steelhead, cruise by paying no attention to our flies. On the way home we had tacos and burritos in Estacada. Our boys were tired out and asleep in the back seat well before we got home after 10pm. It was a good trip, we caught a bunch of fish and did about 150 miles on less than a tank of gas.

June 1, 2001
Two of the neighborhood girls knocked on our door wanting to trade tadpoles and small tree frogs for fishing flies. One girl chose a salmon fly the other a deer hair frog bass bug. We now have frogs in our goldfish ponds in the back yard. They promised to bring more frogs next year in exchange for flies.

June 7, 2001

I fished with Josh Thompson, a friend from work, for bass in the "back-waters" of the Columbia River without much luck. I hooked a very large carp, which broke off. Next, we fished for Squawfish and the $4 per fish bounty, but did not catch any fish. It was getting late so we tried our luck for White Sturgeon, and were successful. We hooked four sturgeon within an hour. We fought one fish for a half hour before bringing it alongside the boat several times before landing it. I put its upper body under my arm in a headlock and held its tail with my other hand, the whole time the fish was thrashing to get free. It was a struggle to remove the hook. All sturgeon less than forty eight inches and over sixty inches must be released unharmed; our fish was one inch over the legal limit. We measured it several times. We reluctantly released the fish. The sturgeon weighed over sixty pounds. We hooked her about 150 yards below the Highway 14 bridge near The Dalles Dam. We used about twelve ounces of lead three feet above the 3/0 hook, on twenty pound test braided line. For bait, we had a fist size chunk of shad we found floating in a back eddy. When we ran out of bait, we ran shad jigs down the sturgeon line, hoping to pick up a few bait fish before the jig reached the sinker.

June 9, 2001

Grady and I fished Faraday Reservoir and caught a dozen rainbows. We drove up the canyon and fished Harriet and only caught one trout. The day was sunny and hot. On the way home we fished the "kid's pond" at Promontory and Grady caught a dozen stocked rainbows on #14 Wooly Worms.

June 17, 2001

Five guys from work (one retired) and I floated the John Day River in north central Oregon. We each took small pontoon kick boats with camping gear in waterproof packs. We put in at Thirty Mile Canyon after paying a rancher for access and got out at Cottonwood Bridge on Highway 206, covering forty four river miles in four days. The flow was unusually low at 800 cfs. We had to drag our pontoons over several gravel bars. The best flows for rafting were around 1,200 cfs. There were no road access points the entire trip so we either had to float or walk out. Most of the riparian area was managed by BLM with several private ranch holdings along the river. We fished

for small mouth bass and each caught over 100 fish per day. Most fish were in the ten to fourteen inch range. My best fish was over four pounds and twenty inches long.

Smallmouth Bass, John Day River, Oregon

We also caught several squawfish and saw many large carp. There were no trout in the lower John Day River because the water was too warm in the summer, but there was a fairly good run of fall steelhead that head up river to cooler headwaters. The best flies for bass in the hot 80 degree afternoons, when there was calm water, were #6 Deer Hair Mice and #8 Chernobyl Ants. The bass would hangout near the grassy banks or at the base of cliffs waiting for mice, lizards, baby swallows, or grasshoppers to fall into the water. The water temperature was about 65 degrees so we wet waded the entire trip. During the mornings and evenings, when the wind kicked-up, the bass would cruise the main channel readily taking rabbit hair leeches. The best colors were black or purple with fluorescent red thread or chenille and brass bead heads. Every afternoon around 3pm the wind would begin blowing upstream in forty mph gusts, which made rowing difficult on the flat stretches of water. Several times I had to row through rapids because the wind would catch and hold the boat in rough water. Most of the rapids were class I and II. As we floated around tight bends in the river we could hear rocks tumbling off the cliffs in the distance. We saw over 100 head of bighorn sheep, in small bands of twenty to thirty head. I was able to row within forty yards of four sheep drinking along the stream bank before they spooked and ran up the cliff. We saw a lot of ewes and lambs but no mature full curl rams; they must have been more cautious.

July 9, 2001
Todd Wilson, Don Welch, and I took our Boy Scouts on a whitewater float trip on the Rogue River in southwestern Oregon. We camped at Lost Creek Reservoir at Four Corners campground, which was a one-third mile hike in from the road. We had the campground all to ourselves until Friday night when another small group moved in. We had to haul water to the camp, and poison oak was everywhere, but besides that it was a very nice camp. In the evenings we caught smallmouth bass in the reservoir where most fish were less than a pound. The bass took small bead head marabou leeches. I did catch two skinny trout, one fourteen inches the other about twelve inches, but the lake was managed as a warm water fishery. We had lightning storms the first three nights, and saw a small lightning-strike fire across the lake which a helicopter quickly put out with water from the lake. The Rogue River was having the best Spring Chinook run in the past fifty years. I watched four Chinook hooked and landed the first two miles on the river. Most fish were in the thirty pound range and a little on the dark side. The first day of our float trip we put all the young men in six-man rubber rafts to teach them white water basics. The second day we took two man kayaks, a little more difficult but the boys could handle it. On the next two days we took one man kayaks. We had a great time running the class I-II rapids. We kayaked twelve miles a day on the river for a total of fifty two miles for the week. We didn't make time to fish the river because we were focusing on teaching river running skills. On the trip home we visited Crater Lake National Park. We kept the cost of the trip to $100 per person, half of which was the raft and kayak rental.

July 23, 2001
My family camped on the North Fork of the Middle Fork of the Willamette River, near Oakridge, Oregon, at the Kianeham USFS campground. We almost had the entire campground to ourselves for the week, sharing 19 sites with only one or two other small groups. It was quiet and peaceful in the old-growth Douglas fir. Our campsite was right on the river, where we waded and swam every day. The fishing was excellent. I averaged over fifty fish each day during the three hours per day I was able to fish. The river is managed for native fish and was fly fishing only, with barbless hooks and catch and release. Most of the trout were rainbows, but there were a few Cutthroats as well. All the fish had beautiful, bright colors. The best fly was a #12 Elk Hair Caddis. Most fish were in the eight to ten inch range. When I was catching too many small fish I switched to a larger fly, #10 Madam X. In one hole I caught three fish in three casts and another seven fish in a dozen casts. The biggest fish was sixteen inches, a relatively large fish for the North Fork. The Rainbow solidly hit a yellow elk hair caddis, stripped line out of my reel, jumped several times on my two pound leader before being landed in the shallow gravel and released. I only saw one other fisherman the entire week. We had a nice drive home, crossing over the ridge to Cougar Watershed and following the McKenzie River to Eugene.

August 1, 2001
A few guys from work and I fished McKay Reservoir, near Pendleton, Oregon after work. We caught a dozen crappie and a few small perch casting flies from shore. A few migrant farm workers filled a five gallon bucket with fish.

August 18, 2001
I fished with the International Fly Fishing Association in Alaska. We'd been planning the trip for months, and one of our members, Dan Holly, had a connection with a lodge owner who gave us a great deal. I caught a flight from Portland at 10pm and arrived in Anchorage at 2am, and slept in the airport. At 7am I met several other IFFA members at the dock on Lake Hood. We packed seventy pounds of gear per person in the floatplane and took off on the forty five minute flight to Three Rivers-Lake Creek Lodge located on the Yenta River, northwest of Anchorage. We flew over Cook Inlet and miles of wet tundra and boreal forest. We saw a dozen moose and a couple of bear on our flight in. The plane landed on the

river and taxied onto the sandy beach in front of the lodge. We formed a line and unloaded our gear in the shallow water, then carried it to our small A-frame cabins.

Lake Creek, Alaska

Within an hour of landing we were fishing. Throughout the week we caught four species of salmon: Pinks (humpies), Chum, Sockeye, and Coho (silvers). I lost count how many salmon I caught, but if we were not catching a salmon at least every thirty minutes we moved to another spot. We wore out arms and shoulders.

Sockeye Salmon, Lake Creek, Alaska

We had three fishing guides who shuttled us up and down Lake Creek. We concentrated on the first two or three miles of Lake Creek and the confluence with Yenta River. We had breakfast at 7am and at 8am the guides took us up river and dropped us off for the morning. The guides picked us up for lunch around noon and took us to another spot for the afternoon. At 5pm we met back at the lodge for dinner. We hired a cook off

the streets of Anchorage for the week, to take care of all meals and clean up. After the second night we had problems with the cook. He drank a large portion of the others guy's alcohol. We could not fire him because the plane was not coming back for a week, so we banished him from the lodge, except when he was cooking and cleaning. One afternoon five of us were fishing a nice run, taking turns casting and hooking Pink, Chum and an occasional Coho salmon. The first guy would take a half dozen casts, hook a salmon, lead the salmon down river and play the fish while the next guy in line would repeat the process. We fished this run for about three hours with at least one or two fish on at all times. The Pinks had been in the river for several weeks and were getting a little "dark", running four to five pounds with an occasional seven pounder. We caught so many Pinks that toward the end of the week we had to cast to avoid them.

Pink Salmon, Lake Creek, Alaska

The Chum were fairly fresh and averaged seven to fifteen pounds. A bright Chum would put up a nice fight and would take you into your flyline backing in several seconds if you were not careful. Chum would jump several times when first hooked and then again when brought to shore, but most of the time they would "hunker" down and swim back and forth until they tired. I fished with eight pound tippet and rarely had a fish break-off. Having a good fly reel drag was the key to successfully landing a large salmon. By mid-week, the silvers began showing up in greater numbers. Silvers were the best fighters, mostly because they were freshest to the river. They averaged eight to fifteen pounds, and were feisty. A typical Silver would scream across the water, jump several times and then take off in another direction. They were difficult to land in the water and most had to be beached. My most memorable Sliver took my fly while I was standing in four feet of water and took off directly at me. On the third jump I had to stand a side or be run over. I could have put down my rod and caught him underneath my arm.

Chum Salmon, Lake Creek, Alaska

Once I hooked a very large Silver in the Yenta River, or it could have been a late Chinook, who fought valiantly and spooled my fly reel and broke-off. I brought my fly in and found a large spinner attached to my fly. The best flies for salmon were heavily weighted #6 Cerise Tyrant Bunny Leeches and #6 Purple Egg Sucking Leeches with a lot of flash. Towards the end of the week we decided to pursue trout, which were gorging on salmon eggs. We flipped egg imitations in fast water below spawning salmon and were rewarded with many fine trout. We caught several twenty inch trout, which were fatter than any I'd seen in the lower forty-eight states. They were shaped like footballs and very aggressive. Once hooked, they ran downstream, jumped several times, and were fairly difficult to land. I was able to land one fish for every five I hooked. Locally they were called leopard rainbows because of their beautiful large black spots on their backs, and the rainbow on their sides were a brilliant rosy red. Several in our group were lucky enough to catch grayling. Bears appeared in camp the last three nights. The first grizzly took a fish off the boat landing in front of the lodge, and was scared off by two bottle-rocket fireworks. The next evening another grizzly came to the lodge and ate twenty

five pounds of dog food from the kennel. The dogs were barking, but the bear ignored them. The lodge caretaker fired a couple of shotgun rounds over the bear, which scared him off for a few minutes but he came back looking for more food. At one point there were three or four bears milling around camp.

Lake Creek, Alaska

Bears were difficult to see in the heavy brush and timber in the evening shadows. The dogs were let loose each afternoon, not necessarily to scare off the bears but to let us know where the bears were. We could hear the dogs barking at bears all night. One night there was a grizzly rummaging through the buried trash five feet behind our A-frame cabin. We could hear him breathing deeply and snorting in the darkness. Luckily there was little food so he took off before morning.

Rainbow, Lake Creek, Alaska

We saw few bears on the river while we fished, but saw many tracks. I kept whistling at each new fishing run, kept "bear bells" on my pack and carried bear pepper spray. About mid-week we met a camper on a large island next to a good fishing hole. The next day all his gear was scattered around and several tent poles bent. The camper was not around; apparently he was surprised at night by the bear and took off. We did not see blood or a body so we assumed he was not in trouble. We watched his camp for the next few days, he did not come back to collect his gear. On the return trip to Anchorage, I met Bill Daley, my retired boss, and we discussed work over Chinese food. My 1:30am flight home was over-booked. I gave up my seat to the airline for $400, an excellent deal since my ticket was only $325. Total trip costs: Airplane: $325, Meals: $200, Lodge-Shared $275, Miscellaneous Expenses: $300, seven days, Total Cost: $1,100

September 8, 2001
Todd Wilson and I took our boys fishing on the Salmon River near Zig-Zag, Oregon. We caught two dozen small wild rainbows, and a few native cutthroat trout, on #14 Elk Hair Caddis. We watched a few old spawned-out salmon chase each other around a small pool.

September 14, 2001
I took my son Grady fishing at Trillium Lake on Mt. Hood, Oregon. Several fly fishers in float tubes were catching eighteen inchers, but we only caught ten inch fish from shore. It was difficult to get an eight year-old in a float tube. We caught about a dozen rainbows and kept two fish. At sunset we built a fire and cooked the trout in tin-foil over the coals, ate smores and drank sodas. We talked about bears until he fell asleep. I packed him into the back seat of the car and we got home after midnight. I needed some quiet time to think about the New York, Pentagon, and Pennsylvania airline terrorist bombings. It was a horrific tragedy.

October 26, 2001
The alarm went off at 4am and my wife sleepily asked what I was doing. She had forgotten that I was going fishing. I took the last half of the week off to go elk hunting, but caught a cold and cancelled the trip. Not wanting to waste vacation time I slept off the cold the first day, installed a wood stove the second day, and fished the third day. I quickly headed out the door trying not to

wake the rest of the family. At 5:30am I passed Government Camp on Mt. Hood. The highway department had recently installed snow markers expecting early, heavy snows this winter. We could use the snow to help the fishing and end the drought this year. I had breakfast sausage and eggs in Madras at my favorite Scottish restaurant - McDonalds. Just outside of Prineville, I jumped two four-point bucks along the highway. Wonder where they were during deer season? I had my waders on and fly rod rigged before sun up on the Crooked River. There were several fish rising at the first pool and the caddis were in the air. They could have been blue wing olives, I couldn't tell from a distance. I tied on an elk hair caddis and started casting. A half hour later I was still casting to rising fish. I had several takes but still no fish in the net. It was still a little too cold and frosty. A short hike to the next pool warmed me up. The first cast produced a feisty, foot-long rainbow trout. He took a #14 Tan Elk Hair Caddis about three feet from shore next to a small bunch of watercress. The Crooked River is always slightly off-colored from the silty soils in the area and contrasts nicely with the native brightly colored Redside trout that live there. When the sun came up over the canyon walls and on the water, it was a good time for nymphs as the caddis and mayflies were becoming scarce. The Crooked River below Bowman Dam is relatively slow flowing with a lot of aquatic vegetation. A #18 Tan Scud worked nicely in the murky spring creek. On the next riffle I landed four trout and three whitefish. The trout were active and challenging to land amongst the rocks and vegetation. The whitefish were big for a small creek, running two to three pounds. Mid-morning I met two other fisherman, they were intent on catching fish and not too friendly. They appeared to have just walked out of the Orvis Shop and had out-of-town license plates on their sport utility vehicle. They were fishing downstream as I was heading upstream. Later, I met a nice gentleman with a German accent and we traded a few flies. The more flies I gave him, the more fishing information he shared. He was interested in smoking whitefish for the holidays, and was filling his creel. I had Spam & cheese sandwiches for lunch in the sun while I watched a retired couple float worms and bobbers through a nice hole. In November the river becomes artificial lures only. They caught enough trout for dinner and left. I fished the riffle at the head of the pool (which they had ignored) and caught the biggest trout of the day in about six inches of water. A sixteen inch beauty gave my two pound tippet a workout. After releasing her I headed back to the car to fish the lower river. The day was starting to warm up, so I left my jacket in the car and fished in short sleeves. After several more trout it was time to head home with a packet of sunflower seeds to keep me awake. The sun went down while I was driving along the Deschutes River toward Warm Springs. I noticed Treg Owings' pick-up truck and stopped to check on his luck. As we were talking he hooked a nice steelhead on his Spey rod. Fifteen minutes later I had the fish by the tail in the shallows, a nice twenty nine inch fish caught on an egg sucking leech tube fly. We released the fish. Later, a Warm Springs tribal lady met up with us to get an elk hide and hoofs from an elk Treg had shot earlier in the week. Treg promised the next fish to me and a few minutes later I landed a nice 19 inch rainbow. It was getting late as I passed the Fly Shop in Welches on the way home, something I rarely did. Dinner was ready when I got home at 9pm. It was nice to be with my family again.

2002

February 22, 2002
I sold four framed classic Atlantic Salmon Flies to a gentleman in Singapore and one framed fly to a friend in Alaska.

April 9, 2002
I could hear the rain pounding the tarp over the woodpile outside our bedroom door, but decided to get up anyway. Even though it was a steady downpour, I had arranged to take the day off and go fishing. I had a burrito for breakfast and was out the door at 5am. Two hours later, in a torrential downpour, I had my rain gear on and pontoon boat in the water. Lost Lake had been stocked last fall and again a month ago with rainbows and a few leftover hatchery steelhead. I must have spooked a steelhead while launching my boat. It flew out of the water, skittered over a large floating log and fell on the other side into the water with a splash. This year there were more floating logs than I had seen before. There must have been a terrible windstorm over the winter. Lost Lake is about fifteen acres and about twenty feet deep, on the Coast Range in Oregon. Doug fir and alders grow right up to the waterline on the steep banks. This natural lake has no inlet or outlet and is spring fed and always the same level. A nice breeze is always blowing on this lake which sits in a bowl near the top of the ridge. I could hear chain saws several miles away. Loggers rarely take a day off in Oregon. I began casting a #12 Carey Special and had one short tug. Next I tied on a #12 Black Leech and had no fish twenty casts later.

Carey Special

I tried my two best lake flies with fish jumping everywhere, and caught nothing. I tied on a bead head prince nymph and immediately hooked a fish. A minute later I had a twelve inch hatchery rainbow coughing up nymphs in my hand. I could not identify the nymphs until I got home; they were Alderfly nymphs. I switched to a #14 Pheasant Tail Nymph and caught fish the rest of the day. The trout that were stocked last fall averaged about fourteen inches and had light blue backs and silver sides. Most had picked up the color of the sand in the deeper parts of the lake during the winter. The foot long rainbows stocked the month before had mossy dark green backs and red sides. An older gentleman arrived late in the morning and left before lunch. He must have been too cold in his float tube. It was still raining. We avoided each other, each wanting privacy on this trip. He reminded me of my last fishing trip with Clyde Scott here several years ago. Clyde was a good friend of mine, and we car pooled to work together for years. After working for years as a fishery biologist for several natural resources agencies, Clyde now has his name memorialized on a brass plaque on Henry's Lake, Idaho. I made a quick lunch of onion bagels when the sun came out briefly. A short time later another fisherman launched a small pram and began trolling a fly around the shoreline. We spoke for a moment about the weather and steelhead and it started to shower again. I asked him with a grin "it looks like it might rain?" he replied "just a little". Native Oregonians never take their rain too seriously. A few fish later, we called it quits. Catching two dozen trout was a good day. I kept four trout for my wife who chided me the day before about never bringing home any fish. My new friend emptied the rainwater out of his boat. I packed up and headed home. Three hours later, after a hot shower, I was helping my son learn his multiplication tables. Third grade can be tough some days. The next day I met a friend of mine who had hooked four, and landed two twenty pound spring Chinook, trolling hardware in the Columbia River. I wondered if I should have fished the Columbia yesterday.

April 13, 2002
We took the Boy Scouts camping on the coast and spent the day at the Whisky Springs Fish Hatchery. We helped fin-clip over a hundred

thousand fall Chinook smolts. On the way home we took a few casts for surf perch but did not catch any fish.

April 20, 2002

Kai Thompson, a neighbor friend, and I fished the Deschutes River, upriver from Maupin, at the locked gate. It was a two hour drive from Portland, Oregon. The Deschutes Club owns the land beyond the locked gate, but allows fishermen to walk through their property. Club members can drive or ride bicycles but the rest of us must walk. It was a sunny day. We preferred clouds though because they produce an abundance of blue wing olives and small caddis flies in the early spring. There were few insects today. We began fishing large, black, heavy stonefly nymphs. The Deschutes is a large, fast river about 150 to 200 feet wide and four to eight feet deep. We were content to fish near shore in the back eddies and boulder fields. We didn't pick up a fish until mid-morning, when I caught an eight inch trout.

Redside Trout, Deschutes River, Oregon

We had lunch three miles past the locked gate near the Deschutes Club House in the shade. It was about 60 degrees outside but hot in our chest waders. We found a pod of trout rising in a large back eddy and picked up a dozen fish on small blue wing olive emergers at the foam line. None of our fish were over twelve inches. We did catch a few salmon smolts with adipose fins clipped from the tribal hatchery up river. Our first big redside trout came midafternoon. I was swinging a large black crystal bugger through a boulder field. The sixteen inch Redside went screaming downstream, upstream and across the river. A few jumps later I had him in a back eddy ready for a photograph. He was a beautiful dark trout with crimson red sides. We picked up a few more small trout, until the wind picked up and the sun went below the volcanic canyon walls. The last few hours of daylight on the Deschutes were the best for fishing. I picked up half dozen more sixteen to eighteen inch trout. All on #10 Black Wooly Buggers, fished below a small corky & toothpick strike indicator on a nine foot leader. Our methods were simple: we cast slightly upstream on the far side of a back eddy and let the line float downstream. At the end of the drift the line swung into the back eddy and headed upstream. We were either playing out line, or stripping in line as fast as we could. Somewhere during the drift we hooked fish. No hatchery trout were allowed in the Deschutes, it's managed for wild trout. We didn't get into any twenty inch fish, maybe next trip during the salmonfly hatch. We made it back to the truck in the dark. We only saw five other fishermen during the day. This was my friend Kai's second fly fishing trip and he caught fish. He drove his new truck and bought gas in exchange for flies. I don't know who got the better deal. He lost over two dozen of my flies (plus a few extras for his next trip). I suppose I got the better deal. We had a great time and I began planning our next trip.

May 11, 2002

My son Grady and I attended the annual fathers and sons campout at Scouter's Mountain. We slept in a long house and had a great time with others from our church. I was asked to give a ghost story at the campfire. The next day we fished with one of Grady's friends and his father. We fished Faraday Reservoir, Harriet, Timothy and Little Fry Lakes and only caught three fish.

We also tried for steelhead on the Clackamas River but had no luck.

June 17, 2002

My coworkers and I completed our second annual float trip down the John Day River in north central Oregon. Six guys that I work with, and one retired, did some serious smallmouth bass fishing. We took our pontoon kick-boats with waterproof packs strapped on back. We covered forty four river miles in five days. The flow was average at 1,300 cfs. We each caught over seventy five smallmouth bass per day. The fish were bigger than average this year. Most fish were in the fourteen to fifteen inch range, the biggest fish was seventeen inches. We also caught several squawfish and saw many thirty pound carp. The best flies were deer-hair mice, foam-disk mice, and Chernobyl ants. During the windy afternoons rabbit-hair leeches worked the best.

John Day River, Oregon

The water temperature was about 65 degrees so we wet-waded the entire trip. I have never seen such a variety of aquatic insects on the water at the same time. The John Day is a very productive river. There were at least four species of Mayflies ranging from pure white, to olive, to bronze. Midmorning mayflies were all over the calm water and between the riffles the bass were cruising in pods slurping them up. I didn't bring any trout flies, so we cast big ants into the foray and hooked a lot of bass. Big dragon flies were catching mayflies mid-air and landing on my pontoon boat to consume them. They were veracious eaters. Dozens of giant stoneflys left their exoskeletons cemented to our boats as they emerged overnight, taking flight as we walked through the shoreline brush. Small golden and yellow stoneflys floated

with us during the morning, but disappeared in the afternoon. A few clumsy craneflys crashed into the water during the windy afternoons. We found leeches and a few scuds during our afternoon swims.

John Day River, Oregon

The John Day is a very productive river, ideal for smallmouth bass, but too warm in the summer months for trout. Steelhead thrive in the upper reaches of the river, but only if they make it through the gauntlet of bass and warm water. Last year we saw over 100 head of bighorn sheep, but this year we saw only four ewes. There was more rain this year so I suppose the sheep stayed up away from the river. Towards the end of the trip several F-15 fighter jets flew up the narrow canyon (probably on a training mission). Seconds later their sound caught up with them. The noise was deafening as the sound bounced off the canyon walls.

June 29, 2002

My son Grady and I fished the Nestucca River, not far from McMinnville, Oregon. During the fall and winter months the river is crowded with big fish anglers looking for forty five pound Chinook or twenty pound steelhead. Anglers come from around the world to fish these famed coastal streams, and locals assert their God-given-right to fill their freezers with fillets. They all disappear during the summer months when we fish for native cutthroats weighing less than a pound. I like big fish as much as the next guy but will trade a lunker in a crowded stream for an afternoon on the river all to myself pursuing native trout. We occasionally meet the summer steelheader picking their way up river fishing the deeper holes. I ignore the deeper holes and fish the faster water, enjoying the solitude of casting to rising trout under shaded old-growth firs and cedars. Occasionally we pick up a stray steelhead. I once fought a seven pounder for twenty minutes on a #16 hare's ear on my five weight rod. I'll never forget that fish. We never catch more than a dozen trout a day. The summer flows were a third less than winter runoff. The low flows make catching trout more challenging in the quiet, clear waters. An insect hatch is rare, but there were always spotted caddis, midge and grasshoppers on the water. I suppose the trout get fat on salmon eggs in the spring, the rest of the year there were relatively few aquatic insects in the river. Our best flies were elk hair caddis, Griffith's gnats, and pheasant tails. I'd rather catch rising fish under difficult casting situations on quiet water than brave the crowds of plunkers lining the bank and fleets of drift boaters' intent on catching big fish. On some rivers, nothing brings out the worst in people more than the news that "the salmon have arrived." Fortunately, there were plenty of opportunities for all anglers. Solitude can sometimes be found early in the morning on weekdays. For the most part, I prefer fishing the off-season.

July 6, 2002
Grady and I took the neighbor kids fishing to Vernonia Pond. We caught several small bass, crappie, and bluegill on spinning rods, casting bubbles and #16 Woolly Worms. These were the first fish the neighbor boys had ever caught.

August 20, 2002
I attended a conference in Bend, Oregon and stayed at the Riverhouse Motel. The Deschutes River ran through the motel property. We fished the swift, cold, bouldery pocket water a cast from our balcony rooms. I caught a dozen rainbows on #14 Elk Hair Caddis and a #16 Dry Renegade.

August 24, 2002
Steve Stephenson and I took a few scouts backpacking in the High Cascades. The fishing was fair - we only caught a few small trout. We began at Cultus Lake and hiked up to Teddy Lakes near the Pacific Crest Trail. We scared a black bear out of camp the first evening. A thunderstorm hit at sun down and we watched the lightning from our tents. The next day a bigger storm began moving in so we hiked out to Crane Prairie

Reservoir and set up camp. Lightning hit 200 yards away from camp and knocked a pine tree down. We saw several smoky spots in the mountains surrounding the lake the next morning, but they were out by mid-day. On our drive home we saw a black bear that had been hit by a car along the road. It probably was the same bear we saw earlier in the week. We also fished Lava Lake and caught a dozen trout. We stopped at Timothy and Trillium Lakes on our way home and had limited success.

September 27, 2002
I fished the Williamson River near Klamath Falls, Oregon. I had been getting reports and photos of huge rainbows from friends of mine all summer and I promised them a couple dozen flies for a fishing trip. Chris Mundy and Ryan practically blindfolded me as we drove out of town. The Williamson River flows through mostly private land with very limited public access. We fished south of Collier State Park and hiked a short distance up the river. The river was cold and relatively shallow over dark gravel. As Klamath Lake warms up in the summer, the rainbows either find cold springs in the lake or move up into the Williamson and hold there until they spawn in late winter. There were few resident trout. Apparently the fish put on most of their weight in the lake and have a subsistence diet in the river. The river is flat with widely dispersed holding water. We fished one long, narrow hole, which was difficult to locate unless you had a guide. The river was 100 feet across and about two feet deep, with the hole dropping off sharply to about four feet deep up against the far riverbank. The wading was easy on the gravel bottom. Fish were rising throughout the hole. Monster four and six pounder trout were doing belly flops chasing small fluttering caddis flies. The recommended fly was a large #10 heavily weighted bead head pheasant tail nymph. Chris hooked the first fish, a dark eighteen inch rainbow. The river stratum is dark lava, and the fish's back was equally black. The fish was strong, and hung at the bottom of the river for about fifteen minutes before we brought her to the net. We took a few pictures then released the fish. I hooked the second fish and lost it after a short fight. The three pound tippet snapped on the rock ledge at the lip of the pool. Chris hooked the third fish and after a long struggle landed a twenty four

inch rainbow. The hen had a huge strong lower jaw, not common on the typical rainbow. There were several scars on the fish's head indicating its old age and struggles living in the high desert.

Rainbow, Williamson River, Oregon

We hooked several more fish before it became too dark for fishing. We tried midges and small caddis flies but the fish were too large to land in the shallow water. We fished again the next evening with similar results. On a large log in the river we noticed a brass plaque in memory of a deceased fisherman and we thought it was a beautiful spot to remember a lost friend.

September 30, 2002

I attended Steve's and my annual deer hunt-fishing trip to the high Cascades of Oregon. It was a four hour drive from Portland and rained most of the way, there was little snow on Santiam Pass. Steve Stephenson set up camp at North Twin Lake (west of Bend, Oregon) and we shared the campground with four other deer hunting parties. When I arrived there were already three deer hanging in the campground. There were six of us in our party: two of us were fishing and the other four were strictly hunting deer. After pitching my tent in the pines, I put my pontoon boat together, loaded it on the trailer, and drove two miles to South Twin Lake. It was cold and showered occasionally throughout the evening. I caught a nice rainbow on my second cast on a maroon marabou bead head leech, with a full sinking line. That was the only fish for me, but Doug Healy caught a four pound rainbow just a few feet away. It was a very nice fish. The fish were about twenty feet deep and hugging the bottom.

October 1, 2002

Doug Healy and I fished Hosmer Lake. People come from around the world to photograph and fish this beautiful lake. Several outfitters from Bend, Oregon rent kayaks and shuttle people to the lake in old school busses. It is one of the few waters west of the Mississippi stocked with Atlantic salmon. I put on a sinking-tip line, twelve foot leader, two pound tippet and tied on a #16 Green Metallic Caddis Nymph. I made a short cast and began stripping out line to prepare for a longer cast when a fish hit my fly. He was on only for a moment: I had too much slack line out and quickly lost the fish. My adrenaline was pumping. It was another hour before I caught my first Atlantic salmon dredging the bottom of the lake. That day I caught five Atlantic salmon, three of which were over twenty inches. Each fish hit hard, made a short run, jumped a few times and then pulled hard on the lake bottom until they were brought to the net. The best fishing method in the cold, clear, shallow water was to let out most of your flyline and slowly kick your float tube or pontoon around the lake. Trolling was best because it was difficult to cast a flyline when the water was calm. I could see fish scatter with every cast. Each Atlantic was silver bright with small red spots on their backs.

Atlantic Salmon, Hosmer Lake, Oregon

At dusk on the way home we saw a large three point buck grazing along the highway. Back at camp there were no deer hanging and we considered returning with a rifle. By the time we found Steve, it was too dark to shoot.

October 2, 2002

Doug Healy and I fished the channel between upper and lower Hosmer Lake. During the hot summer months the fish migrate to the colder waters of upper Hosmer. In the fall they migrate to the warmer shallower water in lower Hosmer Lake. The key to catching the wild brook trout is to find them migrating through the mile long channel. My timing was perfect. I saw several dozen brook trout at the mouth of the channel and several of them looked to be over five pounds. I kicked up the channel about a quarter mile and parked my pontoon in the thick aquatic vegetation near the bank. Brook trout were rising to midges in the sunny afternoon. They were not interested in my pupa imitations. I switched to small bead head flashback pheasant tails and green caddis pupa. Almost immediately I hooked a fat fourteen inch brook trout. They were strong fish, feistier than the Atlantic salmon. They took the fly and headed for the bottom weeds, making it difficult to land them. It was a slow day with only half a dozen fish. On my way out of the channel a bald eagle flew twenty feet directly over my head. Once out of the channel I put on a Mickey Finn and trolled it back to the boat ramp. Another Atlantic hit and jumped completely out of the water and fought valiantly until he was in my hand. He was my best fish at Hosmer, over twenty inches and strong willed. After I released him I called it quits and thawed my frozen feet in the car on the drive back to camp. There were no deer hanging in camp. We had beef stew and dutch-oven cobbler for dinner.

October 3, 2002

Doug Healy and I fished the Fall River. This spring creek bubbles up out of the ground at the base of a lava flow. The water is cold and crystal clear. Water cress and other vegetation grow abundantly in the slower backwater and provide habitat for aquatic insects. Fish were seasonally distributed throughout the river, which is about ten miles long between the lower falls and the headwater springs. The winter winds cool the shallow river water to near freezing so the fish migrate to the warmer headwaters, where the water is a constant 55 degrees. Fishing can be good in mid-winter if you can keep your line guides free of ice. In the summer the fish migrate to the lower river to take advantage of the abundant insect populations. We fished the campground area and did not see a single fish. We tried the hatchery access and found all the fish. I began with a #18 bead head flash back pheasant tail nymph and immediately picked up a nice rainbow. I could see at least a dozen fish in each hole and all were actively feeding.

Beadhead Flashback Pheasant Tail Nymph

Most were rising to very small, cream colored mayflies. Several trout were picking up small nymphs by rolling into their sides an inch above the gravel stream bottom, inhaling a nymph and then rolling upright again. You could literally see the whites of their mouths. After casting to each trout I could see in the hole I switched to a small olive scud and picked up a few more fish. It was fun to catch a fish that refused the first fly on a second fly pattern. It was apparent these fish were familiar with seeing anglers because we could get within ten feet before they would swim for cover. They were not afraid of our shadows or wading in the river. I finally switched to a small blue wing olive parachute and caught a few more fish. All three fly patterns worked on different fish in the same hole. This was the place to get an education on trout behavior. We spent an hour on each hole repeatedly casting to the same fish. Most fish were twelve to fourteen inches but we could see larger fish. We continued to fish within about a half mile of the fish hatchery until sundown, repeating the same process at each hole, until we each had caught several dozen fish.

October 4, 2002

The last day of our annual deer hunting-fishing trip I left the group and headed to Prineville, Oregon to fish the Crooked River. I arrived around ten in the morning and began fishing a #14 tan scud in the deeper holes. Within an hour I had three hefty whitefish and one small trout. By noon the caddis fly hatch was on. I stood in three spots in a fifty yard stretch of river and caught fish the rest of the day. I'd see a fish rise within casting distance, throw an elk hair caddis slightly upstream, and wham another fish. The fish all averaged about twelve inches. The fish were rising when it was cloudy and stopped when the sun was on the water. I am not sure if the fish quit rising because the sun was in their eyes or if the caddis stayed off the water when it was sunny. By the end of the day I must have hooked at least four dozen fish. I arrived home after dark and learned that Steve Stevenson got his deer, a small spike mule deer. I spent the next day cleaning, salting, and preparing the hide to tie more elk hair caddis for our next trip to the Crooked River.

October 8, 2002

A couple of us from work fished the Powder River, upstream from Baker City, Oregon. The river was relatively low. The farms must have been taking irrigation water out below the reservoir. We fished near the USFS boundary and caught a plump rainbow on the first cast. We caught a couple of fish in each pool using #16 elk hair caddis and hare's ear. The trout were on the small side, averaging eight inches, but we had the river all to ourselves and caught about two dozen fish.

December 21, 2002

The weekend before Christmas I got a call from a lady who lives at the end of our road. Her husband recently passed away and they wanted me to have his fly tying materials. I had tied a few flies for him, and didn't know what to say to such a generous offer. My daughter and I spent the afternoon visiting with her as she showed us newspaper clippings, photos, and notes about her husband's fishing trips. He had fished all over the Pacific Northwest and was quite successful. He started fly tying before zip-lock bags were invented, all his fly tying materials were in glass quart jars with mothballs (as a preservative). It took several hours to go through a lifetime's worth of fur, thread and feathers. He had polar bear, seal, and junglecock all packaged before the Endangered Species Act made them illegal in the USA. There were over fifty boxes of Mustad hooks, thirty spools of silk floss, and a dozen flats

of tarnished tinsel. He had bear, goat, buffalo, reindeer, moose, elk and other assorted hair and feathers from almost every bird you could imagine. It completely filled the backseat and trunk of our car. I told her the collection was worth hundreds of dollars, but she wanted the material to go to someone who would appreciate it, rather than sell it. I was very grateful for her generosity. What a blessing to associate with such nice people.

2003

January 3, 2003

I fished the Crooked River, near Prineville, Oregon. I left home at five in the morning and drove over Mt Hood on wet pavement. There was not much snow this year and the temperatures were in the 40s. I began fishing at eight thirty and had two nice rainbows before nine. The fly shop owner in Lebanon, Oregon showed me a new technique for the Crooked River. Tie a #16 light orange scud at the point, a #12 bead head soft hackle twenty inches above the scud and a corkie indicator three feet above the soft hackle.

Crooked River, Oregon

The water is turbid in the Crooked, so the fish hang in the middle of the water column. They don't hug the bottom because they feel safe from predators. I met Scott Robbins from work mid-morning and by noon we each had caught and released a dozen fish. After noon the river became crowded as other fisherman appeared. We took a lunch break and let them compete over the good riffle water. I found some solitude on some slow flat water and caught several fat whitefish - one over three pounds. Mid-afternoon we had a nice midge hatch and switched to a #20 parachute and caught another dozen trout. The fish feeding on the surface were not large, eight to twelve inches, but casting to rising trout is much more rewarding than nymphing. By late afternoon the crowd thinned out and we had the nice water to ourselves again. We only fished about a mile of water today around Cobble Rock campground. I caught several more trout on nymphs as the sun went below the rim rock. I made it home at 10pm.

February 21, 2003

I fished with the International Fly Fishing Association in New Zealand. We had ten IFFA members from Australia, Maryland, Montana, New Zealand, Oregon, Pennsylvania, and Singapore. I caught a flight from Portland, Oregon, at 6pm and arrived in Christchurch, New Zealand, 14 hours and 6,500 miles later, at noon. The flight was bearable with six in-flight movies, a full dinner and breakfast, a CD player, and a good book. I rented a car in Christchurch with Wendell Ferris, my friend from Pennsylvania, for the rest of the week. It was disorienting driving on the left side of the road at first, but we got used to it. The exchange rate was $.55USD to $1NZ, very affordable. Christchurch is very British, we walked around town Sunday visiting the Arts Center, the Cathedral, and the River Avon in Hagley Park. Later that evening we met two other members of our group, Tom Wilson and Wendell McConnell, and had a nice visit.

February 24, 2003

Monday we had an early breakfast of sausages and eggs and drove to Twizel. We took the scenic route south through the Rakaia Gorge with the snowcapped Southern Alps to the west. Mostly land was grazed with a few orchards, vineyards and row crops. Pastures were lined with neatly trimmed hedgerows and were stocked with sheep. We also saw farmed Red Deer and Rocky Mountain Elk. Australian possum were everywhere, mostly flattened on the road. The South Island is about 40 degrees south of the equator, with a climate similar to eastern Oregon. We visited the Church of the Good Shepherd at Lake Tekapo and saw several salmon farms on the hydro-electric canals below Lake Pukaki. We arrived in Twizel mid-afternoon and checked into our room at the MacKenzie Country Inn. I was amazed when the lady at the reception desk did not run our credit cards and said the key was in our room door. We could not wait to hit the water so we grabbed our gear and a map and headed to the Twizel River south of town. After taking a few wrong turns and five miles of rough gravel road, we made it to the river. Within minutes we had caught our first New Zealand trout, small rainbows six to ten inches. They readily took #14 Royal Wulffs on the surface. I spooked a large trout in a riffle by almost stepping on it. By the time the sun went down we had fished a mile of water and were having a great time. We drove by the endangered Black Stilt bird refuge. There are less than fifty Black Stilts surviving in the wild, the stilt is the rarest wading bird in the world. We saw one Black Stilt feeding on the edge of a small pond. Later that night, we met the rest of our group at the Inn and planned the next day's fishing. Everyone was having a good time, except for Bob Kloskowski who had a bad head cold.

February 25, 2003

Tuesday Wendell Ferris and I fished the Tekapo River, several miles above Lake Benmore. We followed the road along the hydro canal below Lake Tekapo until we reached the Tekapo River and then followed the river south thirty kilometers until a small river crossed the road.

Tekapo River, South Island, New Zealand

The road was rough on our small rental car and I didn't think we could cross the river, even though Wendell wanted to give it a shot. We parked the car in the shade of large willow trees. We hiked another three miles along the road before beginning to fish back to the car. From the road above the river, we spotted several trout in the five to ten pound range. Fish were not abundant, but they were big and you could see them clearly in the shallow water below each riffle and fast run. The river was all gravel and cobble stone. There were few places for fish to hide. We fished hard and picked up a few small rainbows. We sight cast to several large browns but could not put a hook into them. I crept up to one large brown trout in a small, flat side channel. The water was about three feet deep and crystal clear. The trout was rising to mayfly emergers in the middle of the pool. I watched him for several minutes and tied on a

#14 NZ Blow Fly and cast a fourteen foot leader on my five weight rod. He rose to the fly, followed it for two feet and then went back to his holding pattern. I immediately changed flies and tied on a #16 Adams. Again he followed the fly for several seconds and ignored it. The third cast was a #14 Foam Beetle. The trout saw the fly splat heavily on the water and charged the fly. Before he could reach the fly, a small trout darted in front of the large brown and took the fly. The brown chased the small trout around the pool, with my line attached, until I pulled the small trout from the water. By then the brown was spooked and headed down stream. At the end of the day we had a rough hike out, pushing through a half mile of thorny gorse, wild rose, and acacia. We caught no big fish, but we learned a lot and were ready the next day.

February 26, 2003

Wednesday I met up with George Lincoln, Nick van Weelden, and our guide Wayne and fished the Ahuriri River where it empties into Lake Benmore. We drove east of Omarama and took a small jet boat across the lake.

Lake Benmore, New Zealand

George fished the morning in the boat with Wayne, casting to cruising trout in the shallow flats and moss beds. They picked up several nice rainbows. Nick and I fished the lake delta, sight casting to large rainbows. Nick picked up a few nice fish on heavily weighted small nymphs, casting fifty to seventy feet. After a lunch of kiwi fruit, chicken, and beetroot sandwiches we headed up stream to fish the river. Wayne showed me a new casting technique, the "short line, only leader over the fish" cast. I tied on a heavily weighted

#10 Gold Bead Copper & Hare with a heavily weighted #16 Caddis Nymph point fly, and cast directly up stream. The heavily weighted flies immediately sank to the bottom and bounced along the gravel. A yarn indicator signaled any movement. When my fly drifted the length of the leader, I lift and recast my line upstream again. I kept the line tight by slowly lifting the rod and pulling the line in with my left hand as the fly drifted back toward me. After two or three casts I walked upstream and repeated the process. The key was a short cast, not running the fly line over the fish, and keeping the line tight. After a ten minute lesson I was into my first large New Zealand Rainbow. He hit hard, jumped three feet into the air, stripped thirty yards off my reel, and fought for five minutes until he was in the net. He was only three pounds but what a thrill.

Rainbow Trout, Ahuriri River, New Zealand

A few minutes later I had another rainbow. Convinced I had the technique, Wayne and Nick headed upstream to chase a ten pound brown they spotted. The next hole was fantastic. It was a long run with riffles and a small ledge running diagonal across the top of the pool. The fast water was on the far side and shallow water directly in front of me. After two casts, bouncing my nymph rig across the ledge into deeper water, I hooked a five pound rainbow. He jumped four feet into the air almost hitting the branches of a willow tree over hanging the far bank. He made a strong run toward the root wad of a fallen tree at the tailout out of the pool, turning just before fouling the line in the debris. For the next ten minutes he

hunkered down, weaving among the boulders at the bottom of the pool. I could see him in the crystal clear water. Finally, I brought him to the net, took a photo, and released him. That's what I came for. Over the next hour I caught four more rainbows and one nice brown out of the same run. The fish were all over four pounds with the largest close to six pounds. Not trophy fish for New Zealand, but what fun. We left when the wind started to pick up in the late afternoon. We had white caps on the lake as we loaded the boat onto the trailer. That evening I had lamb for dinner and our group had the rod drawing, where we drew for gifts donated by IFFA members. I won a nice book written by a member of our group.

February 27, 2003

Thursday I fished with Wendell Ferris, Dave Cameron (Camo), and George Hadler (our New Zealand host) on the Ahuriri River, west of Omarama. We had to get permission from the landowner before we could fish. The river ran through a very wide flood plain that was all cobble stone and had very little topsoil and vegetation. The best fish holding water was near the steep, cut banks of gravel, pocket water, and riffles. Deep holes were few and far apart. I began casting a #12 NZ Blow Fly in pocket water close to the bank and picked up a three pound brown on the third cast.

Brown Trout, Ahuriri River, New Zealand

He took off into fast water, tired in a few minutes and I beached him in a back eddy. He was a nice colored fish. We caught many small rainbows throughout the morning on dry flies. Most of the rainbows were under a pound but great sport. It was a hot, clear, sunny day. After lunch I watched

Camo catch a large rainbow in a deep pool. As he was leaving he jokingly said to me across the river "I've caught all the fish in this pool." I could see another trout at the head of the pool, made a quick cast, and I was onto a nice two pound rainbow. I received a mild scolding from Camo about catching a trout that was not there. We walked three miles back to the car in the late afternoon, scattering hares and Australian possum as we hiked. I did not see a blade of grass taller than three inches. Rabbit pellets were everywhere. There was a serious overpopulation problem. That evening George and I hiked around one of the small reservoirs just south of Twizel. We only cast to one fish, but had a good talk. That night I had a nice meal of fish and chips and we met with the local Fish and Wildlife Commissioner, Gramme, who spoke to our group about his game warden experiences. He was very entertaining.

February 28, 2003
Friday our guide Wayne took Wendell Farris and I to the Waitaki River. We put into the river below an old bridge downstream from Lake Aviemore. Wayne maneuvered his jet boat through the gravel bars and willows to several backwaters to sight-fish large cruising trout. Wendell had the first large fish via a #18 soft-hackle emerger cast several feet in front of a nymphing rainbow. Wayne said "he's moving away, cast again… no, he's coming back, he's going to take it… he took it, set the hook, set the hook!" Wendell fought the four pound rainbow around snags, aquatic weeds and rocks in the clear shallow water until he brought it to the net. Wayne took me to a secluded backwater to visit "Mr. Brown", he said "some of these fish have addresses". He was right, an eight pound brown was right below where a small creek entered the river. We carefully moved closer and I tied on a #18 Pheasant Tail Nymph, fourteen foot leader and sixty feet of line and cast … short three feet. I slowly drew my line in and cast again… behind the trout a foot. The third cast I hit him right on the nose and spooked him. He turned to look at us and slowly swam away. I swear he smiled and laughed at us. We're not going to put a hook in him today. I later caught a five pound brown on a #14 Bead Head Caddis Nymph in fast water next to a long riffle. He wore out easily in the fast water. Wendell hooked another nice fish in the big water that took him into his backing and got hung up on a snag. Down river, in the

mainstream, I caught five rainbows over three pounds in the same hole. The fast, deep water came around a bend and dropped over a small gravel bar, where fish were holding on the downstream lip of the bar. A heavily weighted #10 and #14 Bead Head Copper & Hare did the trick, bumping along the gravel bottom with a yarn indicator. After each fish was landed and released I searched the entire gravel bar by wading waste deep in the river and casting upstream. These fish were powerful and took off downstream stripping my line into backing every time.

Brown Trout, Waitaki River, New Zealand

The deep cold water felt good in the hot afternoon. In the evening we found a large backwater that was like a small pond. We crept up the willow lined bank and saw several large trout picking up rising nymphs. We cast to these fish for the next two hours with no luck. We'd cast several feet in front of a cruising fish, which turned to inspect our fly and reject our offering. It was frustrating and exciting at the same time. Following a harrowing jet boat ride upstream as the sun was going down, we had Chinese food with the rest of the IFFA group that evening and shared experiences. Tom Wilson and Wendell

McConnell announced that they each had caught nine pound browns today, the largest fish from our group so far.

March 1, 2003
Early Saturday morning, Wendell Farris and I visited the Twizel Fly Shop. There were a dozen hare and possum skins drying on the laundry line between the owner's home and the fly shop/garage. They appeared to be road kill but could have been shot (we heard shooting all week in the foothills). The shop smelled of mothballs and had a nice collection of trophy fish photos and a small inventory of flies and gear. There were dozens of fishing club pins from around the world stuck on the wall. We purchased some dubbing, a few flies, picked up a business card, and chatted with the owner. We drove south to fish the Ahuriri River again. Since we had no access to a boat, we hiked two miles along a wet meadow at the north end of Lake Benmore to the river. I fished the same hole we caught several fish at the Wednesday before, but had no luck. I picked up a nice rainbow in a small, very deep hole under a large willow tree. I could see him darting around the smooth gravel bottom. I cast a small nymph into the middle of the pool. Misjudging the depth of the pool, my nymph never reached the trout but settled in the shallow gravel near the bank. I was about to retrieve my line when the trout slowly swam up toward my fly, inhaled it, turned, and was hooked. A big fish in a small pool meant a fight. I turned him before he made it to the root wad of the willow tree and again from the shallow tail of the pool. Finally, we brought him to the net, a nice fat three pound rainbow. He had beautiful colors, bright red sides and a dark green back. We caught another half dozen two-pound rainbows in riffle water during the early afternoon. Wendell spent an hour stalking a dozen three-pound browns that were circling in a large calm backwater. I could see the fish thirty yards away rising to hatching mayflies. It was a hot, clear, calm day and we could not bring a fish to our fly. I hiked upstream and climbed a cliff thirty feet above a large hole. At the bottom of the clear, off-green colored water I saw a fifteen pound brown and several other large trout. After watching them, and eating the remainder of my lunch, I cast a large heavily weighted nymph at the head of the hole. All the fish scattered. I let the nymph drift through the deep, calm water into the foam in a

back eddy, and retrieved my fly. I felt a bump, and set the hook. Nothing except a large fish scale stuck on my fly hook. A few minutes later the fish returned to the center of the pool out of reach. It was time to move onto the next hole. The next fish was a nice rainbow I saw feeding in a clear, slow run. He was easy to see in the lightly colored quartz gravel. I cast, watching the gold bead head nymph drift through the gravel. The trout did not hesitate and directly took the fly and made a strong run downstream, taking all my fly line and fifty feet of backing. He was using the current to gain the advantage. I let him run, not in a hurry to land him. I thought this would be my last trout of the trip and wanted to enjoy every minute. I admired him in my hand and slowly released the two pound rainbow. I went and found Wendell and we hiked back to the car.

March 2, 2003
Sunday I caught a ride to Christchurch with George Lincoln, who was on his way back to Australia. We had a nice ride and saw some new country. I spent the afternoon wandering around Christchurch. I visited the Maori cultural art center, where I was invited by a bone carver to watch the last hours of the America's Cup. Switzerland won first place and New Zealand's ship won second place. Later I watched cricket on TV at the motel, but didn't understand the rules of the game. I had a late dinner of fresh bread and cheese from a sidewalk vender. Total trip cost in US dollars: $2,100. Airplane ticket $1,200, rental car (shared) $150, motel (2 days) $100, lodge (six days, shared) $125, guide (2 days, shared) $250, meals and snacks $150, miscellaneous $125. The exchange rate was $.55 USA to $1.00 NZ.

April 22 2003
I saw a half dozen fishing boats on the Willamette River out my thirteenth floor office window. When I saw a fish hooked I grabbed binoculars and ran to the window to watch. During my lunch breaks, I occasionally walked over the Hawthorn Bridge and look down at half a dozen fishermen in boats. When the Spring Chinook are in, the river is full of jet boats and sleds.

May 16, 2003
I took my nine year old son Grady and Todd Wilson and his sons Michael and Brett camping on the Deschutes, upriver from Maupin, Oregon.

The Golden Stoneflies were all over the stream side vegetation. The boys caught several dozen for their bug collections. Deschutes Stoneflies were beefy insects, three inches long, thicker than a pencil, and heavy. It was raining and hailing in Portland, but clear, sunny, and windy in the Deschutes canyon. We fished for two hours and managed to catch one nice Redside trout. On the way home the boys insisted on stopping at the fly shop. I didn't object. Back in Portland it was still raining and hailing.

May 21, 2003
The office spent the day upgrading our computers to a new operating system. I took the day off and went fishing. I called a few fly shops and did not like their recommendations. Lost Lake on the coast range is always good this time of year. I had breakfast and hit the road at 5:30am and returned home fifteen minutes later to get my forgotten waders and boots. An hour later I was barreling up an old logging road toward the lake through burned over clear-cuts and old growth timber, with small alders brushing both sides of the car. The fog was moving down the canyon as I swerved to miss several black tail deer loitering on the road. I reached the lake just as the rising sun burned the fog off the lake. I had the whole lake to myself, all fifteen acres. Several small rainbows were jumping out of the water at midges as I put my pontoon boat together and pushed aside several floating logs at the boat launch. There were a hundred floating timbers (some over sixty feet long) moving across the lake with the early morning breeze, excellent hiding places for cruising trout. There must have been a heck of a storm a few years ago because there were fallen logs everywhere. I let out about thirty feet of line and began kicking my fins toward the far side of the lake. I had my first trout in five minutes, a beauty barely six inches long. Over the next three hours, I had a fat little rainbow every ten minutes, none over eight inches. They sure liked my #16 Bead Head Pheasant Tail. The big ones must be waiting for something better. Just before 10am I heard an old truck lumbering up the road and moments later an older gentleman appeared off the point with a cooler and rod. We exchanged "good mornings" and he promptly began to tell me his life story. I did not want to appear rude so I listened while slowly finning out of earshot. His story got louder the further I moved away. The

lake was only so big. On my next pass he hit his limit we said "adios" and he packed up and left. I could hear him tromping through the brush on his way out. Moments later I heard a large fir tree crack and fall to the ground with a loud thud. I hoped he was OK. As I was heading to shore I heard his truck engine start up. Good thing, the nearest help was over an hour away. By noon the clouds were gone and it was starting to get hot. As I applied sunscreen, I noticed several caddis flies around the lake. When a small rainbow gobbled one up a few feet away it was time to switch my nymph for a #14 Olive Elk Hair Caddis. My first cast was next to a floating log, where I let it sit for ten seconds. I gave the fly a small twitch and it was sucked down by a fish that was under the log. A moment later I netted a monster fourteen inch rainbow, big for this lake. Another cast, twitch and another fish. Throughout the afternoon trout hit my caddis fly with reckless abandon, they acted as if they had never seen an Elk Hair Caddis before. The fish were on average bigger than those caught on nymphs. As a pod of fish moved close to my pontoon, I dropped the fly near them and they all darted at my fly. As the sun went behind the hills, the fishing slowed down. It started to get a little chilly and a few mosquitoes came out. I remembered to eat my forgotten lunch and get home before my wife called the sheriff to come find me. I suppose twelve hours of fishing is enough for one day. On the way home I almost hit a fat cotton tail rabbit that would have made nice dubbing.

June 4, 2003
After work I fished the Columbia River, near the bridge in The Dalles, Oregon. I caught several Smallmouth Bass and Squaw Fish from shore. Later, Josh Thompson, a friend from work, invited me to go out on the river for Sturgeon and Shad. We had several Sturgeon hits and schools of Shad bumped into our lines, but no big fish this trip.

June 9, 2003
I completed my third annual John Day River float trip. Over five days and almost fifty river miles I caught dozens of smallmouth bass. The bass were running on the large size this year, averaging about fourteen inches. The water was 2,400 cfs, almost twice last year's flow, resulting in a cast every twenty feet of shoreline rather than every ten feet.

Most of the bass were in the grass along the flooded stream bank in less than a foot of water, making accurate casts essential. I exclusively used foam flies, all the action was top water. I remember one fish. I made a bad cast to a small back eddy behind a boulder and quickly pulled my fly over the rock to avoid a snag. A twelve inch bass followed the foam cricket up the rock, out of the water, and took the fly on a small ledge and flopped back into the water. He was hooked and put up a good fight. We caught a lot of fish.

Smallmouth Bass, John Day River, Oregon

I saw twenty bighorn sheep on the third day, they scattered when we floated by but regrouped minutes later. I watched them drink from the river for over an hour before they headed back to the high country. One bighorn had a broken leg, and later we saw several coyotes following the herd. I also saw dozens of chucker, a couple of otter, and one beaver. The wind picked up every late afternoon giving us an opportunity to set up camp early and relax. We limited our gear to less than thirty pounds per person, only three of us in kick-boat pontoons (no raft this year for luxuries). The morning of day two, Jay Gibbs loaded his gear and pushed his pontoon off into a large calm pool and began to tie on a new leader and fly. He began screaming. We looked up to see a large rattlesnake swimming away from his kick-boat in the middle of the river. Somehow the snake was sunning himself on his pontoon boat and could not get off before becoming a castaway. Later that evening we debated whether he should have stayed on board and fought the snake or abandoned ship. He was pretty lucky either way. It would have been a two day trip to get out of the canyon and to a hospital. On day four we hit a good run and the fish were cruising in pods in the middle of the

river. For half an hour we tested our skills by closing our eyes and casting blind and striking when we heard fish take the fly on the surface. We had great fun and hooked most of the fish. By the end of the trip we were sunburned, had a dozen tattered flies, sore muscles, and memories of another great trip.

June 21, 2003
I fished the Salmon River near Zig Zag, Oregon and caught several small wild trout on #14 Renegade and #16 Elk Hair Caddis in between rain showers. The river was clear and cold. I fished near the road and did not go too far up the canyon. This was my first trip with my new Sage SP three weight rod. It was a very easy rod to cast and threw a perfect loop.

July 2, 2003
Cliff Mair, a neighbor friend, and I fished Lost Lake, near Lolo Pass on Mt. Hood. We caught and released five dozen rainbow and 1 dozen brook trout. All fish were ten to fourteen inches. The best set-up was a weighted #8 Wooly Bugger or Carey Special with a small #14 Pheasant Tail on two feet of tippet and tied to the hook bend of the larger fly. About ninety five percent of the fish hit the smaller trailing fly. We used pontoon boats to fish the lake shore and shoal areas, typical "cast and retrieve" lake fishing. Most of the fish were in four feet of water. Late in the afternoon we fished #12 Elk Hair Caddis and had great surface action in sheltered areas out of the wind. We caught all the brook trout on dry flies.

July 11, 2003
Don Welch, Todd Wilson, and I took several Boy Scouts on a float trip down the Rogue River in southern Oregon. The boys took kayaks and we took pontoon boats. We camped at the Four Corners Campground, a primitive hike-in campground, on the south side of Lost Creek Lake. We floated the same stretch of river for three days covering a total of forty six miles, between Cole River Hatchery and Dodge Park. Most of the water had Class II rapids. There was one Class III rapid. In the mornings and evenings we caught small mouth bass in the lake and trout in the river during the day. I caught four large trout between eighteen and twenty inches. The guys at the fly shop in Shady Cove said this stretch of the Rogue is famous for half pounder

steelhead, and that large trout were really steelhead. No wonder they fought so well. The largest steelhead hit on my third cast of the day, jumped several times, and was difficult to land on four pound tippet. Eventually I brought him to shallow gravel and released him. All the steelhead were in fast water behind large boulders in the middle of the river. During our daily runs down the river we watched several Spring Chinook being caught, the largest of which was about thirty five pounds. It was late in the season for Chinook, but it looked like good sport. All the Chinook were caught on very small "Glo Bugs", #14 bright red yarn and quarter ounce lead to keep it deep. We watched several dozen osprey working the lake and river picking up fish. It was exciting to hear a swoosh overhead, see a big splash, and watch the large birds lifting fish into the air just a few yards away. I was able to fish one evening on the "Holy Water", one mile of very productive, fly-only, catch and release water on the Rogue River. It was hot and sunny but I did pick up two fish (twelve and eighteen inches) on a #6 heavily weighted Kauffman's Stonefly Nymph and a #14 Flash Back Pheasant Tail Nymph. Both fish took the pheasant tail, the heavy nymph must have put the trailing small nymph in the feeding zone. A similar rig worked for the steelhead, except they all took the larger stonefly nymph. I hooked many small trout, and eventually removed the small nymph and focused on the larger fish. On the way home we took a one and half mile hike through the Oregon Caves (National Monument) to cool down. Later the boys took a jet boat ride through Hellsgate Canyon on the Rouge below Grants Pass, Oregon.

July 19, 2003
During the last few days the steelhead counts over The Dalles dam were 2,000 fish per day. I decided it was time to head to the Deschutes River. I pulled out of my driveway at 2am and met Tom Wilson, a friend of mine from West Virginia, at the motel in The Dalles at 4am. The last thirty miles of gravel road into Macks Canyon was rough and dusty; we were lucky not to get a flat tire or hit any mule deer. We arrived at the river at 5:30am and met Adam Haarberg, from work, at the boat ramp. He guided the Deschutes for several years before coming to work for us. We loaded our gear in his friend's jet boat and headed down river. The best steelheading is before or after the sun shines on the water. Several miles downstream, just below some class III-rapids the river split and we tied-up behind a small island. They call the west bank run the "ice box" because it produced so many steelhead in such a small area. Tom headed for the upper pool and I fished the lower run. Within half an hour I felt a tug, let the fish run until he hooked himself, and set the hook. A twelve inch Redside flew several feet in the air before splashing back into the water. Disappointed, I released the trout and began casting again. A few moments later I heard shouting upstream and saw a nice steelhead leap several feet into air. I watched from a distance as Tom played with and landed a nice steelhead. Later I learned they had released a seven or eight pound native steelhead. As the sun hit the water, we decided to head down river and fish another shaded run. I told everyone "just one more cast" while everyone was getting in the boat. I took two more casts and on the second hooked a strong steelhead at the tail end of the boulder strewn pool. He hit my fly, turned hard, and took a strong run across the river.

Steelhead, Deschutes River, Oregon

He never jumped, but took line out several times and gave my drag a workout. After a few minutes he tired and we gently grabbed him by the tail, took the fly out of the corner of his mouth and released him. He was a healthy native steelhead and slightly smaller than Tom's steelhead. I fished a #6 Purple Peril on a seven weight rod with a floating line, nine foot leader, and eight pound tippet. I cast one quarter downstream, let my fly swing slowly and steadily toward shore, with my rod tip low and following my fly in the water. Sometimes I had to mend the line upstream once or twice, after my line first hit the water, to keep the line straight. I was told to never strike in order to hook a Deschutes steelhead because the fish are directly downstream and you'll pull the hook out of its mouth. Always wait for the fish to take the fly, and turn and hook themselves. We always began casting at the top of the run, swung our line a couple of times, then took a few steps downstream and repeated the process until we reached the tail end of the pool. Ideally, fly fishable steelhead were found in three to six feet of relatively slow water with lots of large rock for cover. Water conditions have a lot to do with catching summer steelhead on a fly. It's best when the sun is off the water and the water temperature is below 65 degrees. The water temperature was almost 70 degrees when we caught our fish. It was hot and sunny the last few days, lower 50's at night and upper 90's during the day. It got up to 102 degrees today. We headed downstream, chasing the shade and fishing another long run below a series of rapids and riffles. I switched to a sinking-tip line when the sun was on the water. When the sun was directly overhead we took a break for lunch. Adam had set up camp several miles below the put-in just upstream of a place called "Dike". He and his friends were staying for several days. Adam cooked breakfast burritos and we relaxed in the shade for several hours. I received my first lesson casting a Spey rod. Within a few minutes I realized it was going to take several days for me to master the fifteen foot rod technique. I practiced casting for a few hours then switched back to my nine foot fly rod. I swung a fly through a long run just upstream from camp with no luck. I then tried a heavy stonefly nymph, small prince nymph, and indicator. We caught no fish. Finally, I switched to a foam grasshopper and caught a nice rainbow in a back eddy. The lower Deschutes is primarily steelhead water because it gets too hot for resident trout from over a hundred miles of sun-baked basalt canyon. There is also more sediment in the lower Deschutes, mostly from the glacially laden White River, which makes for poor spawning habitat. The good trout water is upstream where the steelhead spawn. By late afternoon the wind kicked up, making it difficult to cast. Just as the sun dropped below the canyon wall, we tried to fish the "Ledge" run, a long narrow solid rock ledge on the outside bend of the river with deeper, slow pocket water within easy casting distance. It was too windy to get a good cast and drift, the wind was blowing with gusts of twenty mph. We headed up river to Steely Flats, one of the best steelhead runs in the lower river. The flats were about a half mile long and about five acres of slow, shallow, fishable water full of small boulders. The wind was still blowing and the water temperature was over 60 degrees, not in our favor. We practiced casting for another hour and packed up our gear and headed back to the put-in at Macks Canyon just as it was getting dark. We thanked our friends for a great trip and headed back to the highway. I dropped Tom off at the motel and got home at 1am. What a great day, good company, nice water, two big fish, and memories to last a lifetime.

August 6, 2003

A couple of guys from work and I fished McKay Reservoir, east of Pendleton, Oregon several nights after work. It was hot, in the upper 90's, and perfect for evening boating on the lake. Matt Drechsel brought his boat up from Klamath Falls. We caught several dozen crappie, perch and smallmouth bass on heavily weighted white bucktails. The fish were schooling. When we caught one fish we were assured to catch a dozen. The biggest crappie were close to two pounds, the perch were around a pound, and the bass were less than ten inches long. Each afternoon convection thunder storms moved in. We fished until we could count ten seconds between lightning flashes and the sound of thunder, then motored back to the boat ramp before the downpour (slow boating with the four of us in a ten foot rowboat with a one HP electric motor). The storms came like clockwork each evening; it was good to be off the water when the lightning hit. It was exciting to see your buddy's hair stand up from static electricity in the air and then see lightning hit within smelling distance. Each morning there were several lightning caused fires in the surrounding wheat fields and foothills.

August 11, 2003

I had the chance to take my son Grady and my nephew Douglas fishing where I fished as a kid, up Farmington Canyon in northern Utah. We began with fly casting instructions at a small pond at the base of the canyon. In minutes each boy could cast ten feet and within an hour we caught about two dozen bluegill on small #18 Copper Nymphs. All the fish were within six feet of shore and the boys could sight cast to them without spooking the fish. Next, we graduated to the creek and fast water. Northern Utah was going through a drought, but the creek was in good shape, running about five cfs of clear, cold water. At the widest point, Farmington Creek was only ten feet across, full of fast riffles, and plunge pools. I put on a #16 Elk Hair Caddis and we started walking up the creek. At first the boys were distracted by a small water snake, chasing and catching it - until I caught the first fish, a wild rainbow trout about eight inches long. I had the boy's attention now and they were ready to fish. A road follows the first mile of creek and the rest of the canyon was pristine national forest with barely a deer trail for twenty river miles. There was plenty of brush, poison ivy and rattlesnakes to keep the casual fisherman or hunter out. I don't think the creek has ever been stocked (since pioneer times). Occasionally a few trout slip downstream from the beaver ponds near the summit, beyond that the creek is all natural trout reproduction. We had at least one fish rise in every hole, and hooked many of them. I suppose we caught two dozen trout during the afternoon (but who's counting). These rainbows were brightly colored, healthy and ran eight to ten inches. They were the right size given the limited environment they lived in. The boys took a swim and shower under a small waterfall to cool off late in the afternoon. As they were drying off, a mink surprised them and they stared each other down. I whistled and the mink took off, he could smell a meal and was willing to challenge the boys for their fish. The boys wanted to chase the mink up the creek, but he quickly lost them in the thick willows. We hiked back to the car and we each took a small trout home for Grandma to cook for dinner.

August 14, 2003
I finished work early and wanted to take a look at the Owhyee River, close to Ontario, Oregon near the Idaho border. I've heard there were monster brown trout in the tailwater below the Owhyee Reservoir. My rod and fly box were in the trunk of the car but it was too hot to fish, upper nineties, or so I thought. There were several fishermen camping along the ten miles of river below the

dam, so I pulled over to talk to a few who were packing up their gear. They caught several large browns on small #18 PMD Mayflies and Midge patterns and encouraged me to take a few casts. I didn't have waders, but found some flat, shallow riffles about a mile below the tunnel. Leaping to several dry boulders in the creek, and avoiding the poison ivy, I rigged up and tied on a #18 PMD emerger. Fish were rising steadily and I hooked a nice trout within ten minutes, a sixteen inch brown. Fifteen minutes later, in the same hole I hooked and released a strong eighteen inch brown on a #18 Flash Back Pheasant Tail Nymph. He made a strong run, but became entangled in the aquatic weeds and came in easily.

Owhyee River, Oregon

A quarter mile downstream, a fisherman's dog spooked a deer, which crossed the river in the hole I was fishing. The fish stopped rising for about fifteen minutes. When the fish started rising again I hooked two large browns and lost them as they headed for weedy cover. I finally hooked another nice brown and released him just as the sun was going down. What a nice river. I have to make another trip and stay a little longer.

September 12, 2003
I skipped work on Friday, the Coho salmon were running in the Columbia River. Steve Stephenson and Steve Lowe picked me up at 3am and we headed for Astoria, Oregon. Within two hours we turned off Highway 30 at Knappa Junction, changed into our waders under a street light at the gas station and parked at the rail road crossing a mile or so down the road. After a short hike along the tracks and through the wetland muck, we reached the mouth of Big Creek, only to find a trawler with gill nets spread across the slough and

the mouth of the creek. They shouldn't be here. When the boatmen saw us, they quickly began hauling in their nets and moved away from shore until they were further than rock throwing distance (they knew they were breaking the law). Gill netting is legal on portions of the Columbia River, but not completely across the mouth of a stream. We thought the fishing was ruined by the trawler. We were wrong. Within half an hour I had my first silver salmon on, a strong brute that pulled thirty yards of line and dogged up and down river for about five minutes, breaking off when my ten pound line nicked a timber poking up out of the water. It was still a bit dark and I could barely see the snag in the water. The tide was receding as the sun was coming up. We started getting more hits.

Chinook Salmon, Columbia River, Oregon

I hooked a fifteen pound Chinook that was injured by the gill nets. He came in easy and I put him on my tag. Steve hooked a very large "Tule" Chinook that jumped completely out of the water three times, snapped his line, and continued jumping for a quarter mile down river. I hooked two more large fish but was unable to land them. These Columbia River fish were tough. The slack water at low tide exposed the channel and the fish schooled-up in the deep hole at the mouth of the creek. A few fishermen in boats were catching fish further out in the main channel of the slough. Between the three of us, we hooked seven salmon and had a great morning.

September 20, 2003
We spent the day helping the Boy Scouts chop and stack wood for Nanich Lodge on Mt. Hood. The deal was if we chopped and stacked wood during the summer, we got to spend a weekend at the lodge in the winter. On the way home, Steve Stevenson and I fished Clear Lake and Frog Lake. We caught no fish. Trillium Lake was not fishing well either. I caught three small stocked rainbows.

October 10, 2003
I had been planning on fishing the Owhyee River since August, but at the last minute several of my fishing buddies canceled and I was on my own. After a nine hour drive from Portland, Oregon I pitched camp on the Owhyee River, south of Ontario, Oregon. I had a rocky camp just below the road tunnel about five miles below the dam. The Owhyee River is known for its large numbers and size of brown trout. The Owhyee is like a large spring creek, consistent temperature, shallow, lots of aquatic weeds, and slightly off-color. I saw hundreds of fish rising and only caught one trout the first evening. I was disappointed. The next morning I awoke to a small herd of cows running through my camp, spooked by another fisherman downstream. The cows knocked over the portable latrine I had set up in the willows and made nuisances of themselves. Luckily I was not in there at the time. A few hours later I met the gentleman who spooked the cows, we traded a few flies and he explained the fishery to me. The Owhyee Reservoir was built to store irrigation water and has a thriving warm water fishery. At the beginning of the irrigation season the reservoir spills thousands of crappie fry to the tail water below the dam. Brown trout grow large on the small fish. However, fish fry were only available in the spring and the large trout had to resort to feeding on grasshoppers, mayflies, midges and scuds the rest of the year. As a result, the large brown trout were feeding continuously on small insects which made an excellent fly fishery. There is a fair amount of fishing pressure, mostly from Boise, Idaho fisherman, which makes the trout selective in their feeding habits. The fly pattern must be a fairly good representation of the insect to catch fish. I started to catch fish once I changed from a #16 Pheasant Tail Nymph to a #18 Black Midge Pupa. My best set-up was a #14 Elk Hair Caddis with the #18 Midge Pupa on an eighteen

inch dropper. Fishing was very relaxed and I fished about two hundred yards of water each day. The best water had slow runs with lots of pockets in the thick moss. Fish were rising everywhere. I made two dozen casts to rising fish in one place, moved upstream a few feet, and repeated the process. I fished for the whole week within one mile of my camp. I saw the best fish of the trip, a twenty inch brown, rising to midges in a slow run between two fast riffles. My first thought was "I can't catch that fish, don't get your hopes up". I saw his dark back as he "porpoised" several times randomly through the run. I took a deep breath and began casting upstream of the last ring he left in the water. He took my midge hard and stripped ten yards of line before I knew it. I struggled to keep him out of the moss and finally brought him to the net.

Brown trout, Owhyee River, Oregon

A beautiful fish, a little on the lean side with bright red spots and yellow underbelly. I quickly snapped a few photos and released him. I had several big fish strip line and fight hard only to be lost in the aquatic weeds. Another memorable fish was lurking under a mat of floating algae, popping in and out snatching mayflies as they floated by. I watched him for several minutes before making my first cast. He came up, looked at my elk hair caddis, then turned and followed my midge pupa and sucked it in.

Brown Trout, Owhyee River, Oregon

He exploded into a fast riffle and I landed him downstream several minutes later, a nice eighteen inch brown. After releasing another sixteen inch brown I heard an awful screech and looked into the sun on a rock ledge a few yards above my head to see what looked like a prehistoric pterodactyl with a six foot wingspan. Actually it was a very angry Great Blue Heron. I didn't mean to invade the bird's space and moved upstream. Throughout the trip I averaged about twenty brown trout a day, most running fourteen to eighteen inches. I only caught one rainbow trout. By the end of the week I was getting a little lonely, a week of solitude was a bit much. I began working my way home. I stopped at the Snively BLM Rest Area on the lower Owhyee River for a short dip in the hot springs and the river. I left clean, refreshed and with the faint odor of sulfur. I spent the night in the sagebrush somewhere between Burns and Bend, Oregon. I fished the Crooked River below Prineville at sun-up and caught three small rainbows and two whitefish. It was not fishing well. I got home late Friday afternoon in time to do some yard work and take the family out to dinner.

December 10, 2003
I fished the Crooked River for about two hours, on the way home from working with a rancher who lived above Bowman Reservoir. I caught two foot long Redside trout on a #14 Orange Scud before hurrying home for my wife's birthday.

2004

January 30, 2004
I worked in Sisters, Oregon for a few days and decided to fish on the way home. I visited the guys at the Redmond Fly Shop and had three choices: The Crooked River, the Deschutes near Maupin, and the Metolius River, near Camp Sherman, Oregon. Having visited the Metolius several times in the summer and leaving because of the crowds, I thought I'd give it a try in the winter. There was supposed to be a small black stonefly hatch around noon every day, midges all day long and maybe a few blue wing olives. It was snowing when I woke up Friday morning and by the time I reached the turn-off to Camp Sherman it was a blizzard. I decided I was going to fish anyway. Not another soul was in sight, and my car made the only tracks in the snow as I drove past the closed Camp Sherman Store. I parked just below Allingham Bridge. The spring-fed Metolius was running about 45 degrees and the stream banks were clear of snow and ice. There was almost two feet of snow along the trail to the river, several steps increased my height as inches of snow collected on the felt of my wading boots. I had to stop and break off snow blocks every few minutes. Once in the river I tied on a heavily weighted stonefly nymph and a small #18 Olive Bead Head Hares Ear on 6X tippet. I cast to every likely looking hole and intently watched my indicator. By noon I noticed several small black stoneflies in the snow and switched to a #14 Black Parachute Stonefly and #18 BWO Emerger. It was difficult to see if fish were rising in the snow storm. Snowdrifts near the water's edge were peppered with hundreds of midges that were knocked down by snowflakes. The snow was really piling up as I fished the mile back to my car on the opposite side of the river. After the stoneflies disappeared I put the stonefly nymph and hare's ear back on and began casting along the undercut bank of a deep hole. I hooked a large fish. At first I thought it was a large whitefish because he hunkered near the bottom for a few minutes and hardly moved. I gently hauled him near the surface and was excited to see a large trout. He took the #18 hare's ear on three pound tippet. He spooked and took off across the river trying to make the current. Several minutes later he rolled on the surface, I had a large Bull Trout.

He came to the bank several times, saw me and high tailed it back to deep water. Finally I brought him to the net. He was a nice healthy twenty four inch fish. The problem with fishing alone is that no one can take a photo for you. He took off quickly when I placed him back in the water.

Bull Trout, Metolius River, Oregon

Back at the car I could not see the road, the snow was too deep, and the road must be in the clearing between the trees. I passed the sheriff just past Camp Sherman, he was closing the road because of the snow, and I made it with minutes to spare. Back on the highway visibility was about twenty yards so I put chains on my tires. Just as I was getting back in my car, two older ladies pulled up, jumped out of their van with a box of chains and smiled at me. It took me another fifteen minutes to get chains on their van. We caravanned over Santiam Pass at twenty miles per hour in a total blizzard and forty mph winds. What a day.

February 4, 2004
I attended the Washington County Fly Fishers meeting in Beaverton, Oregon for the first time. The club was organized a couple of years ago by Pete Priepke and a couple other fly fishermen. I'd heard about the group for years, but could not attend because I was volunteering with the Boy Scouts Wednesday nights, the same night as the club meetings. I resigned from the Boy Scouts when my son became a scout because I wanted him to have another role model and did not think it was right for a boy's father to be his scout leader. It was a good club meeting. They had monthly meetings, service projects, and fishing trips. I made a few contacts and paid my $20 annual membership dues.

March 17, 2004

I used Saint Patrick's Day as an excuse to take the day off and go fishing. I also invited Chris Martin from work and a neighbor, Roger Smith, along for the ride. We hit the road at 7am with two pontoon boats tied on top of my small utility trailer. It was hard to believe that eighteen years ago, when Jean and I got married, everything we owned fit into that trailer and the back of a station wagon. An hour later we were at Lost Lake in Clatsop County, Oregon. We met two guys from Hillsboro who were just leaving with their limit of trout. They left home at 4:30am thinking they had to be on the lake early to catch fish. What were they thinking? We loaded our gear onto the pontoon boats, pushed aside several floating logs at the boat launch and within five minutes Chris was into the first trout. We each caught and released four to five dozen trout running six to thirteen inches. The best fly, actually the only fly we used, was a #10 Bead Head Carey Special. Around 2pm it was getting warm and sunny, unusual for this time of year. I was day dreaming and slowly kicking my pontoon boat around with about twenty five yards of line out when I hooked a large fish. The line started buzzing off my reel, rod tip bending into the water and I sat up straining to hold onto the rod. The line cut through the surface of the water with a whooshing sound.

Steelhead, Lost Lake, Oregon

After five minutes I got the fish close to the net, but he took off again to deep water. My friends laughed and kept getting in the way. I finally got a net over his head and pectoral fins, only one third of his body could fit into the net. He flipped out of the net as I lifted him out of the water. I finally wore him out and got my hand around his tail. He was about thirty inches long and an estimated seven pounds. He was a beautiful fish with good color and a bright red spawning strip. We took a few pictures and spent the rest of the day catching more foot long trout and hoping for another monster fish. We got home just before dark, lucky for us because the lights on my trailer were broken.

April 24, 2004

I fished with the Washington County Fly Fishers on the McKenzie River. Our expectations were low because it was unseasonably warm and sunny. The anticipated caddis fly hatch would have to wait another day. We put in at Hendricks's Bridge and floated about five miles to the takeout. There were a few March Brown Mayflies and caddis flies, but not enough to bring many fish to the surface. I caught and released about a half dozen small rainbows on nymphs and Elk Hair Caddis. Mid-day was really slow. I looked for a challenging area to practice casting and beached my pontoon boat where the river was braided around three small islands. Standing at the tail-end of the middle island I could see a few fish rising downstream along the far stream bank. Catching these fish required a drag-free drift downstream across two faster currents. The key was to cast straight across, mend the far end of the line upstream, and a second mend downstream at the line's mid-point, within the first few seconds of the drift. I stood there for about two hours trying to get it right and finally my persistence paid off. Nice trout began rising about every ten minutes to caddis. I greased up my Elk Hair Caddis and cast, mend, mend, mend, the fish took it and I missed setting the hook. I waited another fifteen minutes and cast again. My diligence paid off with a five foot drag-free float. The trout took the fly again and headed for the deep pool, until I played him to the net. A nice thirteen inch native Redside Trout, biggest fish of the day. It was a good day even though we caught no huge fish and got a little sunburned. We were home before dark.

May 8, 2004

I took my ten year old son Grady to Dorman's Pond on his first pontoon boat fishing trip. He was excited and nervous as I pushed him off into the lake. By the time I had my pontoon and fly rod put together he had figured out how to row and was half way across the pond. It was cloudy with an occasional shower. All the trout were on the surface and hungry. I caught a half dozen fish before my son noisily splashed over and asked if he could use my fly rod. His best casts were about twenty five feet. Within minutes he had a small trout on. He wanted to keep a few fish for his mom, so I kept the first four and pretended to lose the rest into the water as I unhooked them. It took my son about a dozen fish to realize I was releasing his fish and not really losing them. We spent the rest of the morning following pods of stocked rainbows around the pond, chasing geese, picking water lily flowers, and having a great time.

Dorman's Pond, Oregon

May 22, 2004

I fished with the Washington County Fly Fishers. We met at Mecca Flats on the Deschutes early Saturday morning. Most of the club came the day before and camped overnight. They were ready to hit the water when I arrived at 7am. There were clear skies overhead and dark thunder clouds heading over the Cascades. By noon we had several short showers in between bursts of sunshine. Thousands of salmon flies covered the willows and rabbit brush along the river. Some were over three inches long. Amazingly, the trout were not keyed onto the salmon flies, we began fishing deep nymphs. I tied a #18 Copper John onto a dropper behind a large heavily weighted stonefly nymph and promptly caught two small trout in the slow water behind a small island. The next riffle was a little more exciting. We found a submerged gravel bar in the middle of the river, anchored our pontoons and drifted nymphs over a ledge into deep water. My friends promptly

hooked and landed a half dozen two pound whitefish while I watched. When the guys moved upstream searching for trout, I cast a #14 Red Wire San Juan Worm into the same hole and hooked a very large whitefish. He rolled on the surface just to look at me and headed downstream in the fast current. When I reached the backing of my fly line, I broke him off with a snap of my leader. He must have been three or four pounds. On the next run we met several others from our group. One guy caught several large trout below two small islands. One was over twenty four inches and could have been an early steelhead. I also got a brief lesson on improving my tuck cast, upstream mending and shaking line out during the downstream drift significantly increased my drag-free drifts. Several guys in our group were former guides and willing to teach us a few tricks. We all met for lunch and exchanged stories, we have a pretty good group. There were quite a few people on the river, about ten people per mile. That was typical for a Saturday. Most were rushing through and not fishing the water thoroughly. We did not have to wait long for the good holes. We split up for the afternoon. The trout began rising to salmon flies. I found a large back-eddy and parked my pontoon on a pile of rocks at the base of a steep talus slope. Several large trout were clearing the water, jumping for caddis flies in the middle of the pool. I tied on a #14 Elk Hair Caddis and sight cast to several trout in the fast, upstream back eddy next to the shore, and promptly caught two nice trout. Next, I tied on a large, black foam stonefly and blindly cast a little further out into the back eddy. My fly swirled around for a moment and disappeared in a small splash. The fish stripped line out on his first run, but I had him because all he could do was go round and round in the large back eddy. We fought each other for a few minutes until I tailed him behind a large boulder. He was eighteen inches long, dark, deep shouldered and had crimson red sides, a beautiful native Deschutes Redside Trout (I forgot my film in the car). The barbless hook came out easily as I released him. We fished a few more runs before the take-out at Trout Creek. We shuttled the boats back to Mecca Flats. I headed home, because I had to get back before my daughter's 14th birthday tomorrow.

June 7, 2004

I'd read in a guide book about the upper
Williamson River and wanted to give it a try. It
was raining in the Willamette Valley in the early
morning and snowing on Willamette Pass near
Odell Lake at noon, but was dry east of the
Cascades. Driving across Klamath Marsh, I was
surprised to see a large herd of domestic buffalo.
Off the pavement on a dirt road several miles
from the river a large flock of buzzards were
circling. Not a good sign for something or
someone. At the river I pulled out my maps and
located the public access points. One of the
bridges had been washed out (or removed) so I
parked my car at the end of the road and began to
hike upstream. In the distance I could see several
shanties and run-down campers permanently
parked along the river. I was a bit concerned but
did not see any people or vehicles around. Upon
close inspection, I realized they were Indian fish
camps. Each had a large fire pit, outhouse and
Indian symbols painted on plywood. This area
used to be part of the Klamath Indian
Reservation. Several decades ago the tribal council
voted to sell the Indian property. Now they were
trying to get it back. Later in the week I spoke
with the Inter-Tribal Fish and Wildlife Officer
who told me the tribe had a USFS special use
permit to keep structures on ancestral land, even
though it was now US Forest Service land.

Williamson River, Oregon

The upper Williamson is a thirty-five mile spring
creek. Today it was a little off-color from the
recent rains. I noticed a few Grey Drakes on the
river and tied on a #14 Deer Hair Parachute
Drake. The water was dead calm, flowing
smoothly through a large wetland-meadow. No
fish were rising so I started walking upstream,
casting to likely looking undercut banks. It was
too early in the season for the aquatic vegetation
to grow and provide much fish cover. I had one
fish hit my fly, but did not hook him. I came to a
large back-eddy and saw several fish rising to
emerging nymphs. I tied on a #16 Pheasant Tail
Nymph and made a downstream presentation to a
consistently rising fish. He took on the second
drift and I promptly landed a fat one pound
Brook Trout. I cast to several other rising fish and
got takes but no hook ups. Further up the
meadow I noticed a fish rising in an undercut
bank below a stunted pine tree. The only possible
cast was downstream. I hooked several caddis fly
cases with a heavily weighted peasant tail nymph
so I tied on a #14 Gold Bead Caddis Pupa. On
the first cast, at the end of the drift as my fly was
rising, I hooked a nice Rainbow. He shot across
the river (only thirty feet) and jumped several
times before I landed him in the shallow water on
the sand and released him. Storm clouds were
building from the west and I wanted to see more
of the river. I hiked back to my car through
several other fish camps and had an uneasy feeling
like I was invading someone else's privacy. I took
the road on the east side of the river for about ten
miles, until it was flooded and washed out by a
side creek. I back-tracked and took the forest road
on the west side of the river. It began to rain and I
was worried about getting stuck in the mud, thirty
miles from a paved road and a phone. I suppose I
could have stayed at a fish camp until the Indians
rescued me. I finally made it to a paved road and
the campground where the Williamson River
bubbled out of the ground in several large springs.
It really started raining. I'd had enough, time to
get back to work. I arrived in Klamath Falls,
Oregon just as it was getting dark.

June 14, 2004

My son Grady and I took a few days off to go
fishing. He had just turned 11 years old. We drove
to East Lake, southeast of Bend, Oregon and
camped in the Newberry National Volcanic
Monument at Hot Springs campground. We were
surprised to find snowdrifts in the campground.
There were signs warning campers to beware of
black bears. My son thought it was cool. We
quickly put up our tents and dumped our pontoon
boats in the lake. The wind was blowing strong
and immediately blew my son a quarter mile out

into the lake. I finally caught up with him and we trolled Olive Wooly Buggers back to shore. My son caught the first and biggest fish of the trip, a fat sixteen inch rainbow. He must have been an old fish because he had a hooked jaw. I fished Callibaetis nymphs and caught a half dozen small Rainbows and one Brown Trout. The next morning the wind was still blowing and there were white-caps on the lake. We fished for two hours and caught two landlocked Atlantic salmon. We rowed our pontoons to the lodge and took a break. I was amazed that the lodge was charging $3 per fly. The wind blew us back to the boat ramp on our return trip and we picked up a couple more small rainbows. We had enough of the wind and packed up camp. East Lake is just too big and open to fly fish when it's windy. We headed to Lost Lake on Santiam Pass, in the Cascades. This lake was smaller and had high ridges with thick forest surrounding it. There was a forest fire through the area two years ago, and the campground had only just re-opened. We thought the fishing would be good, it was not. I only saw two fish rise and we did not catch anything. My son lost his hat in the lake. They must not have stocked the lake the previous two years because of the fire. We had a big campfire to keep the mosquitoes away and relaxed for the evening. At 2am my son woke me up. He had lost one of his baby teeth and had to show me. We slept in and drove home the next morning.

June 2004
Don Nelson invited me to teach a monthly Atlantic salmon fly tying class at the River City Fly Shop in Beaverton, Oregon. The class was limited to four students, was held on Saturday from 10am until 4pm, and cost $65.

"Sunset Highway" Classic Salmon Fly

We tyed married-wing, Spey and Dee salmon flies. I had read all the old books about Atlantic salmon flys, but never had a proper lesson. I did watch Harry Lemire tye Atlantics at the Fly Tyers Expo in Eugene several times, but his table was always crowded and it was difficult to have a personal conservation with him. I took notes and tried to keep up with his instructions and picked up a few tricks. Teaching a class forced me to accelerate my learning and I spent hours experimenting and practicing until I got the flys tyed just right.

June 19, 2004
I fished the Salmon River, near Zig Zag, Oregon, with Cliff Mair. We caught a dozen native cutthroat trout and a few steelhead smolts. They were hammering small #16 Elk Hair Caddis.

July 7, 2004
We took our annual Boy Scout float trip down the Rogue River in southern Oregon. I am no longer the Varsity Scout Coach, but was invited along anyway. I fished, they kayaked. I watched several fishermen catching twenty five pound spring Chinook salmon on salmon eggs and hardware below the Cole River Hatchery weir. I gave it a try with my fly rod. I waded in at the tail-end of the large pool and began casting a heavily weighted #8 Stonefly Nymph and a #16 red Copper John with my five weight fly rod. Of course I was under-sized, but what the heck, it was a challenge. After two hours of catching three dozen foot-long rainbows (or they could have been steelhead smolts), who were feeding on salmon eggs, I hooked my Chinook. What a rush. He took the Copper John and jumped completely out of the water. He turned and made three jumps toward me. I was standing in three feet of water, reeling in like crazy, wondering what to do if he got any closer. A few fisherman stopped fishing as my fly line crossed their lines. One guy shouted to his friend "that's how it's supposed to be done". After a half dozen jumps, the Chinook settled down in the lower river and swam slowly in a ten foot circle for about ten minutes. My arm was wearing out. I'd had my sport and knew it was almost impossible to land the twenty-five pounder on six pound tippet. I horsed him more than I should have. He headed across river and broke off. It made my day just hooking a large salmon. That afternoon I hooked and lost two nice steelhead. They both leaped several feet into the

air and headed upstream while I floated downstream on my pontoon. At the end of two days fishing, I had hooked five steelhead and landed two. They were about six pounds and beautiful, bright fish. The last evening as we were relaxing in camp after dinner, a large rattlesnake crawled behind my lawn chair and into the brush. A few moments later, he crawled back toward me! This snake had to go. We quickly disposed of him before he became too tempting for one of our scouts. Next year we were thinking of bringing seven weight fly rods for the salmon.

July 18, 2004

I fished with the International Fly Fishing Association in Montana. I left Portland at 4am and arrived in Bozeman, Montana at 4pm. Not a bad drive, except traffic was slow where a car hit a moose near the Continental Divide in the Lolo National Forest. We met for dinner at Bob and Judi Kloskowski's house, and then a few of us headed for the East Gallatin River. I watched Matt Wenzel catch a nice sixteen inch Brown Trout on an Elk Hair Caddis in the rain. We spent the night at Dean and Margaret Larsen's home and had a huge breakfast in the morning. Monday we fished the ranch pond near Wheat, Montana. There were about two dozen in our group and about half of us fished. Most caught fish, a few on dry damsel flies. I had the best luck with #14 nymphs. The pond was shallow, the bottom covered with thick aquatic weeds, and very productive. We caught several twenty inch rainbows. We had a nice lunch under a large canvas canopy. Bob, Judi, and other Montana members of our group did a great job organizing our outing at the pond. I found half of a flint arrowhead in the sagebrush near the lake. In the late afternoon the storm clouds appeared over the mountains to the west, along with thunder and lightning. The wind kicked up so we hurriedly started packing our gear, but we still got soaked when the rain hit. On Tuesday we drove to Gardiner, Montana and entered the north entrance of Yellowstone National Park. Within an hour we saw a large herd of buffalo and three black bears. We stayed near the northeast entrance of the park in Cooke City, Montana. That evening we fished for an hour on the upper Soda Butte River, I caught one small cutthroat on a #16 Tan Elk Hair Caddis. On Wednesday I fished with Tom Wilson and Kevin Griggs on the lower Soda Butte, above the confluence with the Lamar River.

Tom had fished this area for the last ten years, and put us in some nice spots. My first fish of the day was a challenge. I cast a #10 Black Foam Cricket with a #16 Flashback Pheasant Tail dropper into a small back eddy below a riffle. On the third cast an eighteen inch Yellowstone Cutthroat came up and looked at the cricket, dove, and took the pheasant tail. He took a couple of nice runs and I netted him a few minutes later. I caught a few more fish on the cricket in the pocket water along the grass riverbanks. Later in the day Kevin and I fished a long, fast, deep riffle. Nothing would rise to my cricket, so I switched to a #14 Tungsten Bead Red Copper John with a #16 Pheasant Tail dropper. I picked up another half dozen trout in the fourteen to sixteen inch range. We did not get the expected Grey Drake hatch around noon. The day was partly cloudy with widely scattered showers. The river was slightly off-color because of the recent rains. It appeared that most of the rivers in Yellowstone were running high and off-color. There were a lot of fishermen on Soda Butte Creek because it was running clear. That night we had a group barbecue at Tom and Dottie's rented cabin in Silver Gate. They put a lot of work into feeding us and we all appreciated the great meal and camaraderie. Thursday morning on the drive to Slough Creek we saw a black wolf and a large buffalo bull next to the road. They ignored us and were focused on each other. At the trailhead we met the outfitter with the horses we had rented for the day.

Second Meadow, Slough Creek, Wyoming

We saddled up after a brief rain shower and rode about ten miles out of Wyoming to the third meadow of Slough Creek in Montana. The outfitter hobbled the horses while we ate lunch.

We had sunshine for most of the morning. Several in our group caught some very nice twenty inch plus Yellowstone Cutthroats. We had a small hatch of green and grey drakes and PMDs, until it began to thunder, with lightning, rain, and hail. Throughout the day I caught about a dozen fourteen to twenty inch trout, and brought up much bigger fish that swirled on my fly before disappearing. I fished #8 Black Chernobyl Ants, #10 Black Crickets, #16 Pheasant Tails, and #14 Parachute Extended-Body Green & Grey Drakes.

Cutthroat Trout, Slough Creek, Montana

Most fish were next to the steep, grass covered banks in deep water, where they had a lot of time to look a fly over. It stopped raining for our ride out. We had three coyotes follow us for about a mile along the trail. There were six inch drifts of hail on a stretch of highway in the Lamar Valley on our drive back to Cooke City. Friday I fished with Tom again on Soda Butte. Within minutes I caught two nice eighteen to twenty inch fish on nymphs, in a deep, fast hole next to the road. An hour later a man, who was watching wolves with a telescope, motioned me over and pointed out three large cutthroats rising in a stagnant back-water slough. The fish appeared to be nymphing to rising mayflies. I followed a cruising trout along the shore until I could cast a #20 Pheasant Tail Nymph at him. On the second cast he took the fly, I nicked him on the lip and he would not take the fly again. I started working on the second trout, but he would not budge. I cast a #10 Black Foam Cricket to the third fish. He looked at my fly for a few seconds when it hit the water and turned away. I slowly stripped the fly. He turned and followed it for about ten feet and slowly rose and gulped it in. I waited for him to turn before setting the hook. I landed him quickly in the

shallow water, a beautiful bronze 18 inch cutthroat. I caught a few more trout along the grassy bank with my cricket.

Soda Butte River, Yellowstone, Wyoming

After lunch, we had the first real hatch of the week, Pale Morning Duns, Callibaetis and a few Grey Drakes all at the same time. It was cloudy with a few short showers. I fished a long narrow shelf of water below a short, shallow riffle. The fish were stacked up against the lip of the shelf in about ten inches of water. I could see a half dozen fish rising or turning sideways as they inhaled rising nymphs. I put on a #16 Parachute Adams and caught a dozen sixteen to eighteen inch cutthroats on about every third cast. I was amazed. We fished this water two days before and could not raise a fish. The hatch ended an hour later. On the drive back to Cooke City we saw another wolf. We fished briefly in upper Soda Butte River where it entered the forest. I caught two eight inch cutthroats on a #16 Elk Hair Caddis. Saturday was hot and sunny, how Yellowstone was supposed to be this time of year. We fished Soda Butte again. The morning started slowly with few fish. Around noon we had a nice PMD hatch with a few large Grey drakes. Some in our group caught a lot of nice fish. I was not in the right spot. I hooked four fish on a #12 Parachute Extended Deer Hair Grey Drake, but only landed one fish. I switched to a #16 Parachute PMD and promptly caught three trout in the middle of a slow, deep pool. The hatch subsided three hours later. I began stalking trout along the river bank, and caught two more fish on a black cricket. We had a group dinner at the historic Roosevelt Lodge and had a good time. On the last day in the park, Dany Groeten, Tom, Dottie and I headed back to Soda Butte to fish until dark. Dany and I headed downstream to fish a long flat run. We ran into a buffalo, which began walking slowly towards us. Dany had a fish on when the buffalo was within fifty yards, I didn't wait for him and I headed to the safe side of the river. When the sun was behind the ridge, large caddis and crane flies appeared above the water. Dany put on a large #8 Stimulator and promptly caught a dozen sixteen to eighteen inch trout. I caught a few fish on a #12 Elk Hair Caddis.

Cutthroat Trout, Soda Butte River, Wyoming

Fish were popping out of the water everywhere. At any given minute, three or four fish were leaping into the air in the thirty yard run. On my hike back to the car, in the fading light, I could hear Dany whooping with each new fish. Earlier that day a black bear had crossed the river where we were fishing, I didn't want to take any chances. Dany returned a short time later because he was not able to see his fly on the water anymore. That was the best way to end a fishing trip. Sunday morning we had a small group breakfast in Silver Gate and headed our separate ways. I went sightseeing in Yellowstone and saw one bear, a small herd of elk, and a buffalo herd that stopped us on the road north of Yellowstone Lake. The traffic was slow around Old Faithful. It began raining in West Yellowstone and I spent the night in Belgrade, Montana. Tom had reserved two rods for us Monday morning at DuPuy's Spring Creek, just outside of Livingston, Montana. It was a bit expensive, but well worth it. The water was extremely clear with thick aquatic plants. It was sunny and the fish were rising in pockets between the weed beds. It was tough fishing. Mid-morning we had a Pale Morning Dunn hatch that lasted

until early afternoon. I hooked and lost three large fish in the aquatic weeds. Most upstream casts spooked fish, so we made across or downstream casts to individual rising fish on 7X tippet. Most fish did us the courtesy of looking at our flies, but we had few takers. In the hot, bright afternoon I cast a #18 Parachute PMD to one rising trout with no takes, a moment later the same fish took my foam cricket with him and broke off in the weeds. In the early evening Tom yelled for some help, I found him on the other side of a clump of willows and watched him fight and land a very healthy twenty two plus inch brown trout. He caught him on a #10 Black Foam Cricket. We quit fishing around 8pm near the fishing hut. I washed-up in the creek before beginning my 700 mile trip back to Portland. I took a nap at the rest area outside of Deer Lodge around midnight and another nap around St. Regis, Montana, two hours later. In Washington I missed the turn-off at Ritzville and took the long way home though the Yakima Indian Reservation. I got home to hot, 100 degree weather around 2pm the next day. It was another great IFFA trip. Budget: Transportation: $125, Car, Miles Driven: 1,800, Meals: $150, Motel $375, Miscellaneous Expenses: $50, nine Days, Total Cost: $700

August 7, 2004
I took my son Grady fishing for the day. He's getting pretty good with his fly rod, casting about thirty feet from his pontoon boat. I put a small corkie on the end of his fly line, before the leader, to prevent the fly line from falling through the line guides, which had given him problems casting. We fished Vernonia Pond and caught a half dozen, eight inch Perch and one small Bluegill. After fishing an hour we found out that they had a fishing tournament the day before. We now knew why we were doing so poorly. We packed up, had lunch at the Timber Junction Cafe and drove to Lost Lake. I caught a small rainbow on my second cast. Fishing was slow the rest of the day, it was clear and hot. It was nice to hang my feet in the cool water. Grady caught two small rainbows and I caught four more. The big fish must be sulking on the bottom waiting for cooler water.

August 14, 2004
My brother-in-law Sheldon Munns was in town and wanted to go fishing. It was a hot, ninety degree, cloudless day, the worst possible time to

go fishing. We decided to fish Lawrence Lake, on the north slope of Mt. Hood. There was a slight wind from the Columbia Gorge as we pushed our pontoon boats into the lake. My son was happy to get into the cool water. We began trolling #14 Pheasant Tail Nymphs toward the east end of the lake. When we passed over a ridge of shallow shoals, in three feet of water, cluttered with old tree stumps, we began catching fish. I caught four rainbow trout, fourteen to sixteen inches, during the first hour. Then the fish stopped biting. I headed toward the shade of a bridge over a creek entering the lake. Several small native cutthroat trout were taking midges on the shaded, leeward side of the bridge. I put on a #16 Parachute Ant and caught three trout, on the small side but very colorful. After a brief lunch, we headed to the west end of the lake, hoping for an evening Callibaetis hatch. I immediately caught two sixteen inch rainbows near a sunken snag in the old stream channel where the creek enters the lake. For a short time, the water was completely calm. I put on a #14 Black Foam Beetle, cast it thirty feet and let it sit still for five minutes. The water erupted as a cruising trout hit it hard and fought well. We caught another dozen fish over the next three hours before the sun sank below the steep talus ridge to the west. Within minutes of being cast into shadows, fish started jumping like popcorn. The speckled mayflies were thick, crawling on our faces and covering our boats. We caught another two dozen fish, eight to fourteen inches, before dark. I had little luck with dry flies, but they were killing our pheasant tails. I did catch one small Bull Trout, my first one from a lake. We got home around midnight, Sheldon's wife was not happy. She had wanted to go shopping.

August 17, 2004

I was working for a week at the National Conservation Training Center near Shepardstown, West Virginia, putting a course together for our new employees. The Potomac River was a short hike away through the woods. It was hot and humid. The first night after work I fished a #10 Tan Foam Hopper and soon learned the smallmouth bass were not taking terrestrials. I put on a #8 Black Leech and caught a four inch fish. The next evening I headed down river, swinging a small streamer. At dusk I heard animal screams in the thick undergrowth next to the river, I continued to fish, a little concerned with what was

going on. A short time later on my way back, a small raccoon rolled into the river and a large raccoon grabbed him and threw him back on shore. The large male proceeded to pummel the screaming small male to death. I had never seen this before and was amazed at his brutality. I did not catch any fish. The third evening I saw a fish rise and promptly cast and caught a ten inch fish, on a #16 Adams Parachute. I crossed forty yards of river, on a limestone ledge, to a small island (where I saw three deer cross the night before). On the back side of the island I found a school of smallmouth bass. The bass were chasing smaller fish into shallow riffles where they scattered like mice from a burning barn. I could see at least a dozen bass working the riffle. I cast a #12 Beadhead Krystal Flash streamer across the riffle and promptly caught a foot long smallmouth. He put up a decent fight and I quickly released him. I caught another five bass, twelve to fourteen inches, over the next half hour. I spooked a deer on my hike back in the dark and almost stepped on a slider turtle on my wade back across the river. Sure glad it was not a snapping turtle. I later learned the island had played a small role in the battle at Antietam, which had the most casualties in one day during the civil war. Perhaps this explains the old male raccoon's behavior.

September 4, 2004

Since the summer was coming to an end and it started to cool down, the fall Chinook were in the Columbia River. Steve Stephenson and his son Daniel picked up my son Grady and me at 3:30am and we headed down the Columbia River towards Astoria. We hiked in to Big Creek along the rail road tracks in the dark. We arrived early at high tide and had to sit along the flooded trail for an hour until the water level was low enough to get out of the willows to the Columbia River. The boys had an adventure when large decomposing Chinook salmon, floating with the high tide, bumped into us along the flooded trail in the dark. We started fishing at first light. I hooked the first salmon, which leaped, rolled twice, and threw the hook. Six hours later, at low tide, we hooked our second fish. A large salmon, probably around thirty pounds, took my lure on a short cast, and jumped and stripped thirty yards of line on his first run. Over the next ten minutes my finger was on my reel's drag as he slowly stripped line out on his way back to the Pacific. He finally began to tire and I put most of the line back on my reel. Just as I pulled him across the channel lip towards shore, the line went limp and he was free. My son accused me of hooking a log. Steve hooked the next two fish. Both were foul hooked, but gave strong runs, jumped four feet in the air, and were terrific fighters. I foul hooked my third fish of the day. He leaped several feet from where I was standing, headed across the channel, and almost beached himself on the mud flats, only to brake free moments later. At the end of low, slack tide, the fishing abruptly stopped, so we packed up our gear and hiked back to the truck. We each had a logger burger at the cafe in Knapp Junction and headed home. There were about a hundred boats on the Columbia at the mouth of the Lewis River. Fishing must also be good down there.

September 25, 2004

After teaching a class in West Virginia, I met Tom Wilson and we drove up to central Pennsylvania. A visitor could easily get lost on the forested back roads in this part of the country. We dropped off our gear at Tom's cabin, near Hartleton in Union County, and were fishing Penns Creek within minutes. The previous week several residual storms from the Florida hurricanes flooded the northeastern states and filled most streams beyond flood capacity. We swung #8 Black Wooly Buggers through the off-colored water and picked up a few nice brown trout. I landed a twelve to fourteen inch fish. Tom also caught several browns, the biggest a little over sixteen inches. The autumn leaves were turning orange in the thick deciduous forest. Squirrels were everywhere.

Brown Trout, Penn's Creek, Pennsylvania

The next day we headed north to the state forest and fished the fly-only section of White Deer Creek, a free-stone mountain creek much smaller and clearer than Penns Creek. We got a few rises on #18 Adams Parachutes. The fishing was slow. I switched to a #16 Beadhead Flashback Pheasant Tail and bounced it through a deep pool. I hooked three fish and landed a ten inch wild brown. These trout were heavily fished and cautious. It was a challenge to catch them. Hunting lodges were common in this part of the country, I suppose city folks on the east coast purchase cabins to secure hunting and fishing opportunities. Along some roads that we traveled, there were several lodges per mile, something not common in the western states. Whitetail deer were everywhere, almost too many. Next we headed west to State College and fished Spring Creek, the first fly-fishing-only designated water in the United States. This river was also high and flood debris littered the stream bank. We fished a short while and did not catch any fish. We passed several Amish communities on our return trip, and had to be careful to avoid their horse drawn carriages along the highway. That evening, we fished Penns Creek again and had a few hits but no fish. I left for the airport the next morning and wished for more time to fish those beautiful limestone creeks.

September 29, 2004

I hiked a mile up the John Day River from Cottonwood Bridge (near Condon, Oregon), and took a few casts for smallmouth bass. I usually catch a lot of fish in this section in June. The river was fishing poorly this fall. Foam grasshoppers did not bring a rise in the back eddies. I switched to a small #10 Krystal Flash Streamer and caught three very small bass.

October 1, 2004

I stopped at the fly shop in Prineville for some advice and picked up some leaders and headed up the Crooked River. I parked at Bison Butte (second campsite from the dam) and put on my waders. I crossed the river and had the river to myself. The river was calm, normal flows with a few mayflies and midges in the air. No fish were rising. I began casting a #22 Black Midge Pupa, on an eighteen inch dropper, below a #14 Bead Head Pheasant Tail Nymph, five feet below a yarn indicator. At the head of the pool was a deep, fast chute. I hooked the first fish within minutes and landed a fat two pound whitefish, on the #22 midge. Over the next half hour from the same hole, I landed another half dozen large whitefish. The largest was about three pounds and eighteen inches long. The whitefish were schooling. When you catch one, you were bound to catch others in the same area. By noon several other fishermen appeared just as the fish began rising for midges and blue wing olives. I swapped the weighted nymph and indicator for a #12 Elk Hair Caddis and began casting to the rings in the river. Moments later I picked up a nice Redband Trout on the #22 midge, he was well hooked. From noon to four in the afternoon I hooked a dozen trout an hour, all on the midge pupa. The fish were running large this year, most were in the fourteen to sixteen inch range and hefty. A few larger fish broke my 7X tippet, but they could have been big whitefish. By late afternoon, the fishing slowed and I headed home.

October 6, 2004

I arrived on the Owhyee River at 8am. Storm clouds were threatening from the west. It was overcast, which was normally perfect weather for a midge, blue wing olive, or PDM hatch. I like fishing the flat, slow moving frog water where you can see big browns taking insects on the surface and get long, drag-free drifts. The best areas have large boulders randomly poking above the water dispersed amongst islands of aquatic vegetation. I immediately rigged up a #22 Black Midge Pupa on an eighteen inch dropper below a #14 Elk Hair Caddis. I began blind-casting to likely looking water. Few fish were rising, so I concentrated on pockets along the bank. I hooked a fish on the midge after three casts across the current, a sixteen inch brown trout. He was taking insects behind a mat of floating algae. I continued wading upstream, casting to fish midstream, hooking and releasing a dozen browns before lunch. The trout were running big this year, ranging from sixteen to eighteen inches. After lunch the sun came out and the fish moved into the boulder water surrounded by thick weedbeds along the streambank. The Owhyee has always been turbid, but the fish were easy to see in the shallow water if you know what to look for. I began stalking a large brown who was aggressively taking emergers. I put my midge right on his nose, which he promptly ignored. The next cast was two feet to his right and slightly upstream, he turned, inhaled my fly, and I set the

hook and he exploded. He made the main current before I could tighten the drag, and buried himself in a mass of weeds and algae. I kept the tension on and he came free from the weeds. A few minutes later I got half of him into my net, a 22 inch, scared, hooked jawed brown trout. I cut my thumb on his sharp teeth while removing the hook. I hooked and released another dozen browns before the sun went behind the ridge. All the good camp sites were taken (there were very few tent sites in the rocky canyon). I parked near the river in a grove of cottonwoods, fixed a sandwich for dinner and slept in the back of my Toyota station wagon. I used a piece of plywood under an inflatable mattress to make a level bed.

October 7, 2004

I rose early, had another sandwich for breakfast, and headed back to the Owhyee River. I'll never win a culinary award for meal planning on my solo fishing trips. The fish were rising early. I stalked several huge browns in the shallow water and took my best fish on the Owhyee that morning. I could see him clearly taking midge emergers. I put on a new #22 midge pupa and cast twenty feet to his side to estimate the correct casting distance. My first cast was right on target, slipping into the water five feet upstream, my tippet laying right over the top of his head.

Brown Trout, Owhyee River, Oregon

I could see the silver ribbing on the small fly sparkle as it drifted toward the trout. He scooted upstream and took the midge without a second thought. I set the hook and he took off, stripping thirty feet of line upstream before taking another ten feet downstream. He was a wild ride until I beached him in the shallow rushes five minutes later. He was twenty five inches, about five pounds and no one was around to take a picture. I released him and took a break. The rest of the morning, I took another dozen fish, averaging sixteen to eighteen inches. Most took the midge, a few the caddis. I met a gentleman taking a lunch break high on the river bank. We exchanged flies. He pointed out several large browns working the tail-out of a large pool. We chatted for a few minutes and then he spotted for me as I hooked and released two more trout.

Brown Trout, Owhyee River, Oregon

The largest brown kept rising as I cast to other fish, but hid under a large algae raft when I cast to him. This happened several times until we gave up on him. We fished to the top of the run together until we ran into several other fishermen. I went looking for new water. Downstream was a half mile of riffle water, I cast small nymphs with an indicator and picked up one fish. It was sunny and getting hot, maybe 70 degrees, the fish took the afternoon off so I headed upstream. I didn't want to miss the evening hatch. I found a long bend in the river, with a deep run on the outside curve with fish rising. I cast a #18 Parachute Adams and picked up another half dozen browns and one small rainbow. I was surprised to foul-hook an eighteen inch brown in the tail with a dry fly. He fought like a demon stripping my line well into the backing. It took ten minutes to net and release him. I caught my last fish in the dark, hearing the "gulp" as he took the fly from the surface. After releasing him I happily headed back to the car and

slept in the back seat, too tired to look for a camp site.

October 8, 2004
On the drive home from the Owhyee I took a 200 mile detour to check out the Donner and Blitzen River. I'd read about the Steens Mountains for years, but have never been there. I was surprised to find a fancy resort near Frenchglen and a large campground half filled with recreational vehicles. At first I thought they were deer hunters, but most were sandal-wearing backpackers preparing for a sunny weekend. I met two other fishermen at the trailhead just after 9am. One told me the best fishing was above the dam-irrigation diversion, a mile or so up the trail. I quickly hustled up the trail, keeping an eye out for rattlesnakes along the rocky trail.

Donner and Blitzen River, Oregon

It was about 70 degrees, I wet-waded because I only planned to fish for a few hours. I tied on a #16 Olive Elk Hair Caddis and quickly hooked a six inch native Redside Trout. The pressure was off. I can enjoy the rest of the day. I hooked a half dozen trout over the next two hours, each one a jewel of red, green, and black spots. The small creek ran through a basalt canyon that was unlike anything else I'd fished in Oregon. The area was more like southern Utah or northern New Mexico, lots of juniper, sagebrush and sand. I hiked out mid-afternoon and arrived home after midnight

October 14, 2004
I arrived early on the North Umpqua River. The mouth of Steamboat Creek had a half dozen fisherman at six in the morning. I hiked downriver about a mile until I found my own run where I

could swing a salmon fly. Even though it was late in the season for summer steelhead, I tied on a #1/0 Purple Peril Spey and began casting. For years I'd wanted to fish this famed river. I swung a dry flyline, cast three-quarters across and downstream, and guided my fly as slowly as I could through the run. I've been told that weighted nymphs or indicators were not allowed on this river. I did not interest any fish in the first fifty yard run and headed to the next hole downstream. I began casting at the head of the pool. Halfway through two fishermen appeared out of the underbrush and asked if they could fish. I begrudgingly said yes. They began fishing the best water and left a half hour later. I let the pool rest for a while and ate my breakfast. All the fog had burned away and the sun was almost on the water when I began casting. I was rewarded for my efforts with a beautiful buck steelhead jumping out of the water and rolling at my fly. I never even pricked him. He appeared to have been in the river for some time with bright red sides, a little on the dark side and about ten pounds. I fished hard the rest of the day. He was the only steelhead I saw. Later I cast to and hooked several small resident trout who were taking mayflies on the surface. It was fun catching them in this historic water, but what I really needed was a steelhead. I'll have to come back earlier in the season, study a little harder and find someone to teach me how to fish this beautiful river.

November 3, 2004
I arrived on the Crooked River at noon and quickly tied on an #16 Tungsten Bead Pheasant Tail Nymph and #22 Midge Pupa dropper with indicator yarn about six feet up the leader. I began casting into a fast, short run between two large boulders. Within minutes I hooked a very large whitefish on the midge. He stripped fifty feet of line downstream while maneuvering into the fast current. He broke off just before I could get a net around him in the fast water. I returned to the same slot and began dredging my nymphs through the run. I caught another half dozen, two to three pound whitefish from the same spot; all on the midge pupa. The hole finally played out and I headed upstream, switching to a midge pupa below a #14 Elk Hair Caddis. I hooked a fat sixteen inch Rainbow on the caddis. He was hiding alongside the watercress a foot from shore. He looked like a skipped rock in the shallow water

as he took off. I gave him a lot of slack so he wouldn't get hurt on the rocks. I landed him on the sand a few minutes later. The next three hours I landed another dozen trout, most on the midge. The technique was simple: spot a fish rise, wade within casting distance, place the fly ten feet upstream, minimize line drag, watch the caddis indicator and lift the rod at any irregular indicator movements. I experimented with the distance between the caddis and the midge. Six inches was too short, the midge was too high in the water column. Two or three feet was too long, the fish could spit the midge out before being hooked. The best distance was about eighteen inches. I left the river at dusk, hungry and tired.

November 5, 2004
The Crooked River was cold and windy, but there was not a cloud in the sky. I tore the gravel guard off my frozen waders as I pulled my stiff wading boots on. Next time I'll soften them in the river and not let them freeze in the car overnight. I spent most of the morning casting into a stiff canyon wind and only caught one whitefish on a midge pupa. The wind got really bad around noon. I sat in the shelter of a tree stump in the sunshine and waited for a midge or blue wing olive hatch to begin. About 1pm the fish started to rise, I put on a #16 Elk Hair Caddis and #22 Midge Pupa and began casting to rising fish. Within an hour I caught and released five Redside Rainbows, most on the midge. The fish were average, fourteen to sixteen inches and fat. I shared the run with a retired gentleman from Bend. We talked about the recent presidential election and problems in the school system (he was a retired school teacher). The fishing all but stopped around 3pm so I headed home and saw about thirty head of mule deer in an alfalfa field at the mouth of the canyon.

December 2, 2004
It had been snowing in Bozeman over the past few days, I wasn't sure we'd get some fishing in. The temperature was hovering in the low 20s and was supposed to rise to the upper 30s by the weekend. Bob Kloskowski picked me up at the motel and we headed to Livingston, Montana to fish Armstrong Creek. We arrived to strong winds and below freezing temperatures. We paid our $20 fee to the lady at the ranch headquarters. She gave us that "you crazy fishermen" look. Upon Bob's

recommendation I tied on a #16 peach egg pattern, he called it an "ova emerger". Bob cast below a small riffle and hooked and landed a nice rainbow. Shortly thereafter I hooked and lost a small rainbow. A few fish began rising to midges, I switched to a #14 Elk Hair Caddis with a #22 Midge Pupa dropper, a rainbow rose to the caddis twice but no hook-up. The wind blew my hat off into the water. I slipped, stumbled and finally dove after it before it floated too far downstream. I didn't get too wet, but did tear half my thumbnail off.

Armstrong Creek, Montana

We headed upstream where I noticed several large Brown Trout working the shallow riffles. I hooked a sixteen inch Brown on the caddis and a few minutes later a four inch rainbow on the midge. A little further upstream, below a large culvert, I cast a midge into the tail-end of the plunge pool and hooked an eight inch rainbow. Bob caught several nice fish on eggs below the large springs and a nice brown swinging a brown wooly bugger in slow slough water above the culvert. It was getting dark as we headed back to the truck. I walked down the middle of several slower runs, swinging a #8 Mickey Finn through the channels of thick aquatic weeds. At one point, I cast across a small island of matted vegetation into a fast run. At the end of the swing I hooked a large Cutthroat Trout. He must have come up the creek from the Yellowstone River a half mile downstream. It was a struggle to keep him out of the weeds, but I finally beached him thirty yards downstream. He was over eighteen inches long and darker than the cutthroats we had caught in the park last July. I should have brought my camera, he was a

beautiful fish. Bob had the truck warmed up when I met him in the parking area.

December 3, 2004

I awoke to a clear, cold morning ready to go fishing. Bob Kloskowski picked me up at 9:30am and we met Dean Larsen and Bob Abrams at the Wheat Bakery for breakfast. Dean was a little grumpy because they did not have free coffee any more, but softened-up with a sweet roll. We arrived at Plunkett Lake, an hour west of Bozeman, Montana with a stiff breeze out of the south. It was very cold as we got into our polar-fleece and waders and launched our pontoon boats into the slightly warmer water. Within minutes Dean and Bob both had fish on; they shouted "eighteen to twenty two inchers". I put on a white #6 Wooly Bugger and stripped it through the thick aquatic weeds. After a half hour Bob insisted that I switch to a #6 Chartreuse Krystal Flash Streamer, I had my first fish a few casts later. He jumped twice and then dodged through the weeds before I brought him to the net. This rainbow was a twenty inch football shape with dark crimson sides.

Rainbow Trout, Plunkett Lake, Wheat, Montana

I released him as Dean hooked into another fish. The action slowed the rest of the morning. We took a break, ate our lunch in the truck, and tried to warm up. In the afternoon Bob and Dean caught a few more fish, and I hooked and lost two fish. Around 3pm we called it quits because of the strong winds. I was wind burned but felt good about our success.

2005

February 2, 2005
I gave a slide-show to the Washington County Fly Fishers club about our trip to New Zealand. Several in our group had fished there and we all agreed that you had to fish there at least once before you died.

February 12, 2005
I was invited by the River City Fly Shop to tie flies at their booth at the Pacific Northwest Sportsman's Show at the Portland EXPO center. I tied classic Atlantic salmon flies for a day and a half. We met some interesting people and heard a lot of fishing stories. I traded salmon flies with Lee Clark (of Clark's Stonefly fame), Denny Rickards (Oregon author), and Chuck Stranahan (Montana guide) for flies they tied and their autographed books. I was invited by several Federation of Fly Fishers board members to tie at the Fly Tyers Expo in Eugene, Oregon the upcoming spring. I also sold several framed salmon flies for $75 each.

Akroyd Classic Salmon Fly

February 26, 2005
I fished the Clackamas River with the Washington County Fly Fishers. We put our pontoon boats in at McIver Park and floated eight miles down to Barton County Park, it took about six hours. Our expectations were low. It was 60 degrees, sunny, and not a cloud in the sky. We were in a drought period and had just broken the February record with twenty rainless days, very unusual for this time of year. It felt like we were summer

steelheading. Dan hooked the first steelhead within a half hour, our hopes improved. I started out with a #6 MOAL String Leech and switched mid-morning to a #6 Purple Egg Sucking Leech.

Steelhead, Clackamas River, Oregon

Ten minutes after switching flies, I cast to the slow water between the bank and the swift water at the top of a run. I began stripping to keep the heavily weighted fly off the bottom when I hooked a fish. She was well hooked and stripped line out as I followed her down the swift shoot of water. I kicked furiously to a gravel bar, keeping my rod high, and beached my pontoon. A few moments later I had her in the net, a nice crimson streaked hen, over two feet long and about seven pounds. A friend took a few photos then we were off looking for more fish. We found fish, but were unable to hook any the rest of the day. The water was too low and clear for steelhead. We passed over many fish in the deep, slow runs, who scooted out of the way as we passed overhead. Not a bad first day on the Clackamas.

March 17, 2005
I picked Shann Jones, a friend from Alaska, up at the airport at 6am and headed to the Deschutes River. It was cloudy in Portland and we hoped it would be the same on the river, it was not. There were a few clouds but mostly bright sunshine and unseasonably warm. We stopped at the first meadow upstream from Maupin and fished a nice run. I tied on a heavily weighted #8 Black Rubberleg Stonefly Nymph with a #16 Green Rock Worm (tied twelve inches below the stonefly). It took an hour to hook my first fish, a nice trout. He took the stonefly just below a

submerged boulder in a short riffle and headed for the main current. I got him to my feet, where he slipped the hook and was gone. The second fish, a large whitefish, took the rock worm in a slow, muddy run next to a weed bed. He didn't fight much. I went looking for Shann upstream, he had also caught fish. We drove up river to the next campground and fished near the boat launch. We both picked up a couple of fish. The largest was sixteen inches and fat. Two other people had fished the run an hour before, and I fished the run twice before I hooked my first fish on a #18 Bead Head Flashback Pheasant Tail Nymph. These fish were used to people. Fly presentation and pattern is everything. The third and last run we fished was the best. It had a long glide below a fast riffle with many seams and cobble areas. Clouds briefly shaded the sun for a half hour and the Blue Wing Olive and Caddis flies exploded. We even saw a few Golden Stoneflys, two months early. The insects were not out long enough to produce a rise, but the fish were hitting our pheasant tail nymphs.

Redside Trout, Deschutes River, Oregon

I hooked four trout and one whitefish. The action slowed considerably when the sun reappeared. I was not paying attention and stepped into a deep hole and flooded my waders. It was cold and I was

through fishing for the day. I changed my pants and watched several rafts and pontoons float by, with the drought and nice weather people were getting an early start on the river this year. We left the river around 3pm and I dropped Shann off at his motel just after 5pm. On my way home I was stuck in Portland traffic for over an hour because of a wreck on the bridge over the Willamette. It sure was nice to spend the day on the river without a care in the world.

March 26, 2005
I was invited by the Oregon Council of the Federation of Fly Fishers to tie at the 17th Annual Northwest Fly Tyers Exposition. I tied Atlantic salmon flies for two four-hour sessions. There were over 150 tiers from around the country and about 1,000 visitors attending the convention. I met a lot of nice people, traded a few materials, and learned some new techniques from other tiers.

March 26, 2005
I fished Lost Lake in Clatsop County, Oregon with Roger Smith, Phuc Vu, and Chris Martin. It was raining, cold, and windy- we almost did not get out of the car. We each caught a dozen or two of stocked rainbows, mostly on #12 Carey Specials. We got home just before dark, cold and hungry.

April 2, 2005
I was invited to tie Atlantic salmon flies at the second Annual Northwest Fishing and Flyfishing Show in Vancouver, Washington.

"Green Highlander" Classic Salmon Fly

The show had low attendance but was a success for me. My son Grady and I sold two framed flies for $70 and traded a fly for a pen and an ink fishing drawing, a fly for tying materials and three framed flies for two very nice carved cherry wood fly boxes. I always get a better deal bartering than paying cash. I made several good contacts with other local fly tiers.

"Lady Caroline" Classic Salmon Fly

April 19, 2005
I fished the Rogue River "holy water" in the late afternoon between thunder storms. I caught three trout over seventeen inches: one on a dry fly, one on a nymph, and another on a soft hackle. There were a few midges, caddis, and stoneflys on the water but no hatch. Few fish were rising. After casting for an hour a lone golden stonefly struggled to fly across the river and plopped in the water a rod's length from where I was standing. Immediately a hungry trout slurped it from the surface. Within seconds I instinctively cast my fly to the same spot and was rewarded with a solid hook-up with a #18 Bead Head Pheasant Tail. A fat trout stripped line on several runs and jumped a few times until I beached him on the sandy shore. I watched the next fish rise several times on the far side of the fast current in the middle of the river. I took several casts before I got the drag right and hooked him on a #14 Elk Hair Caddis. He came in easy because the line was wrapped around his nose. When the sun was off the water I swung a #14 Partridge Soft Hackle downstream (quarter cast downstream, swing fly, retrieve, take two steps downstream and cast again) while heading back to my car. The third fish took my fly near the end of the swing and fought hard for a few minutes. I released him and was grateful for a good day.

April 23, 2005
I fished the McKenzie River with the Washington County Fly Fishers. It rained the whole day (quarter inch an hour) and we all got soaked. Most

of us floated the river in pontoon boats, but my son rode in Tom Wideman's drift boat. I caught a half dozen fourteen inch rainbows on a #14 orange Elk Hair Caddis. We blind cast and sight cast to rising fish. Most fish were caught at the pool tail-outs. I did hook an eighteen inch native cutthroat in fast water that stripped thirty yards of line and made me chase him downstream to the next hole. I let a friend borrow my spare fly rod and he dropped and lost it in a deep hole (he later wrote me a check to pay for the rod). It was a good day, except for the lost rod.

May 14, 2005
I took my son Grady on his first solo white-water float trip down the Wilson River. We hired a driver at the Guide Shop to shuttle our car from Mills Bridge to Sollie Smith Bridge, about four miles. Grady was excited and I a little nervous as we launched our pontoon boats into the river. He insisted that I not take my fly rod but teach him how to float the river. We had a great time and he learned all the basics during our three hour float. Grady was challenged on one fast run that swept him into a willow tree that was half submerged in the river. He survived. We stopped at the Tillamook Creamery for lunch on the way home.

May 20, 2005
I had the day to fish the Deschutes River and was welcomed by a pack of howling coyotes as I drove into Mecca Flat. I parked next to a fisherman and his dog sleeping in the back of their pick-up at the trail-head. It was 8am and I apologized for waking them up as I walked down river. It was calm and partly cloudy but changed to wind and rain later in the day.

Redside Trout, Deschutes River, Oregon

I rigged up a #6 Kauffman's Stonefly Nymph with Rubber Legs with a #18 Flashback Pheasant Tail Nymph dropper. Within minutes I hooked a three pound whitefish on the pheasant tail. He caught the current and stripped line halfway to my backing. A few minutes later I beached and released him. I was using a new ten foot seven-weight rod and was finally able to roll-cast and Spey cast forty feet. On the way to the next hole I ran into a rattlesnake on the trail, I heard him before I saw him, and used my rod to direct him out of the way. I fished several riffles and picked-up a half dozen ten to fourteen inch rainbows on stonefly and pheasant tail nymphs. Adult stoneflys were everywhere on the bushes, but the cold weather kept them grounded and the trout were not keyed on them yet. With some hot weather the stonefly action should pick up. I got caught in a downpour and spent a half hour getting soaked beneath a large bush. After lunch I began fishing the rocky streambank on the way back to the car. I switched to dry flies and began with a #14 Tan Elk Hair Caddis and hooked a fourteen inch trout on the first cast. I noticed a guide boat was parked in a large back-eddy pool for over three hours. They left as I got closer, apparently not wanting to disclose any secrets. Fish were rising throughout the pool in the constantly changing eddys and foam lines. I waded out and almost flooded my waders, retreated back to shore and found a sand bar leading to the upper end of the pool. I put on a #20 Midge Emerger and cast over several trout. I switched to a #18 Bead Head Pheasant Tail and hooked a strong seventeen inch Redside Trout on my first cast. He went deep and used the currents to avoid my net. I released him and picked up two more trout on the same fly. The back eddy currents shifted every time the wind changed, it was difficult to get a good drift without mending the line every few seconds. The wind was getting stronger and my arm weaker. I headed back to the car. At Mecca Flat I met a few friends from Washington County Fly Fishers and we barbequed hamburgers, watched the sun set, and had a good chat. I helped shuttle their vehicles to Trout Creek for their float trip tomorrow. I had a long drive home and finally hung up my waders in the garage at 1am.

June 2005
I tied ninety dozen #12 Elk Hair Parachutes for a fishing guide from Springfield, Oregon. He and his son guide the McKenzie River and were looking for only one particular pattern, a #12 parachute with over-sized hackles. I sold the flys for $.90 each.

June 1, 2005
I caught the midnight flight from Portland, Oregon, and arrived in Washington DC before noon the next day, picked up a rental car, and met Tom Wilson in Mifflinburg, Pennsylvania. We stowed my gear in his cabin and by four that afternoon we were hiking in our waders toward the Fish Commissioner's Cabin on Penns Creek. There were several pick-up trucks at the trail head. We hurried along the old railroad grade to prime water. Penns Creek is a classic limestone creek, full of ledges, drop offs, and slow runs. We passed several other fishermen and found a nice section of river. Tom took the tail-out and I took the head of a nice long pool. Tom had a cigar while we waited for the hatch. A few green drakes were in the air, but not enough to interest the fish. In fact, we saw very few fish rise until after sun set. I began drifting a #14 Pheasant Tail below a #8 Extended Tail Parachute Green Drake and caught a small trout on the nymph.

Penn's Creek, Pennsylvania

An hour before dark everything broke loose. Three other fishermen crowded our run on the opposite bank as the drake spinner fall began. I've never seen anything like it. The two inch, fat, white bodied, grey winged mayflies began dropping from the trees in mass. They flew in waves, at any given moment a dozen were within reach of my nine foot rod. I knocked several into the water casting my fly line. The trout also made their appearance, what was barren water an hour earlier now had rising fish. I switched to a big dry drake pattern and cast to feeding fish. I became frustrated. An hour of casting into the feeding frenzy yielded no fish. I put a #14 Pheasant Tail back on and hooked a sixteen inch brown trout on the second cast. That was it for the night. Tom explained that these fish see a lot of flies and were very cautious. He wasn't kidding. We tripped through the dark with our flashlights, trying to find the trail back to the truck. The next morning we visited the Coburn Fly Shop and headed back to Penns Creek south east of town. It rained most of the morning. We did not catch any fish but we added several beautiful Green Drakes to our bug collections. After lunch in town we headed two miles downriver and fished near a bridge. Tom worked a nice run and pool above the bridge. I headed downstream where there were fewer people. Tall oak and maple trees grew right up to the bank, it was impossible to back-cast. I collected several tippet adorned flies from low hanging branches. I was able to Spey cast, without a back-cast, and cover most of the river. Others were not willing to put up with the tall trees so I had a forty yard run to myself. The far bank had swift, deep, tree limb covered water. The near bank was slow water with rubble and small boulders. I tied on a #6 Coffin Fly and could not produce a rise. A #8 Extended Body Green Drake produced the same results. The fish were rising on the far bank. I had good long drifts, but no hits. I switched to a large #10 Pheasant Tail Nymph and cast to a rising fish on the far bank and hooked a fish. A moment later I landed a fat fourteen inch brown trout.

Brook Trout, Penn's Creek, Pennsylvania

Over the next few hours, amidst a cloud of Green Drakes I landed five more brown trout ranging from fourteen to seventeen inches long on the nymph. I sight casted to each fish with a downstream, slight swing, presentation. Apparently the fish were hitting emerging green drakes and ignoring the adults. I hooked and released the last fish in total darkness and went looking for Tom. He had similar luck and saw over a hundred fish in the shallow riffle at the head of the pool. On Saturday we fished where Cherry Creek empties into Penns Creek, near Tom's friends place. I deep-nymphed the fast water along several limestone ledges most of the day and caught a large sucker. Just before sundown the Blue Wing Olives and Midges appeared. I sight cast a half dozen Blue Wing Olive patterns to a consistently rising fish on the far side of a semi-submerged boulder, before I found the right pattern. He took a #18 Moose Maine Body Blue Dunn Parachute BWO and headed below the boulder and hunkered down. I coaxed him around the boulder and landed a fat foot long Brook Trout. He was a beautiful native trout in his historic habitat and not common these days. An hour before dark, fish exploded out of the water everywhere on the river. I had never seen a hatch like we experienced. There were hundreds of Green Drake spinners, yellow Sulphers, Light Cahills, Caddis, and Great Red Spinners in the air.

Drake Hatch, Penn's Creek, Pennsylvania

I have never seen so many different insects, in such numbers, at one time. The humid air was thick with bugs, they were pouring out of the trees and brush. The fish were keyed into one insect and only one phase of emergence. We had less than an hour to figure out the hatch, and we failed miserably. I switched patterns every few casts. There were so many flies in the air and fish were jumping everywhere, I was confused and humbled and only hooked and lost one fish the rest of the night. Luckily, Tom hooked a few fish and saved the day. We had a late dinner in Mifflinburg at a small Italian restaurant. The next morning I thanked Tom for a great trip, headed down the Susquehanna River to work in Washington DC.

June 25, 2005
My son and I fished Lawrence Lake, in Hood River County, Oregon with the Washington County Fly Fishers. Grady had his own fly rod and pontoon boat and caught a nice trout before I could get my line in the water. We were using a #12 Grizzly Peacock Wooly Worm and a #10 Cary Special. Fishing was slow until the Callibaetis began emerging around 11am. We caught a dozen rainbows near the mouth of Clear Creek on the stump strewn flats. At 2pm the wind kicked up and blew hundreds of mayflies inland, they hovered over our group as we ate lunch. After lunch we headed back to the water and fought white caps on the west end of the lake. My son seemed to enjoy the rough water. He laughed when he caught the first fish of our group in the afternoon. We left before dark and picked up a few pounds of fresh cherries in Parkdale for the ride home.

Rainbow Trout, Lawrence Lake, Oregon

July 12, 2005
At the prompting of my mother, I took five of my nephews, ages 4 to 13, fishing up Farmington Creek in northern Utah. She said they did not get out fishing enough. We caught six to ten inch trout all morning on #14 Elk Hair Caddis. I'd cast for the younger boys, hook a trout, and hand them the rod. I taught the older boys to cast on their own. We caught about two dozen rainbows. It was hot and we enjoyed wading up the small, steep, cold creek. I was a little concerned about poison ivy, rattlesnakes, yellow jackets, fast water, and sharp rocks, but everything went well. We also shot at a few tin cans with my .22 pistol. I got in trouble for that later from a few of their mothers. On the hike back to the car we met James Wakely, my nephew-in-law, whom I'd invited to fish with us. After dropping the boys off at my mom's house, we returned to fish the same stretch of river again. We picked up another couple dozen fish each and caught a few larger fish, several a foot long.

July 13, 2005
At my wife's family reunion my nephew James Wakely told my brother-in-law Sheldon Munns and I about a little known creek with huge trout that few people knew about. I've heard that before. But he insisted it was true, even though he had never been there before. We later met in Provo, Utah, and drove south on I-5, turned east on Highway 6, took the road past Diamond Campground, and turned off on USFS road #029 towards Sixth Water Creek. We parked on the ridge above the creek and hiked down the steep canyon. Our goal was to fish up the river to the bridge and walk back to the car. I rigged up a #14 Elk Hair Caddis with a #18 Bead Head Pheasant Tail Nymph and began casting to likely looking water. We wet waded. Sheldon's thermometer showed 103 degrees. The creek was fast with many rock ledge pools and shallow riffles, and was about two rod lengths wide and three feet deep. Hundreds of caddis flies were in the willows waiting out the hot afternoon. We fished hard for two hours with no luck. We didn't even spook a fish. We began to think James had given us some bad advice. I was disappointed and began collecting horn coral fossils along the streambank. Finally I noticed a large trout feeding in the shadows of a willow above a small pool. He was rising consistently to emergers. I held up my hands to signal Sheldon that I'd seen a trout and that he was a big one. I took several casts and finally got a good drift, he took the nymph, and I set the hook. He took off downstream past Sheldon and held in a small pool. A few minutes later I beached a beautiful eighteen inch

Bonneville Cutthroat on the sand. It's hard to believe a trout could grow that big in such a small creek. He must have come downstream out of Strawberry Reservoir. The creek was a little alkaline and had good aquatic plant growth and tons of caddis fly cases. Maybe he did come from the creek. An hour later a thunder cloud dropped a little rain on us, we were lucky to miss the lightning strikes.

Cutthroat Trout, Sixth Water Creek, Utah

Sheldon hooked the next fish, another large trout, but lost him in the submerged brush. I landed the next fish, a twelve inch cut-bow trout. He took the Elk Hair Caddis. James hooked a large trout and lost him. Sheldon found a small pool below a rock ledge in the middle of about 100 yards of fast riffle water. There had to be a bunch of trout holed-up in there. A large trout flashed and Sheldon tied on a #16 Black Metallic Caddis and drifted the nymph through the hole. He immediately hooked a very large trout that took off downstream and wrapped his leader around a rock and broke off. Sheldon cast again into the same hole and hooked and landed a nice eighteen inch brown trout. I tried to take a picture but the trout slipped away before I could get my camera to work. Sheldon caught the last trout in the hole a few minutes later, another large brown. This

time we got a good picture. I hooked another brown before it was time to go. At the bridge we found James' girlfriend taking a nap. She gave us a ride back to our car. On the ride home we found and harassed a rattlesnake in the middle of the road. He got tired of us and slid into the tall grass in the road ditch. We didn't follow him. James was right in the end: we caught some nice fish and saw little evidence of others fishing this desert creek.

August 19, 2005
I fished in Alaska with the International Fly Fishers Association. I flew into Anchorage and met Bob Kloskowski at the rental car desk in the airport. His plane was about two hours late. We drove up the Parks High (Hwy 3) past Willow, and turned east at Sheep Creek and drove up to Caswell Lake. We met Linda and her husband Larry who own and operate the Gigglewood Inn. We checked in and met Camo (Dave Cameron) from Australia, Andy Killian from Wisconsin, and Wendell Ferris from Pennsylvania. We also met our hosts Dan and Heather Holly from Anchorage, who drove up in their new Hummer.

August 20 2005
Linda prepared a great breakfast in the morning and made each of us a sack lunch. Dan recommended we fish Sheep Creek in the morning. We parked just off Highway 3, rigged up our rods, put mosquito dope on and spread out downstream. Sheep Creek was slightly blue with glacial silt. Within minutes Bob yelled "fish on". I didn't see Bob land his fish. Seconds later I had a fish on myself.

Rainbow Trout, Sheep Creek, Alaska

A strong fish took a #6 Purple Flash Fly at the head of a deep pool, jumped and headed downstream. It was a twenty inch trout. After a five minute tug-of-war I beached him, took a photo, and released him. Already this was a good trip. My next fish was a large Chum Salmon. I spotted him in a shallow run below a tree that fell into the river. He took my fly on the third cast and played hard in the shallow fast water. He weighed about fifteen pounds, had a large hooked jaw and red strips. He had been in the river for some time. About a half mile downriver from the highway we found a hundred yard run of fast, deep water that held a lot of fish. We took turns working through the run and caught over a dozen nice fish. We caught Rainbow, Chum, Pink, Dolly Varden, Grayling, and one Whitefish. Bob caught the best fish of the day, a beautifully spotted twenty four inch Rainbow.

Chum Salmon, Sheep Creek, Alaska

The best set-up for Trout was plastic beads cast below spawning Chum and Pink salmon. We tied on a #8 Egg Hook, slid a bead on the line and secured it to the tippet an inch above the hook with a toothpick. Eighteen inches above the bead we crimped on a split-shot or tied on a heavily weighted egg pattern (such as a Babine Special). At the tip of the fly line we used a large corkie as an indicator. The best bead colors were clear orange beads spotted with pink fingernail polish or dull light pink beads. The beads were very effective. Once I flipped my bead setup and ten feet of line downstream out of the way while un-hooking a trout. While I wasn't watching a fresh humpy took the bead and pulled my rod and line downstream. I caught up with my rod and landed

a nice fish. That evening Dan and Heather took us out to dinner at the Sheep Creek Inn. It was a real dive, but Dan wanted us to experience a "real Alaskan bush diner." We sat outside on the patio because the locals at the bar looked pretty scary. The manager told us the cook was only doing hamburgers tonight and did not even offer us a menu. The waitress told us she was "working to pay off her camping fee" and was not real friendly. Needless to say the meal was very bad. Late that night we met Shann Jones from Fairbanks, he slept outside on the porch with his dog.

Pink Salmon, Sheep Creek, Alaska

August 21, 2005
It rained hard last night and most of the day. Linda fixed moose sausage for breakfast and we got a late start on fishing. We fished Goose Creek, above and below the Parks Highway. Luckily there were no mosquitoes. The river was relatively clear with all the rain. Wendell and Dan caught nice Rainbows and the rest of us caught a few Chum and Pink salmon. Goose Creek was shallow with lots of old spawning Pinks and Chum salmon. We were glad to get out of the rain at the end of the day.

August 22, 2005
It stopped raining this morning and was partly cloudy. We headed north toward Talkeetna, turned east onto Yoder Road, and began fishing Montana Creek, downstream from the bridge (about four miles downstream from the falls). Fishing was poor because the salmon had not made it up the river this far. Shann caught a Grayling and Camo found several large bear tracks

in the sand. We had Linda's Caribou sandwiches for lunch and then headed down river. At Sunshine (near the Talkeetna and Parks Highway junction) we turned onto Commercial Street and followed Main Street to Montana Creek. We wondered why there were no buildings on Main Street. Fishing was much better. We each caught a few fish. Andy caught a nice twenty inch Rainbow on a flesh fly, Bob caught the first Silver salmon of the trip, I caught an eighteen inch Rainbow and Camo and Wendell caught Chum salmon. I broke a rod after hooking a large Chum, the drag on my reel jammed and my rod snapped in two places from the sudden torque. I'm not sure a seven weight rod is strong enough for these fish. That evening we had musk ox, caribou and crab burgers, and caribou chili for dinner at the West Rib Pub and Grill in Talkeetna.

August 23, 2005
We awoke to rain (again) and headed to the lower portion of Montana Creek. We noticed a pod of Silvers below the railroad bridge, half of us stayed at the bridge and the rest went to the river's confluence. Bob hooked the first fish but lost him a moment later. All of us began catching fish, big strong Silvers. I had to chase my first two Coho downstream and lost both of them in the fast water. The third fish stayed in the pool, fought hard, and I beached him on the gravel bar. He was a slightly pink, twelve pound buck who took a #6 Purple Egg Sucking Leech.

Coho Salmon, Montana Creek, Alaska

By late morning it stopped raining and the crowds appeared. We kept close to our pool, several fisherman were circling and waiting for a chance

to elbow us out. I don't enjoy this kind of fishing, but we were catching a lot of nice big fish. We caught over a dozen Silvers, a few big Chums and a several Pinks. The best flies were a #6 Cerise Rabbit Leech, an Egg Sucking Leach and a Bullet Head Red Crystal Bugger. After lunch the crowds thinned out and Wendell, Andy, and Camo came back from the confluence where they also had caught many large, bright Silvers. Shann showed up late in the day and caught a nice Chum. The Silvers averaged ten to twelve pounds, Chums ten to fifteen pounds, and the Pinks five to seven pounds. We kept a few Silvers to barbecue for dinner.

August 24, 2005
It was raining in the morning and the rivers were high and off-color, the Talkeetna Mountains got a lot of rain the night before. Montana Creek was our best bet and we returned to the lower river. There were several German tourists fishing at the confluence, Wendell and I waited our turn and fished a good hole after they left. Wendell caught the first Coho, a bright silver fish. I hooked the next fish and released it because it was foul hooked in the tail. An hour later I cast slightly upstream and let my heavily weighted fly sink and swing across the current. Near the end of the swing, as my fly rose to the surface, a fresh Silver hit and ripped out line. She pulled in the current and rolled to loosen the hook. After a few minutes Dan helped me beach her on a sandbar, another bright hen.

Coho Salmon, Montana Creek, Alaska

A short while later a flock of mallards and gulls near us started squawking and madly flew away. Something was wrong and I began looking for a bear in the nearby willows. Seconds later a Bald Eagle swooped down and picked up a dead salmon off the mud flats and flew right over my head. Glad it wasn't a bear. The fishing slowed and we went back to the bridge to have lunch with the group. There were fewer people on the river than the day before. We heard the whistle from the Alaska Rail Road engine and watched the train pass on the bridge above our heads.

Coho Salmon, Montana Creek, Alaska

We fished the hole below the bridge and all caught Silvers. I caught my largest Silver, a thirty inch buck, on a #6 Conehead Cerise Rabbit Leech. Camo had an acrobatic Silver do summersaults several times before breaking off. Bob caught a huge Chum over fifteen pounds. By late afternoon the water began to turn brown from the iron in the soil and decayed plants leached from up river. We had an early dinner of barbecue chicken, corn on the cob, salad, and salmon.

August 25, 2005
It rained again overnight so we decided to fish the mouth of Sheep Creek. The campground was almost deserted as we walked down the steep trail to the confluence. The few fishermen there were having minimal luck. The water was high, a light tan color, and the visibility was less than two feet. We hiked up stream about half a mile hoping for better conditions, it looked pretty bad. Wendell rigged-up and began casting, the rest of us watched not too excited about the water. Dan recommended that we leave and Wendell said

"just one more cast." The next thing we hear is Wendell's drag spinning, fish on. He hooked a fresh Coho on a Bullet Head Silver Bugger. We watched him land a bright salmon as we hurriedly rigging up. Andy hooked the next fish moments later, another bright sliver. That was it for the next few hours. Dan, Andy, and I waded across Sheep Creek to fish the pool near the confluence. We came within an inch or two of the top of our waders. Andy and I both caught large Chums and waded back across the river when the Silvers were not biting. After lunch we fished Caswell Creek, which was more like a slough than a river. The Silvers were stacked in pretty thick. There were several pods of fifty fish or more. A dozen fishermen were harassing fish near the confluence with lures and catching a few fish. We headed up stream. Dozens of fish erupted out of the water as we cast our flies toward groups of fish. Within an hour we each landed a fish, Camo caught the first Silver. These fish were tough to catch and too spooked to provide much sport. Just before we left I caught a foot long Jack Chinook salmon. We took a look at Sunshine Creek and found a pod of fish in the slough water. Larry Csonka was filming a fishing show and attracting a crowd so we moved on. We went looking for new water along the highway but each creek we passed was blown out. We had Caribou Chili and burgers for dinner in Talkeetna.

August 26, 2005
We went looking for water that was fishable and headed an hour north to Moose Creek, a tributary to the Deshka River. The river was the color of root beer. We rigged up anyway but caught no fish. We watched a helicopter for a few minutes lift lumber off a semi-truck and fly it into the bush. Next we headed south on the highway and checked out Rabideux Creek but it didn't look good. We stopped at Montana Creek for lunch, it was high and off-color. Andy put his rod together and headed up the creek to a spot where he had seen fish hiding beside a sunken log two days earlier. He came back moments later with a big smile. He had caught a large Trout. His friend had passed away not long ago and his wife had given Andy a few of his flies to take to Alaska, he could now report success back to his friend's wife. After lunch we gave Goose Creek one more chance, even though it was still high and off-color. On the hike in we found a Spruce Grouse in a tree and

were able to get close enough to poke him with a fly rod. We located a pod of Silvers in the dark tan water about a mile downriver from the Parks Highway. I could see several dozen fish milling around the head of a deep hole. Andy hooked a large Chum and scattered the fish. A short time later I hooked a large Silver that gave my rod a workout. He jumped several times and broke off when he got into fast water and headed downstream. This was my last fish of the trip. Late that night we heard dogs barking near a cabin down the road and heard a bottle-rocket explode. They were chasing off a bear.

August 27, 2005
We drove back to Anchorage Saturday morning. It was sunny and we saw Mt. McKinley clearly for the first time. A fisherman needs to spend at least a week in Alaska to ensure enough dry days to fish and allow rivers to clear-up after rainy days. I caught a flight back to Portland at 6pm and got home after midnight. The total trip cost for me was $1,000; airfare $475, car rental (split four ways) $100, gas $25, groceries $50, and the lodge (including breakfast and lunch) $350. It was a good trip.

September 7, 2005
While replacing the furnace in our home, a salesman noticed several framed flies hanging in our living room and struck up a conversation about fishing. Before long he knocked $300 off the price of our furnace in exchange for several dozen flies. Jean encouraged me to begin tying more flies.

September 17, 2005
I helped the Washington County Fly Fishers teach fly tying and casting to the Boy Scouts at Butte Creek Scout Camp. We had about a hundred boys visit our booth.

September 20, 2005
It was a sunny cool day on the Crooked River. I arrived at 9am and waited for the caddis flies to warm up. At 10am bugs were everywhere, fish were jumping, and I began catching fish. I tied on a #16 Tan Elk Hair Caddis and a #18 Midge Pupa and caught fish on both flies. I fished a half mile of river in seven hours, from Cobble Rock to Post Pile campground. Just about anywhere on the river would have been good. In the morning, most

of the trout were caught within ten feet of the bank in the slow water behind boulders. The fish moved into the main current in the afternoon, rising randomly throughout the river. I caught three dozen Redside trout. Three fish were seventeen to eighteen inches long, and were caught in the fast water where the canyon narrowed. It was a successful day.

Redside Trout, Crooked River, Oregon

September 22, 2005
I returned to the Crooked River and fished the area around Bison Butte Campground. It was a repeat of last Tuesday, lots of caddis and lots of trout. It was fifty-fifty between the dry caddis and the bead head midge pupa. I sight cast to several whitefish, but no hook-ups. This was my first trip to the Crooked without catching any whitefish. A doe and two fawns followed me around most of the day, sometimes grazing within twenty yards. I met a retired gentleman from Bend and we fished together for an hour. We talked about New Zealand and fly patterns. Around 3pm our part of the river was in the shadows of the canyon and the fish were mid-stream. It was easy to get a drag-free drift. I took the bead head midge off and put on a #20 un-weighted midge pupa and cast into the shallow weed beds. The fish came readily. We had hook-ups on every third cast. It was one of those days where we caught so many fish it was pointless to catch any more.

September 24, 2005
Grady and I fished the Siletz River with the Washington County Fly Fishers. We met at the River City Fly Shop at 6am and three hours later were on the river. We put in at Morgan County Park and took out eight miles downstream at Strome Park. We caught small trout and smolts

the first three miles until we got below Cedar Creek. The river was down and we had to scoot our boats across several gravel bars. When we watched a fisherman land a large fall Chinook, our hopes improved. In a stretch of slow water between riffles, I cast next to a stream bank stump and a large sea-run cutthroat rose and hit the end of my fly line. I cast again and hooked him on a #10 Black Reverse Spider.

Sea-run Cutthroat, Siletz River, Oregon

He jumped several times and tried to swim behind the snag. I finally landed him, a skinny bright sixteen inch blueback. A short time later Pete Priepke was fishing a big pool with a slight back-eddy and hooked and landed an active summer steelhead, I'd guess about five pounds. A mile downstream I cast and stripped my fly parallel to a sunken tree trunk. I hooked another feisty cutthroat. A bit smaller than my first fish, but a little stronger. He pulled a little line off my spool but eventually came to my hand. These fish were few and far between but nice to catch on a warm sunny fall afternoon. I hooked and lost a few other fish and that was it for the day. We rowed our pontoon boats through the last three miles of frog water. Grady was getting worn out until he noticed a large seal following about thirty yards behind us. He began rowing a little faster. The seal popped his head up to watch us every few minutes. We had dinner at the Dairy Queen in Lincoln City on the way home.

October 8, 2005
I met two guys from Portland who were just learning to fly fish. They complained about paying a guide $300 for a day on the river and only

catching two small trout. I offered to fish with them, but they insisted on hiring me as their guide and offered $250. I felt a little uncomfortable but agreed to take them for a day on the Crooked River. The fish and caddis flies cooperated and they each caught two dozen trout and a few whitefish. I spent the day untangling their leaders, tying knots, showing them where to cast and talking about fish. We had a great time. I suppose they got their money's worth, they were happy and bought me dinner on the way home.

October 17, 2005
I wanted to fish the North Fork of the Middle Fork of the Willamette River, but there were dark storm clouds above the canyon in the morning. I parked south of the storm at the first boat ramp above where the Willamette dumped into Lookout Point Reservoir, and saw two fish rising. It was cold and windy but I rigged up anyway and began casting an Elk Hair Caddis around the rocks and tall grasses next to shore. After an hour of casting I caught one small trout. The storm began to dissipate so I drove to Westfir, Oregon and headed ten miles up the canyon. The river was cold and clear and the maple leaves were turning yellow and orange. No one else was on the river. I chose a long section of pocket water and immediately spooked two nice fish in the first hole. After heading upstream and fighting the streamside brush and swift water I cast a #16 Elk Hair Caddis and landed a nice native Redside rainbow. It was slow fishing the next 100 yards until I got away from the trail and found fish. I hooked and released a dozen trout within twenty yards, ranging from eight to twelve inches. I had one large trout, maybe sixteen inches, follow my fly for six feet and ignore it. I could not bring him up again. It was getting late, I bush-whacked back to the road and was offered a ride by a retired couple who were sightseeing. I declined and enjoyed the walk back to my car. It turned out to be a bright, beautiful sunny day.

October 21, 2005
I fished with the Washington County Fly Fishers on the Crooked River. We camped and fished near Big Bend Campground just below Bowman Dam. The first afternoon was slow. I caught a half dozen rainbows and a few whitefish. They were taking #16 Tan Elk Hair Caddis and #22 Midge Pupa. I had the best success in the swift water,

behind boulders within ten feet of shore. The sunny day brought out the fisherman, one about every one hundred yards. That evening Ralph Brooks cooked cheeseburgers over the grill for our group. It was a cold, clear night. We huddled around a campfire and saw stars that were not visible in Portland. Fish started rising the next morning about 9am, just before the sun hit the water. I rigged up with a #18 Flashback Pheasant Tail Nymph and a #16 Ray Charles (light orange scud) and within ten minutes caught three nice whitefish. When the sun hit the water, I switched to an Elk Hair Caddis to match the hundreds of small, dark caddis that were flying above the water and caught another half dozen trout. We met again at noon for lunch, compared flies and headed our separate ways. I noticed Ralph's truck along the Deschutes on the way home and later learned that they had caught a few trout and that Pete had hooked a steelhead.

November 7, 2005

I picked Scott Robbins, a friend from work, up in Salem and we fished the Crooked River. We parked the car under a large juniper and changed into our waders in the rain. The base of Bison Butte had a light dusting of snow, the wind was blowing, and it was cold. I rigged up an orange #18 Ray Charles Scud and a #18 Pheasant Tail dropper and began deep nymphing. Three feet separated my yarn indicator and single split-shot, any deeper got caught up in the moss and weeds. I had two whitefish within an hour, both on the scud. Mid-afternoon I picked up two trout; the largest rainbow was fourteen inches.

Crooked River, Oregon

It started to snow and stick to the ground. I missed several strikes while fumbling with cold hands. My line was starting to freeze in the rod guides and it became difficult to cast. We left just before sundown. It was just too cold to fish.

November 9, 2005

The snow storm passed and Prineville, Oregon was sunny, bright, and cold. My wet wading boots (from a few days earlier) froze solid in the car overnight. I soaked them in the Crooked River before putting them on. My boots were frozen again before I could get back into the river. I was determined to fish dry flies and rigged up a #14 Elk Hair Caddis and a #18 Black Midge Pupa dropper. I lost a nice fish after several casts. I just wasn't paying attention. The fly floatant froze my fly in between casts, but softened up when it hit the warmer water. An hour later I landed my first rainbow. I saw him rising and tricked him with the pupa. The fish seemed to be rising slower in the cold temperatures. They followed my fly several feet before slowly inhaling it. I usually set the hook too fast and lost a half dozen fish before noon. I switched to a #16 Soft Hackle and swung a fly downstream for a change and to warm up. I hooked and lost one fish before switching back to dry flies. Just after noon the fish started rising in the back-eddies and slack water next to the steep grassy banks. It took an hour to fish up to an old Blue Heron. He let me get within a rod's length before flying off his sunny rock. I checked to see if he'd left me any feathers, he didn't. I hooked the best fish of the day below the rock where he was fishing, a bright sixteen inch rainbow. It felt good. I hooked a few smaller trout in the slow water and noticed a nice fish consistently rising just below the steep bank next to a large boulder. I knelt behind him just out of sight. He was not interested in my caddis, pupa, midge, gnat or anything else. I cast five different flies, each a size smaller down to size #22. He continued gulping what I assume were minute midge emergers from the surface. I finished my frozen fried chicken for lunch as Scott gave him a try. He snagged a bunch of tall grass above the pool and the fish spooked. That was it for the day. We visited the Sisters Fly Shop on the way home and found nothing we couldn't live without.

November 12, 2005
I tied at the Northwest Fly Fishers Fly Tying
Rendezvous in Troutdale, Oregon and was seated
between Jim Teeny (creator of Teeny Nymphs)
and Don Nelson from River City Fly Shop. I tied
Woolhead Sculpins; purple for steelhead and olive,
tan, and brown for trout. We had a great time and
visited with a couple of hundred attendees. The
Rendezvous makes several thousand dollars each
year and they donate it to conservation activities in
the Pacific Northwest.

December 10, 2005
I fished with the Washington County Fly Fishers
on the Sandy River. It had been cold and clear the
last few days and the temperature was in the
twenties when we arrived at Ox Bow Park before
sun up. The sky was clear and the wind was
blowing strong. I was grateful Tom Wideman
invited me to fish in his drift boat. We swung
streamers and drifted egg patterns for steelhead.
We fished hard the first few hours until we
realized there were no fish in the river: too early in
the season. We floated over several spawned out
salmon that were in bad shape. At times it was
difficult to cast in thirty mile wind gusts and with
sand blowing in our eyes. There were white caps
on the river when we took out at Dabney Park. It
took the rest of the day to warm up.

2006

January 24, 2006
I tyed 100 dozen dry flies for a guide in Montana. The pattern was the Purple Haze, a parachute pattern with a forked tail, violet super fine dubbing body, white poly post, and blue dunn hackle in sizes #14, 16, 18 and 20. We agreed to $.90 per fly. Some interesting statistics: A spool of 200 yards of thread tied thirty five dozen flies, a packet of dubbing fifty dozen, 1 pack of Microfibetts fifty dozen (four strands per fly), and a Whiting quarter saddle hackle tied twenty five dozen flies. Without interruption, I averaged fifteen flies per hour.

February 11, 2006
I was invited by the River City Fly Shop to tie flies at its booth at the Pacific Northwest Sportsman's Show at the Portland EXPO center. I tied classic Atlantic salmon flies for a couple of hours over four days, met some great people and had a good time.

Sportsman Show, Portland, Oregon

March 6, 2006
I fished the Nehalem River with Panos Lampros, a guy I met at the fly shop. There were three boats ahead of us as we put in at Beaver Slide, and two more boats quickly caught up from behind. The word was out: fish were in the river. It began raining first thing in the morning and did not stop the rest of the day. This was my first trip with my thirteen foot Spey rod, and I spent most of the day learning to cast. I really needed an expert to show me how to Spey cast. By the time we reached the gravel pit take-out, we were drenched.

We did not raise a fish and to our knowledge no one else did either.

March 25, 2006
I was invited by the Oregon Council of the Federation of Fly Fishers to tie at the 18th Annual Northwest Fly Tyers Exposition, in Eugene, Oregon. I tied perfect parachutes and woolhead sculpins for two four-hour sessions.

Perfect Parachute

There were over 150 tiers from around the country and a thousand visitors attending the convention. I was also asked to be in the tiers video and tied my sculpin pattern. I met a lot of nice people, traded a few materials, and learned some new techniques from other tiers.

April 22, 2006
My son and I fished the McKenzie River with the Washington County Fly Fishers. On the trip down I had two flat tires. We were rescued by John McNally who fixed our tire in Springfield, Oregon. While we were waiting along the highway for John, two fishermen from the Sanitam Fly Fishers pulled over to see if we needed help. They had seen our pontoon boats on the trailer. From now on the boat trailer goes everywhere, guaranteeing help if we breakdown along the road. We got to the river an hour late and put in at Hendricks Bridge and floated to the Bellinger take-out. This was my son Grady's second major river float by himself in his own pontoon boat. He did very well. It was an unusually sunny day. The March Brown hatch was a little slow this year, around 1pm a few fish started rising. I caught a half dozen trout on a #14 March Brown emerger fished deep behind a heavily weighted Hare's Ear

on a nine foot leader with a yarn indicator. Two fish were sixteen inch native cutthroat, a little bit skinny, and the rest were twelve inch rainbows. I did catch one fish on a #14 Comparadun. He was rising next to shore as we floated by. After a quick cast, he inhaled and ripped down stream. I kicked to shore and landed a nice fat rainbow. The rainfall was unusually high in February and flood waters scoured most of the river clean. Fishing was a little slow, but Grady did catch a nice rainbow on a #10 Brown Grizzly Hackle Wooly Bugger. We spent most of the day on a large pool with a nice back-eddy, where the river split around a gravel bar and entered the pool from two directions. We had to rescue one of our group's drift boat as the anchor pulled free from the loose riverbank gravel and floated downstream. It's tough pulling a drift boat upstream with a pontoon boat, but I did it. At the end of the day we were tired and a little sun burned. On the way home we bought John dinner for helping get our tire fixed.

May 8, 2006

I've wanted to fish the southern Appalachian Mountains since I was a kid and finally had the chance. Jeff Wilkins picked me up in Greensboro, North Carolina at 6am and we arrived at Stone Mountain State Park, near Roaring Gap, two hours later. We parked near the old wooden church on the East Prong Roaring River near the confluence of Widow's Creek. There was a sporadic sulfur hatch and a few yellow stoneflies and crane flies. It was partly cloudy and in the mid-60s, perfect weather. The trees made a closed canopy above the creek so I suppose the clouds didn't really matter. I began fishing a #16 Sulfur Dun, an old Catskill pattern, and was immediately rewarded with a twelve inch brown trout. I caught several more of his twins on a six foot three weight rod, before catching a beautifully colored fourteen inch brook trout. We worked our way up the free-stone creek catching several fish in each pool. It was obvious the fish were aware of fishermen. They only accepted near perfect presentations and were not spooked by fly lines or wading. We saw several twenty inch fish but could not interest them. We had lunch where Widow's Creek fell over a thirty foot high solid granite slab creating a deep plunge pool. Mid-afternoon we fished some pocket water and caught our first rainbow and a few more brookies. The last pool

near the church had a dozen trout holding at the head of the pool below a large submerged boulder. It was easy to cast over the fish but difficult to get a rise. After several casts I switched to an Elk Hair Caddis with a small Bead Head Pheasant Tail Nymph on a three foot dropper. I cast upstream and let the rig float over the boulder, swing around in the back eddy, and let the current suck the nymph deeper toward the fish. After a short drift I hooked a fish.

East Prong Roaring River, North Carolina

A moment later we landed the largest brook trout of the day, a jeweled sixteen inch native. A few casts later I hooked another hefty brookie on the caddis. We wanted to fish another river on the way home, so we headed upstream from Kapps Mill near Dobson and parked along the Mitchell River. Several land owners graciously provided fishing access to this beautiful river. We were hoping for a sulfur blanket hatch but were disappointed. A few flies were on the water and we saw a dozen fish in the first pool consistently rising. We started picking them off at the tail-out and hooked half-a-dozen foot long browns the first hour. One large brown kept rising underneath the limbs of a large maple tree and sulking back into the partially exposed root wad. I lost several flys trying to get the right drift and finally got a rise, but only pricked him. A few minutes later he started rising again and I hooked him on the first cast on a #14 Orange Spinner. He was a strong fish and stripped line out of my three weight before getting tangled in a small sunken tree limb. I yanked the limb in and released a very nice three pound brown. It would have been more sporting without the tree limb. As it was getting dark we picked up a few more rainbows and brook trout on a #14 Black Gnat Parachute. Jeff hooked an eighteen inch rainbow stripping a wooly bugger, in the dark, as we waded back to the car. Jeff dropped me off at the motel at 11pm after we had a great day.

May 20, 2006

My son Grady and I made our annual pilgrimage to the Deschutes River, with the Washington County Fly Fishers, to greet the emerging salmon flies. A thunder storm and cloud burst welcomed us to Harpham Flat and we ducked inch thick hail running for the cover of John Stalcup's truck canopy. A few minutes later the sun came out and it was 80 degrees. Our tents were set up before the next wave of storm clouds passed overhead, then we headed for the river. Paul Skelton was not so lucky, he got pounded with hail and his half put up tent got soaked. That evening we fished two set ups; a #6 Clark's Stonefly and a #6 Kauffman's Stonefly Nymph, both with a #16 Beadhead Nymph dropper. We hooked several small trout but did not land any fish. Just before dark, Ralph Brooks caught a very nice three pound Rainbow just below the campground boat ramp, on a Tan Caddis Sparkle Pupa, fished deep. We all met for dinner, but discovered that someone forgot to pack the hamburger. Everyone, except Grady and I, headed for the Café in Maupin for dinner. They returned with an unfavorable report on the food and the service. It started raining about midnight and did not let up until breakfast the next morning. We got drenched. First thing in the morning someone pointed out a rising fish near our tent, I got my rod and hooked a fish on the third cast. It turned out to be a large whitefish and I received a few jeers from our group. Hey, it's a native fish and fun to catch. After donuts for breakfast we shuttled our boats three miles upriver to the locked gate and began our float. This was Grady's first time down the Deschutes alone, he was excited. The river was high and off-color, we fished large rubber leg stoneflys nymphs and a March brown emerger dropper. The water was so swift that the only place to get a good drift was next to the cut-banks, along the meadows on the west side of the river. In the first meadow we hooked two small trout, the next meadow was much better. We hooked three trout in 100 yards, fishing upstream, casting into the under-cut banks,

fighting root-wads, and grass stems. Most fish took the emerger even though the stream bank sedges and rushes were covered with huge black adult stoneflys and slightly smaller golden stoneflys. In many places there were more than a dozen stoneflys per square foot of vegetation. On the downstream trip we waded in water up to our waists-a few feet out from the undercut-bank - and found the big fish.

Redside Trout, Deschutes River, Oregon

I hooked a large Redside, about twenty five feet out, in deep water, about forty yards below a fast riffle. My reel screamed as he took twenty yards of line downstream, and stopped just above the next fast run and slowly headed back up river to the slower water. I would have lost him if he made it to the fast water. We pulled each other around for a few more minutes before I tailed him in the shallows. He was a bright hefty seventeen inch rainbow close to three pounds. He took the Kauffman's Rubber leg Stonefly Nymph. On my second cast into the same run we had another large fish who repeated the action of the first fish, except Grady fought and landed the fish. He was eager to point out that his fish was two inches larger than my fish and a bit heavier. This time he took the March Brown Nymph dropper. The salmon fly season really brings out the big fish, but they do not always feed on stoneflys. I suppose fish like a variety of foods. That was the last fish of the day. Grady practiced running the rapids and I followed to keep an eye on him. He did pretty well for a twelve year old. By noon the wind had dried out our tent and gear, we packed up, had lunch, and headed home.

May 24, 2006

First thing in the morning, I fished the Deschutes River at Mecca Flat, concentrating on the area around the campground. It was cloudy and looked like rain. I tried a LaFontane's Sparkle Pupa for the first time as a dropper behind a heavy stonefly nymph, and caught a nice trout on the second cast. With all the salmon flies around, and salmon fly fisherman, I suppose the fish were looking for something different than a salmon fly imitation. This next fish was a lunker whitefish, at least three pounds. He took the heavily weighted stonefly nymph and gave my fly rod a workout. I almost lost him in the fast current. Over the next two hours I caught a half dozen more whitefish ranging from fourteen to twenty inches and weighing two to four pounds. These were big, strong fish. Several fishermen across the river were paying close attention and asked what I was using. I caught two more foot long trout before I had to leave. They both took the caddis pupa. I fished the afternoon at Trout Creek where the Deschutes was swifter, had fewer grass-banks, and less people. Hiking upstream three miles past the campground I picked up three nice trout. It was partly sunny after a week of rain and high water. The fish were not aggressive. A pod of fish was feeding in a large back-eddy where the current converged from three directions. My indicator and flies rode in one position until a fish took. I caught a half dozen trout in the same spot in just a few minutes. This was too easy. I hiked back to the car before dark.

May 26, 2006

I made another trip to the Deschutes River. I wanted to catch some trout on dry flies and was tired of nymphing. I could not raise a fish the first half hour and switched to an indicator and nymphs. Several casts later I hooked a large fish that slipped into the fast current and broke off twenty yards downstream. At the next hole I lost another large fish who also found the fast water. He jumped, identifying himself as a trout, a very big trout. I picked up a few more small trout on a #16 Sparkle Pupa dropper below some riffles. Fish were rising in a large back-eddy. I eagerly switched to an Elk Hair Caddis and pupa dropper and began casting to rising fish. No takes. I switched to a #18 Bead Head Flashback Pheasant Tail and immediately hooked a nice trout. Apparently Caddis Pupa were found in the fast water drifts and May Flies were more common in calmer back-waters. I caught a half dozen Redside in the large back eddy, all less than a foot long,

before the action stopped as it began raining. I headed to a tree for cover and ate my lunch. The sun came out moments later and I dried my rain jacket on a sagebrush and almost stepped on a large bull snake, which was camouflaged as a rattle snake. I began working my Elk Hair Caddis and Pheasant Tail Nymph upstream, hearing imaginary rattlesnakes along the way.

Elk Hair Caddis

A nice trout rose to my caddis in a small run below a half-submerged tree. I cast again and got another good look at him, a large beautiful Redside, as he refused my caddis the second time. He disappeared after the next few casts. He did not appreciate the Black Parachute Gnat presented to him either. I switched to a #6 Clark's Stonefly and hooked him on the first cast. He charged the fly, flew out of the water, and jumped several times before tiring in the fast water. He measured seventeen inches, a beautiful fish. Another dozen cast-lengths upstream I hooked another fish in similar fashion: an eighteen inch hooked-jawed male a little on the dark side. He must have been a late spawner. Three other fish took the dry stonefly imitation in the same run. These fish were over looked, getting a break from the fishing pressure because of a popular riffle on the other side of the river near Dry Creek. A lot of hiking fishermen also passed this area heading downstream to easier-to-cast waters. I headed back to the car when lightning strikes started hitting the canyon rim and thunder was five seconds away. It started raining just as I pulled off my waders. I raced up the road hoping to make it past the clay inclusion in the narrow part of the canyon before it became too slick. I was too late, the area was soaked and I slipped between the road ruts and slid sideways before hitting solid gravel. The car was covered with mud from the spinning tires, but after backing up and running forward several times I finally made it out safely. A downpour at Government Camp on Mt. Hood washed most of the mud off my car.

June 19, 2006

My son Grady and I went camping for a week on the Rogue River. We caught the tail end of the salmon fly hatch. The air was full of three inch long bugs that kept landing on our heads and shoulders. We fished the "holy water" below Lost Creek Reservoir in the evenings. There were a dozen other fishermen along the mile long tail-water. We had to wait our turn for the good riffles. The other fishermen would wade deep (through the best water) and cast mid-current to rising fish. We had the most success casting a #6 Clark's Stonefly along the current seam nearest to shore, but we had to rest the water from the previous fisherman's wading. We caught several fish each afternoon. The biggest was a thick seventeen inch rainbow. We floated the river one day and caught a dozen ten to fourteen inch rainbows. The most memorable fish was caught on a Clark's Stonefly, cast into the shadows of a large alder tree. He jumped completely out of the water the second he saw my fly, jumped twice and broke-off. He must have been at least five pounds and looked dark, almost black. I was disappointed to lose him.

June 22, 2006

Grady and I camped and fished at Gold Lake on Willamette Pass, southeast of Eugene, Oregon. This is one of the few fly fishing only lakes in Oregon. We set up out tents mid-afternoon before the mosquitoes swarmed our camp. They were pretty bad. The lake was choppy and the wind blew us to the far end of the lake. We tried emergers, damselflies, streamers, and soft hackles to no avail. The lake was relatively shallow, about four to five feet deep where the fish were rising. The bottom was mud with aquatic weeds growing in the shallower areas where the sun could reach the bottom. It was early in the year and the aquatic plants were just greening-up. In desperation I tied on an indicator and four feet below (in five foot deep water) a Bead Head Midge Pupa. Within minutes we began hooking fish. We caught two dozen twelve to sixteen inch brook trout during the rest of the afternoon, and three rainbows. This

was easy fishing. We cast our lines thirty to forty feet, kept the line straight and watched our corkies. With any movement, we set the hook. We trolled Carey Specials back to our campsite and Grady hooked a very nice sixteen inch rainbow. We kept three brookies for dinner and cooked them in tin-foil over the fire. The next morning the lake was as calm as glass. We slowly trolled #16 Black Midge Pupas around the lake and picked up a few fish, but it was really slow. Fish were rising for midges all over the lake but our lines and pontoon boats spooked the fish. There were a few winged ants on the surface and the fish made splashy rises for them. I caught a seventeen inch rainbow on an unweighted #18 Midge Pupa on the surface, but the fish were few and far between. Around noon we could see the wind approaching from the far end of the lake. I switched out the midge and tied on a heavily weighted #16 Gold Bead Head Pheasant Tail Nymph, and began casting and stripping near the lake bottom. Within minutes of having riffled-water we both had fish on. The next half hour we caught a dozen fish. The change in the water surface made a big difference in the trout's attitude. They readily took our flies. By late afternoon we had caught two dozen brookies. After dinner the weekend crowd appeared so we headed home.

July 22, 2006

It reached 108 degrees this week, too hot to stay in the valley. My son Grady and I and the Washington County Fly Fishers met at Lawrence Lake to cool off. We arrived to a flotilla of inflatables with people of the same mind. Before we could rig up our rods, a fish & game officer checked our licenses. The first time I'd been checked in several years. There was no wind, the lake was flat and the water was just starting to green-up with algae. We trolled #12 Carey Specials on floating lines and a nine foot leaders to the far end of the lake and caught a half dozen trout. At noon we had lunch with the group. Around 2pm the Callibaetis hatch and spinner fall began. I could not tell if they were coming or going. We maneuvered into the grassy shallows near the inlet stream and watched dozens of fish go nuts over the bugs. I rigged a #16 Parachute Adams up for Grady and watched him cast and bring several fish to the surface. He even hooked a few. They were beautifully spotted native cutthroat, eight to twelve inches long. Clouds of spinners were dancing inches above the water for about two hours until they abruptly disappeared. There was still no wind, the lake was calm and it was hot. We beached our pontoons and found a shady spot to wait out the heat of the day. I fell asleep on a large rock and Grady made a walking stick. As the sun dipped below the ridge, the wind kicked-up, the mayflies returned and the fish headed to the shallow flats to feast. I tied on a #16 Callibaetis Nymph and Grady tied on a #16 Beadhead Soft Hackle. We caught another dozen fish the first half hour of dusk. I landed a beautiful sixteen inch rainbow that had more chrome than a fresh steelhead. Grady hooked several nice fish and broke-off a heavy fish. When it became too dark to see the submerged tree stumps, we headed back to the car. Most of our group had already left, missing the best fishing of the day. We got home just before midnight. It was still about 80 degrees outside.

July 27, 2006

I fished the Trask River in the late afternoon until dark. Mitch Cummings took me up past the Dam Hole and we cast #14 Elk Hair Caddis and caught dozens of native cutthroat trout and a few steelhead smolts. The fish were not big, six to eleven inches, but they made up for it in spunk. It was fun to wet-wade crystal clear water in the forested canyon with not a soul in sight. The caddis were hatching and fish were jumping everywhere. We chose which fish to cast to. I hooked a substantial fish that took line off my three weight reel. He barely poked his nose above the water to take my fly and was headed across the stream to fast water when he broke off. He could have been a summer steelhead, but probably was a large sea-run cutthroat. I had a late stream bank dinner near the peninsula among the nosy bullfrogs, raccoons, and other night critters.

August 4, 2006

When Mt. St. Helens erupted in 1980, the eruption created Coldwater Lake by damming up a small creek. I met Paul Skelton at the fly shop and Chris Roe at Ralph Brooks house at 5am. By 8am we were on the lake chasing large rainbows. Chris had the first fish on in fifteen minutes, a silver sixteen inch rainbow. The lake was deep and clear, I could see aquatic plants on the fifteen foot bottom. It was sunny and calm, with very little

wind. Damsel flies and mayflies were everywhere, but no fish were rising. I fished an unweighted #14 Rickards Callibaetis Nymph and a long #14 Pheasant Tail Damsel Nymph on a full-sinking type III line with eight foot leader and 5X tippet. Near the put-in there was an island formed from one huge rock, about fifty feet wide and another fifty feet tall. It blew out of the volcano about fifteen miles away and landed in the soon to be formed lake. We headed opposite the boulder around the east side of the lake where there were shallow flats. We found fish just off the shoals in about ten feet of water. My first fish hit deep on the dragonfly and pulled like a bulldog and gave my seven weight a workout. I finally netted a flawless, chrome silver, eighteen inch rainbow. I released the fish just as Ralph yelled "look at the mountain." The volcano sent up a huge column of steam, several thousand feet into the sky.

Mt. Saint Helens, Washington

We sat and watched for several minutes. If this was an eruption we were goners, what a way to go. Mid-morning fish started rising to emerging midges. I switched to a floating line and cast ahead of several trout. These gulpers were predictable, heading in a straight line and sucking in insects off the surface every few feet. The only problem was keeping up with them, they were moving faster than I could kick my U-boat. I finally got within range of a nice fish and cast twenty feet ahead of him. Gulp, gulp, he took my fly. He was big and broke-off after a few strong head twists. The next fish was hooked while stripping a Callibaetis nymph from deep water over a shallow pile of rubble. He took a strong deep run and stripped out twenty feet of line. He then circled several times and lost his energy when I pulled him into the warm, oxygen depleted, shallow water. He was a fat twenty inch, four pound rainbow. We each caught another half dozen fish, with at least one twenty inches or better each. It got a little windy mid-afternoon so we called it quits around 4pm. We slowly kicked past a bus load of camera waving tourists on the boardwalk. They wasted a lot of film on us and asked a lot of silly questions. I enjoyed talking to two ladies from Britain. We got home about 8pm.

August 9, 2006

I met Steve Stephenson and some other friends at Lava Lake. It was hot, clear, and windy. There were several large forest fires in the high Cascades and the air smelled of smoke. I was on the lake by 10am and had a seventeen inch rainbow the first half hour. He took a #10 Carey Special on a full sinking line, trolled slowly over a sunken ridge of lava rock. It took six more hours to hook the next trout. It was lousy fishing. Last month a twenty pound rainbow was caught at Lava Lake and the fish photo made it in all the local newspapers. Hundreds headed to the lake and apparently the lake was fished out. Besides all the fishermen, the hot weather put the fish deep and they were not biting. I headed to the far end of the lake where there were fewer motor boats and cast over aquatic weed beds near shore. I was day dreaming, not really thinking about fishing. I noticed a small log floating near my fly. I twitched my fly line out of the way to avoid getting snagged. Seconds later the log turned into a four pound trout and slammed my fly. He took off, spun, jumped and headed deep. He was a beautiful fish, dark back, crimson sides and white belly. He broke off when I got him near the boat. I caught three more fish before the sun went down, and decided to fish elsewhere tomorrow.

August 10, 2006

I fished Hosmer Lake for two days. People come from around the world to bird watch, fish, and tour this scenic lake. Hosmer offers unique challenges. In mid-summer the lower lake is relatively warm and slightly green with algae. The upper lake is crystal clear, cold and relatively sterile. The two lakes are separated by a hundred acres of shallow reed beds and a mile long channel connects the two lakes. Dozens of canoeists, kayakers, and other boaters keep the channel free of weeds as they travel to the upper lake. During

hot summer days, the channel is where most of the fish are. You would think the fish would be spooked by all the commotion - not true. Every watercraft that passes through the small channel stirs up the water, scattering aquatic insects and small fish. Large brook trout and Atlantic salmon cruise the channel, following the turbulence. Fish especially enjoy float tubers because they dig deep in to the water column with their fins, sending small tornados through the weed beds. In the day, the brookies hang out along the sides of the channel, near the reeds and lily pads where there is cover. They even hold their positions when noisy party barges float overhead. Occasionally they will rise noisily to the surface, taking a damsel fly or some other terrestrial insect. These are the fish the unseasoned angler focuses on, has little success with, and goes home frustrated. The Atlantics roam mid-channel, avoiding the older and more aggressive brookies. They dart about behind the watercraft, flashing as they pursue dislodged nymphs. I usually pick up a half dozen fish with each pass through the channel, mostly Atlantics mid-day and brook trout in the evening. I only needed two flies to have success, a #10 Carey Special for the brook trout and a #16 Green Metallic Caddis for the Atlantics. Both flies were fished with a sink-tip line, twelve foot leader and 5X tippet. I fished the Carey Special downstream, with the current, like a dragon fly nymph or a baitfish, twitching and darting it through the weeds. I slowly trolled the caddis upstream, against the current, the caddis rising and falling with every push of my fins. I only caught one fish in the upper lake, where the lake bottom is white with volcanic ash and the wind-blown current forms dark lines of sunken twigs, leaves and other debris along the lake bottom. Some of the debris lines were hundreds of feet long. I trolled a fly along and over a debris line and caught a chunky three pound brookie. I caught my best Atlantic salmon at twilight near the mouth of the channel in the lower lake. I was stripping a Carey Special deep on the way back to the boat ramp when my fly was bumped and bumped again. On the third hit I hooked a big fish. Moments later I landed an eighteen inch Atlantic salmon, only after he tangled up my line trying to hide under my pontoon boat.

August 12, 2006
I checked out Three Creeks Lake, south of Sisters, Oregon. The lake was a carnival with boaters, sun bathers and the regular Saturday afternoon beach crowd. The lady at the lodge said fishing was lousy. I headed back down the rough road and fished Three Creeks Creek near the campground, and caught a dozen very small brook trout on an Elk Hair Caddis. I explored a forest road several miles downstream and got lost. My forest map was years out of date. I finally found the lower Three Creeks Creek and caught a few stunted brookies. There were too many fish in the river and not enough habitat.

August 19, 2006
I taught a three week class in Corvallis, Oregon and invited several of my students to fish Salmon Creek, near Oakridge, over the weekend. Four students took my offer. It was a hot day and felt good to wet wade in the clear mountain stream.

Coastal Cutthroat, Salmon Creek, Oregon

Two of the students had never cast a fly rod before and after ten minutes of instruction they were catching small native cutthroats and rainbows. One student was missing a left hand and compensated by using his upper arm; he caught a dozen fish. We used #14 Elk Hair Caddis all day long. Most fish were in the eight to ten inch range, but we hooked a few twelve inchers. Most fish were in the fast, pocket water and a few were in the slow pools where there was less cover and fewer bigger fish to chase them. We had greasy chicken fried steak near the lumber mill on the way home and were the only customers in the

place. It took a few anti-acid tablets to make it the rest of the way home.

August 25, 2006
It was 95 degrees and hot. I wet-waded the Nestucca River on the way home from work to cool off. The river below Elk Creek is "fly and artificial lure only" water and two miles below the confluence I had the river to myself. I hooked a small trout on the first cast using an Elk Hair Caddis. Over the next three hours I caught several dozen small cutthroat and rainbow trout, mostly six inches long and two cutthroat thirteen inches long. Most fish were at the head of pools, hiding in the rough, oxygenated water. I fished a long, deep pool with no luck, until I noticed a large fish nervously circling, looking for a place to hide. I looked closer. There were a dozen large summer steelhead hugging the pool bottom. They were crowded where a small spring emptied cold water over a rock-face on the far side of the pool. After resting them for an hour, I came back and tied a small, weighted pheasant tail nymph four feet below an indicator caddis and slowly drifted it through the pod of fish. I sat on a rock at the head of the pool and let the fast water pull my fly line downstream through the calm pool. It took about ten minutes to get a good drift. I could feel steelhead bumping in to the line, but no hook-ups. For one of the few times in my life I became less interested in catching small fish and was fixated on hooking only large fish. I quit fishing early and left before dark to avoid the logging trucks that were taking timber out from the east slope of the Coast Range.

September 21, 2006
I was invited by the Rainland Fly Casters, of Astoria, Oregon, to teach their "Tie with the Masters" program. I invited Don Nelson from River City Fly Shop along for the ride. They bought us dinner and I demonstrated how to tie a Tyrant for Coho and a Blue Charm for sea-run cutthroat. They videoed taped the program and we had a great time.

September 25, 2006
My Spey rod had been sitting idle too long and it needed a work-out. Grady and I left at 6am and arrived at Sherars Falls, on the Deschutes River, a little after 8am. The washboard road rattled our teeth and filled our car with dust. We parked the

car at Beavertail Campground and hiked upriver around the peninsula to a nice drift we saw high above the river from the road. I swung a #4 Purple Spey through a fifty yard run and did not raise a single fish. The sun was low to the water and directly upstream. We would have to wait until the shadows returned in the evening to swing flies again. I put on a heavy stonefly nymph with an indicator and Spey cast through the run again. It's amazing how much line control you have with a thirteen foot rod and heavy line. Fifty foot drifts were easy and mending the line was a snap. At the top of the run, in a deep slot next to a small island, I got a solid hit. A second cast produced a steelhead. He was boxed in by the island and large boulders at the head and tail of the pool and could not run. All he could do was swim in circles which wore him out easily. I beached him on the grass and Grady helped me release a native two foot long, five pound fish. At the next pool I hooked two Redside trout on a nymph, one was sixteen inches. Mid-morning clouds of small caddis appeared above the water, intent on dropping eggs in the riffles along the shoreline. Several rising trout in a slow run perked Grady's interest. We waded within an easy cast of several fish. He cast a #16 Elk Hair Caddis and missed three fish before he hooked a six incher. His next fish was fourteen inches and gave his five weight a workout. He caught one more fish before we found a shady tree for lunch. In the next run I caught two large whitefish and a fat battle scared eighteen inch trout. It was tough nymphing with a Spey rod and I learned to appreciate my five weight and dry flies even more. We caught a couple more trout before heading downstream to a good steelhead run as the sun disappeared behind the western basalt rim. The run we wanted was occupied so we slipped into the run above the campground and fished until dark. We had no hook-ups, but did see a lot of large trout taking October caddis on the surface. We met a small group of Washington County Fly Fishers at the campground for a barbecue and conversation. No one else in the group had caught fish.

October 2, 2006
I volunteered to host a week-long fishing trip for the Washington County Fly Fishers. Twelve of us met at Page Springs Campground on the Donner and Blitzen River in the Steens Mountains in southeastern Oregon. It was an eight hour drive from Portland to Frenchglen. I stopped for groceries in Burns. The weather was perfect, a few clouds and 65 degrees when I set up my tent and made my way to the river in the late afternoon. I caught an eight inch trout on my first cast on a #16 Pheasant Tail below an Elk Hair Caddis, and it's twin a half hour later. The river was running at 45 cfs, cold and clear. Just before dark I hooked two fourteen-inch Redside trout in a deep pool near the campground, under a large willow limb. They took the caddis. We all met at the campground for dinner and campfire. Everyone caught fish, but John Stalcup caught the best fish, a twenty inch trout on a #18 Blue Wing Olive Parachute. That night several deer inducted me into their herd by bedding down around my tent. I awoke several times during the night to snorting, barking, and farting! They looked surprised when I crawled out of my tent at sun-up. They did not move out of the way until I walked through them on the way to the outhouse. After breakfast we spread out along the river and I hooked my first fish, a fat sixteen inch rainbow, a mile up the canyon at the weir. Several of us hiked another mile upstream before fishing again. The river is made up of many calm runs separated by pocket water and riffles. The best holes were found in the fast water above long stretches of calm water. At one hole I hooked three trout, about a foot long, before hooking the big fish. He took my caddis and spooked the rest of the fish by jumping several times and thrashing around in the shallow water. We both had a great time on my three weight rod. He was a beautiful nineteen inch fish full of fight.

Trout, Donner & Blitzen River, Oregon

The next hole was a long, deep undercut run beneath a high, grassy bank with riffle water running into the entire length of the deep slot, about three miles upstream from camp. There was fast shallow water downstream and a large calm pool upstream, a perfect place to rest, get oxygen and catch bugs. I landed three fish sixteen to eighteen inches before feeling guilty and inviting George Wilson to take a cast. He brought up two fish in the seventeen inch range, and I caught two more sixteen inchers before heading upstream. Upstream fish were taking mayfly and caddis emergers next to the shoreline along a 100 yard slow run. We sight cast to rising fish and landed a dozen large fish. My best fish was 19 inches. We headed back downstream at dusk not wanting to get caught in the canyon without a flashlight. The trail was undefined and wandered all over the floodplain. Back at camp, we had a pot-luck dinner. Everyone caught fish. I did not have the pleasure of sleeping with deer that night. The sky was clear and cold. About 3am a storm came in and pounded our tents with high winds and rain. Now I know why the deer headed for better cover. It was still raining at sun-up. I got soaked running from my tent to the car to get my raincoat. We decided this would be a good travel day. We packed up our wet gear and headed to the Rogue River. The shortest route was through northern Nevada. We saw a lot of open country and a herd of wild burros, several wild horses, and two golden eagles eating road-kill jack rabbit along the highway. We thought about collecting some hare's ear for fly tying, but rejected the idea when the eagles started giving us the look that says "don't even think about it". By the time we had lunch in Lakeview my tent and gear were dry. I kept turning it over in the front seat of the car with the heater blowing it dry. Eight hours later we set up camp at Lost Creek Reservoir, southwest of Crater Lake, Oregon. It was good to be dry again and take a hot shower.

October 5, 2006
We hustled getting our gear ready in the morning, excited about the prospect of steelhead on the Rogue River. George Wilson had a valve problem on his pontoon boat, and headed to town it get it fixed. We launched below the fish hatchery. The river was running low at 900 cfs. Within minutes Ed Sanders caught a small trout. Moments later Mary Myhre yelled for some help. She hooked a big one. Her fish took off all over the river, ten minutes later she landed a twelve pound salmon. It did not have black gums like a Chinook. We think it was a Coho. It took a #4 Purple Wooly Worm, hooked right in the tongue. I fished with my Spey rod, trying to become more proficient at casting. The half-pounders were late this year. We didn't even get a hit. I caught one trout on a #6 Stonefly Nymph with rubber legs. Earl and Doug each caught several small trout, but that was it. A bald eagle flew up river over our heads with a small fish. We also saw several wild turkeys just before the take-out at Rogue Elk Park. The next morning, Doug and Mary woke up to flat pontoons boats and spent the day along shore. George and I floated the Rogue and saw a guide boat pick-up one steelhead, a crimson brute about five pounds. That was the only steelhead we saw on the trip. I took my three weight this time and caught three small trout and a Chinook smolt, in a large back-eddy, on a #18 Pheasant Tail Emerger. They were rising all over, taking mayflies. We left the river early and fished the "holy water" below the dam. No fish were rising and none took our nymphs fished deep. At sundown the situation changed. Fish appeared out of nowhere. Still, they ignored our offerings. In desperation I tied on a soft hackle and began swinging it downstream, working my way back to the car. After ten minutes of cast, swing, and two steps downstream I hooked a nice, strong rainbow, a thick sixteen inch beauty. The rest of the group switched to #16 Olive Partridge Soft Hackles. We cast and swung in unison, heading downstream… and caught no more fish. Back at camp, Ed cooked pork chops for dinner. Earl invited us to visit his cabin in Montana. George smoked a cigar and Mary and Doug went home early. It was a late night. We headed our separate ways in the morning, already planning a trip for next year. We probably won't do this trip again, the driving cut into our fishing time.

October 14, 2006
Friday at the fly shop, Ralph Brooks and Paul Skelton invited me to fish Mt Saint Helens, Washington, on Saturday. We arrived at Hanaford Lake, below Coldwater Ridge at sun up. We had to cross twenty miles of private timber land to get to the lake and Weyerhaeuser only opened the gate during deer and elk hunting season. Because of the limited access, the fish were bigger than

average. The lake sat near the top of the ridge. There was no inlet or apparent outlet, just clean rainwater and snow melt. No fish were rising in the morning. We trolled full-sinking lines deep with #10 Black Mohair Leeches. Paul caught two nice fish in the morning. That was it. About 2pm fish started to rise, Ralph caught several large cutthroats on a #16 Wilted Spinach. I switched to a floating line and #16 Olive Soft Hackle and caught a seventeen inch Westslope Cutthroat on my second cast.

Cutthroat Trout, Hanford Lake, Washington

These beautiful fish were several hundred miles out of their native range. Apparently the park service planted the lake with fish from an Idaho hatchery and a few Yellowstone cutthroats were accidently shipped with the rainbows. Ralph caught a large Brook Trout near some sunken timber, a little on the skinny side. We followed several pods of fish, only hooking fish when casting a fly immediately on the ring of a rising fish. Ralph and I simultaneously cast a fly at one ring and were rewarded with two fish, a double. Several deer hunters stopped by the lake and we heard several nearby gun shots, but saw no deer. A lone coyote howled for a half hour on the ridge below the lake as we ate lunch. We caught about a dozen more cutthroats before racing to the gate before they locked up at sundown. Not a lot of fish, but each one was a quality fish. We'll have to go back next season.

October 28, 2006
My son Grady and I fished with Tom Wideman on the Nehalem River. The sea-run cutthroat season was coming to a close and in a few weeks

the winter rains would come. This was our last chance to chase cutts this year. We drove to the coast in the fog, but as we put in at Beaver Slide, and shuttled the cars, the sun came out. It was a beautiful sunny, warm, fall day. I hooked a nice trout within minutes and Grady soon followed with another cutthroat, both fish about a foot long. He was using a Royal Coachman Bucktail and I cast an orange Reverse Spider. The river was low and we had to drag our pontoons across several gravel bars. Most of the fish were in the riffle-water, but we did catch a few in the frog water. I caught a dozen fish. Grady caught three fish, but was more interested in exploring the river that fishing. Tom was out of sight most of the day. We passed the gravel pit as the sun was going down and struggled against the wind and incoming tide the last couple of miles to the take-out at Roy Creek. We passed some good looking water we did not have time to fish. Grady had a hole in his waders. We were cold and tired but had a great day.

November 4, 2006
After months of planning and bi-weekly meetings, we attended the Pacific Northwest Fly Tyers Rendezvous in Troutdale, Oregon. I volunteered to be on the board representing Washington County Fly Fishers and designed the patch for the event. The last decade one gentleman organized and ran the whole show. This year the show was too much for one person to handle. Five fly fishing clubs pitched-in and sponsored the show. We had two dozen demonstration tiers (I was one of them) and about 300 people attended the event. After expenses we made over $9,000 from raffle tickets and auction items to donate to conservation projects and fishery scholarships. One of my Atlantic salmon flies sold for $80 at the auction. We started planning for next year's event the next month.

November 18, 2006
I'd been working on a watershed project for our Hawaii office and had a late evening flight home. Louie the Fish picked me up at the hotel in Waikiki at 6am after being introduced by a friend of a friend. We launched his kayak into the bay near the Honolulu Airport and were casting to bonefish by 7am. There was no wind, the tide was almost out and the water was calm as glass. Bonefish were tailing all over Triangle Flats. Lou

was a talkative free-lance artist-bone carver and bonified fish-bum who had guided fly fishers the last twenty years in New Zealand, Samoa and Hawaii. We slowly waded through knee-deep water on alternating grey weed beds and white coral sand trying to get within casting distance of bonefish. Most of the fish were solitary but there were a few pairs and triples. We looked for nervous water, slight riffles in surrounding calmer water. We cast at every movement. If a line was cast over a fish it exploded and shot in the opposite direction. Bonefish are unforgiving. I cast a #6 Orange Crazy Charley on an eight weight rod with floating line and a fourteen foot straight leader of twenty pound fluorocarbon. These fish were not leader-shy, but disliked a heavy line splashing overhead. We had only a few seconds to cast at fish before they were out of range. They moved like lightning. I used a stripping-basket to avoid tangled line. Feeding fish were easy to locate. Their tails were several inches in the air and flashed like small mirrors. Fish were easy to see in the bright sunlight, but when a cloud passed overhead the fish all but disappeared in the water. They were easier to see with yellow lens sunglasses than grey or brown. The fish appeared blue green in the water, their presence given away by their shadows. We must have cast to a dozen fish before we got our first hit. I saw tails, carefully approached, and made a sixty foot cast to a feeding fish. He turned and ignored my fly. Before I could retrieve the line, a second tail appeared twenty feet in front of us, heading in our direction. I made a sloppy roll cast ten feet in front of him. He saw our offering, picked up speed, formed a wake and slammed my fly. He then turned and I set the hook. Before I knew it my reel handle was spinning out of control. I tried palming the reel to slow him down, but just banged up my knuckles. Lou yelled "just let him run". And then he laughed. This was a big, strong fish, hooked solid. He headed toward the deep channel, but never made it off the flats. He easily had 100 yards of line out and was well into my backing. At the end of the first run I was able to reel in ten yards, but then lost twenty. This went on for ten minutes before he tired and I got all the backing on the reel. It took another five minutes to get the fly line in. When he got close enough to see us, he was off again on a twenty yard run. This happened several times. I began worrying about breaking off on the coral reef. We finally got his

head up and a hand around his tail. He was a magnificent mercury-silver, twenty eight inch, thick shouldered, ten pound bonefish! We admired him for a short time and released him to the salt.

Bonefish, Oahu, Hawaii

By early afternoon the "Kona- winds" from the south picked up and it was difficult to see fish. We spent the rest of the day casting to shadows, picking up a few smaller fish and one Trevally. We avoided several Sting-Rays and many large Puffer Fish. Apparently the best time to fish the flats was at the beginning of an incoming tide, without a full moon and between April and November. However, Louie said fish can be caught all year. Around 4pm the winds kicked up and the water became turbid. The angle of the sun made it difficult to locate fish. We loaded the kayak on the car and headed to town. It was a good day. The warm water felt nice in the 80 degree sunshine and the soft wind had a nice touch.

2007

January 26, 2007
Steve Stephenson wanted to secure the best run on Big Creek and picked me up at three in the morning. We hiked in with firewood and were cooking breakfast over the fire before 6am. We could barely see the small creek in the starlight and hoped the firelight would not spook the fish. Several anglers warmed themselves by our fire, but they quickly left when they discovered there was no room to fish. We began casting when it was light enough to tie egg patterns to our ten pound tippets. We took turns creeping up and gently casting our rigs into the pool. The fish were wary. We had to rest the pool in between casts. Steve hooked the first fish - a monster steelhead that tore up the small pool - and scattered the remaining fish in all directions. When he was through playing with us he flipped his tail, threw the hook, and was gone. We patiently waited for the fish to re-group before casting again. The creek was about thirty feet across, twenty feet of that was fast water running over a shallow gravel bar. The remaining ten feet of river was a deep, slow pool. A short while later we saw several fish, in the clear water, returning to the pool. I figured a few fish were holding in the cover of a fast riffle below the pool and slowly crept-up and drifted my rig through the short run. On my second cast my yarn indicator stopped and I set the hook.

Steelhead, Big Creek, Oregon

A nice steelhead ripped through the riffle water and headed to the deep water below the cut-bank. He was hooked squarely on the tip of his upper jaw. Several twists later I swam him up the gravel bar and grabbed his tail. He was a crimson-red hatchery fish and he's going home with me for dinner. I had strict instructions from my wife to bring home a fish. A few minutes later, Steve hooked a monster steelhead and fought him around several boulders, root-wads, and gravel bars. We landed him twice, after he escaped through Steve's legs and almost made it back to the fast water. Finally we landed a fourteen pound hatchery fish. By now the sun was hitting the water through the spruce trees. As careful as we were creeping up to the water, the fish could see us as well as we could see them. We quit fishing mid-morning and headed for town. We had logger burgers at Knappa Junction and were home before the kids got out of school. My wife was pleased with fresh fish.

January 27, 2007
Paul Skelton, a friend from the fishing club, invited several of us to fish with him on the Nehalem River. I picked up Roger Smith at 7am and we met Paul and Al at Alice's Restaurant on the Wilson River for breakfast. We launched our pontoons boats before noon in sunny, fifty degree weather. There were only three other vehicles at the take-out, it didn't look promising. The water was off-green and low. The fish wouldn't be coming in on the tide and hopefully they were already in the river. We fished hard all day, throwing Spey flies and drifting egg patterns. We did not even get a hit. I tripped on a rock in six inches of water and spent an hour drying out my shirt. We arrived at the take-out just before dark and took a short-cut home along the upper Nehalem River. The thirty miles of road was un-paved, mostly mud and full of pot-holes. It really took a toll on our car. Hopefully we'll have better luck fishing next time.

February 10, 2007
I tied classic Atlantic salmon flies at River City Fly Shop's booth at the Pacific Northwest Sportsman's Show at the Portland EXPO center for two days. We were across from the duck-call booth and had to endure squawks and cackles all day long. Duck hunters are all nuts. I was able to sell several framed salmon flies and a couple dozen trout flys. It was nice meeting new people and working with the fishing vendors.

February 17, 2007
I attended the Fly Fishing Show in Portland, and took a class from author Dave Hughes: Fly Fishing Writing 101. It was a very good class and limited to four students.

March 19, 2007
I was invited by the Oregon Council of the Federation of Fly Fishers to tie at the 19th Annual Northwest Fly Tyers Exposition. This was the first year the show was held in Albany. I tied perfect parachutes for three sessions over two days. There were over 150 tiers from around the country and a thousand visitors attending the convention. I was also asked to be in the tiers video and tied my Purple Haze parachute. I met a lot of nice people and learned some new techniques. At the end of the show, a gentleman purchased all ten dozen parachute flies I'd brought to the show. I was grateful. Next year I planned on bringing more flys.

March 31, 2007
I tied at the Western Idaho Fly Fishing Expo, in Boise, Idaho. It was a small group and only the third year of the event, but we had a great time. I tied parachutes and met a lot of nice people.

April 6, 2007
Never take a canoe winter steelheading on an Oregon coastal river. We finished work early in Tillamook and Chad Cherefko invited me to fish the Trask River. We left his old pick-up truck at the Highway 101 take out and loaded his canoe on top of the old station wagon and put-in at Loren's Drift. We hit rough water about a quarter mile downstream and luckily caught the current just right and missed the brush lined rip-rap the fast water was pushing against. We spun out into a large back-eddy, caught our breath, and took a few casts. I swung a Spey fly thru several nice runs and Chad dead-drifted nymphs through deeper water. We covered some good water during the four mile drift, but saw no fish. Several hundred yards above the Highway 101 take-out, Chad finally hooked a fish. He dropped his paddle into the front of the canoe and leaned toward the fish just as we hit fast water. We slid sideways through the rapids and flipped the canoe on a submerged log. I touched bottom with my feet before catching my breath and placed my fly rod in the canoe before hitting bottom a second time. We were in a little

more than four feet of water and Chad was able to scramble up the nearest gravel bar with the fish and submerged canoe in-tow. With our gear secure, I lunged for the canoe paddle drifting down the main current and ended up downstream on the far side of the river, completely soaked. We were both laughing, not knowing any better (we did have our life jackets on). I did not see Chad land and release the fish, but was grateful when he picked me up in the canoe a few minutes later. I did not dry out on the drive home. Luckily my wife did not notice my wet clothes when I got home.

April 11, 2007
I invited a few friends to fish Lost Lake on the Coast Range. Roger Smith, Chuck Cooney, Tom Wideman and I waited for a few minutes while a logging crew moved their equipment off the narrow road, less than a half mile from the lake. It was cold and the water temperature was just over 50 degrees. We still caught fish. Everything worked on the stocked trout: Carey Specials, Wooly Buggers and Soft Hackles all brought in 10 to twelve inch trout. Around noon the wind started to blow, the rain-hail began moving up the mountain and the temperature dropped about five degrees to the mid-forties. It was time to go or get soaked. We headed to Fort Stevens State Park and fished Coffenbury Lake. Luckily it was not raining on the coast, but at 200 feet elevation or higher it was pouring. The wind was blowing and we took cover in the sheltered areas of small coves. We cast flies from our pontoon boats toward shore and picked up two dozen rainbows just feet from the bank. Most fish were caught under old snags, trees and shrubs hanging over the water. These were bright silver stocked trout that provided good sport for the rest of the afternoon. The rain washed all the mud off my car and small boat trailer on the drive home.

April 18, 2007
I experienced all four seasons while fishing the Metolius River. After receiving fishing advice at the Wizard Falls Fish Hatchery, I headed upstream with my day-pack. It was sunny with a slight breeze. An hour later a storm front moved up Black Butte, dropping enough rain to require a rain jacket. I fished hard, casting to every fishy looking pocket of water. I fished the deep, fast water with heavy nymphs and a small emerger

dropper. I threw a small Elk Hair Caddis and Pheasant Tail dropper into the shallow riffles and undercut-banks.

Metolius River, Oregon

There was another hour of dry weather, then snowflakes in full sunshine. The clouds caught up a short time later and the snow turned to rain. I hiked half way through The Gorge, where the water was too fast to hold a lot of fish. The weather must have been confusing to the fish, I didn't even spook one. When it started to snow again I headed back to Wizard Falls and changed out of my waders in sunshine. The Metolius River humbled me today. I suppose all the fish were in the deep volcanic-rock slots, few fish were feeding in the shallow riffles. The water around the hatchery was too fast, I supposed that the better water was upstream in the meadows where the water was flatter and slower.

April 20, 2007
I pulled into the Deschutes Canyon Fly Shop parking lot a little after 8am and purchased some tapered leader in exchange for advice. The advice was "fish the slow runs, the water is still too cold for the riffles", "fish where you can't see the water from the road, that's the slow water". The advice was well worth it, I had one of my best days on the Deschutes River in years. I parked at the top of the first meadow and hiked down river a half mile, jumped the fence. I tied on a heavily weighted #12 Bead Head Pheasant Tail Nymph (with rubber legs) and a #16 Tan Flash Back Hares Ear (cased-caddis) eighteen inches below as a dropper. I also tied a yarn indicator five feet up the leader from the nymph. I cast into the slow water, about a hundred feet below a fast riffle, ten

feet from the bank, about where the streambed disappeared from view. After the third cast, I hooked a fish, saw a silver flash in deep water, then my line went slack. A dozen casts later I hooked and landed a fourteen inch Redside Rainbow Trout. Already it's been a good day. Not a cloud was in the sky, there was hardly a breeze and it was 60-70 degrees. I hooked a dozen trout (and a few foot-long steelhead smolts) before noon, and only worked a hundred yards of stream bank. After lunch, fish began hitting my orange-white yarn indicator, one fish hit three times before the end of the drift. A few little black stoneflys were on the water. It was time to switch to a dry fly. I tied on a #12 Peacock-Orange Stimulator and hooked a nice fish within minutes. It was fine sport to watch a big dry fly drift a few yards, see a trout come from the depths and poke at the fly a few times, grab it and turn into the current. Most fish jumped two or three times then hunkered down in deep water below large rocks. I caught another dozen fish on the Stimulator before reaching the top of the meadow and running out of good water. I walked back to the car, carefully avoiding the tall grass and brush not wanting to bring home any ticks. I spooked a few small lizards sunning themselves on large rocks, they sounded like rattlesnakes as they disappeared through the dry leaves as I walked by. Luckily, I did not see any rattlesnakes. I drove the car several miles upriver beyond the paved road and parked next to one of the many take-outs. I immediately hooked and released a nice trout at the gravel boat ramp. On my next cast, a large tree grabbed and broke-off my last Stimulator with one of its many high branches. A few March Browns and Blue Wing Olives were on the water, so I tied on a weighted #16 Olive Soft-Hackle and dead-drifted and swung it downstream. I caught a few more trout and one small Chinook smolt before calling it quits. I bought a large soda in Maupin for the drive home. The next day I got a stern lecture from my wife about my sunburned face.

April 28, 2007
I fished with the Washington County Fly Fishers on the McKenzie River. It was perfect weather, high clouds, no rain, and about 60 degrees. We hooked a few small trout at Hendricks's Bridge where we put-in. There were a few small mayflies and gnats on the water and cased caddis larva all over the rocks. The major flood event last

summer dramatically changed the landscape, especially the gravel bars, but apparently had little effect on the insect population. I wore fins and side-drifted a heavily weighted #10 Rubber Legged Bead Head Pheasant Tail Nymph with a #12 Possie Bugger dropper alongside my pontoon boat. I hooked half a dozen rainbows, mostly in the deeper slack current along the riverbank. They all took the Possie Bugger, a fly recommended by the local fly shop, and a perfect match for the cased caddis larva. Early in the afternoon my orange-white yarn indicator took a few hits from larger trout. I switched to a #8 Clarks Stonefly and took a few small trout from a couple of back-eddies. We fished the last gravel bar at Bellinger for about an hour before taking-out. It was a beautiful run, long and deep and the current was perfect for swinging a fly. If there were steelhead in the river this is where they would be. I put the Possie Bugger back on (without an indicator) and started at the top of the run and hooked a fat little rainbow on the first cast. I slowly and carefully worked downstream through the run, taking several casts and a few steps downstream. I had a hit about every ten casts. They must have been small fish because I had no hook-ups. At the end of the run I did land a nice foot long native cutthroat. The natives were always the best fighters.

Rainbow Trout, McKenzie River, Oregon

That was it for the day. I split gas money with Greg McCarty for the ride home. The next day I learned that another guy in our group hit a snag and was pulled underwater with his pontoon boat. Luckily, he had his life-jacket on and the group retrieved all his gear. All he lost was his lunch. I also heard that Tom Wideman hooked a steelhead

at Bellinger's gravel bar on a soft-hackle, and lost it after a ten minute battle. And to think we fished the same spot only an hour earlier, maybe one of those soft hits I thought was a smolt was really a steelhead. We started to think steelhead for the next trip down the McKenzie.

May 10, 2007

A couple of guys at the fly shop caught a few smallmouth bass on the Willamette River near the West Linn boat-ramp a few days before. They had a large sea lion harassing them, swimming a rods length away, but they caught a few nice fish anyway. I've been looking for a place to fish near home and gave it a try. I picked Ralph Brooks up at the fly shop early in the afternoon. The forecast was for thunderstorms, which are rare in the Portland area. Paul Skelton was waiting for us at the boat-ramp. There was a lot of boat traffic on the river - a dozen Sturgeon boats were within sight. The wind was blowing and it was unseasonable cold, around 50 degrees. We trolled large Wooly Buggers on sink-tip lines for an hour before even getting a strike. Three hours later, after fishing the lower end of the island, gravel points and back-waters, we only had one fish. Ralph caught a foot-long bass on a yellow and brown bugger. The Sea Lion kept to himself on the far side of the river, he looked like he weighed over a half-ton. Around 6pm the wind really began to blow and the rain came down in torrents. We got off the water before it got too bad, avoiding the lightning and thunder. I hoped to come back on a better day.

May 19, 2007

I fished Rock Creek Reservoir on the east side of Mt. Hood with the Washington County Fly Fishers. We arrived around 8am to find a full campground and two dozen boats on the small irrigation impoundment. I began trolling a #10 Carey Special on a sink-tip line behind my pontoon boat. A few guys from our group caught a few fish on full-sinking line, but I only had a few hits before lunch (not catching fish was giving me a complex). At 1pm a few large Callibaetis mayflies floated by and I caught four trout in a row. I fished a large, shallow portion of the lake where the bottom was covered with aquatic weeds. Before long, I was surrounded by other boats. It was hard to keep a secret on a lake. Over the next two hours I landed two dozen bright, hatchery rainbows. They were all fat with mayflies and twelve to sixteen inches long. The wind began kicking up and a few of us headed to the leeward side of the lake downwind of some large cottonwood trees. I stretched my legs and cast from shore and hooked a few more fish in a small lagoon. Bald eagles and osprey were all over the lake and hauling fish back to their nests. Around 3pm the wind really picked up and I headed back to the boat-ramp through white-caps. We caught and released enough fish for the day. I split gas money with Greg and we decided to fish the Deschutes River on the way home (just fifteen minutes out of our way). Poison oak was reaching the three-leaf stage and we had to be careful to avoid it as we walked through the first meadow above Maupin. The golden stoneflys were mating on the tall grasses next to the river. We may get to float a few dry flies if they start hitting the water. I tied on a heavy #10 Pheasant Tail Nymph with a San Juan Worm dropper. The river was a little high and off-color. I hooked a nice trout on my third cast. The Redside threw the hook before I could land him. I swapped out the worm for a #18 Pheasant Tail Nymph and caught a plump trout a foot from shore in a small back-eddy. With a couple of fish under my belt, it was time for dry flies. An Elk Hair Caddis produced four more trout before it was time to go. We met Mary and Doug back at the car on our walk out. They had been camping and also caught a few fish. It was a successful day.

Redside Trout, Deschutes River, Oregon

June 1, 2007

We kept our annual appointment with the Salmon Fly Hatch on the Deschutes River. I fished with Tom Wideman, Cary Maycumber, and a thousand other fishermen. We shuttled Cary's truck to Trout Creek and were on the river before 11am. Every good hole was taken. We could see a fisherman every fifty yards and waited our turn for several good runs. We put Cary's beautiful mahogany-wood drift boat in at Mecca Flat. Salmon flies were thick on the streamside vegetation with both golden and black stoneflys.

Stoneflys, Deschutes River, Oregon

The fish were taking them on the surface, but mostly in mid-river where we could not cast. I tied a heavily weighted #8 Stonefly nymph on and a #16 Tan Hare's Ear soft hackle dropper and cast into a fast run upstream from the Dry Creek confluence. Within an hour, I had several hits and finally connected to a large Redside Trout.

Redside Trout, Deschutes River, Oregon

He took the dropper and headed downstream, stripping twenty yards of line from my reel. It was a tugging match working him back upstream. I yelled "someone bring a net!" Cary brought his camera instead and took a few photos when the fish was a rod's length away. It was a nice Redside, about eighteen inches and bright crimson. He threw the barbless hook as we tried to land him. I cast the rest of the day without another fish. Tom and Cary hooked a few smaller trout, one whitefish and a couple of smolt but that was it. A brief thunder storm and a few strokes of lightning prompted us to get off the water around 4pm. Luckily it never did rain. Just above Trout Creek, where guides camp with their clients, we watched a gust of wind blow two camp chairs into the river and a small tent high into an alder tree. It was entertaining watching their owners run and swim after their gear. We met Pete Prepke and a few other guys from the Washington County Fly Fishers at the Trout Creek Campground. I rode back with Cary to Mecca to get my car and when I returned to Trout Creek, the club had set up a small city of tents. We enjoyed dinner and conservation until midnight.

June 2, 2007

We all slept in late to let the early crowd get on the river first and migrate downstream before hitting the water. Nothing is worse than competing for fishing spots. I was accused by several in our group of snoring all night, but it could have been any one of us. We loaded our boats and shuttled back to Warm Springs. Pete Prepke arrived late with the boats because a couple of oars bounced out of the back of his truck on the rough road, it took them an hour to find them and catch up with the rest of the group. The BLM and Sheriff Deputies were checking float and tribal fishing permits at the put-in, directing traffic and keeping an eye on a couple of Indians looking for handouts. The Deschutes River canyon was calm, cool, and barely had a breeze as we began our float. Salmon Flies were everywhere. I rode with Pete in his drift boat. Half our group stopped at the first island and spread out along a very nice run. Large fish were rising and taking Salmon Flies and what appeared to be large Yellow Drakes. They drove us crazy for over an hour, refusing everything we threw at them while they continued to rise. I fished the back side and tail of the island with no luck. I returned to the top of the run, just as everyone was packing up, to make a few more casts. I put on a #8 Black Rogue Foam Stonefly and cast into the slow water

half way through the run. A nose appeared then disappeared. Now I had their attention. Two casts later after a flashy splash I had a fish on. I could tell he was big as he bent my six weight rod downstream and began jumping and rolling. He did several tail-spins and then hunkered down testing my 6X Tippet. Five minutes later Doug had him in the net, a fat, chrome eighteen inch Redside Trout. What more could a guy ask for. After taking a few pictures and enduring a few snide comments from Mary, Doug, and Pete, we headed down river. Mary caught the next big fish at the top of the island above Mecca Flat, a seventeen inch beauty. We put in at the tail of the island and Pete fished the run while I ate a sandwich. I followed Pete through the run, and hooked another large fish on my third cast.

Redside Trout, Deschutes River, Oregon

He was heavy, almost twenty inches long, a little on the dark side (must have recently spawned) and did not have much fight. I took the foam stonefly out of his mouth and quickly released him. We fished several other good runs, but with the river traffic, never did hook-up with any more big fish. I did catch a foot long steelhead smolt and tail hooked a large sucker (don't know how that happened), on a small Pheasant Tail trailing behind my Foam Stone Fly. By late afternoon black clouds were building up in the west, it looked like we were in for some bad weather. Of course I didn't have my rain jacket when the storm hit and I got soaked. It rained buckets and the wind blew us all over the river. Lightning flashed beyond the canyon rim, so we got off the water. Back at camp all the tents were blown over and many were filled with water. We all packed up and headed home, too soaked to dry out before dark. We decided to have the club barbeque some other time.

June 9, 2007

I wandered through the Hood River Watershed looking for new water to fish. I wanted wilderness water, away from people where I could spend the day alone sneaking up on small fish with a three weight rod. I didn't care if it was open or closed water, I just wanted to get away from it all. The main stems of the Hood River were closed to protect spawning salmon and steelhead. Using my topography maps I found a gem of a small, remote creek off an old logging road. Green Point Creek was cold, crystal clear, a foot or two deep, ten feet wide, and had a closed-in canopy of alder and spruce trees. I parked my car on a logging spur out of sight from the main road and jumped a small berm to the river. Bugs were all over the water. I tied on a #16 Tan Elk Hair Caddis and caught a small native rainbow on my second cast. The canyon was steep and the creek was littered with boulders and large timber. It was rough wading upstream, but always beyond the next log-jam was another nice pool or run. I quit counting after catching two dozen trout, all ranging from six to ten inches.

Rainbow Trout, Hood River, Oregon.

When it started to rain I took refuge under the thick alders and waited out the short, brief showers. I found a shortcut back to the road through a notch in the basalt cliffs that surrounded the creek. I did not hear or see another person all day.

June 18, 2007

My son Grady and I took a three day, twenty five mile, backpacking trip into the high Cascades. Our goal was Eight-Lakes Basin, east of Marion Forks, Oregon. We hiked into Duffy Lake, set up camp and our rods, and only saw three fish rise all evening. Three years ago a fire burned through the area, filling the small spawning creeks with sediment. At least we used that as our excuse for not catching fish. The next day we hiked into Mowich, Jorn and several other small lakes, but still caught no fish. The fire burned a lot of timber up the ridges and left the creeks and lake riparian areas green. We hit snow-drifts at 6,000 feet elevation and could not get all the way into Marion Lake. The Mosquitoes were terrible, but bearable with repellant and netting. On the way back we hiked into the Dixie Lakes and cast to a few rising fish, but with no luck. The water was too shallow, calm, and clear. Our last chance was Santiam Lake.

Santiam Lake, Oregon.

None of the watershed was burned around Santiam Lake - it looked promising. Fish were rising all over the lake. On my third cast I caught a deep orange Brook Trout on a #14 Callibaetis Nymph. The next two were sixteen inch Rainbows fooled by a #14 Black Foam Beetle. We cast as far as possible to where fish were rising, let the line lay still, retrieving only enough to keep the line straight in the current and wind. Cruising fish took the beetle with a splash and put up a good fight. The next day we hiked back to the car and spent the evening camping on the Metolius River, watching others fish.

June 21, 2007

Grady and I tried to fish Lake Creek (outflow of Suttle Lake) but it was too brushy. I was able to poke my fly rod through a mass of vine maple and willows, drop a fly into a nice run and hook a decent Rainbow. Because of the tight quarters, I could not set the hook and we lost him. Next we drove up to Three Creeks Creek, south of Sisters, Oregon and fished the meadow for small Brook Trout. The creek was only two feet wide, two to three feet deep, and full of small trout. There were so many fish many of them were stunted. I tied on a #16 Foam Ant and we caught three dozen fish the first 200 yards. Grady caught four fish on four consecutive casts. The creek meandered all over the alpine valley and was as beautiful as the fish. That evening we met up with Grady's scout troop so he could finish off the week with another twenty five mile hike.

June 22, 2007

I had the next two days to myself and wanted to explore some new territory. I'd heard Quartzville Creek had some nice fish. I drove to Sweet Home, Oregon, and east along Green Peter Reservoir. I felt a little uneasy, it was unseasonably warm and every wide spot in the road had a campsite with several tents and a party going on. Literally every 100 yards of highway along the reservoir had a campfire, four-wheelers, barking dogs, and a beat-up truck or hippie van. I later discovered the area is popular with gold panners and is one of the few places in Oregon where gold mining on public land, without a mining claim, is legal. I camped at the BLM campground, which was clean and quiet.

Quartzville Creek, Oregon.

At sun up I was on the river, which was cold, fast and crystal clear. I wet waded about a mile up from the campground. The river bottom was solid rock and there were several waterfalls and large-deep holes. At the first hole I caught a half dozen wild Rainbows and one native Cutthroat Trout, all around twelve inches long. I cast a #16 Tan Elk Hair Caddis. Working my way up the river I picked up another two dozen trout, four of which were fat hatchery fish. Around noon it started to get hot and the sunbathing crowd began making their way to the river. I explored the upper reaches of Quartzville Creek from my car and will have to return some other day when there are fewer people.

June 25, 2007

I sold twenty dozen Orange Caddis Parachutes to two guides who work the McKenzie & Rogue Rivers.

June 28, 2007

I met John Stalcup at Gold Lake near Willamette Pass. We both arrived a day early to reserve campsites for Washington County Fly Fisher's monthly trip. The Mosquitoes were thick, but kept at bay by our smoky camp fire. It rained off and on during the night and a little the next day. I fished a full-sinking type III line, with a short leader and a #14 Tri-Color Damsel Nymph. I caught a dozen wild Brook Trout, ten to sixteen inches long, throughout the day. It was cloudy and a thirty mile-per-hour wind kicked-up mid-afternoon. The wind brought the cloud layer down to lake level and we had fog, rain, and mist blowing us to the far end of the lake. It was semi-realistic seeing images appearing and disappearing through the windswept fog. The rest of the group arrived late afternoon and we spent the evening fishing in calmer water. I tied on a #14 Rickards Callibaetis Nymph and fished it as an emerger. The lake was glass smooth, we could follow individual fish working a straight line gulping midges and mayflies on the surface. One large rainbow was working toward my pontoon. He made three rises in five foot intervals. I cast five feet ahead of his last rise. He hit my fly hard. I set the hook and he erupted several feet in the air. He put up a good fight and was a beautiful fish. I caught two more Rainbows sixteen to seventeen inches long before it was too dark to see.

Rainbow Trout, Gold Lake, Oregon.

June 30, 2007
Doug and I fished Gold Lake again the next morning, this time in bright sunshine. The high-pressure front blew the clouds away. It was cooler than the night before and the mosquitoes all but disappeared. The fishing was really slow. I only caught three Brook Trout on a full-sinking line, before noon. We watched two Bald Eagles harass a duck and her brood for a half hour before plucking a duckling from the water. After lunch, Doug proposed we fish the McKenzie River on the way home. We took a short-cut up the North Fork of the Willamette, around Cougar Reservoir and put in at Forest Glen above Blue River. After shuttling vehicles, we floated about six miles to Finn Rock. I caught a small rainbow at the first hole we fished. The second hole was classic McKenzie water.

Redside Trout, McKenzie River, Oregon.

A fast run dropped over a gravel ledge and the water slowed as it became deeper. Doug took a few casts at the top of the run, as I worked the slower water. Cased Caddis larva were on the rocks and a few Mayflies were flying around. I cast a heavily weighted #14 Possie Bugger five feet under a yarn indicator. Moments later two trout rose almost simultaneously near my indicator. I quickly re-cast and luckily hooked the larger of the two trout. He was strong and fought well. Doug helped direct him to the net, a nice fifteen inch Redside Trout. The sun set behind the ridge and we had another five miles to float, we quickly fished a couple other runs and hooked no other fish. We picked our way around rapids and submerged rocks in the twilight. I wondered if we were going to make it out alive. I watched dozens of trout rise in a large hole at the take out as Doug retrieved my car and trailer. I got home at 2am after taking a short nap in Albany on the drive home.

July 21, 2007
I fished with the Washington County Fly Fishers on the Middle Fork of the Willamette River, near Black Canyon Campground. I caught a ride with Dave Wesley and we were on the water before 9am. It was cloudy and a little windy, nymphing weather. I tied on a heavily weighted #14 Possie Bugger and #18 Flashback Pheasant Tail Nymph as a dropper, and began casting into a broad, long, deep run. The water was a little off-color because of recent rains. It took an hour to hook into our first fish. He took my pheasant tail at the end of a swing and took off down current. I could immediately tell he was a strong fish. He jumped twice and then twisted in the deep current for a few minutes. Tom Wideman took out his camera and Shane lent me his net (I lost mine in the garage months ago). The eighteen inch rainbow was the prettiest fish I'd seen in months, dark olive back, cherry red sides, and silver belly. We quickly released him and he did not waste any time getting back to deep water. We worked upstream, and hooked a few small fish along a gravel bar-riffle. Dave and I fished the far side of a small island where the river split into a small channel. We switched to dry flies and each picked up another half dozen foot long wild rainbow and a couple of small native cutthroats. We met back at the truck for lunch, swapped stories and drove up river. The next run was a bust, fast shallow

water and no fish. Our next stop was better, a short distance above the confluence with the North Fork. Chuck caught the next fish on a soft-hackle swung downstream. We each hooked a few more rainbows as the sun drifted below the canyon. I hiked upstream, just below the bridge near Oakridge, and fished a nice, fast run. I hooked another eighteen inch rainbow, the twin of my first fish. He was a little more acrobatic, taking four slow, three foot high jumps in succession.

Rainbow Trout, Middle Fork Willamette.

He also took the Pheasant Tail and slipped the hook a rod length away. I fished with a yarn indicator while walking upstream, trying to get a dead-drift. On the way downstream I took the indicator off and dead-drifted and swung the nymph at the end of the drift. By 6pm we were tired and done for the day. We all met at the Oakridge A&W for root beer floats on the way home.

July 24, 2007

I stopped by the fly shop on the way home and Tim suggested we fish the Willamette River for smallmouths. As my family was out of town, I hustled home for my gear and met Tim at the West Linn boat ramp at 7:30pm. Tim had it all figured out and caught three nice bass before I knew what was going on. I hooked the forth bass on a #12 Olive Brown Wooly Bugger. He was a scrappy two-pounder who tried to hide under my pontoon boat. Tim caught two more bass before my next fish, one almost three pounds. I caught another bass and a crappie as it was getting dark.

We made our way back to the boat ramp by the light of a half-moon. It was a good trip.

July 31, 2007

A group of us from work fished the Umatilla River downstream from Rieth, Oregon. The river was turbid with irrigation water returns and a feed-lot just upstream, but cold enough to cool us off in the 100 degree weather. We ate a bucket of fried chicken as we watched the water for rising fish. We had no luck casting deep nymphs, so switched to dry flies. Phuc Vu caught the first fish, an eight inch trout.

Rainbow Trout, Umatilla River, Oregon

Phuc is a scuba spear fisherman from Vietnam. He chided us on the small size of the trout and questioned us about the worthiness of our prey. I caught the next fish, a twelve inch Chinook salmon smolt. He took a #14 Elk Hair Caddis and struggled against my three weight rod. We were fishing a fifty yard long gravel bar, with fast water on the far side, a nice deep center run and slow, boulderly water on our side. As soon as the sun went down, fish were rising everywhere and extremely picky. Scott Robbins caught the next fish, another smolt. The three of us caught a few more fish while Russ Hatz was getting discouraged. It was his first trip with a fly rod. I gave him my rod and guided him toward a small pocket below a submerged boulder. I kept yelling, "fish-on, fish-on" as several fish took his fly and spit it out. Finally, he hooked one and it pulled the drag out and headed toward a section of semi-submerged irrigation wheel-line on the far side of the river. The wind or high water must have blown the pipe into the river from the adjacent alfalfa field. It took Russ a few minutes to figure out the fly reel and he finally landed the fish in the shallows, another foot long smolt. By now it was dark and we headed back to the motel.

August 1, 2007
After work, we returned to the Umatilla River for another evening of fly casting. Phuc Vu was not fast enough getting his gear together and we had to wait ten minutes for a freight train to pass before he could cross the tracks. The train engineer was not happy seeing us run across the tracks and wailed on the train whistle, letting everything within a mile know of his displeasure. I hoped he didn't scare the fish. The fishing was a repeat of the previous evening. We each caught a few fish. At dark, a night-hawk took my fly on the back-cast. He circled around my head a dozen times with thirty feet of fly line. Finally, both of us dizzy, he landed on the shallow water. We caught and calmed him down, and removed the fly from his wing feathers. Luckily the hook did not penetrate his skin. We held him in the air and he flew off, none the worse for the experience. We did not have to contend with a freight train on the return hike back to the car.

August 2, 2007
Phuc Vu and I picked up Loren Unruh on the Umatilla Indian Reservation and headed to Milton-Freewater, Oregon. We wanted to fish the South Fork of the Walla Walla River. We shouldered our day-packs and headed up the two track rutted road. I'd heard the best fishing was three miles up the canyon, near a group of rustic cabins. On the hike in we could not pass up a nice pool and caught a few small rainbows on #14 Elk Hair Caddis.

Rainbow, Walla Walla River, Washington

Loren caught his first fly rod fish, a three incher. Another mile up the trail a pick-up truck barreled out of the forest, scattering us into the thick brush. The rancher stopped to see if we were OK and we bummed a ride with him another two miles up the road. Loren rode in the cab (local guys have all the luck) while Phuc and I sat in the truck bed. The road was bad and much of it was in the stream bed. During one stream crossing, the truck spooked a very large fish. I thought it was a Bull Trout because it was over ten pounds. After seeing several others spawning in the shallow water, we realized it was a spring Chinook salmon. At the end of the road at the cabins, we thanked our driver for the ride with a few flies and he invited us to stop by anytime and visit. Maybe we will someday. We caught a few ten inch trout near the cabins and began hiking up stream looking for better water. We met two hikers heading downstream in a panic. They ran into a sow black bear and her two cubs. Neither the hikers nor the bears were pleased to see each other. We decided not to tempt fate and followed them downstream. We began fishing in earnest about a half mile below the cabins and picked up some nice rainbows. We caught one or two in every hole, ranging from six to fourteen inches long. The canyon was narrow, brushy, and steep. There were very few holes and a lot of fast runs. I had trouble landing my best trout, a fourteen inch whopper. I hooked him along a small back eddy in fast water. I was standing on a large windblown fir tree that was laying four feet in the air above the river. My rod was above a limb of vine maple and the fish decided to head down river, beneath the log I was standing on. I finally sorted things out, grabbed the line and landed the fish below the log, with the rest of my gear all tangled up in the brush. Luckily I didn't break anything (including my leg). By the end of the day we each had caught a dozen fish. We dropped Loren off at his house and Phuc and I took turns driving home. I crawled into bed around 2:30am and was back at work at 10am the same day. I slept in over the weekend.

August 6, 2007
After working almost eighteen years in the state office, I took a job promotion to the regional office (still in Portland, Oregon) as the West Region Agricultural Economist.

September 3, 2007
It was Labor Day so I had the day off and went looking for "work." I met Paul Skelton at his place at 5am and we headed to Mt. St. Helens to fish Coldwater Lake. We had a lousy egg-sausage burger at the gas station in Castle Rock, Washington. Not a good way to start the day. We woke up several illegal campers at the day use area as we unloaded our gear. The USFS rangers arrived a short time later and dealt with them. The valley was dead calm with a thick mist across the lake. We put in just above the outlet stream where there was a nice gravel beach. The land across from the outlet was posted "No Trespassing" because a cougar had regularly been seen there in the thick willows. I hooked and landed the first rainbow about 100 feet from the put-in. He took a #14 Peacock Rickards Callibaetis Nymph, on full-sinking line, slowly trolled behind my U-boat. He was on the small size for this lake, about twelve inches long, but full of fight. The lake surface was calm so we focused on the deeper water, about eight feet deep, where you could barely see the moss at the bottom of the lake. I hooked the second fish about an hour later, a seventeen inch beauty, who helped himself to thirty yards of line off my reel.

Rainbow Trout, Coldwater Lake, Washington

Paul held him for a photo before we released him. The wind started to pick up and we assumed the fish would move into shallower water. I started to fish the shoreline. A bald eagle chased a smaller osprey around the west shore, hoping he'd drop the small trout he was carrying. I noticed several fish rising along the weed beds and hooked and lost several nice trout. I saw one rainbow tailing like a bonefish in about ten inches of water. I

finned within casting range and threw my nymph in his next wake. I swear, before the fly hit the water he took it and jumped two feet into the air. I could see the water drops scatter off my line, as he straightened out my flyline. The tippet snapped before the line hit the water, and the fish was gone. I had never seen this before. We picked up a few more fish, in the fourteen to sixteen inch range, after noon. Paul took a nap on a large log in the cougar posted area and was woken up and yelled at by a park ranger. It just wasn't his day. By late afternoon the volcano started shooting up huge billows of steam as the snow melted and drained into the cauldron. For most of the day there were about a half dozen fishermen on the water. The fishing really shut down around 3pm and we decided to leave.

September 22, 2007
My sister in law Kathy and niece Kelly were in town to visit my wife. I had to sneak out early without waking them and missed breakfast. I picked up a couple of hot dogs at the gas station in Salem, the kind that sit for weeks in the slow-cooker on the counter and turn green. I occasionally take a chance with cheap, lousy food and usually pay dearly for it. This time it was different. The hot dogs helped me catch fish. I split a ride with Greg McCarty and met a few other Washington County Fly Fishers at sun up at the Allen Springs Campground on the Metolius River. In spite of abundant insect populations, cold, clean water, and a healthy fish population, the Metolius is not an easy river to fish. We headed downstream and spread out along the river. I hooked and lost a rainbow on the first run. He threw my #18 Pheasant Tail as it rose at the end of a swing. I used a heavily weighted #14 Possie Bugger to get the small nymph deep in the fast water. I rested the pool for a few minutes and enjoyed the sun in the cool morning air. The maple leaves were just tuning orange from the frost a few days earlier. We saw a few tourists and hikers, but not too many fishermen. A couple of guys from Montana were frustrated because caddis flies were all over the water, fish rising everywhere, but they were not catching fish. I began casting again and hooked and landed a foot long whitefish. I took him up stream and released him near Doug so he could catch him again (he didn't see the humor). We worked downstream and spread out around a large pool. Doug almost

stepped on a large Bull Trout and went back to camp to get his eight weight rod and bunny leeches. I waded out along a submerged ridge of gravel at the head of the pool and spooked several Kokanee that were moving upstream to spawn. One was bright red and the others were mostly pink with green heads. Fish were rising randomly all over the pool for large mayflies and caddis flys. I cast for an hour to rising fish with no luck. No one else caught fish and Dave fell in the water up to his neck and went back to camp to change his clothes. Doug, Mary Myhre, and Greg had lunch under a large juniper and gave me casting instructions, and other unsolicited advice, while I continued to flog the water. Finally, I had enough and cast my #10 Orange Stimulator into a slow, back eddy and let it spin while I pulled my lunch out of my pack (by now a few October Caddis were hitting the water). I was halfway through my hot dog when a large trout took my fly off the surface and took off. I shoved the hot dog in my mouth, wrapper and all, and pulled in the slack line. The trout turned and headed toward me creating more slack. I walked backward in the fast current trying to get control of the situation, spewing mustard all down my shirt. The lunch crowd under the tree must have enjoyed my performance given their hooting and screaming. I finally got the line on the reel, brought the trout to the net and finished my hot dog. Any rainbow on the Metolius is a good fish, the two pounder I held in my hands was exceptional.

Rainbow, Metolius River, Oregon

Mary held the fish in the net while I snapped a photo and we released him. Fish continued to rise the rest of the day, but we did not catch them. Chuck Cooney sent stew, fresh bread, and drinks

with Dave Wesley for dinner, even though he could not fish with us (something about having a new grandchild). We enjoyed a meal together and took a few more casts before the sun went down. Greg drove the whole way home as we solved the world's problems. My niece, the gourmet chief, had an excellent meal waiting for me when I got home, a lot better tasting than hot dogs. It was a perfect day.

October 1, 2007
I really enjoy muddy waters, so much so that I drove 500 miles to see them. I'm not talking about the blues singer (although I did see him in concert in the late '70s). I'm talking about the Owhyee River on the Oregon-Idaho border. It was our second annual Washington County Fly Fishers week-long fishing trip. I met John Stalcup at Owhyee State Park on the Owhyee Reservoir, set up my tent, and headed to the river. The river was not really muddy, more of a light green-grey cloudy color from the clay and volcanic ash soils.

Owhyee River, Oregon

There was a major flood event the previous spring which scoured the riverbed and cleaned out most of the muck and aquatic weeds. I was surprised to see so much gravel in the river, which previously had been hidden by silt. I parked my car just downstream from the White House Hole and cast through the thick willows before I waded into the river. Casting upstream beneath the willows, a big brown rolled on my #14 Elk Hair Caddis and was hooked. He barreled downstream. I fumbled to get line back onto my reel until he promptly took it all back and more. We were having a great time. I finally got him in the net, a handsome eighteen inch Brown, and quickly released him. I cleaned up my fly, greased it so it would float high and added a #18 Midge Pupa as a dropper. Fish began rising all over the river as the sun went down behind the large cottonwoods. I targeted a fish a short cast away and floated my rig over his head once, twice, and on the third pass he took the fly and immediately exploded from the water. He jumped three more times before I realized he was a big rainbow. I had only caught one other rainbow on the Owhyee, and he was only a foot long. This one was special, about four pounds, twenty inches, and bright as a fresh coastal steelhead. He fought stronger than a brown. I finally netted him and he was so big his tail did not fit in the net. After removing the midge from his lower jaw he took off with a splash. Muddy waters were easy to fish because you can get closer to fish, use heavier tippets, and kick-up mud and not spook downstream fish. I hooked and lost three more fish before calling it quits and drove back to the campground. George Wilson built a roaring fire and the rest of the group spread out to warm themselves and recap the day's events. Everyone caught fish.

October 2, 2007
We awoke at McCormack Campground to strong winds, cloudy skies, and the possibility of rain. After breakfast it did rain and we took shelter under the locus trees until the storm passed. Matt Avila, Chris Roe, and I fished the rock garden run and spread out over a half mile of water. I had fished this stretch several times before and the fish were not in their usual haunts along the shoreline. I blind cast mid-stream behind every submerged boulder and deep run, and did not even see a fish until after noon. In desperation I cast into the most unlikely water - shallow, flat gravel bottom with no cover water. A fish hit like a freight train and took off upstream creating a wake in the shallow water. I struggled to keep him away from sharp rocks and finally put his nose in the net. Matt waded across the river to take a photo of the beautiful twenty one inch brown trout. He took the Elk Hair Caddis. An hour later I caught another brown, about eighteen inches long, uncharacteristically in mid-river. This one took the Midge Pupa. We caught up with the rest of the group for the evening hatch below the White House Hole. We spread out along a slow moving run and watched fish rise everywhere.

Everyone caught at least one fish and I hauled in a nice fat seventeen inch fish.

Brown Trout, Owhyee River, Oregon

There must have been strong winds back at camp because Chris's tent had blown over and Rodger Lehman's tent collapsed in the wind (he was camped on the river). A hot shower, cup of spicy Japanese noodles, and a large campfire felt good in the cold desert air.

October 3, 2007
A skunk managed to get into Matt Avila's tent (a canopy with plastic tarp walls tied together). He awoke several times to the beast rummaging through his groceries and gear. Matt showed the skunk the door with a flashlight and ax-handle. The next night he slept in his truck. We fished a half mile below the tunnel and spent most of the day casting to a pod of fish occupying less than thirty yards of water. I hooked half a dozen large fish but only landed one fish. Because we could see so many fish rising and not spooked by our casting, we stayed longer than we should have. I fished an Elk Hair Caddis with a Midge Pupa dropper all day long. In the morning and evening I kept the dropper about ten inches below the dry fly, mid-day I lengthened the length to twenty four inches when the fish held a little deeper and were more cautious in the bright sunlight. In the evening most of our group fished below the island near the White House Hole. Over a dozen fish were rising when we arrived, but we had too many people in a small area and spooked most of the fish and did not catch anything. We still had a good time. Back at the campground we had a large campfire, shared dinner and swapped flys late into the night.

October 4, 2007

We went back to fish the rock garden hoping for better luck than two days earlier. As we walked along the road, high above the river, we saw a dozen huge browns in the slow pocket-water near the shoreline, right where they were supposed to be. This was bound to be a good day. Why they weren't there a few days before we'll never know. I stalked an eighteen inch brown for half an hour and must have cast to him two dozen times. I rested him every few casts by drifting my fly through an adjacent slow, deep run. Finally, casting no different than the previous casts, I got him to turn and inhale my #18 Midge Pupa. He ripped into the strong current and I landed him fifty yards across the river. I caught two more fish, around twenty inches, who must have attended the same school as the first trout, playing hard to get. Feeling a little tired, I sat on a large rock in the middle of the river, ate my lunch and watched Matt hook and land another twenty inch brown. I lazily cast while sitting on the rock, not expecting to interest any trout. I was wrong and hooked another seventeen inch fish that made me wade through deep water, almost over my chest-waders, to net him. I also hooked another small brown a few minutes later from the same rock. It had been a pretty good day, landing five fish, three over twenty inches, within a quarter mile run.

Brown Trout, Owhyee River, Oregon

As the sun was going down we met the rest of the group a short distance below the tunnel, where we saw dozens of fish rising along a glass smooth run. These were picky fish, they had plenty of time to inspect and reject our flies. I focused on one particular fish, regularly taking what I thought were midge emergers. I floated six different flies

several times over his head to no avail. Even a #22 Pheasant Tail did not do the trick. In desperation I tied on a #20 Disco Midge which he inhaled on the second pass. The run was shallow with smooth gravel. He could not go deep, so he went every other direction including into the air. I finally put a net under him, another beautiful eighteen inch brown. On the drive back to camp we saw a skunk running along the road, heading to Matt's tent.

October 5, 2007

The campground was getting a little too crowded for our taste. Deer hunters, chuckar hunters and bass fishermen (preparing for a weekend bass tournament) noisily filtered into the campground during the evening. One deer hunter was asking everyone if they had seen his deer rack that disappeared during the night. It must have been Matt's skunks. They were stealing everything else at the campground. Al Halverson and I decided to hit the road and fish the Crooked River on the way home. The recent storm front brought cold temperatures and many of the mountain tops along Highway 20 were dusted with snow.

Crooked River, Oregon

I arrived at Bison Butte around 3pm, quickly rigged up the same caddis and midge we used on the Owhyee, waded across the river and began fishing. The rumor that the Crooked was dead following an early season release of non-oxygenated water from the dam was not true, fish were everywhere. I caught two dozen Redside trout before Al arrived just after 5pm. Most fish were about a foot long, but I did catch a monster seventeen inch fish (one of the biggest I've seen on the river). He jumped all over the river, even leaped over a partially submerged boulder, until he turned side-up. Glad I was using my six weight rather than my typical three weight rod on the Crooked. Al and I caught another dozen fish before calling it quits. We had sandwiches in the dark at the campground and called our wives from Prineville on the way home. It was time to start planning next year's trip.

October 20, 2007
The brochure and web-site showed huge Kamloops rainbows and the owner of the "pay to play" fishing pond was all too willing to give our fishing club a half-price deal to fish for the day. A half dozen of us met at the Red Hills south of Dundee, Oregon, on a rainy Saturday morning. We fished the three acre pond hard and only caught a few fish, but the biggest was only ten inches (nothing like the brochure). In fact, all the fish we caught were smaller than the average smolt. We tried a handful of fly patterns on full sinking, intermediate and floating lines to no avail. The result was always the same: small hatchery fish. We huddled under a huge weeping willow to keep out of the rain while Chuck Cooney cooked everyone lunch. Most of us went home mid-afternoon, disappointed that the fishing was not even close as advertised. The glossy brochure showed big fish, nothing like we were catching.

October 29, 2007
I was not sure we really needed a guide, but because Dany Groeten was visiting from Belgium and wanted to fish, I arranged for one of the better coastal river guides to take us for the day. I'd known Dany for several years through the International Fly Fishers Association. We met Adam McNamara at Alice's Restaurant on the lower Wilson River and were on tide-water on the Trask River an hour before sun-up. The tide was going out as we anchored the sled about a quarter mile below the Hospital Hole, where the deep channel turned around a bend and became shallow below a slough. We cast ten weight rods with forty five foot, 150 grain, sinking lines and level running lines. I tied on a #6 Black and Light Green Clouser Minnow and Dany tried a chreise and pink minnow. Adam said fishing was best when you see fish rolling. We saw few fish roll. We cast across the river, counted down the sinking line from ten to fifteen seconds, and

slowly retrieved the line in arm-length strips. After two hours of no action we headed down to Tillamook Bay and tried to head up the Wilson River, but did not make it because of the low tide and shallow mud flats. We headed back to the mouth of the Trask River and anchored up along the rip-rapped shoreline near the ten foot deep channel. A flock of Canadian Geese were spooked by two Bald Eagles and circled several times, bombarding us with goose grease. Luckily we avoided getting hit (while the green poop splashed all around us) and wished we had thrown a few shotguns into the boat. After high-slack tide, and no fish, we decided to head up the Wilson River. It rained heavily the previous week and pushed a lot of fish up river. We hiked down to the slide hole hoping for late summer steelhead but instead found a dozen bright Chinook salmon lounging at the bottom of a deep, slow pool, below a fast riffle. Salmon are not like trout, they may scatter when first approached but quickly settle down and return to their original holding pattern within minutes. If not harassed too much, they accept a fly line dragging over their heads and go back to establishing a pecking order and prepare to spawn. Salmon fishing is a numbers game, it's best to fish holes where there are lots of fish because only a few will take a fly. When salmon are crowded into a small area, they become more aggressive and will more readily take a fly. The odds are not in your favor if you are casting to only one or two fish. Now that we knew where the fish were, we pulled out the heavy lines, headed to the top of the pool and cast upstream – far enough to get the line to sink and swing slowly through the deep run. It was tricky at first figuring out the currents and getting the line to mend just right, but we finally were able to put a fly within fish range. Standing above the pool on a large rock, we could see every fish in the hole. A few scattered when they first saw our #8 Bar-Bell Purple-Pink Rabbit Leeches, but after several casts two fish began to show an interest in our offering. Apparently we had to put the fly right on their nose before they would take. They would not move more than two feet to inspect a fly. Twice we watched a large salmon take Dany's fly. We yelled "set the hook" but Dany was not fast enough. After two dozen casts the fish became bored and ignored us. We headed up river to the next hole, below prison camp road. A dozen Chinook were pooled-up below a small rocky waterfall. We switched to seven weight rods, floating line, twelve foot leaders and used the same #8 Bar-Bell leeches. Once again, the fish spooked as we approached the pool, settled down after ten minutes and approached and refused our flies over the next hour. Dany finally hooked and quickly lost a large fish at the head of the run. Adam needed to go and we thanked him for the trip. It was getting dark but we wanted to try one more spot. We drove down river, just past Lee's Camp, and walked the muddy road to the river. We immediately saw nice fish in a slow run. Dany waded across the river to the far side of the hole and on his third cast hooked a Chinook in the upper jaw.

Chinook Salmon, Wilson River, Oregon

The fish circled for a few moments before Dany beached him on a gravel bar. We took a few photos and admired the bright, healthy, eight pound native hen. After all our hard work, we were finally rewarded with a nice fish. As far as needing a guide, we learned a lot and enjoyed his company, but it was interesting that we only caught fish after he left.

November 3, 2007

For the past few years I have been the fly tyer chair for the Pacific Northwest Fly Tyers Rendezvous. Usually we held our event in an old wooden building near the Sandy River in Troutdale, Oregon. This was the first year we held the event at Mt. Hood Community College. Several hundred people attended for a day of tying, auctions, and raffles. I was amazed that one of my shadowbox framed Spey steelhead flies auctioned for $230. The event was a success. We made over $7,000 for conservation activities and fishery student scholarships.

November 17, 2007

I went fishing with Tom Wideman, but he couldn't fish all day and needed to get home early, something about a dinner engagement with his wife. Chuck Cooney and I didn't really care as long as Tom was driving we'd go anywhere. It was raining and we enjoyed the drive to the Deschutes River. We passed several other WCFF Club members along the river, south of Maupin, parked, and rigged-up at the locked gate. Tom was in a hurry to fish a secret run and hustled up the trail. Chuck and I took our time and poked along the river until we caught up with him a half hour later at the cattle guard. Tom thought he had two hits on his Spey rod, but was not sure. Chuck headed up river and I went down river from Tom and we all swung large streamers though a long, fast run. Moments later we heard Tom yell through the thick willows. He did not respond to our inquiries and I didn't see him float by in the river. We figured he must have been OK. It began to rain as Tom emerged out of the brush soaking wet. He'd fallen in the river and was heading back to the car to change clothes. Chuck and I fished a few more runs on our way back. I picked up a small trout and a large whitefish on nymphs. Just above locked gate we ran into Tom again, this time in jeans without waders, casting from shore. He hooked a bright steelhead right in front of us and lost him. That was more than we could take. We headed home and began planning our next trip.

November 24, 2007

I mowed the lawn for the last time until next year. The frost was thick on the garden, seeing as it's winter. The next day, Steve Stephenson picked me up in his beat-up Honda. A fish cooler took up the entire back seat and his rods, reels and other gear permanently stashed in the truck. He'd been catching Coho Salmon on Big Creek since September and thought we might get lucky with an early steelhead. It was just after 5am when we pulled into the day-use area at Big Creek, just beating another car by minutes. We took first dibbs on the best hole, rigged up our rods and built a fire to stay warm. The guy behind us stopped by for a short visit just to let us know he was there. The poor guy drove all the way from Oregon City to get to the hole first. At first light we began drifting egg imitations through the hole, switching patterns every few casts. After an hour of covering every square foot of the small stream we knew there were no fish. I climbed a small ledge above the river and could not see a fish in the low, clear water. We gave it another try down by the ball park, and below the private land in the swamp. We were a few weeks too early. We stopped for chili dogs at Knappa Junction, which were good, but I regretted eating them a few hours later.

2008

January 5, 2008
My Atlantic salmon fly tying class at River City Fly Shop has been very rewarding. Most recently, I've been tying with a retired brain surgeon from England. He is a very detailed perfectionist, as one would expect, and prefers to use his surgical instruments rather than his fingers. The conversation is always interesting and wanders from big game hunting exploits in Africa to hospital humor. I also tied with a retired nurse from Alaska, who ties for several Alaska fishing guides. We had one class together and I learned that doctors and nurses have very differing opinions of each other, and our class discussions often turned frigid.

January 21, 2008
Steve Stephenson had been bugging me for the last few days to fish Big Creek again. I wondered about his sanity. The radio said it was 17 degrees, well below freezing, but dry with no forecast of snow or rain. He picked me up at 2:30am and we hauled a twenty gallon cooler full of firewood a quarter mile into the Deadline Hole. At 5am we had a roaring fire and our first guest, another fisherman wanting our rock by the river. Steve invited him to join us. We fished hard until noon. At sunup Steve foul-hooked an eight pound bright steelhead buck, and released him. I didn't even get a hit. The crowds, lack of fish, and little elbow room make Big Creek one of my last choices to fish, unless everything else is un-fishable. Though sunny, it was below freezing and nice to get back home.

January 25, 2008
I got a call from Don Nelson at the fly shop. Hilary Hart, from Spokane, Washington, saw a few of my framed Atlantic salmon flies at the fly shop and wanted to use them in lingerie advertisements. We gave her a few flys for a photo shoot. Hilary sent us a copy of her work. The photos were interesting.

February 9, 2008
I attended and tied flies at the Pacific Northwest Sportsman's Show in Portland, Oregon. Friday I tied at the Fly Tyers Demonstration Booth and Saturday I tied Atlantic Salmon Flies at River City

Fly Shop's booth. I was also invited to tie at the Fly Tyers Theater Saturday morning and tied four flies representing the Mayfly life cycle in front of a video camera, thirty guests, and herds of people walking down the aisle. I met some interesting people and made some good contacts.

February 18, 2008
The moon was full and bright as Tom Wideman drove me and two of his real-estate clients over Mt. Hood early on President's Day morning. The highway was clear with a little melting snow water on the road near Government Camp. We stopped for windshield wiper fluid in Madras, skipped breakfast because none of us were hungry and headed to the Crooked River. The weather report promised a sunny 50 degree day but by noon it was almost 60 degrees. I stuffed my extra fleece jacket in my day-pack. There were a half dozen bald eagles roosting and sunning themselves along the lower few miles of the quality fishing water. The fishing began well, I hooked three fish the first half hour in front of Bison Butte Campground, but only landed one lethargic seventeen inch Redside on a #16 Orange Flashback Scud. He was a little on the thin side, probably because he was hanging out in a fast riffle in cold mid-winter water. There were no bugs on the water, not even midges. That was it for me. The rest of the day was casting practice. Another fisherman was having success drifting an indicator and midge pupa through slow deep water below a turbulent riffle, catching several six to eight inch fish. About 3pm we gave the last riffle one more try in the "wild and scenic section" of the river before heading home.

Whitefish, Crooked River, Oregon

Lucky we did, Tom hooked a nice Whitefish on a #16 Tan Flashback Caddis Nymph. The weather was great, the company enjoyable, and the fishing poor. One of Tom's clients bought us dinner in Madras on the way home. The moon was so bright on the snow over Mt Hood we didn't need headlights. We blamed the moon for poor fishing.

February 23, 2008
The ninety six year old Marmot Dam was removed from the Sandy River last fall so the Washington County Fly Fishers decided to fish the river and check things out. Removing the dam re-created access to an additional 100 miles of salmon and steelhead habitat, and Coho salmon were observed migrating past the dam site three days later. The Sandy River runs through huge volcanic ash deposits created by Oregon's tallest volcano, Mt. Hood. Removing the dam released several thousand tons of sediment and debris down river, and during high water several stream banks downstream of the dam were severely eroded as the river found new paths. There were large flats of sediment that would take years to disperse down river. Dozens of ancient large cedar trees and stumps were exposed as more than 200 years of sediment washed away. Some trees were well over twenty feet tall.

Sandy River, Oregon

We looked for good water and fished hard all day throwing Spey rods, sink-tips, and indicator-egg patterns. It was unseasonably warm and sunny, perfect for a float trip, but there was too much sediment suspended in the water and on the river bottom to hold fish. I suspect all the fish bypassed their usual haunts and headed up river to the

newly accessible pristine habitat. In a few years we'll catch more fish, but not this year.

March 1, 2008
I was asked by Jack Hagen at NW Fly Fishing Outfitters to demonstrate tying classic Atlantic salmon flies at their shop. About a dozen people showed up for the three hour Saturday morning session. Two guys stayed after the demonstration and we tied until late afternoon.

March 7, 2008
I tied Forked-Tail Parachutes at the Fly Tyers Expo in Albany, Oregon.

March 29, 2008
It snowed for two days (which was very unusual) and was still snowing Saturday morning as Chuck Cooney and I headed to Veronia Pond. We passed one car upside down in the ditch, surrounded by several sheriff deputies trying to figure out what happened. It was cold with a strong east wind as I launched my pontoon boat into the frigid lake. The rest of the guys from Washington County Fly Fishers were reluctant to get their feet wet, until the wind and snow let up. Once we were all on the lake it started to hail but it was too late to turn back. We started to catch fish an hour later but not where we usually caught them. They were in the middle of the lake. I hooked a dozen fish before noon on a #12 Carey Special. Everyone caught fish.

Veronia Pond, Oregon

Chuck fixed chili and hot dogs for lunch and we headed back to the water. It rained, snowed, hailed and the sun shone during the afternoon. A few fish were rising to an unknown bug during the calm between changes in wind direction. I tied on a #14 Elk Hair Caddis for kicks and hooked an anxious trout. A few minutes later we were plastered by a wall of water and headed towards the boat ramp. The rain cleared up moments later and we turned around and fished another two hours and caught another dozen fish. Then it started to rain again. We decided this was nuts and we all went home.

April 4, 2008

I'd met Noel Gollehon several years earlier at a meeting in Washington DC. When disinterested in the meeting we talked fishing in the back row. I called Noel before my next trip back east and he invited me to fish Beaver Creek in rural Maryland. He and his wife Leslie met me at the end of the Metro light rail line in Shady Grove and in less than an hour we were on the river. He introduced me to Doug who had been working with the Chesapeake Bay Foundation and Trout Unlimited to restore a half mile to creek that surrounds his property. It had been raining the last twenty-four hours but the water looked good. I tied on a #14 Possie Bugger with a #18 Pheasant Tail Nymph and walked down the clay bank and into the small spring creek. I cast upstream into a fast riffle and promptly hooked a fat wild Brown Trout.

Brown Trout, Beaver Creek, Maryland

The limestone creek was less than three feet deep and I easily brought the fish to my hand. We fished upriver through a series of fast riffles and slow deep pools. I almost stepped on a nesting Canadian goose, who hissed and flapped her wings to scare me away. I didn't want to mess with her and passed up a good hole to give her some room. Noel and Leslie fished the next hole

beneath a small bridge but saw no fish. I followed them, put on a heavy tungsten beadhead Possie Bugger and hooked a sixteen inch wild brown on the second cast. An even larger brown followed him to the surface to see what all the commotion was about. I quickly released him and made a few more casts for the second brown with no success. Noel hooked a very nice brown on the next hole and we took a few photos. It began to rain, so we called it a day and went out for crab cakes for lunch. On the way to the airport we took a side trip from the Lincoln to the Jefferson Memorials in Washington DC to see the cherry blossoms. After exchanging a few flys I thanked Noel for the trip and caught my flight home. This trip changed some of my perceptions about east coast fishing. There was some good out-of-the-way water with excellent fishing, and the area was not as congested as I'd imagined.

April 17, 2008

Never forget your net when fishing the Owhyee River. The fish are too big. I had a couple of free hours on the way home from working in Boise and took a little detour across southwest Idaho. The irrigation district raised the flows from the Owhyee Dam the week before and the river was a foot higher than usual with a fair amount of free floating debris. The Skwala stonefly hatch was over, it was too early for the caddis and the blue wing olives were sporadic. I tied on a caddis pupa and began casting to deep water. Across the river I noticed a subtle rise but thought it was nothing until I saw a large tail poke out of the water. I tied on a #14 Elk Hair Caddis and a #18 Pheasant Tail Nymph dropper and began casting over the fish. A rod's length upstream, another fish began rising. Was it the same fish? I cast to the new spot with no response. The first fish's dark shadow reappeared downstream and inhaled my Pheasant Tail after a short drift. He exploded down river, looped around a large mat of aquatic weeds, and headed toward me. I cornered him between the weeds and the stream bank until I could get the line back on my reel. After a few minutes he wore himself out and turned side-up. When I grabbed the leader, he exploded again, straightened my hook and was gone. Where's a net when you need one? The second fish was still rising and I quickly hooked him on the Caddis. Playing him a little longer, I managed to beach him on a small gravel bar. I thanked the eighteen inch brown for taking the larger hook, took a photo and released him. I hooked six more fish during the afternoon, all over eighteen inches, but only brought three to my hand.

Brown Trout, Owhyee River, Oregon

I've got to remember the net next time. The fish were evenly split between the Elk Hair Caddis and the Pheasant Tail. Four fish were hiding along the shoreline in deep pockets surrounded by thick moss and the other two fish took the nymph below a shallow gravel shelf in deep water. I don't know why the fish took the caddis, there had been no caddis since last fall. Maybe they were just hopeful it was spring. I got a little sunburned but had a great time on the river.

April 22, 2008

I had a free morning and fished solo on the Deschutes River. Sometimes it's good to spend time alone on the water, unfettered from discussion and with quality time to think. There were no other fishermen on the river from Maupin up to Long Bend. Rumor was that the fishing was pretty good the past two weeks. However, it snowed above 2,000 feet last night and discouraged a lot of fisherman. Over the morning I caught a dozen ten inch steelhead smolts before it started raining. Smolts were everywhere and congregated in the prime water. Where were the Redsides? I wondered if the large smolt population that was moving through this section of river had put the Redside down or pushed them out. By mid-afternoon I grew tired of smolts and spent the rest of the day exploring the river before I headed down the road home.

April 25, 2008

The weather improved the last few days and the Deschutes was a balmy 60 degrees. I caught three small trout on a #14 Elk Hair Caddis at Harpham Flats before Paul Skelton showed up around 10am. We strapped our pontoon boats to the roof of Paul's vehicle and headed up river to Nena. We barely made it to the put-in before the boats slid off the car. We launched and fished the first riffle downstream and quickly hooked several ten inch trout. I fished a heavily weighted #12 Beadhead Possie Bugger with a #18 Pheasant Tail Flashback Beadhead Nymph dropper. We hooked up with another dozen small trout over the next few hours. We had one good run left before the takeout. It was just opposite and upstream of Harpham Flats. A guide had worked his two clients there earlier in the morning, and another guide and clients were just leaving as we floated into the run. There were only two hours of daylight remaining. Paul fished the main run and I headed upstream to the riffle. I hooked two foot-long Redsides in three casts and yelled to Paul to come up and take a few casts. A few casts later I hooked a big fish. He took the Possie Bugger and stripped line across and downstream. We definitely needed a net. This was a twenty inch Redside Trout.

Redside Trout, Deschutes River, Oregon

We finally got most of him in the net and Paul volunteered to take a photo. I removed the hook from the tip of his nose and carefully lifted him from the net. The fish remained calm until he was clear of the net and then flipped into the water. I was disappointed about not getting a photo of my best Redside ever. We rested the hole for half an hour before we began casting into the slot again. We worked the water carefully knowing there was at least one big fish in the run. Against all odds I hooked another fish about the same size, maybe a little bigger, in the same place as the previous fish. Paul insisted that it was the same fish. This time he took the #18 Pheasant Tail Nymph. I've never caught a Redside with as deep a crimson-red color as this fish. We got a photo this time. I speculated that the previous guides and fisherman had pushed the fish up to the top of the run to the deep and fast water. At dusk we floated into camp and met several other Washington County Fly Fishers who were setting up camp, and enjoyed a campfire together and hit the sack early.

April 26, 2008

Between the freight trains across the Deschutes River and the loud snorers in our group I managed to get a good night's sleep. Paul Skelton and I only saw three other fishermen on the drive up river and no guides were on the water. The guides had apparently given up after the slow day yesterday and headed further down river. We put in again at Nena and caught two dozen fish and a lot of smolts on the float down river. Paul caught a very nice sixteen inch trout in some fast riffle water. I tail-hooked and broke off a big fish that was probably a whitefish or sucker. We fished the twenty inch fish hole again, but only caught small fish.

Redside Trout, Deschutes River, Oregon

Back at camp we polished off a pot of hot dogs and chili for dinner and discussed the day's events with the rest of our group. I left early and got home at dark.

April 29, 2008

I was working in Heber City, Utah and stopped into the local fly shop. The middle Provo River emptied below Jordanelle Reservoir and provided several miles of quality tail-water fishery. I purchased a map and tippet in exchange for advice and headed to the river. The river was just below the snowline and there were several snow drifts at the sportsman's access parking lot. It was obvious that a lot of restoration work had been done along the river including several ponds, plantings, and rock work. The wind was blowing in gusts up to forty miles an hour and it was difficult to cast. The top of a large cottonwood tree broke-off in the wind and barely missed hitting another fisherman in the head just upstream from where we were fishing. He left and I moved closer to the center of the river to avoid windfalls. After an hour I had worked up to a large meadow. The wind was still blowing and a few snowflakes dotted the air. If there was any surface insect activity, I could not see it through the white caps on the water. I began looking for deep-nymphing water. At one point the river flowed over a large, steep gravel bar into a deep, narrow hole. I tied on a heavily weighted #12 Possie Bugger with #18 Pheasant Tail Nymph and began dredging the bottom of the hole. I took off the indicator yarn because the wind was blowing it around too much on the water. As I worked up the slot I hooked and landed a slim fourteen inch brown trout. Several casts later I caught another sixteen inch brown. Both were lethargic in the cold air and water and I quickly released them. It was getting cold and I could see a curtain of rain heading my way across the valley. I almost made it to the car before getting wet. I planned to give it another try tomorrow.

April 30, 2008

The afternoon began with less wind and more cold. The Provo River was still running cold and clear. I parked at the sportsman's access about a mile below the Highway 40 Bridge and began hiking up river. Another fisherman said the fishing was poor and the mid-day blue wing olive hatch only lasted thirty minutes. An Osprey dove and took a small trout at the first hole. Perhaps this was a good sign. My line began freezing in coils at my feet and it was difficult to strip line. I passed up a lot of good water looking for deep nymphing runs. I stood above a deep undercut bank and dropped my heavily weighted nymph straight down into a deep hole and hooked a small brown. He flipped off before I could land him. The wind kicked-up and I began walking to stay warm. I found shelter below the highway bridge and began casting below a small island where the current seams came together. It looked like good holding water, I knew fish were there. After two dozen casts I got a bump.

Brown Trout, Provo River, Utah

A couple of casts later I was into a nice brown. He went deep and put up a good fight relative to how cold the water was. I released him just as it started snowing. I'd had enough and hiked back to the car in a mild blizzard. It was good to land one fish.

May 1, 2008
I woke up to an inch of snow on the ground and it was still coming down. By late afternoon the snow had melted and there were even a few sun-breaks through the dark clouds. I made a quick visit to the fly shop for advice and they recommended fishing across town below the water treatment plant. This part of the Provo River appeared to have less traffic and was surrounded by pastureland. I hooked a foot long brown on a #18 Grey RS2 emerger dropper behind a heavy nymph at the tail end of a long, deep hole. I fished the run again and hooked a monster. I never saw him but he was strong and went deep. My rod was stressed and the drag was screaming when he slipped the hook. I'll blame it on the small hook and assume that he was hooked only skin deep. The next hole was classic. A hundred feet of fast, shallow riffle water took a sharp angle and compressed down to a tight slot

with an over story of cottonwood and willows. The outside riverbank was deep, the water was fast, the inside turn was slow, and the bottom was sand and gravel. This was perfect water for a drag free drift. There had to be a monster trout in there somewhere. I walked on my knees to get as close as possible and kept my shadow off the water. The first cast went well. The second cast was on target. A fish took my fly and I maneuvered him in the slow tail water and the fight was on. He took the #18 emerger and I didn't want to lose him. After what seemed like a few minutes I beached him in the sand, and the hook fell out. He was a golden eighteen inch brown trout with huge red spots and white tipped fins. He took off like a shot once he realized he was no longer attached to monofilament.

Provo River, Utah

Now that fish were finally taking emergers I took off the indicator and heavy nymph and went looking for rising fish. I found a few in a foam covered back eddy and began casting. I must have spooked them because they stopped rising. I rested the hole and enjoyed a few minutes of the remaining sunshine and watched two deer cross the river upstream. I saw another nose in the foam, made a quick cast, and let the fly swirl in the whirl pool a couple of times. He finally found my fly and hooked himself. He pulled hard in the current before I landed him. It was getting dark – time to go. The two deer were waiting for me in the willows and I followed them along the trail all the way back to the car. They were not spooked and had probably seen a lot of fishermen over the summer.

May 2, 2008

The storm passed, the sun was out, and it froze over night without the cloud cover. I had to soak my frozen boots in the Provo River before I could get them on. I headed up river from the sportsman's access and took a few casts at each likely looking hole. My line froze in the rod guides and made casting difficult. The sun was out and the air didn't feel cold. Perhaps the cold water and wind chill of casting line created the ice on my rod. I began catching fish.

Brown Trout, Provo River, Utah

On one particularly long back-cast I noticed a rod tip stuck on my yarn indicator. I wondered where that came from and soon realized it was my rod tip. I must have chipped my rod with a brass bead head fly. I spent the next couple of hours trying to cast with a broken rod, but it didn't work too well. To make matters worse, the best blue wing olive hatch of the week began. As a cloud passed the mayflys emerged in earnest, when the sun reappeared they shut down. At a particularly good hole I sat on a rock and watched the process repeat itself several times. The spent mayflys and cripples began to fill the back eddies and slack water. Ignoring the broken rod, I began casting during cloud cover and caught a few more fish.

May 5, 2008

I sold thirty dozen flys to two McKenzie River guides in Springfield, Oregon. They liked #12 big, bushy orange hackled parachutes with elk hair tails and posts. They paid $1.20 per fly. Selling flies has kept me in tying materials, fishing gear and the car full of gas.

May 10, 2008

The McKenzie River was fishing well (or so we were told) so the Washington County Fly Fishers gave it a try. We've fished the mid-section the last couple of years and decided this time to fish the lower river. My son Grady and I gave Paul Skelton a ride and we were on the water at Abernathy Bridge before 10am. It was cloudy, 60 degrees and the water was clear but high and running fast. Someone said the river was running above 6,000 cfs. If we were not careful this was going to be a fast trip. We all stopped at the first island below the bridge and caught several small trout. I began indicator fishing with a heavy nymph but quickly switched to a #14 Elk Hair Caddis when a large trout nibbled on my white and orange indicator. I immediately hooked a foot long rainbow. There were a half dozen islands formed by the river breaking away from the main channel through large gravel bars and reconnecting to the main channel several hundred yards downstream. The water and habitat looked excellent, except the water was too high to get a good drift. I began fishing the shoreline where the high waters were flooding the willows and creating small back eddies. Just above the confluence of the McKenzie and Willamette River I hooked a nice native resident cutthroat, maybe a foot long, with beautiful spots and a deep red slash below his jaw.

Coastal Cutthroat, McKenzie River, Oregon

I had to drift downstream about thirty yards until I could find a safe place to park my pontoon boat and land him. The river really picked up speed when it merged with the Willamette. We tried to fish but it was not working. We put our rods away and floated the rapids just for fun. There were entire trees in the river from major floods two years ago which made great perches for the many Osprey and a Bald Eagles along the river. We were off the river before 3pm, covering about seven or eight miles of river.

May 30, 2008
The road to Davis Lake was plowed the previous week but snow continued to cap the surrounding mountain tops. Greg McCarty and I arrived just before noon on a relatively warm, cloudless day. We quickly set up tents and headed for the water. We'd heard rumors of five pound bass in the lake, which was the best early in the spring. I tied a five foot, ten pound leader to the floating line on my seven weight rod and attached a large Chernobyl Ant. On a back-up rod I put on a weighted Carey Bugger just in case the fish were deep. We put in near the Lava Dam on the NE side of the lake and began casting towards shore into the tulle and reed beds. We joined another half dozen boats smacking the water with our flys. Within a few hours everyone had left, without catching a single fish. Greg briefly hooked one fish but it quickly broke-off. The clouds appeared, the wind kicked up, white caps began forming, and we headed back to the boat ramp disappointed. We tried for trout at the mouth of Odell Creek, but saw and hooked nothing.

May 31, 2008
We woke up late on our second day at Davis Lake. Based on yesterday's experience there was no reason to hit the water early. Around 10am Paul Skelton and Chris Roe pulled into the campground. We told them our pitiful story and they laughed and said they would show us how it's done. They told us the fish were in the weedy water, and avoided the open water with no cover. Within an hour I was into a four pound Largemouth Bass. I borrowed a large orange and chartreuse foam popper from Paul and pushed my pontoon into the reeds. The fish liked cover, but not so thick that they could not move around easily. The water was about four feet deep and the tulles were barely sticking out of the water like small pencils. The reeds held my boat in place in the light wind and I cast around a semi-circle, covering all water, and then moved forward twenty feet and began casting again. The bass exploded out of the water seconds after my fly hit the water and was pulled toward dense cover. I was glad I had a seven weight rod, Paul and Chris

both had nine weight rods. After a brief struggle I netted a fat and beautiful fish.

Largemouth Bass, Davis Lake, Oregon

It then began to rain. Over the next two hours I landed another five bass, all were over three pounds and the largest about five pounds. All were caught within about a 200 foot radius. It seemed each fish was protecting its territory and did not move around much. Each of us caught fish until the thunder clouds moved in and the lightning scared us off the water into the pines. Much of the forest had been burned over the previous year from lightning strikes so we did not take any chances. The rain and lightning did not let up within an hour so Greg and I decided to call it quits and head home mid-afternoon. It's amazing what a little knowledge can do to turn a bad fishing trip into a productive one.

June 7, 2008
Our daughter Bethany graduated from high school with honors and will attend Utah State University in the coming fall.

June 14, 2008
I taught a beginner's fly tying class at River City all day and was invited to fish Barney Reservoir in the evening. Barney was closed to fishing for over twenty years but the county raised the dam and the reservoir was opened for fishing about three years before. Very few fishermen were aware of the Hex-Mayfly hatch on the reservoir. I'd heard it was a tough fishery but very good at times. I met Paul Skelton and Laura Martinez at the shop at 5pm and we were on the water by 7pm. The hex hatch is not good until the sun is off the water.

The road to Barney was rough and sometimes the private forester locked the gate to prevent vandalism and fires. We were lucky, the gate was open. I trolled a heavily weighted #12 Possie Bugger as we kicked our U-Boats to the other side of the Reservoir. I picked-up a nice trout midway - a sixteen inch chrome blue trout. The reservoir had been stocked many years ago and the fish were basically wild fish. Paul landed another fish trolling a big foam deer hair hex-emerger. I thought he was nuts trolling a big dry fly, but it worked for him. We spent the rest of the evening fishing a small, wind protected cove on the west side of the lake. Paul picked up two more fish and Laura and I hooked and lost a couple of fish. I tried a foam deer hair hex emerger when a few fish began rising along shore, but it didn't work for me. Around 9pm it was too cold and too dark to fish. We packed-up and were home before midnight. We'll come back when the water level is lower and the temperature higher. Hopefully the hexes will also like it better that way.

June 23, 2008
We made a fourteen hour drive to Fletcher Lake, British Columbia, Canada. Stan Smith talked most of the way, Tom Wideman kept things interesting with jokes, and Chuck Cooney just drove. We had lunch at a greasy-spoon restaurant in Shaw Creek, BC. It was bad, the beef stew had no beef and the catsup was watered down. We watched a black bear run along the hillside across from the restaurant. Even the bear had enough sense to avoid the food at that restaurant. At Williams Lake we tracked down the only fly shop in town and met the owner fixing his Harley motorcycle in the garage with a few of his biker friends. He had temporarily shut the shop down because of the poor exchange-rate between the USA and Canada, but was willing to share advice. He answered our questions and was very helpful. We thanked him and met the rest of the Washington County Fly Fishers at Fletcher Lake an hour later. Battling hordes of mosquitoes, we set-up our pontoon boats and unloaded our gear into the small, woodstove heated, cabin. I was a little concerned about the place during my first trip to the outhouse. It only had three walls, no door and the opening was facing the road. I was tired and went to bed early.

June 24, 2008
We woke at sunrise to the smell of Chuck fixing a huge breakfast of eggs, hash-browns, and bacon. He even made enough for the landlady's stray dog begging at our door. The lake was mostly shallow and a little on the warm side for June. I dumped my boat into the lake and spent the next ten minutes looking for my sunglasses that had fallen into the water.

Fletcher Lake, British Columbia

I headed for a shallow shoal that was covered with reeds and surrounded by deep water. I fished a full-sinking line and nine feet of leader and picked-up a brightly colored seventeen inch rainbow on a #12 Pheasant Tail Damsel Nymph (with red flash in the tail). I spent the rest of the day slowly trolling my line around the small reed island and picked up a dozen trout.

Rainbow, Fletcher Lake, British Columbia

All the fish were between sixteen and twenty inches and a little on the skinny side. The damsel flys were just starting to hatch with the promise of each day getting more prolific. It sprinkled a little mid-afternoon but not enough to get drenched. I caught two nice fish on a floating line with a #12 Carey Special. I tried to skate an Elk Hair Caddis to imitate the traveling sedge that were beginning to appear on the water, but it did not interest any fish. We called it quits around 6pm and Chuck fixed steak and coleslaw for dinner. The camp shower was terrible. I have had more water leaking into my waders than what came out of the shower faucet. And the water was cold. I suppose that's what you get when you were last in line.

June 25, 2008
Seven out of ten in our group headed west past Big Creek to find Kloacut Lake, which was recommended by the Williams Lake fly shop owner and the local guidebooks. Our map was inadequate and we promptly got lost. Luckily we flagged down a logger (who happened to be a caretaker for several cabins on the lake) and he took us to the lake. The mosquitoes were especially bad as we rushed to get on the water and away from the bugs. Almost immediately we began picking up fat, bright healthy rainbows. These fish were in much better shape than the trout in Fletcher Lake. I caught eight fish from seventeen to twenty inches, all with a full-sinking line and Pheasant Tail Damsel Nymph.

Rainbow Trout, Kloacut Lake, British Columbia

They were all in deep water because of the higher elevation and the damsel migration to shore had not yet begun. We spoke to the care-taker again when he returned in the late afternoon, a German fellow who immigrated to Canada to find solitude.

He sure found it in this area. That evening we enjoyed a group campfire and dinner at Ed Sander's cabin. The area was recently infested with pine beetles and hundreds of acres were affected, so we had plenty of firewood. We stuck pretty close to the fire to avoid mosquitoes and stay warm from the cool breeze off the lake.

June 26, 2008
We fished the north side of Fletcher Lake, about a half mile directly across the lake from our cabins. I picked up three fish in the middle of the lake on my full-sinking line while fin kicking across the lake. We fished the shallow water near two small coves most of the day. The cloudy weather and wind kept the lake surface riffled, and the fish came into shallow water. I caught another two dozen trout with a floating line and Pheasant Tail Damsel Nymph. The damsel activity was picking up and several actually hatched on my pontoons.

Rainbow Trout, Fletcher Lake, British Columbia

By late afternoon it was a rough row back to the cabins in the wind. I tried to get back early to be first in line at the showers hoping to get some hot water. The electricity had been out all day and it was another cold shower for me. Chuck fixed taco stew for dinner and as usual it was excellent.

June 27, 2008
We headed to the far side of Fletcher Lake again in the morning on glass-smooth water. Chuck and I sight-cast to rising large trout in the small, shallow cove until the wind kicked up mid-afternoon. We had a great time and each picked up a dozen fish. The cruising fish were larger than what we'd been catching and most were twenty

inches long and strong. The bottom of the lake was carpeted green with aquatic vegetation and I lost several fish in the weed beds. The damsel migration was in full-force by late afternoon. The shoreline was covered by nymph husks and adult damsel flys. Some areas had over a hundred bugs per square foot and it was impossible to avoid crushing hundreds when walking inland. I had at least a dozen damsels hatch on my chest-waders while I sat on the shoreline eating lunch. By mid-afternoon the breeze stopped. There were no clouds and the water was glass smooth and calm. The fish quit biting. Chris Brooks tied on a midge and deep fished with an indicator with no success. Next he put on a damsel nymph and began hammering fish. Soon we all followed suit and dead drifted nymphs a foot off the bottom of the weed beds, usually in five to eight feet of water. We picked up a lot of fish the first hour until we fooled all the easy trout. As the wind kicked up we returned to the traditional cast-and-strip method and began catching fish again. Late afternoon I picked up another dozen fish taking a tour around the south-east end of the lake on the way back to the cabin. We can't get much better lake fishing than that.

June 28, 2008
We woke up early, packed up our gear, and headed home. It had been a great trip, but we needed to recuperate from our sunburns and sore casting arms. We needed to head home so we could tie more flys to restock our depleted fly boxes. Total trip cost in US dollars: $320. Cabin (five days) $120, meals and snacks $50, Gas $100, Canadian fishing license $50. The exchange rate was $1.00 USA to $1.06 CAN, not as good as it was a few years ago but doable.

July 8, 2008
I fished White Pine Creek, a tributary to Logan River, Utah, over twenty years ago while attending college in Logan and thought I'd give the creek another try. I parked my car up river from Red Banks Campground. I took a quick look at the map posted at the trailhead billboard, and briefly spoke to a Forest Service employee counting cows off the forest, before heading up the trail. I must have missed the fork in the trail and continued climbing straight up the hillside. Five miles later and 3,000 feet higher I could hear a small creek through the poplar and pine trees. A half mile

later I could see the creek in a deep rock gorge and it looked fishy. Another mile further the trail bisected the creek. I checked every undercut bank and pool but spooked no fish. I followed the creek another mile up into a beautiful sagebrush-lupine meadow. This was not White Pine Creek and appeared to be ephemeral and poor fish habitat. I decided to bring a map next time. I was exhausted and dehydrated when I got back to the trailhead and drank a warm bottle of water from the trunk of my car. Still looking for fish, I followed a gravel road up the Logan River and found one isolated pool along a mile of fast water. This resting water was full of fish. At least a dozen trout were working the small pool for rising Pale Evening Duns. I hooked a half dozen trout, but did not land any fish, before calling it quits. I stopped at Ricks Springs on the drive back to town and drank a pint of cold, clear water before noticing a sign warning of potential Guardia contamination on the trail away from the spring. We didn't have a water quality problem twenty years ago. Things have changed. I re-introduced the water back into the road ditch and had an upset stomach the rest of the evening.

July 9, 2008
I headed up Logan Canyon, Utah, in search of native cutthroat trout. There were several small beaver ponds at the base of Little Bear Canyon (near the Tony Grove turn-off) rumored to be full of trout.

Logan River, Utah

I wet-waded across the Logan River and pushed through the thick willows surrounding the ponds and immediately saw several rising trout. There were a couple of small openings in the willow thicket where casting a fly rod was possible. It was tough casting but I managed to throw a line at two rising fish. I tried an Elk Hair Caddis, Griffiths Gnat, Stimulator and RS2 Emerger and got nothing but refusals. A #16 Parachute Adams did the trick and I caught my target fish on the second drift, a beautiful twelve inch cutthroat.

The second fish had a green Fish & Wildlife tracking tag stuck in his back that appeared to be several years old. I quickly released him not wanting to mess up someone's research. A half dozen fish later I had spooked all the rising fish in the lower beaver pond and moved to the upper pond. The Parachute Adams was still working and I pulled in another half dozen cutthroats before they became wary again. I moved back to the lower pond where the Adams did not work and I caught one fish on a foam beetle.

Cutthroat Trout, Logan River, Utah

I figured it was time to rest the fish, eat lunch and take a nap in the shade. I must have slept and hour. I became more selective during the afternoon's fishing, popping in and out of the willows, sight casting once or twice to rising fish. I caught another tagged fish and recorded the tag number and phone number to call in later. After spending the entire day on less than a half-acre of slow moving pond water it was time to call it quits. It was time well spent on the water, catching some beautiful trout and enjoying the solitude.

July 17, 2008
I gave a slideshow on our Fletcher Lake trip and lake fishing to the Rainlanders Fly Fishing club in Astoria, Oregon.

July 23, 2008
I had won the privilege to fish Dean Larsen's pond near Augusta, Montana in a raffle from the International Fly Fishing Association several years ago. Augusta Pond was Dean's private retreat from the world. We drove from Bozeman and arrived at the pond late in the afternoon. Dean asked how long it would take to set my tent up, I answered "about five minutes", and he responded "hurry up the fish won't wait much longer." He was in a rush to put me onto fish. I quickly put up my tent because his twelve foot camper trailer only had room for Dean and the mice. While I rigged up my five weight rod, Dean picked a #12 Tan Foam Hopper from my fly box and I tied it to my nine foot leader. I stepped up to the water and then noticed the trout. Not one or two, but at least a dozen fish were swirling in the shallow water below the feeder creek behind the trailer. It was almost as if Dean had parked the trailer there to hide the fish from view, even though the pond was at the end of a mile long private unimproved dirt road about forty miles from Great Falls, Montana. To get the distance right I made a false cast into the weed bed to avoid spooking the fish. The second cast landed the heavy floating hopper hard on the water. I gave the fly a couple of short strips to get the rubber legs working and then whoop, a trout sucked it in, I responded with a light strip and the fight was on. The fish put his nose into the gravel and exposed a huge golden tail, a big brown. He careened across the pool, my leader collected pond weeds as he reached deeper water. I took a few steps closer to the bank and quickly got my feet wet. Dean later said it was not wet there last week and apologized for not giving me time to put my waders on. After a heroic fight by the brown, Dean threw me a net (he didn't want to get his feet wet) and I landed the fish. He was a little over twenty inches long and weighed three pounds. I quickly removed the hopper, Dean took a photo, and we released the fish. By now it was getting dark, not because it was late in the evening, but because a storm was heading our way. Yesterday in Bozeman it rained almost a half-inch of hail. The wind blew down tree limbs all over town. We ducked for cover under his trailer awning just as the heavens let loose a torrent of rain. We got a little wet, but our main concern was the lightning strikes heading our way. I was glad Dean rushed me in setting my tent up, at least I'll sleep dry. The rain stopped, we didn't hear

thunder for a few minutes so we hit the water again. My first cast was short and landed in the moss. I took another cast to the side to get the distance right at our targeted fish. The third cast was on target. Another fish took my hopper, this time a monster rainbow. He put up a bigger fight than the brown, jumping several times and rolling in the floating weeds.

Rainbow Trout, Augusta Pond, Montana

I finally landed him in the net along with several pounds of pond weed. This time we weighed him, four pounds and just short of twenty one inches. By now the storm returned with a vengeance. There were three seconds between lightning hits and thunder claps. Dean recommended I put my graphite rod down as he hustled into the trailer. We warmed up over the gas stove, talked for a bit then I retreated to my tent. We were too tired to eat dinner. A couple of cheeseburgers in Helena en-route were enough to tide us over until breakfast. This was a great start to two days of fishing.

July 24, 2008

Dean began banging around his trailer at six in the morning, a signal for me to wake up. We had a bowl of oatmeal for breakfast and headed out behind the trailer for another few casts. The sun was not quite on the water and only a few clouds dotted the sky. The storm dropped a little rain on my tent last night, but not much. We could see two fish working the shallows near the inlet, probably taking midges. I still had the foam hopper tied on and took a dozen casts up current from the rising fish. Finally, after several rejections and swirls, a large brown gently took my fly. I set

the hook and he took off towards the far bank, and then headed directly toward me. I had a little trouble keeping him on the reel but managed to keep the line tight. We landed him just as the sun hit the water. I've never seen a more golden brown trout. The clear morning air and the angle of the sunlight made a perfect picture. We released the fish and headed to the boat launch for a day of fishing. Fish were jumping all over the four acre pond, not just taking insects from the surface but literally jumping three feet into the air. We could not figure out what they were taking, but assumed they were midges. I tied a midge pupa dropper two feet behind the hopper and went stalking trout. I picked up two trout in the two pound range before Bob and Judi Kloskowski drove through the gate. I took off the hopper, wind drifted the midge, and picked up two more browns.

Brown Trout, Augusta Pond, Montana

Judi positioned her pontoon boat near the inlet and picked-up a half dozen fish on a #16 Black Parachute Ant before the rest of us realized that she was catching all the fish. We shared the water as fish became more selective under pressure. I put on a #16 Parachute Adams and hooked two more three pound browns in the slow moving water about fifty yards down from the inlet creek. It seemed as if we had caught all the rising fish because they disappeared around mid-afternoon. Bob staked a large rainbow that was taking mayfly dunns several feet up the feeder creek and finally hooked him on a #16 CDC Mayfly Emerger. The fish was not happy and wrapped the line around a submerged fence post holding up a broken fence in the middle of the creek. The line went slack.

Bob shrugged his shoulders as he pulled the line off the post. His footwork must have spooked the fish because he became untangled and shot between the fence boards into the pond, pulling off twenty feet of line and straining Bob's reel. By the time Bob came to his senses the rainbow had rolled several times in the thick weeds and the line went slack again. I walked over and scooped up a mass of weeds at the end of the fly leader and found a five pound, twenty four inch rainbow. We took a few photos and released the fish to be caught again. The inlet-fish needed resting so we headed to the put-in for a quick lunch and cold drinks. The fishing slowed in late afternoon and we cast hoppers into the shadows of willows and tall grass next to shore. The big browns were inches from the shore. Often their dorsal fins were rubbing the shoreline vegetation. I even saw one brown take an insect off a grass stem inches above the water. We caught another half dozen fish before Bob and Judi headed home in the late afternoon. The catching stopped and we just fished. I tried a heavily weighted sink-tip and damsel nymph, speculating the fish were on the bottom, but only caught two fourteen inch fish. We called it quits when a few storm clouds moved in as the sun went down. It was another good day on the water.

July 25, 2008

Late afternoon the day before, Dean Larsen cleaned the pond weed off the outlet pipe which lowered the pond about a half foot overnight. As a result the fish stopped congregating on the now shallower flats below the inlet creek. A few fish were rising at the far end of the pond towards the dam. Dean hooked a few browns, stripping his hopper in the middle of the pond as I dead-drifted a midge pupa without any luck. I became restless and began casting a #10 Foam Hopper towards shore. Weed beds completely surrounded the pond and large fish sometimes held in the shadows taking adult damsels and other terrestrials in the hot afternoon sun. I quickly picked up two eighteen inch browns that fought violently to make it back into the weeds. I lost a large brown that was lurking at the back of a small bay. I watched his dorsal fin breaking the water surface in the weed beds for several minutes before he was in weed-free water. I made the cast and he savagely took my hopper and simultaneously broke my tippet as he somersaulted in the air. He

would have been the fish of the trip if I'd landed him. The fishing slowed and we headed back to the flats near the inlet where fish began rising again. We had dozens of refusals casting to individual fish, trying midge patterns, emergers and terrestrials. Finally, in frustration, I tied on a #16 March Brown Comparadun that was about the size and profile of what we thought the fish were taking. On my second cast he savagely took my fly and a few minutes later I landed a beautiful eighteen inch brown.

Brown Trout, Augusta Pond, Montana

On my next cast I hooked and broke off his sister in the thick weeds. We solved this mystery, but with all the commotion the fish stopped rising. As a last resort I headed up the feeder creek and noticed four actively rising trout taking emerging adult Pale Morning Dunns in the lower thirty yards of the small creek. I cast a #16 Forked-Tail Parachute Adams three feet above and to the left of the closest fish. He only saw a few feet of tippet as he turned and gulped in my fly. I set the hook. He jumped twice and I turned his head back toward the pond and the fight began. He criss-crossed the flats several times before he stuck his nose in the weeds. I netted a silver twenty inch hefty rainbow. The next fish in the creek was a repeat of the previous fish, except that he was a twenty inch brown. I felt a little guilty approaching the third fish and told Dean this was too easy. He responded "You came here to fish didn't ya? Well, go fish." The third fish in line up the creek hungrily took the Adams on the first cast and immediately knew he was in trouble. He did not want to leave the creek and jumped several times, rolled up the grass stream bank, and even tried to tangle the line in the submerged fence post. After all his antics I finally turned his head toward the pond and he reluctantly passed me heading to deeper water. By now he was worn out and I prayed my five pound leader would hold long enough to haul him to the net. It did and I proudly held a twenty four inch, five pound rainbow in my trembling hands.

Rainbow Trout, Augusta Creek, Montana

Dean took a photo and we revived the fish and turned him loose. He did not return to the creek but headed to deep water into the shade of a stand of cattails. There was only one fish left in the creek. I straightened the bent fly-hook from the previous fish and headed upstream. The last fish was clearly a large brown holding just behind the riffle water below several small rocky waterfalls. He was well oxygenated and actively moving throughout the creek taking mayflys. He had no competition from other trout and had the whole creek to himself. He took my fly on the first cast and without a second thought headed straight for the pond. I've never seen a trout move so fast and ride so high, his lateral-line to the top of his dorsal fin was out on the water as he jetted down the creek and a flylines length into the pond. He wore out easily after taking flight and I landed another handsome brown trout, pushing five pounds and twenty two inches. I retired my fly, a tattered #16 Forked-Tail Parachute Adams that caught four trophy trout in a few short casts. Dean and I headed back to the pond and picked up a few more two pound browns before it was time to head home. What a great trip. Dean invited me to sleep in his back-room in Bozeman and dropped

me off at the airport Saturday morning. I hoped to fish with Dean again soon.

August 8, 2008
The hex hatch was still on at Barney Reservoir so Al Halverson and I piled all our gear into Paul Skelton's vehicle and headed to the coast range. Luckily the gate was unlocked and we put in just as the sun went behind the ridge. I trolled a #12 Tri-Color Damsel on a full sinking line and picked up a sixteen inch rainbow in deep water in the middle of the lake. Paul and Al fished the far shoreline with Hex emergers with no luck, even though a few of the large yellow mayflies were floating on the surface. I gave up after an hour and headed back to the middle of the lake with my sinking line and hooked two fish and landed one fat rainbow. In the short time I was gone; the fish started taking Hexes along the shoreline. By the time I made the half mile back into position Al and Paul had hooked a half dozen fish. After a few casts the fish stopped rising. I'd missed all the action. Apparently the Hex rise only lasts a short time on this lake. Next time I'll stick around a little longer and be more patient.

August 22, 2008
I finished moving our daughter Bethany to student housing at Utah State University and went looking for trout water. I'd fished Box Elder Creek, Utah over fifteen years ago and had caught a few fish. Since then the highway department had widened and straightened the highway, the small creek all but disappeared into a culvert pipe. A couple hundred yards were left intact and I speculated they had to hold a few trout. I parked my car off the busy highway and scouted for fish up the creek out of sight from the road. Two brown trout were taking terrestrials in a small pool in the bright sun shine. I hurriedly stripped a long willow branch of twigs and leaves for a rod and accidently smashed a couple hundred aphids on my hand (got to be more careful next time). I tied a length of fly line and leader to the tip of the willow and put my fly reel in my pocket. The first cast with my #12 Tan Foam Hopper spooked the trout nearest to shore. The second cast was right on target and the trout followed the hopper downstream and took it midway through the pool. A willow rod does not have much action so I just lifted the ten inch flopping fish into my hand and quickly released him. I had a 700 mile trip home

this evening, I'll be back soon to fish this creek again.

August 23, 2008

I spent the night camped below Anderson Dam on the South Fork of the Boise River, not far from Mountain Home, Idaho. The river looked high and I only saw one fisherman amongst several dozen rafters. I arrived too late to get an Idaho license so it was off to fish Oregon (after a brief stop at the Boise fly shop). The Powder River below Phillips Lake looked good so I pulled over at the interpretative wayside and rigged up my rod. Grass hoppers were everywhere, but I only got two rises and no hookups on my foam hopper at the first hole.

Powder River, Oregon

Next I tied on a #14 Elk Hair Caddis and began catching fish. I was surprised that few fish were in the back eddies or stream bank-water. They were all mid-stream in fast water. I must have caught three dozen six to thirteen inch rainbows over the next two hours in less than a quarter mile of river. Fish were everywhere and hungry. It only took a few minutes to dry my wading pants in the hot sun before heading down the road. I almost hit a dozen wild turkeys crossing the road between Service Creek and Fossil, Oregon. I took the long way home, enjoying the back roads, good weather, and listening to old county western songs broadcast from several small eastern Oregon towns. I miss the dry climate, smell of sagebrush and juniper and open landscapes at our home in western Oregon.

August 29, 2008

I needed a few pointers on Spey casting and offered Paul Skelton a ride to fish the Deschutes River in exchange for his casting expertise. The canyon was hot and the rubber hatch was in progress. Rafts, kayaks and inner-tubes owned the river. Our first stop was in the shade of the canyon walls a couple of miles below Beavertail Campground. We swung Spey flys through a 100 yard run for an hour with no luck. I did learn that to throw a nice D-Loop with little effort I needed a leader-tippet that was one and a half times the length of the rod (in my case twenty feet). The best leader was a poly-leader that hovered in the surface film. The idea was for the leader to stick on the water surface and temporarily anchor the line for the roll-cast forward. Once I figured this out casting became a breeze. We fished a few more runs upstream to Maupin and had a bad hamburger at the Oasis Resort. We visited the Deschutes Fly Shop on the way home. 90 degrees was too hot to fish.

September 3, 2008

I gave a slideshow on our Fletcher Lake trip to Washington County Fly Fishers.

September 6, 2008

Sea-run cutthroats had been in the river since July but it was a busy summer and we finally got around to chasing them. Mark, Paul Skelton, and I had breakfast at Alice's Restaurant on the Wilson River then paid our two dollars to park at the county park on the upper Trask River. There was a nice long run adjacent to the park that usually held fish and this morning was no exception. Paul headed to the fast water at the top of the run, I took the mid-section and Mark waded into the slow water at the tail-out. Mark hooked the biggest cutthroat of the day on his third cast, a beautiful bronze twenty inch native. He was fishing a #8 Pink Body Elk Hair Streamer with a braided leader, three feet of tippet, floating line on a four weight rod. I hooked a few small fish on a #10 Hot Orange Reverse Spider but did not land any fish. When the sun hit the water I walked down to the next hole and saw a nice fish take a caddis fly on the surface. On the next cast I hooked him and shortly landed a bright sixteen inch sea-run. Mark caught another nice cutthroat at the top of the run in the fast water. We adequately fished the hole and moved down river to the Dam Hole. Mark took the slow water again and hooked and lost another nice fish. I think I can learn a lot from this guy. He's had years of experience chasing cutts and knows how to fish for them. I hooked and lost a twelve inch fish in the plunge pool at the base of the natural rock dam. Paul lost his fly and a section of tippet to a large fish in the slow water Mark had just fished through. Mark smoked his pipe and Paul headed down stream while we rested the slow water tail-out. After about half hour I stepped up for my turn and cast downstream to the far side of the river. My un-weighted spider drifted over a shallow boulder field, into deeper water and was carried about four feet down by the slow moving current into the clear, deep water. A large cutthroat slowly came out of the depths, looked at my fly, and then gulped it down. I don't know if he followed the fly from behind a submerged rock in the shallow water or came up from the bottom of the deep water, either way, he was hooked firmly to my line. He tested my five weight rod and light tippet for a few minutes, and then turned side-up as I landed him on a sandy depression in the solid rock shoreline. He was the biggest sea-run cutthroat I'd ever caught, pushing eighteen inches. He was sleek, firm and handsomely spotted.

Sea-run Cutthroat, Trask River, Oregon

I quickly released him and he headed back to the depths. We stopped at Loren's Drift and fished the next two holes upstream. By now the river was in full sunlight and we hooked nothing. A large fungus-head spring Chinook circled the run several times until we spooked him. On the way back to the truck I hooked a twelve inch cutthroat

in the fast riffle water at the top of a run and quickly released him. We were not sure he was going to make it as he floated belly-up in the tail water. Several buzzards who had been circling us the last hour (probably following the old salmon) saw the trout and perched in the alders above the river, waiting for us to leave before having lunch. They had hoped for a salmon meal but will have to settle for trout. We packed-up and headed home, stopping to take a few casts on the Wilson River at the Boy Scout Hole. It was too hot, the river too low, and we saw no fish.

September 9, 2008
Chuck Cooney and Tom Wideman rescued me from the office just after lunch to fish the Klickitat River, across the Columbia River in Washington State. It was hot and cloudless as we rigged up our Spey rods. We'd met another fly-rodder that caught two steelhead the previous day. He used a Muddler Minnow in the tail-out of a large, deep pool. I tied on a Muddler for the first couple of hours but caught no fish. We moved upstream a couple of miles and fished a short run. Chuck was able to get a steelhead to roll at his fly, but no hook-up. Tom and I got nothing. It was getting dark in the canyon as we headed up river and parked at the water treatment plant below town and walked a quarter mile to a long, fishy looking deep riffle. I switched to a #8 Green Butt Skunk with white polar bear wing and began swinging downstream. We each hooked a couple of small trout but could not interest any steelhead with our offerings. We ate our sack lunches in the dark at the city park in beautiful downtown Klickitat. Several stray dogs joined us but refused scraps from our bologna sandwiches. We enjoyed the entertainment a small rural town provides as kids ran through the streets and old folks walked beneath the stars. We got home just before midnight.

September 10, 2008
I gave a presentation at the Stonefly Maidens club in Portland about Victorian Salmon Flys, their history, and a tying demonstration. It is the only women's fly club in the Portland area, and a fun group to work with.

September 13, 2008
The Washington County Fly Fishers met at Timothy Lake on Mt. Hood early Saturday

morning. We'd seen photos and heard rumors that the fish were getting fat on crayfish. The sun was out and it was a beautiful calm day - when we launched our pontoon boats. Within minutes the wind kicked up white-caps and blew us off the lake. Greg McCarty, Ron Reinebach and I retreated to a small cove trying to get out of the wind but it was no use, too rough to fish. A few big yellow Hex mayflies managed to emerge but they could not get air borne and drifted like sailboats to shore. We packed up and headed to Trillium Lake a few miles up the mountain. The lake was over-run with tourists. I'd guess there were over one hundred rafts, canoes, kayaks and small boats on the 100 acre lake. It was bedlam. The camp hosts (guards) were even rude when we tried to park and launch our boats. We caught a dozen fish in about two hours and left, vowing never to return if there were more than a couple of boats on the water.

October 6, 2008

Phil Oliver and Pete Prepke picked me up early Monday morning for our third annual week-long fishing trip with the Washington County Fly Fishers. We filled Phil's camper with groceries in Ontario and were parked at the Owhyee State Park campground before sundown. A dozen guys from the club were already there, and many of them had caught some nice fish. We had dinner and shared stories over a big campfire.

October 7, 2008

We waited for the sun to come up and warm the canyon before we headed to the Owhyee River. We fished just above the tunnel near the White House, but it was too windy to cast. There were no bugs on the water and we saw no fish. We headed down river below the tunnel to the Camp Hole looking for rising fish. The river was a little more sheltered and after about an hour three large brown trout started working across the river in a back eddy. They floated counter-clockwise in the current and were taking what looked to be Blue Winged Olives along a floating mat of algae. I tried a Caddis-Pheasant Tail dropper, a BWO Parachute and finally had success with a #18 Mahogany Sparkle Dunn. A large brown was gulping emergers about every three feet. I put my fly six feet ahead of him and he took it two gulps later. He was not happy and struggled in the cold water before coming to my net. He was twenty

inches and a little on the skinny side. The rest of the fish in the pool scattered and we headed down river to check out one of my favorite reaches of the river, what I call the Rock Garden. Pete walked down the road a half mile to fish a slow bend in the river. He caught two nice browns. Phil headed up river to fish a nice riffle leading into a deep hole. I bush-wacked down the steep bank and through the willows and waded into the middle of the river where it was only two feet deep and the river bed was large gravel. A few fish were rising to midges along the riverbank, but they were difficult to see in between the wind gusts. I put on a #14 Tan Elk Hair Caddis and a #18 Black Midge Pupa dropper and stalked the first trout. He took the pupa on the second drift and I landed him on the far side of the river, hoping not to spook the other fish. He was a fat twenty one inch brown. I released him. I hooked another fish in the same slot as the previous trout, but he broke off after scraping my tippet across the rock he was hiding behind.

Brown Trout, Owhyee River, Oregon

Phil became interested in all the action. I waved him downstream and gave him a few pointers on where the fish were and what they were taking. He drifted his rig over a couple of fish, but he could not keep the drag out of his fly line and spooked fish. I gave him a few more pointers about line management and demonstrated the technique by hooking and landing a twenty two inch brown that should have been his fish. After he took a couple more casts, I followed up catching another twenty one inch fish. This was a great run. After watching me cast, he got the technique down and a few moments later hooked a nice fish that promptly broke off. It was getting dark and he was disappointed. We planned to do better the next day. Back at the campground a herd of does and yearling bucks were grazing on the lawn, even though a few of their brothers were hanging from a tree at the far end of the campground.

October 8, 2008
We spent the day fishing the flat water below the Camp Hole. Fish were rising and we did not need to move all day. In fact, I fished about ten linear feet of water, two feet deep, and cast thirty to fifty feet in all directions. We began using #18 Black Midge Pupa and caught a few fish, not as many as we should have because we could see them rising all over the river. I switched to a #18 Beadhead Flashback Pheasant Tail Nymph and hammered fish. Phil begged for a fly and he began catching fish. Pete was a little more reserved, but finally he could not take it anymore and requested a fly. Fish apparently were taking mayfly nymphs and we had a fish on at least every half-hour all day long. When the rises slowed because of wind or spooked fish, we took short breaks along the grassy shore in the willows. It was a good day. I've developed a theory on the Owhyee that fish take midge pupa on long, shallow, relatively flat runs and mayfly nymphs in deep runs below riffles. Maybe that is where the insect populations were the densest I don't know, but those were the flys in each location that took fish. That night Greg played his guitar and sang a few old cowboy songs at the campfire.

October 9, 2008
We woke up to a cold, windy morning- not the best conditions for fishing. Phil cooked up a heart-stopping breakfast of eggs, bacon, sausage and hash browns. It was a cold one on the Owhyee today. We took a few casts at the run we fished the previous day with no luck. The wind blew all the bugs off the water and no fish were rising. We explored a new run just upstream of the bridge, (where the wind was not blowing so strong) but saw no fish. Pete and I tied on streamers and swung them downstream through a long, deep hole. I caught a ten inch brown, the smallest fish of the trip. We had lunch huddled out of the wind behind a clump of willows, it was 40 degrees cold. We took one more look at the river and I noticed a large brown rising on the far side of the river next to a sheer rock wall. The

current was perfect to drift a fly downstream to where he was hiding. I cast an Elk Hair Caddis across the river, stripped all the fly-line off my reel and let the current do its work. The plan worked, I was ten feet into my fly-line backing when his nose poked above surface and my fly disappeared. Because there was so much slack in the line I had to take two steps upstream, strip in line, and haul back on my rod just to set the hook. The fish took off to deep water, fought for a few minutes and rolled as I brought him to the net.

Brown Trout, Owhyee River, Oregon

He was another twenty inch gold colored brown trout. I quickly released him and we headed back to the truck to warm up and find another spot to fish. We next parked at a large, deep hole just above the sagebrush flats, one of the few large rock-free areas along the river where it's possible for a large group to pitch tents. The far bank of the hole was a ten foot cliff and the near bank was shallow riffles. A few fish were rising randomly throughout the run. After a few short casts Pete caught the first fish, a small brown. I walked upstream and crossed the river on a shallow riffle. From the top of the cliff I could see every rising trout in the pool, and all were within a short cast. Waves of Blue Wing Olive Mayflys were coming downstream between 1 and 3pm. The fish went nuts when a wave passed by. I thought this was going to be easy, but I was wrong. One fish kept rising every two or three minutes and then ducked behind a submerged boulder in three feet of water. I must have cast to him twenty times. He always took the natural next to my #18 Adams Parachute, or inspected and ignored my fly. Phil caught a beautiful twenty four inch brown, probably the biggest fish of the trip. I was obsessed with hooking my fish, ignoring all other risers. Finally, after at least an hour of casting, he took my fly, acting like it was not a big deal. What an obnoxious fish. He gave a good fight. I worked him along the cliff to an opening where I jumped down to the river and landed him on a sandy bench. At eighteen inches he was not a trophy fish, but was a challenge to catch. I felt content and took the rest of the day off. I waded back across the river and watched Pete catch another nice brown, and relaxed on shore and enjoyed the sunshine during a brief break in the clouds.

October 10, 2008
We woke up late to a windy, cold morning, packed our gear and headed west to the Crooked River. It was snowing in Brothers and did not look good for fishing. On the river it was not so bad, we quickly rigged up our rods and headed to the water. I didn't put on my waders because fish were rising close to shore. I fished a #14 Elk Hair Caddis and a #18 Bead Head Flashback Pheasant Tail Nymph dropper. I quickly caught a dozen fish. Surprisingly two were fat seventeen inches. A young Orvis-dressed woman, who had been fishing the next hole downriver approached and stated in a haughty tone "you're using nymphs aren't you?' I was surprised by her attitude and replied "yes, behind a dry fly, would you like a few flys?" Up went her nose, "No, I have hundreds of flys, this is dry fly water." I was irritated and asked where she was from. Folks from around here don't act that way. "California" she proudly replied, and said she and her husband liked this river so much they were thinking about buying a place in town. I hope not. I wished her a good day, while she was rambling something about the environment, and headed back to camp. I lost interest in fishing for the rest of the day.

October 11, 2008
A few more members of Washington County Fly Fishers arrived early in the morning and we were on the water around 9am. Oregon Fish and Wildlife was doing research on the stretch of the Crooked River we were fishing, and they had a dozen fishers from the Central Oregon Fly Fishers catching and tagging fish. The wind was picking up. It was getting colder and too many people were on the river. The propane cook stove blew-out a couple of times as Dave Wesley cooked

hamburgers for the group. Around 2pm we all packed up and headed home. It was just too cold and windy to enjoy fishing.

October 21, 2008
I gave a presentation at the Northwest Fly Fishers club in Portland about lake fishing.

October 28, 2008
The weatherman forecasted that this would be the last warm, sunny day of the year, and that rain would set in over the next few days for the winter. Paul Skelton and I set out early to fish Coldwater Lake near Mt Saint Helens, Washington. I rigged up a #14 Tri-Color Damsel Nymph and hooked a fish fifty feet from the put-in. I was surprised at his strength. He kept up a good fight for ten minutes, stripping line deep several times. Coldwater is known for its strong fish. I landed a seventeen inch rainbow and quickly released him.

Rainbow Trout, Coldwater Lake, Washington

I caught the next fish twenty minutes later. He was only fourteen inches but ounce-for-ounce just as strong as the first fish. Paul caught four more fish further out in the deeper, open water. In the late afternoon the wind started to blow and it became too cold to fish. The water temperature was in the forties. I caught one more fish in the same location as the first fish, right in front of a group of German tourists. They all wanted photos. We had the same experience during our last two trips to Coldwater, except they were Japanese tourists. We look forward to returning next spring when things warm up. I don't know how long Coldwater will be a secret, but I hope for a long time.

November 1, 2008
We had a successful 11th Annual Fly Tyers Rendezvous at Mt. Hood Community College in Gresham, Oregon. I was the Fly Tyer Chair and responsible for lining up four dozen tyers for the day. It was a fair amount of work, meeting with the board monthly and organizing the event, but we had a good turn-out and a great time.

November 8, 2008
Washington County Fly Fishers scheduled a steelhead trip to the Deschutes River, but because of the cold rain, few people showed up. I was having difficulty casting my Spey rod and stopped by the Deschutes Anglers Fly Shop in Maupin to get a new line that would balance my rod. The shop help said I'd been using the wrong type of line for my rod the past two years. No wonder I was getting frustrated casting. They sold me a new line. Paul Skelton and I parked at the locked gate and hiked up to the cattle guard to fish a long steelhead run. A couple of other anglers were there with trout rods. One had already landed a steelhead earlier that morning. We swung dark #4 hair-wing streamers through the run and had no hits. The new line made casting a pleasure. I finally got the "Snap-T" cast down and had no problems with the Double Spey cast. We ran into Chuck Cooney and Tom Wideman on the walk out and fished together the rest of the day. I watched a guy land a steelhead across the river just upstream from where I caught my first Deschutes summer steelhead almost twenty years ago. Some fish you remember for life. Just about dark I noticed several trout rising to blue wing olives and October Caddis. I borrowed Tom's trout rod for a few casts and hooked a nice trout. The rain turned from rain to showers and we headed home.

December 13, 2008
I was commissioned by Nike Sportswear to tie and frame a collection of steelhead flys for one of their professional snowboarders.

December 27, 2008
We had a break in northwestern Oregon's record snowfall (almost two feet of snow) so Tom Wideman, Chuck Cooney, and I headed to the coast to chase steelhead in the rivers near Tillamook. Not far from Banks, Oregon the sheriff had blocked the highway because of fallen trees. We spent the rest of the day visiting the metro Portland area fly shops.

2009

January 10, 2009
I was invited to tye flys at a fly tying event organized by a student for his senior project at St. Helens High School. He did it as a fund raiser for the American Cancer Society. A dozen of us tied flys all the day for about fifty guests. We had a great time.

January 17, 2009
Tom Wideman and Chuck Cooney needed a fishing trip and convinced my wife that I needed a day off. We headed to the coast a 6am on a foggy Saturday morning. Even though I did not need breakfast, we had hash browns and eggs at Alice's Restaurant. We parked at the top of the mine field hole and rigged-up our Spey rods and waded into the river.

Spey Rod, Wilson River, Oregon

I was trying a new Skagit line with a ten foot sink tip, which cast really easy. I could throw it across the river. According to the water gage the river was about five feet deep and very green. It was a big, bright fly day. I fished a #4 Orange-Purple Marabou Popsicle. By 1pm we had not seen a fish even though several drift boaters had picked up a couple of steelhead on corkies and yarn. We headed into Tillamook for lunch and then onto the Kilchis River. The Kikchis was low and clear. If there were fish we would have seen them. I put on a smaller fly and hiked upstream from the county park and fished a couple of holes. The fish had the advantage in the low water. On the way home we fished the Wilson River upstream of Mills Bridge. We saw no fish but did scare a few gulls off a large Chinook salmon carcass. He would have been a nice catch last fall. It's funny how birds are always a part of fishing, either on the wing or on the hook.

January 31, 2009
Tom Wideman invited me to fish the Wilson River. The real estate market had been slow and he needed a break. The weather was clear, the river was stable, and the water level was slightly falling. While having breakfast at Alice's Restaurant the waitress asked if we were participating in the annual Tillamook steelhead derby. We could not have picked a worse weekend to fish. Gear fishermen rarely allow fly casters enough room to swing a fly. We headed up river where boats could not drift and tried a few holes with no luck. I got some more practice on my Spey rod and could throw a Skagit line almost seventy feet. We'll give the river another try some other weekend.

February 28, 2009
I gave a fly tying demonstration at Jack Hagen's Northwest Fly Fishing Shop in Portland, Oregon. The theme was "a new twist on old patterns."

March 11, 2009
Tom Wideman came over a few days before to drop off a few flys he wanted me to tie for him. We decided to fish the Wilson River and Tom agreed to pick me up early a few days later. Late the night before our trip, Tom called from the hospital – he was being wheeled in for surgery to get his appendix removed. He apologized profusely about canceling the fishing trip. I think he was still under anesthetics as he hardly made sense over the phone. I told him he still had a couple of hours until daylight, but he insisted he could not make it. It's tough finding a good fishing partner.

March 14, 2009
I tied at the Oregon Council of the Federation of Fly Fisher's 21st Annual Northwest Fly Tyers Exposition, in Albany, Oregon. I tied a Living Damsel which had a woven marabou tail. There were over 150 tiers from around the country and a thousand visitors attending the convention. I gave away five dozen flys and met some nice people and learned some new techniques.

March 30, 2009

I flew from Seattle to Anchorage to teach a class in Delta Junction, Alaska. As usual I fell asleep on the plane and woke up to the stewardess welcoming us to Fairbanks. What? We were supposed to land in Anchorage. The Mt. Redoubt volcano erupted (again) and all flights in and out of Anchorage were canceled for most of the week. I called the Fairbanks field office, borrowed a truck and checked into a motel. My class was not for two days so I had a day to kill before driving a half day south to Delta Junction. I tied a couple dozen flys then pulled out the yellow pages to find the closest fly shop, which happened to be less than a mile away. The shop was well stocked and the hired help was bored. We got to talking and discovered we'd grown up in the same town. What are the odds? We spent the rest of the afternoon talking about old fishing haunts, exchanging fly patterns and catching up on mutual friends. He'd wanted to get away from it all and found refuge in the hinterlands of Alaska. He survived on minimum wage, had plenty of work and spent his free time fishing.

April 8, 2009

Work interfered with fishing lately, and took me to Washington DC, Atlanta, Georgia, and Fairbanks, Alaska. Tom Wideman, Chuck Cooney, and I headed for the Deschutes River just ahead of a storm. It was raining in the valley, but the weatherman promised a dry day on the east side of the Cascades. We put our rods together in the first meadow up from Maupin and began casting heavily weighted nymphs and small droppers below indicators.

Redside Trout, Deschutes River, Oregon

I hooked a fish in ten minutes, a ten inch rainbow. Before lunch we each had picked up half dozen fish. The biggest was sixteen inches. The wind really picked up and made casting difficult. We headed up river looking for protection from the wind. Gusts were over fifty mph and dust blew up from the gravel road into our eyes. We fished a couple more take-outs until giving up for the day. I'd caught a dozen fish, mostly on a #18 Bead Head Flashback Pheasant Tail Nymph. On the way home we sat by the fireplace and ate hamburgers at Calamity Jane's Restaurant just outside of Gresham, Oregon.

April 15, 2009

Tax day. Tom Wideman and I fished Lost Lake in Clatsop County, Oregon. I missed fishing Lost Lake last year and was looking forward to fishing this quiet, secluded lake in the Coast Range. A Bald Eagle was circling the lake when we arrived and fish were jumping out of the water everywhere. It was a little on the chilly side and foggy, but no rain. Tom forgot the seat to his pontoon boat so we improvised with a piece of rubber floor mat from my trailer, which seemed to work fine. I put on a #16 Adams and hooked a half dozen fish before Tom got on the water. Hoping to pick up a displaced steelhead, I switched flys to a #16 Callibaetis Nymph and trolled the far end of the lake where I caught a steelhead a few years ago. No steelhead, but I caught dozens of hatchery trout. Looking for a challenge I anchored my pontoon near the middle of the lake, where most fish were rising, and tied on a #8 Yellow Stimulator. Thinking no fish in their right mind would take that fly. I was wrong, the fish went nuts over it. Every other cast brought a ten to twelve inch fish. I began stripping the fly away from fish but they kept coming, sometimes two and three fish at a time. By mid-afternoon we were cold and no longer challenged by the fish. We headed to the Nehalem River for a shot at late winter steelhead. We rigged up at Spruce Run Campground and threw heavy marabou flys into a deep, swift run next to shore. I caught a foot long bright sea-run Cutthroat near where a small creek entered the river, but that was it for the day. We got home around 6pm cold and tired.

April 18, 2009
The Washington County Fly Fishers fished Vernonia Pond. About a half dozen of us spent the day fishing for stocked trout. When the fog lifted we could see several dozen bank fishermen on the far shore. It was a mad-house but we had a great time. I caught and released about three dozen foot long trout on a #12 Bead Head Possie Bugger. I tried a #12 Yellow Stimulator on the surface, but could only entice two fish. Even though these were hatchery fish, they were somewhat selective. They were full of midge pupa, burping them up as we held them in our hands. I suppose a few weeks after being dumped into lakes and rivers stocked fish act like wild fish in the sense that they key in on local insects and learn to avoid unnatural foods. I also caught a couple of hand-size bluegill, a few crappie and one six inch largemouth bass. Late in the afternoon we scouted out boat launches on the Nehalem River around Big Eddy County Park. We planned to float the river for cutthroats after the season opener.

May 1, 2009
I headed out on a 2,500 mile road trip to move our daughter Bethany from winter to summer college student housing. En route I stopped to camp and fish the Owhyee River, a little over half way to Logan, Utah. I had a tail-wind most of the drive as a storm front pushed me eastward.

Brown Trout, Owhyee River, Oregon

I fished about three hours before sundown. The fish were running a little smaller this year. The first fish was a sixteen inch brown, who took my #14 Elk Hair Caddis as soon as it hit the water along the bank. I did not get a rise on the next dozen casts and switched to a heavily weighted #12 Possie Bugger and picked up two more browns with a combination dead-drift and swing through a fast deep hole (without an indicator). I'd planned to fish the next day but it started to rain just past midnight and it was still pouring the next morning. I hit the road toward Utah.

May 5, 2009
I'd wanted to fish the Weber River near Coleville, Utah, but it was running high and off-color so the next logical choice was the Green River. I arrived just after noon and headed up river from Little Hole and fished the A-Section below Flaming Gorge Dam. There were a hundred boat trailers in the parking lot, but only a handful of bank-walkers. We had plenty of room. Fish were rising everywhere on the shallow weed-bottomed flats, taking midges. I noticed a large brown rising no more than two feet from shore and quickly fired an Elk Hair Caddis at him. He took the fly but I was slow on the set and missed him. In this stretch of water most of the fish were in the middle of the river. I cast a dozen different patterns until I found the right one and caught a skinny eighteen inch brown. He took a #22 Midge Pupa that was a dropper behind an Elk Hair Caddis. The fish were at least a forty foot cast away and an indicator fly was necessary to see the fish take. These fish would inhale and spit out a fly in a fraction of a second. If you missed the take you caught no fish. The wind picked up and I hiked upstream and found a deep, short run near shore out of the wind where three fish were taking Blue Wing Olive emergers. I cast for over an hour and had several hits but could not hook a fish. I ran into a stick, sharpened by a beaver, in the tall grass that put a hole through my waders. I desperately headed to the fly shop for wader repair cement, but they were out. The next fly shop was five miles away and I got there just as they were closing. I fixed the waders in the dark with my flash light at Dripping Springs Campground and went to sleep early in the back of the car.

May 6, 2009
The second day on the Green River was much better. I was the first car in the parking lot and took a few casts at the take-out to see if my wader repair worked. It did. I met a fly fishing club from

Colorado who invited me to fish with them for the morning. We exchanged a few flys and they showed me a good place to wade across the river to fish the other side (the riffle was just upstream from the board walk below the cliff). Fish began rising and taking midge pupa just after 10am and I began taking fish. I caught three eighteen to twenty inch browns in about two hours in the same run. They all took #22 Midge Pupa behind a #14 Elk Hair Caddis. About 2pm they began refusing my pupa pattern so I tried several others with no success. I finally realized they were no longer taking midges but had switched to mayfly emergers. I promptly switched to a #22 RS2 Emerger and began catching fish again.

Brown Trout, Green River, Utah

These fish sure were picky and focused. I lost track of the number of fish after the first half dozen, but they all came from the same run. It appeared they would move from mid-stream to shore and back to mid-stream regularly. A spooked fish soon replaced an eager fish. For every fish I hooked, I lost three others that inhaled my fly – I was too slow to set the hook. The water was running at 850 cfs and was so clear I could see every take. Around 4pm the fish stopped rising. I had a late lunch of pork-and-beans, packed up my gear, waded across the river, and headed back to the car. I camped that night on Sheep Creek just above the reservoir. The next morning I awoke to the smell of skunk and hoped it had not sprayed my car. Luckily for me (and not the skunk) it was road-kill on the highway a quarter mile upwind. Next I headed up the Connor Basin Road just outside of Manila, Utah, to see my grandparent's old ranch. There were

deer everywhere and the pasture and range grasses were as green and the soil was red just how I remembered as a kid.

May 8, 2009

On the way home from Utah I camped at Wolf Creek near North Powder, Oregon and drove the long way on Highway 26, through Tygh Valley to the Deschutes River early in the morning. It was hot, not a cloud in the sky, and the river was high and off-color. I fished the first flat above Maupin and did not even get a rise to my Elk Hair Caddis and Pheasant Tail dropper. I also had no luck with a San Juan Worm. I switched to a heavily weighted #12 Possie Bugger and Pheasant Tail dropper and fished the first deep back-eddy above Box Car Rapids. I let my indicator float the fly off the bottom and swirl around in the whirlpool, and quickly hooked and landed a skinny seventeen inch Redside. I put my fly rod under the car's windshield wiper blade and drove up river and parked at Wapinitia, intending to fish up to Harpham Flats. I immediately caught a twelve inch trout at the take-out on the Possie Bugger.

Redside Trout, Deschutes River, Oregon

Fifty yards up river I cast into a fast, deep run next to shore and was rewarded with a very nice eighteen inch rainbow. He jumped several times, hit the fast current, began rolling, and broke off before I could bring him over my net. He took the #18 Pheasant Tail dropper and was a beautiful fish. The next hole up river I cast into the fast current of a back eddy that dropped into a deep hole and caught and landed the previous trout's twin on the Possie Bugger. It's not every trip to the Deschutes you catch three trout over eighteen inches. I landed another half dozen trout on nymphs before dark, all between ten to fourteen inches. I'd put an unopened can of soup on the dashboard of my car to warm in the sun. It was hot and tasted good in the chill of the early evening. I got home before 10pm after covering about 2,500 miles in a week.

May 16, 2009

The weather forecaster predicted the first 90 degree day of the year. It was time to head up the mountain and soak in the lake. I fished with Washington County Fly Fishers and caught a ride with Phil Oliver and Greg McCarty to Rock Creek Reservoir on the back side of Mt. Hood. The campground was full and the lake had a dozen electric motor boats trolling ford fenders or flinging power bait. I put on a heavily weighted streamer and dredged the bottom for trout. After two hours I'd only had three hits and no fish. The fish were in the shallow water under the weeds. It was 80 degrees at noon and not a cloud in the sky. I enjoyed watching the black birds chase the osprey and the osprey harass the bald eagles. The birds of prey were catching fish, we were not. It was still too early in the season for the aquatic vegetation to grow in the shallows and lure trout with insects and cover. Around 1pm the wind picked up and brought a cloud of winged termites over the lake. The bugs were huge, some measuring an inch long. The fish went crazy, rising all over the lake. I put down the anchor on my pontoon boat, tied on a #14 Dark Brown Comparadun and immediately caught three rising fish, each a twelve inch hatchery rainbow. By now there were thousands of ants on the water, about a half dozen ants per square yard. As the ant numbers increased, the fish became more difficult to catch. To interest a fish we had to predict the trout's travel path and put the fly two or three feet on front of the previous rise. Odds were the fish would take a natural so I only hooked one fish every three dozen casts. During the height of the hatch I switched to a #12 Foam Ant and only caught three fish in two hours. There were just too many insects on the water. Later in the afternoon the wind died down and many of the remaining insects were either eaten, drowned or washed to shore. We began catching fish again. I put on a #14 Parachute Adams, cast to rises and caught another dozen fish.

Rainbow, Rock Creek Reservoir, Oregon

By dinner time we were hot, tired and ready to call it quits. We took a short cut home across the White River and through snow banks on Mt. Hood.

June 17, 2009

Chuck Cooney grew up near Condon, Oregon and invited a couple of friends to fish the nearby John Day River for smallmouth bass. Chuck picked me up at 5:30am and we met Tom Wideman and Dave Wesley at Biggs junction for breakfast. We rented a house in Spray, Oregon as our base camp. We scouted state highway 19 for put-ins and unloaded the pontoon boats at Kimberly near the bridge and shuttled the car downriver about eight miles to the state highway gravel pit. I stayed to watch the boats and before the shuttle car returned I'd already caught six bass in a backwater slough. Unfortunately I left my waders at the house and had to wet-wade the river, which was not too bad because the water was about 60 degrees. We had found in the past that the best river level was around 800 csf. This week it was running high and a little off color at 1,300 cfs. We fished cork poppers, Chernobyl Ants, and large foam patterns and all caught fish. I'd guess we each caught three dozen fish before a storm front kicked up in the late afternoon and the wind blew us off the river. At the take-out a large rattlesnake greeted us and was not happy about it. We played with him for a while with long sticks before he coiled up and started hissing at us: time to move on. Chuck volunteered to be the cook and prepared excellent barbecue chicken and salad, Tom provided entertainment, Dave kept things reasonable, and I washed dishes.

June 18, 2009
In the morning we put-in about five miles downriver from Spray at an unimproved campground along the highway. Today I remembered my waders. But they were of no use because I immediately became soaking wet when I stepped into a deep hole in the river and my waders leaked. I'd patched and repaired them several times over the previous months but missed a few holes. I decided that they would go in the trash at the end of this trip. We began catching fish in the backwater of the first hole. We each hooked over a hundred fish over the eight miles downstream. Dave caught the biggest fish, several running about fifteen inches. Most fish were in the ten to twelve inch range and all readily took surface flys. We had the most success floating down the middle of the river, using our fins to keep our pontoon boats pointed toward shore and casting at the shoreline. Where the high water flooded the shoreline grass and provided under water cover were the most productive areas. Where there were grass tops poking out of the water, there were bass.

John Day River, Oregon

The next best water was stagnant back-water pools covered with foam and a thin layer of organic debris. Halfway through our float I cornered a mule deer at the base of a cliff and she swam across the river in front of my boat less than a cast away. We took out eight miles downriver at Service Creek where there were over a hundred vehicles and trailers. There were a few fishermen on the water and almost every boat was filled with joy riders. We'd only seen two other boats on the river today, and were surprised to see so many people at the take-out. We decided not to float from Service Creek to Twickenham tomorrow like we'd planned, but decided to head back up river. Chuck fixed T-bone steaks, fresh asparagus, and ice cream for dinner.

June 19, 2009
This was our last day on the river. We put in at a small campground about two miles up the North Fork of the John Day River. The water was clear until it emptied in the main stem. We hoped to catch a few trout but only caught bass and a couple of Squawfish (Northern Pike Minnow). We enjoyed a few thunder and lightning strikes and a brief rain squall as a storm passed in the late morning. We each caught another hundred bass each before we took out at the state highway gravel pit (about three miles upriver from Spray). We were disappointed that the rattlesnake was not there to welcome us at the take-out. Apparently he was scared off by the hundreds of mosquitoes in the willows. Chuck fixed pork chops and potatoes for dinner. It's been a long time since I've eaten so well during a fishing trip. We re-booked the house for the same week, next year. Total trip cost for three days of fishing was $140.

Smallmouth Bass, John Day River, Oregon

June 24, 2009
A couple of us from the fly club had planned a weeklong Alaska fishing trip for almost a year. The trip began well, but quickly become a Lewis and Clark like expedition. Our group of six consisted of: Greg Kohn who organized the trip with help from his friend from Rainbow River Lodge on Lake Iliamna, Alaska; Pete Prepke from the River City Fly Shop and his brother Ed, both

Pacific northwest coastal river fisherman; Ben Hedberg a steelhead Spey fly fanatic and his father Ralph, an experienced Minnesota Boundary Waters canoeist; and myself. We flew from Portland, Oregon and stayed at a cheap motel in Anchorage the first night. We sorted our gear, studied maps and made plans for our forty mile float down American Creek in the Katmai Wilderness Area of Katmai National Park on southwest Alaska's peninsula.

June 25, 2009

This morning we took a taxi to Merrill Field and caught a small chartered prop plane to Iliamna where we met Chad Hewitt from Rainbow River Lodge at the airport. We loaded our gear into Chad's float planes for a short trip to Rainbow River Lodge for lunch and to reorganize our gear for the float trip. I brought seventy pounds of gear including one change of clothes for every three days on the river, an emergency survival-first aid kit, two polar fleece jackets (in case one got wet), sleeping bag, boots-waders, one six and two seven weight fly rods, three reels with two floating and one sink-tip line, fifteen, ten, and five pound leader and tippet and about fifteen dozen flys packed in small waterproof bags. The lodge provided two fourteen-foot rafts, two six-man tents, sleeping cots-pads, and cooking equipment. It took two float planes to get the six of us and our gear to Hammersly Lake, the headwater of American Creek. We saw several caribou on a high ridge and a couple of large brown bears (fish eating grizzly bear) along waterways on the hour long flight to the lake. We had the rafts pumped up and our gear loaded as the float planes buzzed us on their return flight back to the lodge. We were on our own for the next six days and forty miles of river. The first three miles of river were rough. The water level was low for this time of year (we were later told it was more like August water levels) and we had to push the rafts off submerged rocks every fifty feet or so. Luckily the rocks were rounded by glaciers and river tumbling and had some algae growth which made them slick and less prone to puncher our rafts. The terrain was sub-alpine tundra with granite soils covered with thick lichens, mosses, small brush, short willows, grasses, and not a tree in sight. We stopped at the first large hole and quickly rigged up our fly rods. I cast into the head of the pool and on the third cast hooked and landed an

eighteen inch char that gave my seven weight rod a workout. We were not sure if the fish were resident char or anadromous char (also known as Dolly Varden). We called them char. Pete stepped up next and cast into the same spot and immediately hooked an even larger char. Not to be outdone I cast a few minutes later and hooked an even larger char. We pitched our tents on the only level stop, a swampy area covered with sedges. It really did not matter where we placed the tents because we were off the ground in cots. It rained a little after we set up camp, but the weather quickly cleared. We fished late into the day, caught a dozen big char, and a few rainbows. We had freeze-dried spaghetti and dried fruit for dinner and headed to the tents around 11pm in full daylight.

Char, American Creek, Alaska

June 26, 2009

The next morning we rose around 8am and ate oatmeal and granola bars for breakfast while watching a large brown bear walk across a ridge about a quarter mile behind our camp. We had two hours of darkness the night before. The sun disappeared behind the horizon about 10pm but it was only dark from about 1 to 3am, and the sun rose again around 9am. We had very long dusks and dawns, which were perfect for fishing. We caught over a dozen large fish within a quarter mile of camp. We fished a couple of different streamers and found that the best fly was an olive and white #6 Dolly Llama, tied with two five-inch strips of rabbit hide and bar-bell weighted heads. The fish averaged twenty inches and about eighty percent were char and twenty percent rainbow trout. Another bear walked the high bench above the river downstream from camp where Ben was fishing, but he never saw it. We packed our gear and did another two miles of rock-hopping rafting in gently rolling tundra country before entering a canyon. We tied the rafts to the willows above a class III rapid and scouted the rough water. The situation did not look good so we lowered both rafts through the rapids with long ropes. It was hard work over the next two miles rowing, pushing, and pulling the raft in the shallow, fast, rough water. While pushing the raft off a particularly stubborn rock, I made an acrobatic fall in the cold water and got drenched. Ralph and Ben caught fish in the fast pocket water while I emptied water out of my waders and waited for the other raft to catch up. Ed pointed out a large moose on the side of a hill in the distance, which was being followed by a bear. We scouted the next large hole and found a very good campsite.

American Creek, Alaska

Two bald eagles were nesting across the river near a large cliff. Everyone caught fish in the deep hole and tail-out while I dried my clothes and waders. Ed caught a fat twenty five inch rainbow on a streamer. From camp I watched two large bears walk across a meadow and ridge about a quarter mile away. When my waders were dry I suited up and headed to the top of the run and immediately noticed bear tracks on top of our tracks in the mud along the river. A bear apparently was heading downstream when he saw our camp and detoured in a large willow patch above camp. We decided to set up the portable solar powered electric fence around our tents to deter bears. After dinner, fish were rising throughout the pool on what we assumed to be caddis. I quickly

hooked three large char and landed one twenty two inch fish on a dead drifted #14 Yellow Stimulator.

June 27, 2009

In the morning I caught another four fish on the #14 Stimulator, averaging twenty inches and three to four pounds. Before noon we did another four miles of raft rock-hopping and were grateful for a short stretch of slower, slightly deeper water. At least we were not getting stuck on a rock every hundred feet. We left tundra country mid-way through the canyon and entered cottonwood and spruce forest. The river began to split into side channels and we had to stop often, scout downstream and guess the best channel to float. Log jams, low hanging trees, and sweepers slowed our pace. For the most part we made the right decisions and only had to drag the rafts a couple of times. At least we did not have to back track up river or portage over land. At one particularly large, impassable log jam we had to drag the rafts through a quarter mile of side channel in inches of water. We were tired, but not too tired to fish. Below the log jam I caught three char in three casts. While we were dragging the raft over a shallow section, the safety clip on one of the cans of bear-spray came off and an oar handle hit the button and sprayed red pepper inside of the raft! Small cuts on our hands burned the rest of the day until the pepper dissipated. I was worried the pepper would negatively affect the fishing. At the next hole I thoroughly fished a lightly weighted #6 Green and White Clouser and did not get a hit. I switched to a heavier bar-bell eyed olive and white #6 Dolly Llama and immediately caught two eighteen inch char and a beautiful twenty four inch rainbow in three casts. It was not the pepper spray but the fly that influenced the fishing. We had brief showers of light rain late in the afternoon and quickly found a gravel bar and set up camp. Ralph, Ben and I got our tent up minutes before a barrage of hail. Greg, Pete and Ed were not so lucky. Their tent was flat on the ground and within seconds was covered with quarter inch hail, in some places a half inch deep. We collected hail for iced drinks for dinner, but most of the hail melted within half an hour. After the storm a very wet brown bear visited us across the river and upstream about forty yards from camp. We all stood and yelled and the bear headed into the woods. We had freeze-dried stroganoff for dinner. Ben and I tried to build a fire with wet wood, I gave up early. Ralph found a dry stump and Ben had a fire going within an hour. He'd learned a few fire starting tricks growing up in Minnesota. We caught a few fish in the fast run in front of camp, but it was not the best fishing water.

June 28, 2009

Before we packed our camp and loaded the rafts, I caught three fish in three casts in front of camp. Ed borrowed my rod and caught another fish a couple of casts later. They were all char averaging eighteen inches. It looked like it was going to be a good day. I caught a beautiful chunky rainbow at the next deep hole, twenty-four inches long with a twelve inch girth. The water was much better for rafting; we only had to stop every 1,000 feet to drag off a rock. Ben did a good job captaining our raft. Greg and his crew were scrambling to keep up in their slightly heavier craft. We entered a deep canyon with sheer cliffs on both sides of the river. We parked the rafts at two very deep holes and could see dozens of fish in the crystal clear water. Some of the fish had to be over thirty inches long, but we could not bring them to the hook. I spotted for Ben as he swung his fly within inches of some of the biggest fish on the bottom of the pool. We caught many eighteen to twenty two inch fish, and a few twelve inchers, but no lunkers.

Rainbow Trout, American Creek, Alaska

We stopped at another deep hole a mile down the river and each caught several twenty inch char and rainbow. A few miles downstream we entered the braided water where there were many side

channels, entire trees across the water, and lots of woody debris. We met two guides and five fishermen, who helped get us through a particularly bad section of water. Both guides had stainless steel shotguns strapped to their backs. We had to drag our rafts thirty yards through a side channel in inches of water, up the main river through twenty yards of fast water and through another quarter mile of side channel. We took a break when we got back to the main channel, but stayed too long. A large bear crossed the channel twenty yards behind us where we had been dragging the rafts. Apparently he had been watching us from the tall grass in the side channel and waited for us to pass.

American Creek, Alaska

We immediately jumped in the raft and took off down river, stopping a hundred yards downstream to drag the rafts around another fallen, half submerged cottonwood tree. We past the guide's camp and set up our camp on a gravel bar a mile downstream. We'd had mosquitoes throughout the trip, but they were particularly bad at this camp because of the standing water in the side channels. We found some dry wood and quickly built a smoky fire which helped abate the pesky insects. We enjoyed the fire, had freeze-dried beef stew, and were about to turn in for the night when a large blond bear and her yearling cub appeared sixty feet away in the willows behind our tents. They were as surprised as we were and they quickly lumbered up stream until they were out of sight. We put more wood on the fire. About a half hour later another bear appeared fifty yards up stream and was heading downstream in our direction. He was across the river from our camp when we began yelling at him. He quickly disappeared into the cottonwoods. Apparently the bears were congregating for the anticipated sockeye run from Bristol Bay which was not supposed to happen for another couple of weeks. The shallow braided water and small channels were perfect for a bear to corner and trap a large spawning salmon. Of course the same is true for an unsuspecting fisherman.

June 29, 2009

I left camp earlier than the others to explore several small pools behind our camp and immediately saw the tracks of the bears from last night and also several large wolf tracks. I shouted "Yo bear, yo bear" while walking through a dry channel surrounded by tall willows, birch and cottonwood trees. The shallow slough water was filled with sockeye fry that darted away at the sight of my shadow. Most of the water was too shallow for large trout, except for a few widely spaced holes. I did not see a fish so I returned to camp an hour later. Ben and I rigged up #2 Mouse patterns and headed up the main channel looking for large carnivorous trout. I found a small back eddy behind a sunken log and flung my mouse into the water and gave it two twitches before a large nose appeared and engulfed my fly. I set the hook and the water exploded. The fish jumped twice, darted around the small pool several times, then headed to the main river and downstream, taking me into my line backing.

Rainbow Trout, American Creek, Alaska

I caught up with him five minutes later and landed a hefty twenty four inch rainbow on the sandy beach. A few minutes later Ben also landed a

twenty four inch rainbow, who took his mouse in front of an undercut log jam. We continued to fish a small side channel and picked up a couple of more twenty inch trout before returning to camp. The sun was up past the tall trees and there was not a cloud in the sky. Caddis and small stoneflys began hatching when Greg and I headed back to the channels I'd fished earlier in the morning and saw several fish rising before we got to the water. We tied on #12 Elk Hair Caddis and Greg immediately hooked a large fish who wrapped around a submerged tree branch. I threw my fly into a deep whirl pool and hooked an eighteen inch rainbow that jumped three feet into the air several times before I landed him. Greg hooked and lost several fish to the brush before finally landing a twenty four inch rainbow. I hooked and landed two more five pound rainbows, one from the whirlpool and the other in a pool under a large overhanging willow branch. We rested the pool and fished upstream catching several more rainbows. We returned to the pool an hour later and hooked two large char and several smaller fish. We rested the pool again and returned to camp to learn from the others that three large brown bears had patrolled the water across the river. I encouraged Pete and Ed to check out the pool we had just fished and they returned two hours later after catching several more good fish. We packed up camp and headed downriver two miles to find lots of woody debris and two more bears before setting up camp for another day in the braided water.

June 30, 2009

We awoke at 6am to gun shot. We must be close to where jet boats can reach the lower river from Coville Lake. Ben and I fished the braided water below camp and did not spot a fish in a mile of water. We did locate a parked jet boat that must have arrived very early this morning. We found a nice run with shallow water over fine gravel dumping into a deep hole. We could not bring any fish to the surface with a dry fly, so I tied on a heavy stonefly nymph and landed a large fat char. Fish began rising, but would not take our Elk Hair Caddis. We assumed they were taking migrating sockeye fry near the surface so I tied on a small hair wing fry pattern and hooked two more three pound char. Ben picked up a nice rainbow on a rabbit leech. Around mid-morning the hatch began and I hooked a two foot-long char on an

Elk Hair Caddis. We thought we heard a bear splash across the small channel upstream and knew it was a bear when he appeared twenty five feet away in the willows. Ben yelled and I blew my whistle and the grizzly turned away from us, returned back to the stream bank and finally ran into a small meadow of tall grass across from where we were fishing. Ben headed up stream and I continued to fish the deep hole. I picked up four more fish including a very nice twenty five inch rainbow. I followed Ben upstream and picked up another nice rainbow in a small pocket of slow water next to a fast run and two more rainbows that were rising in a deep slot behind a half-submerged willow tree that had sloughed off the riverbank. Back at camp we learned that four more brown bears had visited our gravel bar. One entered and re-entered the river until he was scared away. Ed and Pete watched another bear chase fish through a shallow run they were fishing four times before heading back into the woods. Everyone was catching fish. Just below camp I noticed a large fish flash in a small slot where fast water formed a small "V" as it flowed out of a large log jam. There was a large submerged root wad on the left and a sunken tree branch on the right. The first cast got tangled in the root wad and I broke off my fly. The fish rose to my fly on the second cast but I could not set the hook. The third cast was right on target and the fight was on. The fish jumped into the submerged tree branch and slid out without getting snarled. He then ran upstream and around the back side of the root wad and I thought I'd lost him. I gave him some slack line and then a short tug and was surprised to find him heading back upstream and around the root wad and into unobstructed water. I held him there for two minutes, pulling harder than I thought my ten pound tippet could handle. He tired out and I netted a beautiful twenty six inch rainbow. I figured it was a good time to stop fishing, enjoy the moment, and pack up camp. We saw three more bear over the next two miles as we floated downriver through a jumble of river debris. We took the wrong channel and had to tow the rafts up river about a quarter mile before getting back to open water. I hooked a four pound rainbow while drifting through a nice run, so we beached our raft to fish. Ralph soon hooked a big fish on a dry fly as Ben swung his Spey rod through the hole. A bear appeared upstream and another bear downstream, both across the river.

We fished two more deep runs and picked up a couple of more fish before entering the portion of the river that looked like it was tidally influenced. We were at least one hundred miles from saltwater so the tidal effect must be from Coville Lake filling and backing up water into the river. It was getting late when we arrived at what we thought was the last riffle and deep run before entering the completely flat water above the lake. A fish rose on the far bank as we set up our rods. Ben fished the tail-out and picked up half a dozen big char.

Char, American Creek, Alaska

I cast dry flys along the slower stream bank water with no luck. Ralph took photos of the sunset and moon rise. Around 11pm the pool erupted, fish were rising everywhere. They were not taking caddis so I switched to a small hair-wing fry pattern and began hooking fish, lots of fish. Ralph and Ben quickly joined me and we swung fry patterns over a gravel lip into deep water, getting a hit on almost every cast. We could walk the shallow water on the gravel bar almost completely across the river, hooking fish in the drop-off and walking the fish back to shore to land on the sandy beach. We literally hooked over fifty three and four pound fish in the next hour and a half. This pool and riffle was the first stopping point for adult fish migrating upstream from the lake. The fish were gorging themselves on waves of sockeye fry migrating downstream to the lake and ocean. We quit fishing around 12:30am so we had enough daylight to make the next two miles downriver to camp and the takeout point. It truly was the land of the midnight sun. The rest of the group had a nice camp fire when we arrived. We quickly set up our tent, battled mosquitoes, and had dinner before hitting the sack.

July 1, 2009

We awoke to full sunshine and quickly packed our gear on the beach before the float plane arrived a little after 9am. We flew to Iliamna, switched to a turbo prop plane, and flew back to Anchorage. A cloud covering the recent eruption of Mt. Redoubt in the Chigmit Mountain Range made the air smell of sulfur. In Anchorage we got a motel room around 2pm for a shower, and a non-freeze-dried dinner, before catching a flight back to Portland that night at 1am. What a great trip. It was more of an adventure trip than a fishing trip. We spent most of the time getting through very rough terrain and difficult water and only had three or four hours of fishing each day. We were constantly on the lookout for predators and did not fish some areas for fear of bears. We floated some very difficult water which dropped 1,500 feet in forty miles. We experienced pristine alpine tundra, forested foothills, rock-cliff canyons, and grass-willow flats. We caught large, healthy, native fish and enjoyed the solitude of the Alaska wilderness. The trip cost $3,000 ($1,700 lodge providing float plane transportation, raft and camping gear; $650 Portland flight to and from Anchorage; $400 Anchorage flight to and from Iliamna; $150 food; and $100 for the motel and fishing license).

July 18, 2009

The summer was getting too hot and a little too humid. Tom Wideman and I headed to the coast range for a morning's worth of fishing on the Nestucca River. We parked the car a mile or so below Elk Creek in the artificial-lure-only water. We tied on #14 Elk Hair Caddis and wet waded up to the first pool. Tom immediately caught a thirteen inch resident cutthroat at the top of the pool in the foam water. It took me another half hour to catch an eight inch cutthroat. It felt good to be standing in water up to our knees in the forest shade. We fished several holes in the early morning with marginal luck, between us catching maybe a dozen trout. The fish were waiting for the day to warm up and produce more bugs. The cool shade of the forested canyon was what we really wanted. We headed home when it started to heat up, probably missing the best fishing of the day.

July 29, 2009

After nearly a week of upper ninety degree weather we headed for the hills to cool off. Chuck Cooney picked Tom Wideman and me up after work and we headed to south central Washington State. The sun was still shining on the top of Mt. Adams as we pulled into the campground at Takhlakh Lake. A cloud of mosquitoes harassed us as we set up out tent and caught a couple of hours of sleep. The bugs were still there in the morning as we unloaded our pontoon boats into the lake. The water was calm and warm. I'd guess about 70 degrees in the upper two feet. I put on an intermediate sinking line and a #14 Tri-Color Damsel and began trolling the edges of the lake. We hooked stocked twelve inch rainbows all morning, maybe catching two or three fish an hour. The fishing was slow. We shared the 300 acre lake with a dozen other fishermen who were mostly trolling hardware or casting bait. Around noon we stopped for lunch and watched several car-loads of people unload inner-tubes and air mattresses into the lake to cool off in the hot weather. It was time for us to check-out a less popular lake. A couple of miles down the road we had Council Lake all to ourselves. We caught a few fish, but it was getting hot in the mid-afternoon sunshine. I must be getting old. I took an hour long nap in the shade along shore. Fish began rising in the late afternoon in the shadows along the shoreline. We cast #14 Elk Hair Caddis and picked up a few stunted brook trout, the biggest maybe eight inches.

Brook Trout, Council Lake, Washington

Someone needed to harvest some of the trout. It was a welcome change from trolling deep for stocked rainbows. By four in the afternoon we lost our cool breeze and it became too hot to fish and we headed to shore. Near the boat launch in the shade of huge fir trees dozens of fish were cruising around in pods and rising to what we thought were midge pupa. Several fish would jump at once to some unseen insects. Between the three of us we tried a dozen patterns from #24 midges to #8 Stimulators. No luck, the fish were frustrating us. They were jumping everywhere, sometimes within a few feet of our pontoon boats. They ignored everything we threw at them. We left the lake defeated and humiliated, but made up for it with huckleberry milk shakes in the town of Trout Lake. We got home just before midnight.

August 15, 2009
Washington County Fly Fishers had a club trip to fish the Willamette River. About a dozen of us met at Begg Park just below the Canby Ferry and spread out along the river. I headed across the river to some old pilings. It took an hour for me to get a hook-up and I caught a nice seventeen inch smallmouth on an intermediate sinking line with a #10 Carey Bugger. I began fishing where rip-rap and vertical metal plates lined the shoreline, protecting an old bridge abutment. I noticed several fish swirl beneath the black berries hanging over the water, not sure if they were taking insects or the berries. A nice bass took my fly on the first cast, and I caught three more within thirty yards in half hour.

Smallmouth Bass, Willamette River, Oregon

The fishing really slowed in the late morning, we packed up and headed down river to Willamette

Park at the mouth of the Tualatin River. We kicked-rowed our pontoons up the river, against the current, a couple hundred yards to a short riffle dumping into a boulder field of deeper water. We fished there for several hours, and only got a few tugs and no fish. We had to try one more spot before quitting for the day. We headed down river again to Cedar Oak Park near West Linn, Oregon. We fished until 6pm and didn't even get a hit. There were a lot of water skiers and joy riders on the water. Our excuse was they disturbed the fish. It was a good day to be on the water even though we caught few fish.

August 22, 2009
Chuck Cooney called me at work and insisted on picking Tom Wideman and I up to go carp fishing. We thought Sauvie Island might be a good place to start. We visited the wildlife refuge headquarters for information and a map. The lady at the counter recommended a mile hike down a closed road to a lake at the north end of the island, which turned out to be a waste of time and just mud flats. The next two lakes were too shallow and the Gilbert River was too deep to spot feeding carp. We finally found a few tailing carp in a small bay next to the road. Chuck and I rigged up rods and Tom spotted for us from a small hill. We got within thirty yards of two carp, but they were not showing themselves consistently enough for us to put a fly on their noses in the muddy water. We gave up an hour later. It was getting dark. We decided to come back when we had more time to explore the island.

September 7, 2009
I got a call late the previous night from Paul Skelton inviting my son and me to put in some volunteer hours at the Trask River fish hatchery. We accepted and arrived at the hatchery to find the stock pen, just up from the fish ladder, full of adult spring Chinook and Coho salmon. Grady climbed down into the concrete pen with the hatchery manager and caught fish with a large square dip net. We released the native fish back into the fish ladder and they escaped back to the river. We sorted the biggest and healthiest fish into male and female pens for future spawning. The rest of the hatchery fish were killed. My job was to run a metal detector across each killed fish's nose to locate an identification tag (which was previously inserted into the juvenile fish's

snout). We processed about 150 fish and killed about 125.

Spring Chinook, Trask River, Oregon

The salmon weighed from seven to thirty pounds each. We kept a half dozen of the brightest Coho salmon for the Oregon Food Bank.

September 11, 2009
The Deschutes River had been fishing really well the first part of the week so Chuck Cooney and I decided to give it a try. We drove to Maupin and hiked up river from the locked gate at 7am. There was not a cloud in the sky and it was about 80 degrees when we reached the cattle guard hole. Chuck rigged his Spey rod to swing flys for steelhead – I figured it was too hot and sunny for steelhead and tyed on a heavy #12 Possie Bugger with a #18 Soft Hackle and yarn indicator. Chuck went fishless all morning, I ran into a rattlesnake. I headed back into the water to avoid more snakes. A short time later I caught a sixteen inch whitefish on the heavy nymph, in fast water, a few feet from shore. On the way back down river I was pushing through heavy willows and sagebrush with my rod pointing behind me to avoid getting caught in the brush. I thought my line was snagged on a limb because the reel sounded like it was clicking though the drag. I looked down and the reel was not spinning but I could still hear the drag, what was going on? A rattlesnake was coiled up three feet away! I slowly backed away, this time getting my line tangled in the brush. Minutes later the snake disappeared into the rocks and I retrieved my line. Downstream I let a large back-eddy do all the work moving my flys and indicator in a large circle. On the third pass a nice trout took my #18

Pheasant Tail Nymph and I landed him without any problems.

Redside Trout, Deschutes River, Oregon

That was the last fish of the day. It was getting hot under the full sunshine. I ran into another rattlesnake while fishing Harpham Flats campground. I've never seen this many rattlers on the Deschutes in one day. In the last hours of daylight we fished the first meadow and caddis were everywhere but we took no fish. Chuck did get a bump on the Spey rod, but nothing else. We picked up snacks in Maupin and made it home before midnight. Next trip we would try to pick a cloudy day.

September 19, 2009
Washington County Fly Fishers had a club outing to Coldwater Lake, Washington. I gave Greg McCarty a ride and we had about a dozen members attend. Mount St Helens was calm the past few months, but we couldn't tell because it was foggy and pouring rain all morning. I caught a ten inch trout first thing in the morning on a #12 Pheasant Tail Damselfly, with a clear intermediate sinking line. My second fish rose to a midge seconds after the fly hit the water. He fought quite hard relative to his size and I landed a very nice seventeen inch rainbow a few minutes later. The heavy rain seemed to improve the fishing. Over the next three hours I landed another half dozen trout ranging from fifteen to seventeen inches. We usually fish the west end of the lake near the boat ramp and the outlet where there is a rocky under-water ridge three to six feet deep that always holds fish. I gave two other guys in our club (who had not fished the lake before) my #12 Pheasant Tail

Damselfly and asked them to follow me around the lake. I wanted to conduct an experiment on fishing technique without them knowing.

Rainbow Trout, Coldwater Lake, Washington

I caught three fish to their one and can attribute my success to only one factor: how I held the rod in my pontoon boat. We all had intermediate sinking lines, the same fly, same tippet, and about the same amount of line out. We were traveling the same speed and did not strip the line but just trolled it behind out boats with the rod tip down a few inches above the water. The only difference was that the other two guys held their rods loosely in their out-stretched arms and I held my rod firmly on top of my oars which were crossed over the front of my pontoons making a solid platform for my wrists. The other guy's arms and wrists absorbed all the shock from their boats when they kicked with their fins or moved with the wind or waves. Because my hands were resting on the oars, none of the boat-shocks were absorbed by my hands and the fly twitched and jerked at the end of my line. I think the fish could tell the difference and I hooked more fish. Early in the afternoon Greg Kohn caught the nicest fish I've ever seen in Coldwater Lake, a twenty inch beauty. Around 2pm it quit raining and the sun poked out between the clouds for a few minutes. It was sunny long enough to dry out our rain jackets. The sun put the fish down deep and they stopped biting. We puttered around the lake after the clouds returned for another hour before calling it quits. We got home around 7pm.

September 22, 2009
I was invited to give a fly tying presentation at Kaufmanns Streamborn Flys in Tigard, Oregon.

The theme was sea-run cutthroat and I tied a Spruce fly for about a dozen beginning fly tyers.

October 5, 2009
Phil Oliver picked me up at 5:30am and Paul Skelton at 6am Monday for our fourth annual week-long fishing trip with the Washington County Fly Fishers. We had breakfast and filled Phil's camper with groceries in The Dalles. We hit three fly shops along Interstate-84, looking for tapered leaders, before we found one open in Island City near LaGrande, Oregon. We picked up sandwiches in Ontario and at 5pm had dinner on a rock ledge overlooking the Owhyee River, watching several two and three foot-long browns gulping mayflys off the water. We patiently left the trout for tomorrow and met the other dozen guys from our group at the Owhyee State Park campground and had a big campfire at sundown.

October 6, 2006
First thing in the morning we headed back to last night's Dinner Hole and found only small fish rising. The lunkers were not showing themselves. We drove back to the White House Hole (above the rapids) and waited for a hatch, which promptly started at 11am. I was having a bad day and lost my first three fish on #18 Beadhead Flashback Pheasant Tail Nymphs fished eighteen inches below a #14 Tan Elk Hair Caddis. A few of the larger trout were rising alongside a floating mat of algae on the far side of the river. I crept within an easy cast and then put my fly several feet upstream of the floating mat, trying to get a good drift to the fish.

Brown Trout, Owhyee River, Oregon

My fly caught the wrong current and it began to float directly into the mess of algae and debris. Upset, I dragged my line away from the algae. Because of the angle my fly line pulled my fly under the mat. I thought the fish was spooked. I was wrong. A twenty inch brown attacked my nymph under the algae mat and hooked himself when he turned to hide downstream. The fish did everything he could to get away. He swam through the algae mat, wrapped around a submerged tree branch and finally tried to swim up the riverbank into some sedges. He finally gave up and I landed my fist brown of the trip. The bright afternoon sun put the insect hatch down. We caught no more fish the rest of the day. The previous week was cloudy and rainy and we had heard the fishing was fantastic, but the fishing was poor so far.

October 7, 2009

Day two on the Owhyee we again fished the White House Hole, this time below the rapids. I was surprised to find another fisherman in the hole because there were no vehicles parked nearby. I later found out he was camping down river and hiked and fished this hole at daylight each morning. We exchanged greetings and he left shortly thereafter. Fish were not rising so I put on a #16 Weighted Possie Bugger, three feet below an indicator, and within an hour caught a beautiful eighteen inch rainbow trout.

Rainbow Trout, Owhyee River, Oregon

Mid-morning blue wing olive mayflies were on the water and a few fish began rising. I caught five more fourteen to sixteen inch browns before the action stopped. We drove downstream and checked on the Dinner Hole and found our big fish hiding. No bugs were on the water. In the late afternoon Phil dropped me off to fish one of my favorite stretches of water, what I call "Walk up the Middle of the River" hole (about two miles below the tunnel). I saw a fish midging and put a #18 Midge Pupa on his nose and immediately hooked a twenty inch brown. He fought hard in the shallow water and I quickly netted him, along with a couple of pounds of aquatic weeds. Over the next quarter mile I spooked four more big browns and hooked no fish. That was it for the day. It was cold that evening and we enjoyed a big campfire and exchanged stories and flys well into midnight.

October 8, 2009

First thing in the morning we headed back to the White House Hole. I hooked nothing during three hours of hard fishing. No insects were on the surface and the fish were not rising. It was another beautiful sunny day, except no willing fish. I decided to take a few casts in the fast water above the hole (where I usually do not fish). There was a large submerged boulder, about mid-stream, that created a fairly long stretch of holding water. I took two dozen casts and drifted my weighted nymph through the run. On my last cast I began putting line back onto my reel when my indicator took off upstream. Because my line was tight the fish knew he was in trouble and he headed downstream through the fast water into the deep hole. I gave him some slack not wanting to break him off on a rock or an underwater branch. This was a mistake because he caught his breath (and strength) and headed towards the fast water and willows near shore where I was standing. He started to get his nose into the willow roots and I put on a little too much pressure and broke him off about a rods length away. I was disappointed. He was a nice fish. I caught up with Phil and Paul just upstream where they were having a blast catching twelve to sixteen inch browns on four foot deep nymphs and indicators. They each had caught about a dozen fish, but no big fish. We had lunch and waited for the hatch to begin around 2pm. Fish began rising everywhere and were taking quarter-inch blue wing olive mayfly emergers. I tried over a dozen fly patterns in #20 and 22 hook sizes to no avail. One eighteen inch brown, who was not afraid of me, was feeding less than a rods length away for over an hour. It appeared he was only taking mayfly emergers that were rising up in the water column. That would explain why I was not catching fish. I may have had an exact mayfly emerger pattern, but my fly's movement was all wrong. The fly should be traveling upwards not horizontally. I tried to add upward movement to my fly, but was not successful. I cast to over a dozen gulping-rising fish but hooked nothing. My excuse was that these fish had been heavily fished over the previous two days and were hook-shy. I looked downstream for more willing fish and found one rising alongside a floating algae mat. My first cast was right on target, the drift was perfect, and he took my pheasant tail nymph on the first pass. A few minutes later I netted a beautiful twenty one inch brown trout.

Brown Trout, Owhyee River, Oregon

A half hour later I found another willing fish and hooked an eighteen inch brown that jumped a half dozen times before I netted him. That was it for me in this hole. Phil took me back to the "Walk up the Middle of the River" hole for the evening hatch. I really love this stretch of water. The water was about knee-deep and the gravel bottom was covered with aquatic plants and a few boulders thrown in to make it interesting. For some reason I've only had success with #18 Midge Pupa in this water. I immediately noticed fish jumping (not rising but jumping completely out of the water), and began wading upstream in the middle of the river. Phil was casting to rising fish in the large hole downstream around the corner. One large fish was repeatedly jumping in a small wide riffle mid-stream. I crept up and began casting and covering the entire riffle. He jumped again and I put the fly several feet upstream. He took my fly seconds later then took off in the shallow water

and rolled a few times in the weeds before I brought out the net. He broke off as soon as I got his head in the net, but he flipped out and swam away before I had a second scoop. I tried for three other jumping fish mid-river with no luck. A few fish were along the shore in frog water like they had been in previous years. I speculated that these fish may have been preparing to spawn in the gravel under the thick weeds. That would explain the jumping and aggressive behavior. Who knows? It was getting dark when Phil picked me up along the road and we headed back to camp. We had a big fire that night and stayed up too late telling stories, laughing, and causing a commotion in the campground.

October 9, 2009

We awoke to another beautiful, cold sunny day. We packed our gear and headed down the highway towards central Oregon. We had lunch at a grocery store deli in Burns and set up camp at Big Bend on the Crooked River around 4pm. We quickly suited-up and I waded into the fast water just below camp. I could not believe it. I hooked a dozen fish within half an hour and landed six Redside trout between twelve and eighteen inches.

Rainbow Trout, Crooked River, Oregon

I love this river. All fish, except the eighteen incher, took the nymph. The big fish had a green plastic tag behind its dorsal fin. I was fishing my usual #14 Tan Elk Hair Caddis and #18 Bead Head Flash Back Pheasant Tail. A half dozen of us from the club camped together and enjoyed another monster campfire and meal together.

October 10, 2009
It was below freezing last night and the fish did not start rising until the sun got on the water around 9am. It was cold and a little windy. The fishing was slow. I only picked up two fish before noon. Around 1pm everything went crazy. Fish appeared out of nowhere and were taking cream colored Pale Morning Duns. I picked up a half dozen fish on a #16 Thorax Dunn with cream hackle, dark biot body and forked tail. Around 2pm a wave of blue wing olives appeared alongside the PMDs. The fish exploded again. Fish were everywhere and we could barely hook any. My excuse was that there were too many naturals on the water and it was difficult to get a good imitation of the profile, color, and movement of an insect that is only a quarter-inch long. We did not give up and worked the water, but only caught two fish among the dozens that were rising within casting range. It was a challenge, and for the most part we failed at catching fish. The hatch tapered off around 4pm and I began catching a few fish on my pheasant tail. Phil and Paul left just after noon wanting to get home early. I caught a ride home with Tom Wideman. It was a good trip.

October 16, 2009
Two more weeks until the close of the sea-run cutthroat season on the coast. Tom Wideman figured the tides were the best on Friday and recruited Chuck Cooney and I to fish the Trask River with him. We had breakfast at Alice's Restaurant on the Wilson River, and were served by Alice herself. Business was a little slow and she took an interest in our fishing and fly boxes. She knew a lot about the river and informed us that the Coho shot up the river last night with the first couple of inches of rain the day before. We put in at the fifth street boat ramp in Tillamook and caught the incoming tide upriver. Floating in our pontoon boats up the middle of the river, we cast #6 Bucktails and Spruce flys into the woody debris that lined the shoreline. I had a few taps from small fish, but did not hook a fish until we reached the South Fork of the Trask River, about a quarter mile up from the put-in. The South Fork was just a dribble of water but the confluence with the main stem was lined with rip-rap making good cutthroat habitat. My cutthroat was only a foot long but gave promise for the rest of the day. It rained off and on for the next few hours as the

tide pushed us up river almost to the Highway 101 Bridge. Chuck and Tom each caught fish and I hooked another small one before the tide turned and we began floating back to the Pacific. There were about a dozen motor boats hop-scotching through each hole, tossing baseball size blobs of salmon roe and lead into the small river. We did not see any caught salmon but did see many spring Chinook and Coho jump and roll in the backwaters. About 3pm we had made a round-trip and loaded out boats back into the truck. We stopped at the Trask River fish hatchery to visit the hatchery manager about my son's "fish egg to fry" Eagle Scout project. We were getting fish eggs and fry from the hatchery to make educational display cases. He was out of town. We had a couple of corn dogs, covered with mustard to hide the taste, at the Glenwood Store and talked with a couple of locals sitting at a card table in the back of the store before heading home.

November 7, 2009
It started raining early in the morning. Not just rain, but pouring rain. The Washington County Fly Fishers planned a group outing to Merrill Lake, Washington and eight of us met on the lake at 11am. Merrill is a fly-fishing-only lake and known for its soft mud bottom and hex-hatch. The wind was blowing and the rain was coming down in horizontal sheets.

Merrill Lake, Washington

We tied a large blue tarp to the trees and the side of the pickup truck and cooked a lunch of chili dogs. We emptied the tarp of rain water every few minutes to avoid structural collapse. A couple of guys wimped-out and went home after lunch but

Chuck, myself, and a couple of others toughed it out. I hooked the first fish not thirty yards from the boat ramp, which turned out to be my best fish of the day, a beautiful sixteen inch full-bodied cutthroat. He took a #12 Cary Special tied as a dropper behind a weighted #10 Black Leech on a clear intermediate sinking line. I headed directly across the lake to a small cove hoping for shelter from the gale force wind and rain, but had no such luck. Over the next couple of hours I picked up a half dozen cutthroats within casting distance of a small creek entering the lake. The rain was so intense the creek ran brown and dumped a fair amount of sediment into the lake. Mid-afternoon during an intense cloud burst I heard what sounded like a bird chirping, but could not see any birds. The sound got louder and louder until I was surrounded by five full grown otters. They were scolding me for fishing their water. Two of the otters were stripping and eating the flesh off of large trout. They were not happy to see me and appeared to be accustomed to chasing fisherman off their fishing grounds. I left without complaint. Around 3pm we were cold and tired of fighting the storm and headed back to the truck. I picked up one more fish in the middle of the lake in deep water. Chuck caught ten fish in a small cove and the rest of the group only caught a couple of fish each. Next time we fish here won't be in November.

November 21, 2009
I attended a symposium at the National Sporting Library in Middleburg, Virginia entitled *A River Never Sleeps: Conservation, History and the Fly Fishing River*. The speakers were interesting and spoke on how fly fishing groups were able through private and political means to restore degraded watersheds back to fishable ecosystems. The crowd was highbrow and the women wore English riding pants and the men sported tweed jackets and ascot silt handkerchiefs. I felt a little out of place in my wool vest and Wrangler jeans. The countryside was spotted with polo fields, stone fences dating back to the Revolutionary War, and a few spring creeks that may hold a few brook trout. We did not get a chance to fish, but did make a few new friends and purchased a few old books. I'll have to get a new silk scarf and brass-tipped walking cane for our next local fly fishing club meeting.

December 1, 2009
I'd been doing some fly-framing projects for a few friends, for donations to fly club auctions and as a part-time business. I was referred to the well-known steelhead fisherman and author, Trey Combs, for some work. Over the past couple of months I've framed a couple dozen frames for Trey with his own tied flys and original photos from his many books. It's been rewarding to get to know him and copy some of his favorite steelhead patterns. He has connections with several rod and reel manufactures and I was able to purchase a top-of-the-line Saracione Spey reel and a Thomas & Thomas #6 Spey rod.

Saracione Reel

December 21, 2009
My son Grady and I have been doing volunteer work for the Trask River Hatchery and invited Chuck Cooney to help. On the way home we took a few casts in the Trask River, up the canyon above the bridge and below the county park. It had been raining for a few days and the Wilson River was blown-out, but the Trask was only a little off-color. I was trying out my new #6 weight Spey rod and quickly realized I was not getting deep enough and needed a longer and heavier sink-tip. Chuck did well and caught a nice seventeen inch sea-run cutthroat. It was pouring rain and we got soaked but it was nice to be on the river.

2010

January 2, 2010

Tom Wideman invited Chuck Cooney and me to a day's fishing. All the local rivers were blown-out except Eagle Creek near Estacada, Oregon. Someone had caught a steelhead on the river a few days ago and it seemed that everyone else and their dog was on the river. A couple of rigs were parked at every turn-out along the narrow forest road. When one truck left, another took its place within minutes. We fished below the hatchery, near Eagle Fern Park and at the mouth of the Clackamas River. Needless to say, no one caught any fish. The Clackamas River did not look too bad so we picked up lunch in Sandy and headed to McIver Park. The Clackamas was running a little high and slightly turbid, but was fishable. Tom fished at the boat ramp so he could watch out for the park ranger because we did not want to pay the $5 county parking fee. Chuck and I headed up river where I took the first pool and Chuck the second hole. I Spey cast the entire run and could not get deep enough in the fast water, so I headed up to Chuck's pool. As I was walking through the willows I heard Chuck yell for help. Through the willows I saw a fish jump in the middle of the river, Chuck had a steelhead on the line. The fish was everywhere in the run and stripped yards of line out of Chuck's spool several times. I thought for sure he'd throw the hook the way he was jumping around. This was a fresh fish, full of fight. He did not want to get close to Chuck or the net. After five minutes he tired out.

Steelhead, Clackamas River, Oregon

I helped Chuck land and photograph the fish, a chrome native nine pounder. The wind picked up and it looked like rain so we called it a day and headed back home. We all could use a couple more days like today.

January 22, 2010

Paul Skelton and I fished the Trask and Wilson Rivers for a couple of hours on a typical overcast, threatening-to-rain, Friday. We hustled up the canyon to be the first to fish the Trask River below the county park. No luck. The Wilson River was a perfect light green and falling after a week of high water.

Wilson River, Oregon

I was surprised to see a few mayflies' on the water. The river was clogged with drift boats so we fished the holes at the top of runs where boats could not hold. Apparently the fish were scattered throughout the river and not congregating. We did not see or hear of any one catching fish. Paul finally caught a small sea-run cutthroat on a black and blue Spey fly. I had a few hits from small sea-runs but that was it. It was a good day to be on the water. I hoped we would do better next trip.

February 6, 2010

I taught a fly-framing class at Northwest Fly Fishing Outfitters in Portland, and had about a dozen students.

February 13, 2010

We had a break between storms and headed to the Deschutes River for a day on the water. Tom Wideman drove and kept Chuck Cooney and I entertained. The weather was not too bad. It was overcast and about 50 degrees. The water was a little low. They must have been keeping a little back in the reservoir for the summer. We began with our Spey rods in the morning and switched to five weights when the blue winged olives appeared just after noon. After swinging a heavy Spey rod all winter the smaller trout rod felt nice. I picked up four, seventeen inch whitefish and three trout in a couple of hours. I fished a yarn indicator between my fly line and leader, an eight foot 5X leader and a heavily weighted #12 Possie Bugger with a #18 Pheasant Tail dropper. I assumed the Whitefish were just finishing up spawning and the trout were thinking about building redds. We probably could have caught more fish with egg patterns.

Whitefish, Deschutes River, Oregon

The hatch really did not amount to much, but did turn the fish onto our #18 Pheasant Tail Nymphs. On the way out of the canyon in the late afternoon we fished the first meadow run. I really like this area because most Deschutes fishers hurry past and head further up the river. It's close to town, and from the road the river looks straight and flat. There are not many parking places but once you get into the river, it had a lot character and good holding areas for fish, mostly within ten yards of shore. I put on a #14 San Juan Worm and drifted it through a deep, slow hole next to shore. A nice trout followed my fly all the way to the surface and then disappeared. A couple of casts later my indicator headed across the river as he took my hook a second time. A minute later I landed a chunky sixteen inch Redside, a good ending for the day.

Redside Trout, Deschutes River, Oregon

February 26, 2010
Pat, a friend of mine at work, was complaining about an obnoxious peacock that took up residence on his small farm a few months ago. I'd been looking for years for a full peacock skin so I offered to solve his problem. At 6:30 in the morning the peacock was roosting in a tall dead maple tree behind his barn and looked huge against the pre-dawn sky. We had to shoot him early to avoid causing a commotion with the neighbors. I carefully walked under the tree, rested my arm on the corral fence and took a shot. He flew off leaving a few feathers floating to the ground. We looked for him for over an hour and finally found him in the neighbors pasture. His tail was about four feet long and the tail feathers bundled together were about six inches thick. The neck hackles were a deep iridescent indigo blue, the saddle feathers were several shades of brilliant green and the secondary wing feathers were unblemished. It took me about an hour at home to skin and salt him. He'll be used and remembered for years. It will take several lifetimes to use all the feathers.

February 27, 2010
I taught an Atlantic salmon fly tying class at the local fly shop for the last six years and met some interesting and unusual people. We once had two people in class who could not have been more opposite. Mike is a young, clean-cut, wireless computer specialist with degrees in physics and electrical engineering, married with two young children and was a fairly good fly tyer. Eugene was a little un-kept, had long hair, was un-shaved, and lived in his car with his dog. He claimed to have

traveled every back-road between Phoenix and Portland and does not fish. The conversation between the three of us was uncomfortable at first until Eugene opened up a box that contained dozens of the most beautiful married salmon fly wings I've seen. He'd watched a few guys tying flys (probably at some campground) and decided he wanted to learn to tye fancy flys. We spent the rest of the day tying, telling stories and having a great time. Pete had to kick us out of the shop at closing, but we continued to talk in the parking lot for another hour. It's amazing how well people can get along when they have something in common, even if it's only tying feathers on a hook. I look forward to tying with both of them again.

March 13, 2010

I tyed my sixth year at the Fly Tyers Expo in Albany, Oregon and demonstrated the Partridge Post Parachute (a dry fly with a hidden post and Hungarian partridge wing). I also did two videos, the first on tying parachutes and the second on the floating dragon fly nymph. I met old friends, made a few new friends and learned some new techniques from other tiers. I caught a ride with Chuck Cooney both days. Chuck wanted to stay for the banquet and auction the second night and bought me a ticket because I was not that interested in attending. During the awards session I received the Oregon Council Federation of Fly Fishers - 2010 Fly Tyer of the Year award.

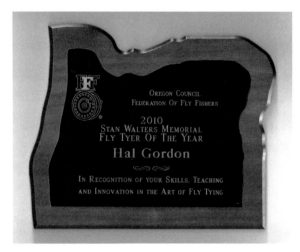

FFF Award, Albany, Oregon

The plaque was engraved "In recognition of your skills, teaching and innovation in the art of fly tying." I was surprised and did not feel deserving of the honor. Now I know why Chuck bought banquet tickets, the committee did not see my name on the banquet list and asked Chuck to make sure I was attending. Now I'll have to act a little more respectable at the fly tying conventions in the future. Along with the award was a life membership to the Federation of Fly Fishers, I was humbled.

March 20, 2010

The Washington County Fly Fishers had a club trip to the coast in search of the elusive winter steelhead. I've failed to hook-up the past few trips and this outing was no exception. We all met at Alice's Restaurant at 7am for breakfast, and paired-up to fish the Wilson, Trask and Nehalem Rivers. The day started nice enough. We put in at beaver slide on the Nehalem River after shuttling our vehicles to the gravel pit takeout.

Nehalem River, Oregon

It was sunny and about 70 degrees, not the best steelhead weather. I fished a weighted purple Egg Sucking Leech through deep runs and swung it through tail-outs. No fish. I did get a bump in a deep slot in a side channel, but it turned out to be a pod of sea-run cutthroat. I put on the smallest fly I had (a number #2), but all the trout did was dart around and bump the fly. No hook-up even though I could see them in the clear water. It's probably good because they were out-of-season. That was it for the Nehalem, except for a storm front that blew us around the river the last mile. Not wanting to give up with no fish, we headed to Cape Mears Lake and dumped our pontoons into the water amidst a dozen shoreline bait-plunkers.

It rained and blew before the white-caps appeared. I didn't bring my oars on the lake and had to kick my fins like a maniac to get back to the boat ramp. I had two hits from a pair of eight inch trout and that was it. Tom Wideman landed three small trout and the rest of the group caught nothing. We were soaked and ready to call it quits. I gave Greg McCarty a ride home and he bought me dinner at a greasy-spoon diner near Glenwood, Oregon. The night help was just one guy: waiter, cook and manager - a one-man operation. He sat with a group of his friends at the corner table and yelled "take any seat" and a few minutes later "what can I get ya?" We had the barbecue pork sandwiches and a pile of fries. Our host yelled "the squeeze bottle has barbecue sauce, use plenty of it, I got more." We felt at home, a little too at home. I was relieved not to be sick the next day. Maybe we'll eat there again on the Tuesday all-you-can-eat spaghetti night.

April 17, 2010

We had a Washington County Fly Fishers club fishing trip to Vernonia Pond, Oregon. This is not the most scenic place to fish, but it is good for beginners who join the club to learn and enjoy each other's company. Tom stopped by my house at 8am and we tied his float tube to the top of my pontoon boat and hauled the trailer up the coast range. The lake was off-color and olive green. The warm weather a few weeks before must have started to turn the lake over and the current cold spell stopped the process and left a lot of algae suspended in the water column. It rained all day in fifteen minutes increments. We each caught a few stocked trout (I caught a dozen) and they were all ten to twelve inches long. Carson Taylor hooked a re-treaded steelhead that was about twenty inches long, but lost him on a #20 fly after the second jump. I hooked and lost a large bass and landed a large crappie. The best flys were #14 Soft Hackles trailed behind a weighted bead-head Woolley Bugger. We were entertained by a couple of blackbirds, who were harassing a pair of bald eagles, who were chasing a half dozen osprey that gave the trout a pounding. Tom bought corn dogs on the way home. The barbecue corn dogs were the worst I'd ever eaten but palatable with enough mustard.

April 23, 2010

Chuck Cooney, Paul Skelton and I fished the open year-long section of the Deschutes River the day before the general trout season opener. The river was high and off-color. Our only luck was going to be with heavy nymphs and droppers. We suited-up at the first meadow and I tied on a #12 weighted Possie Bugger and a #16 BH Tan Partridge Hackle. I hooked and landed a ten incher on my third cast about three feet out from a grassy bank. The water clarity was about two feet and the current swift. I think all the fish were tight to the bank to conserve energy. We had to put the fly right on the fishes nose. About an hour later a few caddis and Blue Winged Olives appeared on the water and we found a small pod of feeding fish. I switched to a #14 Tan Elk Hair Caddis and discovered the pod was Chinook and Steelhead smolts. I quit harassing them after hooking a half dozen. The biggest was eight inches. We headed up river and fished the take-outs at each campground. We had the river to ourselves, but it was poor fishing. I caught a sixteen Redside on a #14 San Juan Worm in a deep slot next to a grassy bank just up river from Harpham Flat.

Redside Trout, Deschutes River, Oregon

He lightly took my fly and headed to the fast water. I had to follow him downstream or lose him. Everything went well until the bottom of the river disappeared on my third step and I slipped a little water over the top of my waders. It was a sunny warm day so it was not too bad. I stripped down and dried out in the sun for a few minutes, trying to change my sox from soggy to just damp. It didn't work. We headed up to Nena to check out one of our favorite runs. I fished the grass lined shore, wading upstream in waist-deep water to avoid the willows and poison ivy, and to get a good cast and drift. In the fast water near the top of a short run, I saw a trout rise to a caddis emerger. I put a tan Partridge Soft Hackle upstream of his rise and I hooked my second respectable trout of the day, another sixteen incher. This time I did not chase him in the fast water. That was it for the day. Chuck caught a few smolts and Paul hooked a few fish and took a nap. We had burgers in Maupin and ice cream in Sandy on the way home. Along the highway we saw a couple of dozen rigs heading to Warm Springs for the opener. I suspect they will be disappointed with the high water.

April 30, 2010

I'd been working in Washington DC for the week and met up Friday afternoon with my fishing buddy Noel Gollehon and his wife Leslie for dinner. We checked out the local fly shop in Arlington, Virginia while waiting for a table at the pizzeria. This town is really different, small shops, narrow roads, well dressed people and everyone looked like they were having a good time all crowded together. The fly shop was much different from what I am accustomed to. This was not a place you could wear your waders into after a day's fishing. Two of the hired help met us at the door and would not leave our sides. "Where are you from, where do you fish, can I get you something, hey you got to see this" When they found out I was from Oregon the dam burst with even more questions about steelhead, Spey rods, and the Deschutes. After fifteen minutes I was worn out and the clerk directed me to the half-off discount bin when another customer walked in the door. Ten percent of the shop was flys and fly tying materials, twenty percent rods and reels and the remaining seventy percent was clothing. Over pizza later that evening, Noel laughed when I complained about the shop. He warned me beforehand that this was a pseudo-shop and that I would not like it, but it was the only fly shop in the DC metro area. A real fly shop is set up like Don Nelson has at River City in Beaverton, Oregon. Three-fourths of the shop space is fly tying materials. All four walls are covered six inches deep with fur, feathers, and various animal parts. This is no place to bring your pet. Don buys up the inventory of going-out-of-business shops

and throws it on the walls. There is at least a dozen of each item so you have a wide selection to choose from. You cannot go in the shop without spending at least two hours looking for just the right size, color, and price (also because Don is sometimes too busy chatting to ring you up at the cash register).

River City Fly Shop, Beaverton, Oregon

The hired help is retired and they all work part-time. It's a great place to spend Friday afternoons, planning trips, getting gear and socializing.

May 6, 2010

Today I set off on a ten day fishing trip, with a little time set aside to visit family. My plan was to help move our daughter in college from winter to summer student housing, visit my mom on mother's day, spend some time with my brother and his family, and fish. I arrived at the White House Hole on the Owhyee River around 2pm and began fishing. There were large spotted caddis ova-depositing on the river and a few blue wing olives but nothing even close to a rise. I tied on my usual #14 Tan Elk Hair Caddis and #18 Beadhead Flashback Pheasant Tail Nymph dropper and began casting along the edge of the willows before I stepped into the water. I jumped when a large brown gulped up a caddis less than a rods length downstream. He must have seen me, what an arrogant fish. The fish had his desired effect of making me jumpy because I hooked and lost four fish in the same hole within an hour. I moved up to the next run and within minutes hooked and landed a nice eighteen inch brown. I hooked and lost another fish before it was time to hit the road again around 5pm. That night I camped in the tall sagebrush along a service road at the Malad River State Park near Bliss, Idaho. It was not exactly camping because I took half of the back seat out of my Toyota Corolla station wagon, laid a two by six foot piece of plywood in the back, and slept on an inflatable backpackers mat. All my gear to the right, I slept on the left, plenty of room. I fell asleep to the nightly news on my portable transistor radio.

May 9, 2010
After moving our daughter to another apartment at Utah State University, and spending Mother's Day with my Mom, I met up with Pete Prepke, Ralph Brooks (from back home in Oregon), Ralph's son Chris, and Ralph's brother on the Provo River. I pulled up to the river access just as they were pulling on their waders. I'd fished the Provo several times and showed them my favorite holes. They caught a few fish but it was not spectacular fishing. I filled up my water jugs with ice at their motel in Heber City and headed to the Green River via Vernal, Utah. I camped at Dripping Springs, just south of Dutch John, Utah, for the night.

May 10, 2010
I was on the Green River before sun up. Two other guys pulled into the take-out at Brown's Hole just as I rigged up my rod. They appeared to be in a hurry to beat me up river (I don't know why), they did not even say good morning when they walked by in the parking lot. There were plenty of fish and room on this river. I headed up river and crossed just up from the board walk. It was cloudy, windy and looked like rain. The fish were not rising. I decided to take a hike and explore the river. I walked up river until a cliff impeded my progress (across from the USFS outhouses) and down river to the take-out (about two miles) without seeing a rising fish. I watched the two previous anglers from across the river frantically hiking and frothing up the water with their casts. They were not catching fish. I hooked and lost my first fish in the whirlpool just below the first boat ramp on a #18 Pheasant Tail Nymph (below a heavily weighted #14 Possie Bugger and indicator). Moments later I hooked a second fish (probably the same fish) and landed a hefty sixteen inch rainbow. It started to rain. I did not want to miss the expected Mayfly hatch so I headed back up river to the boardwalk and deep-

nymphed the fast water and picked up two more rainbows. The first fish was sixteen inches and bright as a fresh steelhead. The second fish was seventeen inches, dark and heavily spotted. I noticed several blue wing olives on my chest-pack and changed flys. The hatch was going to happen. I headed to the flat below the hole and riffles where fish were rising everywhere. From where I was standing on the bank I could cast to at least a dozen rising fish. The fish were picky. I did not have the right fly, but did pick-up an eighteen inch brown and a seventeen inch rainbow after trying a dozen #18 to 20 emerger and dry fly patterns.

Rainbow Trout, Green River, Utah

The two fish I did deceive took the #18 Pheasant Tail Nymph behind a #14 Elk Hair Caddis indicator. I could never catch fish without my old standby Pheasant Tail. The wind kicked up a notch, it sprinkled a little, and the fish disappeared. A couple of guys across the river had a great afternoon hooking a dozen fish (they were not the previous guys I'd run into in the morning). I caught up with them in the parking lot and they shared their fly pattern with me, a #20 CDC BWO Comparadun. I spent a second night at Dripping Springs Campground.

May 11, 2010
I picked up a few of the flys recommended by my new friends from the night before at the fly shop in Dutch John, and met them a second time at the Brown's Hole parking lot the next morning. They were hiking up to Dripping Springs and recommended I fish the run below the second take-out at Browns Hole. The river was running low at about 850 cfs so I was able to cross the

river at the takeout. I had to cross the river three times because I forgot my sunglasses and had to go back and get them. I deep-nymphed the run with a indicator, #14 Possie Bugger and #18 Pheasant Tail Nymph, drifting them through the gravel bottomed slots between the beds of aquatic weeds. I immediately picked up a sixteen inch rainbow on the Pheasant Tail. A half hour later I caught another rainbow about twenty yards downstream on the Possie Bugger. The sun poked briefly though the clouds and the fish catching stopped. I hiked downstream about a mile looking for good holding water and was stopped by a series of cliffs. I fished the first hole again and pressed my luck a little too much and leaked water over the top of my waders. Time for a break to dry out at the parking lot. I hung my waders inside-out and wet clothes under a picnic shelter, ate lunch and took a nap in the sun. My gear dried out fast in the sun and wind and I was back on the river in about an hour. I fished the flat water below the board-walk riffle, where around 3pm the mayfly hatch was in full progress.

Brown Trout, Green River, Utah

The #20 CDC BWO Comparadun recommended by my new friends worked like a charm. I still have a lot to learn about fishing a #20 fly, on a twelve foot leader without an indicator. I was pleasantly surprised to find if I could get my fly within a few feet of a rising fish, they would turn and take it. However, I lost the first six fish by not setting the hook fast enough and straighten the hook on two fish by setting the hook too hard. I finally got it right and began hooking and landing fish. The first was a beautiful twenty inch brown.

I caught two more eighteen inch fish. A storm was building and the wind picked up and made casting impossible. The wind put the fish down just as things were getting good. I headed to Flaming Gorge Lodge for a hot meal and learned from the waitress about an upcoming storm. Around 7pm it started to snow and I decided to head to a lower elevation and camped at Manns Camp on Sheep Creek. The next morning there were three inches of snow on my car and snow was coming down fast. By the time I got to Manila, Utah the snow was up to my Toyota's wheel wells and driving was difficult. At Fort Bridger the snow lightened up and the state police opened the closed interstate highway around noon. I and a couple dozen semi-trucks raced to Evanston, Wyoming and the Utah border. I spent the rest of the afternoon with my brother Keith visiting three flys shops between Salt Lake and Ogden.

May 13, 2010
I arrived at the Owhyee River last night before sunset and camped about two miles below the tunnel. Today was for exploring new water, and I hiked upstream with provisions for the day. The Rock Garden water was not productive and I did not see a fish. The water was lower and clearer than when I usually fish this productive stretch of water in the fall. The next fast water riffle and hole looked good and I deep nymphed it and caught a twelve inch brown on a #18 Pheasant Tail Nymph. A retired couple pulled up in their truck and set up camp where I was fishing. I was not happy to have them invading my space, but they were polite and did not fish the water while I was there. They good humouredly challenged me to catch a fish. I could hardly believe what happened next. It was an arrogant fisherman's dream. I cast behind a submerged boulder on the far side of the pool and caught the interest of a large trout. On the second cast I hooked him and landed a twenty three inch brown, the largest I'd ever caught on the Owhyee. The man quickly landed my fish in his long-handled net and the lady took a few photos with my camera. Jokingly they said, "Catch another one". I cast upstream a few feet above where the previous fish was holding, behind another submerged boulder and brought up another fish, which also refused my fly. He took on the second cast and I landed a yellow-gold twenty inch brown. Two trophy fish in four casts in front of an audience. I started to feel a little

cocky (and did not like it), and quickly excused myself, thanked them for their help, encouraged them to fish the hole and headed up river with a smile. It was hot and sunny and there were few bugs on the water. I passed up a lot of flat water, which usually produces fish during a hatch. I fished the fast water over the next mile and a half with no fish. At the tunnel I waited for a vehicle to follow so I would not get crunched in the dark. I fished another couple of hours with no luck. When the sun hit the horizon I headed back to my car. The retired couple was sitting in lawn chairs at the hole and waved as I walked by on the highway. I opened up a can of tuna fish for dinner and slept in my car that night. In the morning I drove home, planning the next fishing trip in my mind, grateful for the success I'd had the past week.

Brown Trout, Owhyee River, Oregon

May 22, 2010
Phil Oliver called and offered to drive to Rock Creek Reservoir and fish with the rest of the Washington County Fly Fishers. In Portland it was cold and raining and I thought it would be a short trip. We picked up Greg in Tigard, visited the Welches Fly Shop, and found snow before we hit Government Camp on Mt. Hood. There were white caps on the lake at the put-in and the wind was howling about twenty miles-per-hour. It was a challenge to get to the far side of the lake, against a ridge and out of the wind. The fishing was very

good. I fished an intermediate slinking line with a #12 Tri-Color Damsel. The Oregon Department of Fish and Wildlife had stocked the lake at least twice this spring and because of the poor weather this past month most of the fish were still in the lake. I had a bump on my line at least every twenty yards as I kicked my fins and trolled my pontoon boat around the lake. For every half dozen bumps on the line, I hooked a fish. The water was cold and there were a lot of short strikes.

Rainbow Trout, Rock Creek Reservoir, Oregon

I must have caught at least four dozen foot long rainbows in about six hours of fishing. Large Callibaetis mayflies were hatching along the lake edge so I switched to dry flys to make it more interesting. The fish were not rising well, so I went back subsurface. We called it quits around 5pm and I kept my last three trout to take home for dinner, something that I rarely do and should do more.

June 6, 2010
Alaska was calling us back for another week-long float trip, this time on the Alagnak River at Katmai National Park (only a few dozen miles across the tundra from American Creek where we floated last year). I picked Carson Taylor up at his home at 4:30am and we met Harris Cover and Greg Kohn at the Portland airport. I slept most of the way to Seattle and Anchorage. Harris rented a car and he and I headed an hour north to Wasilla to see some un-developed property he'd owned the past thirty years. There was a dirt road to the site but not much else. The neighbors looked a little rough sitting on their outdoor couches surrounded by broken-down vehicles and free-

roaming chickens. We didn't stay to chat. All four of us stayed at a run-down motel in Anchorage and reorganized our gear for the trip.

June 7, 2010
It was light at 3am and dark at 1am and difficult to get a good night's sleep. After a quick motel breakfast we took a taxi to Merrill Field, caught a chartered small plane to Iliamna, and took a float plane to Rainbow River Lodge. We had lunch at the lodge and reorganized our gear into water-proof bags for the float trip. We each were allowed seventy pounds of gear. The lodge provided the rafts, tents, cots, sleeping pads, food and cooking equipment. It took two float planes to get the four of us and our gear to Nonvianuk Lake, the headwater of the south branch of the Alagnak (Nonvianuk) River. The Alagnak is designated as a National Wild and Scenic River and flows out of the Katmai National Park and Wilderness into Bristol Bay. It was windy and the lake had white-caps. Our pilots decided to land the planes on the river rather than chance the high winds on the lake. The river outlet was about 100 feet wide and running about three miles per hour. The pilots put the planes down about fifty yards below the lake and motored up river to a gravel bar near the outlet. The first thing out the plane door was Carson's shoe - which floated down river before I chased it down in a back eddy. We unloaded our gear, pumped up the rafts and said goodbye to the pilots for a week.

Nonvianuk Lake Outlet, Alaska

We hauled the rafts upstream closer to the outlet and set up our tents and camp near the Hammersly cabin, a historic site within the Katami National Park, which was built in the 1940's. For the next few hours we explored the lakeshore and sat in lawn chairs waiting for the 12am trout season opener. Another group of anglers were camped across the river, and they all went to sleep around 9pm, except one guy who kept fiddling with his gear and wandering around camp. I wished this guy would go to sleep so I could fish, not wanting to be caught before the official opener. I finally gave-up and took a nap in my waders in our tent.

June 8, 2010
Greg shook our tent and woke me up at midnight. It was time to fish. I had already rigged up my twelve foot six weight Spey rod with a ten foot type VI sink-tip and a four foot ten pound leader. I fished a #6 Bar Bell weighted olive, and white six inch Dolly Llama rabbit strip streamer. It only took a dozen casts to hook my first fish, a beautiful twenty-four inch rainbow trout.

Rainbow Trout, Nonvianuk Lake, Alaska

The sun had been below the horizon since 11pm and it was getting darker as I landed two more big rainbows and one thirty inch lake trout. I was tired and went to bed around 1am, just as Harris was waking up. He fished the rest of the night and morning and caught eight fish, all lake trout. It was light around 3am and I began fishing at 8am and caught three more rainbows before noon. Carson and Greg also caught a few fish. The Alagnak River is known for its Sockeye salmon that migrate from Bristol Bay up seventy-five miles of river past the lake to spawn. Sockeye need lakes as rearing habitat. The salmon fry and smolt provide a plentiful food source for trout. There were also eels that migrate through the river that also provide an abundant food source. I caught all my fish on the olive and white Dolly Llama, except for one fish on a black and purple Dolly Llama (that imitated the eel). I tried a small hairwing fry pattern but got no hits. The fish wanted big flys. At noon we had a light breakfast, packed-up our gear, and headed down river. There were a few miles of good trout water below the outlet, but the next ten miles were essentially fishless. The river was broad, shallow, fast and offered very poor fishing opportunities. At the confluence of the north and south branches there was a nice hole where we took a break. I caught a twenty six inch Lake Trout and lost two others. The weather was finicky, alternating between wind, rain, and full sun. We entered the islands and braided water around 4pm and began anxiously looking for a camp site. The water was high and the gravel bars and low grass flats were submerged under water. We finally found a small bench a couple of feet above the water, around 9pm, to pitch our tents. We had about 200 square-feet to work with before the ledge tapered off into thick willows and a swampy area. The mosquitoes were not too bad because we had a good strong downstream wind. I took a few dry fly casts with a #6 Black Stimulator trying to entice a couple of fish that were rising to small black stoneflies on the water. No luck. It was difficult to get to good water from camp because of the willows and swampy water. We could only fish about fifty yards of water.

Lake Trout, Alagnak River, Alaska

We had freeze-dried lasagna for dinner and watched the terns dive and take smolts off the water until we went to sleep.

June 9, 2010

We awoke to the sound of gulls and terns arguing over positions to feed. The birds hovered in wide circles a hundred feet in the air, and then crashed into the water as a wave of smolts rolled down river. There had to be feeding fish somewhere in the frenzy. Harris put on a heavily weighted Prince Nymph and drifted it through the water I fished last night. He hooked and landed a twenty inch Rainbow and we all scrambled to grab our rods. What we assumed to be poor water turned out to be productive. We landed a half dozen large trout in front of camp over the next hour, all on large smolt patterns.

Rainbow Trout, Alagnak River, Alaska

At noon we packed up and headed down river, determined to fish the braids. We were disappointed. By my estimate we were a couple of weeks early. The braids were running strong with high, fast water. We did not even spook a fish. We were not going to catch monster rainbows, on dry flys, in this skinny water. It rained off and on all day and we did not see the sun. We surprised a cow and calf moose during the float and were glad to have a little distance between us. Camp sites were scarce but we finally found an island with a three foot high knoll surrounded by flooded grassland. The camp water looked good, but only produced one fish shortly after our arrival. Later Greg and Carson picked up two fish in the channel that divided the island above camp. We used steelhead fishing techniques on the big water, casting across and downstream, mending and slowly swinging a weighted fly across the current over likely holding water. We watched a bald eagle swoop down and take a large fish off the water forty yards away and fly over our camp mocking us. I was last on the water after a dinner of freeze-dried stroganoff and caught a lively twenty seven inch rainbow, swinging through the run with a sink-tip and a Dolly Llama. This fish was a fighter and took out a hundred feet of line twice before even getting close to him. Worn out, he finally came in and we took a few photos before releasing him. We were surrounded by bald eagles staring at us from tree perches, waiting for us to leave them a fish. We were tired and hit the sack early around 10pm in full daylight.

June 10, 2010

After breakfast Carson washed the dishes and lost the coffee pot in the river. After a frantic search he located the pot on the bottom of the river and retrieved it with his fish net. Greg caught one more rainbow below camp before we packed up and headed down river into the unknown. The terns were active in the fast water next to the back eddies, and that's where we caught fish. Harris and I had a double on in the slack water below an island, and we could see Carson on the next island downriver with a fish on as well. We weren't catching a lot of fish, but each one was a quality fish and at least twenty inches long. It began to rain, then rained harder until we had to beach the rafts because of the reduced visibility. The downpour lasted about twenty minutes during which Harris hooked four fish and landed one lake trout below an island. I don't know what Harris was doing but seventy five percent of his fish were lake trout, while the rest of us were catching rainbows. It might be because he was not using a sink-tip while the rest of us were. It was getting late when we finally found a camp site at the tail end of an island. It was the only site this far that actually looked like someone else had used it as a campsite. We put up our tents between rain showers and at 9pm we had full sunshine. We draped our wet clothes over a small willow tree and they dried quickly in the sun and wind. Most of the water was too swift to fish, but was calm and deep next to the bank. We finally got to see up close what all the bird commotion was about. In the bright sunshine, in the deep calm water, we saw balls of hundreds of smolts, turning in circles, slowly drifting down river. There must have been a thousand fish in each ball, and several balls pasted us during an hour of watching from our camp chairs. There were a few fry darting for cover along shore, but the main attractions to the birds were the smolts. We could always tell where the smolts were by the flocks of birds.

June 11, 2010

We left camp late after a mixture of fast moving clouds, wind, and rain passed us early in the morning. We began noticing small black stoneflys. They were everywhere. Every time we rolled up our tents we took a few dozen of them downstream with us. There were also a few caddis on the water as well as hundreds of midges and mosquitoes, but very few fish rising. We fished a few more braids and finally gave up on the small water. The fish were in the main stem river chasing smolts and not the fast-running interconnecting water. We caught a few more two foot long rainbows below islands but the fishing was not so good.

Rainbow Trout, Alagnak River, Alaska

We stopped every half mile or so to read the map. We came upon three forks, with two forks that appeared to dead end in slack water. We misread the map by a quarter mile and discovered what caused the slack water, a half dozen huge beaver dams and lodges. The largest lodge must have been over twenty feet high. The series of beaver dams allowed water to flow slowly under the structures, but also created a backwater about a half mile long. We pulled to the bank to survey our options and decided to pull our rafts upstream about fifty yards and float down a small side-channel back to the main river. It worked and felt good to be out of the mosquitoes and gnats and back on moving water. It was getting late and we were surrounded by either high clay banks or shallow, flooded willow bottoms. After 10pm we finally found a clearing through the willows that lead us to a semi-drained upland flat of mosses, grasses and low growing shrubs. It was a great site, except for the mosquitoes. The bugs were bad. We had to use our mosquito nets and spray for the first time. Before applying bug-dope I counted a dozen blood-suckers on my pant leg within fifteen seconds of brushing them off. We did not fish. The water was too fast and the bugs too annoying. We went to bed early after a meal of freeze dried lasagna.

June 12, 2010

A pair of cranes woke us early in the morning, gawking loudly to proclaim their presence. Today is my 24th wedding anniversary, I reflected momentarily about my wife and family. I'm a very lucky guy for having them in my life. We had a quick breakfast of peanut butter crackers, turkey jerky, and granola bars and got on the river to escape the mosquitoes. The next mile we caught very few fish.

Rainbow Trout, Alagnak River, Alaska

The river was flattening and deepening. We saw two other anglers working the braided water without success. We heard a jet boat a few hours later and assumed they were from one of the remote lodges along the lower river. We were surprised to find one of our best camps within the braids. Somehow a 1,000 square foot island of sand and gravel was created mid-stream, probably by a floating ice-barge pushing up the gravel during the spring thaw. It was flat, dry, and near what looked to be a good fish run. It was a little windy but bug-free. We quickly set up camp and

spread out to fish. Harris quickly caught a very nice twenty three inch rainbow and Greg had a few hits but no hook-ups. I had the beginnings of a head-cold and took it easy in camp.

June 13, 2010

We had freeze dried eggs, covered with Tabasco sauce to hide the taste, and oatmeal for breakfast. We packed our gear, took a few more casts, and headed downriver towards the take-out. We'd learned at the beaver ponds that either our map or GPS coordinates were slightly off, so we quickly found a nice gravel bar campsite near a long, deep run, where what we thought was about a quarter mile up from the takeout. All the pilot told us about the pick-up site a few days earlier were the map coordinates and to look for a tall, steep, hill eroding into the river. We quickly set up camp and caught a few fish in a deep run next to camp.

Rainbow Trout, Alagnak River, Alaska

We could almost sit in camp chairs and fish. In the late afternoon the sun came out and the wind abated, if I was going to take a bath now was the time. I headed to the far end of the island, stripped down, soaped-up and took a plunge into the cold water. It actually felt good. I was wind-dry in a few minutes and ready to associate with civilized humanity again. The other three guys thought I was crazy but they will never know the joy. Besides, we did not have time to clean-up between flights at the airport on the way home. I rejoined our group and caught a couple of more twenty inch rainbows in the back-eddy. Late evening we each had a bowl of freeze-dried stroganoff, green Tabasco sauce, dried fruit and nuts. We watched a moose graze on willows across the river and thought for a few minutes he was heading our way. He disappeared into the brush when he got wind of us. There were very few campsites along the river this early in the season, and we never had enough wood to build a campfire. Beyond that, life was good.

June 14, 2010

We woke up early, packed our gear and waited for the float planes. Harris and Greg used the satellite phone to call home, but at $2 per minute I'll wait until I get to the airport. I caught another twenty inch rainbow just as our pick-up planes buzzed us and headed down river.

Rainbow Trout, Alagnak River, Alaska

Apparently we misjudged the take-out. We headed down river about a mile before we found both float planes waiting on a sandy beach. We quickly re-packed our gear from dry-bags to our original luggage and took off for Iliamna. We were running late. At Iliamna we made our flight to Anchorage by five minutes. The Chigmit Mountains were obscured by low clouds and we missed the spectacular view. In Anchorage we caught a taxi to the airport and learned that a big storm with high winds was heading towards Iliamna and that they might have to close the Iliamna airport for a couple of days. We were lucky to get out just in time. We had a real cooked meal at the airport and caught the 5pm flight back to Portland and arrived home at 1am. The total trip cost was $3,500, but I was able to pay most of it off by tying flys and doing some work for the lodge.

June 17, 2010

I'd read about carp fishing on the Columbia River in a local fly fishing magazine, so I headed to Vantage, Washington to check it out. The water was off-color with snow melt and it was windy. I searched the flats for tails and saw no fish. I will have to try this spot again later in the summer.

June 23, 2010

Chuck Cooney's pontoon boat on the trailer started to lose air just out of Condon, Oregon, and was almost flat by the time we reached the John Day River. Tom Wideman and I assumed it was because he did not let out air as we rose in elevation and because it got hot in the early afternoon. Regardless, Chuck was determined to fish and dumped his boat and pump into the river at the Kimberly Bridge at the confluence with the North Fork. We were off to a four day fishing trip. Fishing started slow. I caught three Squawfish before I hooked my first smallmouth bass. The river was running over 3,000 cfs and a little on the turbid side. It was about 70 degrees. There must have been a gully-washer last night because a Gilliam County road crew was doing road work east of Service Creek, removing mud and debris off the highway and ditch culverts. Chuck had to pump up his boat every 100 yards and finally gave up after an hour. He hitched a ride to the take-out, drove his truck back, and retrieved his pontoon boat. He met us at the take-out a couple of hours later. Fishing was slow. I caught two dozen bass on the eight mile Kimberly to Gravel Pit float. All fish were caught on a #6 Chernobyl Ant. I fished an Elk Hair Caddis for a bit and got lucky and landed an eight inch trout, or maybe it was a steelhead smolt heading down river. We rented a house in Spray, Oregon for $100 per day and split the cost and groceries three ways. We took Chuck's pontoon apart on the kitchen table, found and fixed the leak.

June 24, 2010

The John Day River cleared up overnight and dropped a few inches. We decided to float from the closed gate (about five miles above the gravel pit) into the town of Spray, about ten miles. The weather was perfect with widely scattered clouds, 70 degrees and a light wind. It was a good day to be on the water. The fishing did not disappoint us and made up for the slow previous day. We easily caught four to five dozen bass each averaging twelve to fourteen inches. My biggest fish was sixteen inches. The last mile before town was exceptional, hooking a bass every ten feet along the grass lined shore, all on poppers and Chernobyl Ants. We kept a few bass for dinner.

Smallmouth Bass, John Day River, Oregon

June 25, 2010
There must have been a big storm in the Blue Mountains upriver overnight. The John Day River was blown-out-muddy with only a few inches visibility. The water appeared just above flood stage. Our back-up plan was Bull Prairie Reservoir, a put-and-take lake about thirty minutes north on the Spray-Heppner Highway. I put on an intermediate sinking line with a #14 Carey Special and caught eight to ten inch stocked rainbows and wild brook trout all day.

Brook Trout, Bull Prairie Reservoir, Oregon

The lake was about sixty acres so we circled the lake at least every hour. It was nice to hang-out on the water, relax, enjoy the warm sun and have no

expectations of anything but small trout. I took a long nap after lunch on the grass. We caught a few more fish in the afternoon before heading back to town. Chuck cooked the bass we caught the previous day for dinner, and they were excellent.

June 26, 2010
We packed our gear, paid our bill and headed to the Columbia River in search of carp and anything else we could catch. At the Freeway Ponds a mile down river from the Deschutes confluence we found a pod of the most colorful sun fish I'd ever seen.

Sunfish, Columbia River, Oregon

They were brilliant gold, olive, and yellow with a bright red spot on the gill plate. We fooled them with small nymphs cast in the open water between clumps of aquatic weeds. Further down river we found some monster carp patrolling the slough above Mayer State Park. It was getting late in the day so we did not break out our rods, but marked the spot for a future trip. Those carp must have been over twenty pounds. We got back to Portland just in time for the five o'clock traffic.

July 1, 2010
I was working in Palmer, Alaska and decided to take a couple of days off. I called Bill Daley and he invited me to spend a couple of days at his cabin on the Kenai River. Bill said to call him when I got to Sterling, Alaska. I found his place, but he was not home. He had gotten the days mixed-up when we were to meet and told me over the phone to hustle down to the Kenai River at Bing's Landing where he and a couple of his fishing buddies were getting ready to launch their

boat. When I got there they were having troubles getting the out-board motor started. It was nice to see Bill again. The jumper-cables could not reach from the truck to the boat battery so I pulled my rental car alongside the boat and we got the motor started. We all jumped in the boat and headed up river to catch a few late evening reds (sockeye salmon). A couple of miles upriver we put the anchor in a small willow tree along a steep sandy high bank and began casting. Red fishing is not really fishing because you repeatedly blind cast a sinker and large fly into likely holding water and hope to floss a salmon that swims into the line with an open mouth. The fly is not really a fly but a tuft of yarn tied to meet the definition of a fly. An hour later I caught a small sculpin. We joked about the motor not starting again and it didn't. I became nervous when Bill's friend suggested we "pole" the boat down river to the take-out, but we convinced him that was a stupid idea. We called his neighbor on the cell phone instead, and an hour later he gave us a jump-start with his boat. We were back at our starting point at midnight. Bill cooked a late dinner of bear-meat burgers and we talked about old times and work until 1am. Bill had hired me in 1988 and had been my first SCS boss.

July 2, 2010

Bill and I began fishing for trout on the upper Kenai River just off Skilak Lake Road at Jim's Landing. There was some nice water around the take-out but several boats were unloading so there was no room. I had a couple of hits below the take-out and finally hooked and landed a sixteen inch rainbow on a #6 Dolly Llama and sink-tip line. Next we drove up river and parked at the day-use area and hiked up river to a nice riffle leading into a slow pool with a large tree-snag in the middle of the pool. It took another three casts before I landed another lively rainbow that jumped a half dozen times before being landed. The next spot up river was difficult to get to. We broke trail through mosquito invested willow, cottonwood and spruce trees to get to the next run. We repeatedly yelled "yo-bear" while passing through thick brush. I picked up a third rainbow about the same size as the other two.

Rainbow Trout, Kenai River, Alaska

It appeared like we were not going to get any big fish today. The next hole was about a mile below the Russian River. The far bank, on the inside corner, was filled with salmon fishers flinging heavily weighted lines and barely dressed hooks trying to floss sockeye. We saw others land a few fish, but we had no luck. If there were trout in this area, they were probably following the salmon and looting their eggs. The first of July was the beginning of the sockeye run, but relatively few salmon were in the river this year. Our next and last stop was at the Russian River ferry crossing. Once again the steep bank on the far side of the river was crowded with fishers and the gravel bar on our side had few people fishing, except those who were waiting for their turn across the river on the ferry. I began working my Dolly Llama downriver of the fish cleaning station, quartering downstream and across, and taking a few steps after every few casts. About ten yards into the run I hooked and landed a fourteen inch char and attracted the attention of a couple of kids. The first boy began with incessant questioning about fishing and life in general and the second boy just quietly walked into the river and started fishing my run. There are some things a boy can get away with that an adult cannot. I finished fishing the run and walked back to the top for another try. By then the second boy's mother called him to join his family to cross the river on the ferry. Moments later I hooked, landed and released a second char of about seventeen inches and continued to answer the first boy's questions.

Dolly Varden, Kenai River, Alaska

We'd caught our fish for the day. Bill and I had Salmon chowder at a small restaurant, visited a nearby tackle shop and said our good byes until my next trip. Bill's been good to me and a friend for years.

July 10, 2010
The Washington County Fly Fishers had a club trip to the McKenzie River. I talked Chuck Cooney into driving and we were halfway to Salem before we realized we'd both forgotten the oars to our pontoon boats. We had fins so we decided to take our chances. The river was running a little lower than when we usually float in April, but the water was cold and clear. The forecast was for bright sun, no clouds, and about 80 degrees. We did not expect any hatches. We put in at Hendricks Bridge and shuttled vehicles down to Bellinger. I put on a heavy #12 Possie Bugger with #18 Pheasant Tail dropper and indicator nymphed. The first mile was uneventful because I could not get to the best runs without oars. I finally parked my boat upstream from a nice run and fished about a hundred yards of the edge of a fast run. There were pockets of holding water next to the stream bank about three feet across and another three feet deep. I picked up an 11 inch rainbow on the second cast on the Possie Bugger. He immediately hit the fast water and stripped about twenty yards of line on my five weight rod. I thought he was bigger than he really was. The next run looked good but did not produce. I tied my pontoon to a tree in a small back-eddy and walked downstream a quarter mile to fish back to the boat along some deep rip-rap lined bank water. There were no fish in the deep,

boulder strewn holes. In similar rivers there would have be lots of fish, but not the McKenzie. The fish here like the fast water. I walked upriver another quarter mile to fast, shallow water and picked up three beautiful ten inch cutthroat. The next run produced fish every time I've fished it. The river broke-up into three runs around two small islands and then converged back into one run above a deep hole. I immediately hooked three fish and only landed the last one, a twelve inch rainbow. We spotted two twenty pound spawned out spring Chinook floating down river, barely keeping upright. They were not the only drifters trying to keep upright. A large flotilla of party-rafters caught up with our group. They were riding blow-up doughnuts, inner tubes, inflatable kayaks and whatever would float. None of them had lifejackets and a couple of them were not sober. We watched one large lady in a child's tube get caught in a back-eddy that swirled her around and around a grove of overhanging willows that finally capsized her and washed her downstream. Dave Wesley and I thought for sure we'd have to rescue her and I told him he'd had to give her CPR because there was no way I was going to. Finally they all floated through and we continued to fish.

McKenzie River, Oregon

The next run was my favorite spot on the McKenzie, and I told Greg Kohn so when he beat me there. I patiently waited for him to thoroughly fish the run. Finally, he gave me permission to fish through and I caught a spunky rainbow on my second cast. I don't think he was getting deep enough. He just rolled his eyes and said "whatever". I fish with these guys way too much. I switched to a #14 Elk Hair Caddis the last mile of river and picked up a couple of smolts in the bank-water in the shade. At the last hole before the Bellinger take-out I put the Possie Bugger back on (without the indicator) and swung it down and across the tail of the run, and picked up another foot long rainbow. We'd had a good day, no disasters, and a few fish.

July 23, 2010

As a kid I'd read magazine articles about the famous Miracle Mile on the North Platte River, Wyoming. I had some free time and made arrangements to fish the river for a day. The locals at the fly shop in Casper said the river was running a little high, but fishing well, and recommended the water below Grey Reef. I was on the water at Clarkson Hill by 9am. There was not a cloud in the sky and it was already 90 degrees. The tail-water was cold and a little off-color because of the many farms in the area. The air smelled of alfalfa and the water smelled like livestock. Caddis and trico mayflys were on the water, but not abundant. With the bright sun it was going to be a deep nymphing day. I rigged my five weight with an indicator, weighted #12 Possie Bugger and a #18 Bead Head Flashback Pheasant Tail Nymph dropper. I fished the fast water with no luck and then began focusing on the slow back-eddies where the fish were. The first fish surprised me, taking the hook so fast I heard the loose line stripping out my rod guides before realizing it was a fish.

Rainbow, North Plate River, Wyoming

He was a bruiser and stripped ten yards of line before I could turn him towards the grass-lined under-cut bank. We played give-and-take for a few minutes before I beached him on the grass. He was just short of eighteen inches but fat as a football and strong. I hooked a second fish a half hour later about 100 yards upstream where the fast current boiled over a row of submerged grass-sod. This fish was a little smaller but had every bit as much fight. I worked another half mile of unproductive water before heading back to the car for a drink and a drive down river. I took a two tire-track road along the river through the sagebrush until I hit a locked gate and then hiked another half mile down river to a large back eddy. The river was just below flood stage and relatively clear.

North Platte River, Wyoming

I did not hook a fish in the back-eddy but caught a sixteen inch rainbow at the head of the pool on a pheasant tail nymph. I landed him just as three guided drift boats floated by – the clients were in Aloha shirts, baggy shorts and sandals (must be on vacation). They were side-drifting nymphs with golf-ball size plastic indicators. I hooked and lost two fish a little further upstream and finally landed another sixteen inch cutt-bow, all in slow water next to shore. I continued fishing back to the car and then drove up river to Lusby and had a sandwich under a cottonwood tree. I decided not to fish because the high water was too fast and shallow. I headed to the Grey Reef and parked at the BLM day-use area called The Redds. What a beautiful river, and I had it all to myself. I tried a #12 Tan Foam Hopper and began working upstream and only got one hit from a large rainbow in front of a submerged tree stump. I re-tied on my nymphs and fished the riffle-eddy water. I quickly caught two fourteen and eighteen inch rainbows on a pheasant tail and called it a day. I had to catch my flight home at 7pm in Casper. I've got to fish here again.

August 1, 2010
We'd been planning a fishing trip to Yellowstone with our International Fly Fishing Club and it was getting complicated. A few days ago a grizzly bear and her three cubs ransacked a US Forest Service campground near Cooke City, Montana, where we planned on staying. The bear killed one man and bit two other people and was captured a few days later. We decided to go anyway. I invited Chuck Cooney along for the ride and he picked me up early Saturday morning and we were on our way. We picked up some fresh blue berries just across the Washington border and stopped for gas in Ritzville. We sensed something wrong as we pulled into town. All the gas stations had yellow tape blocking off the gas pumps and there were many people milling around the sidewalks. (This would be the first of many experiences with yellow tape during the upcoming week). Apparently a lightning storm had passed through town a few hours earlier and hit a transformer and blew the electricity out of several rural counties in southeast Washington. We decided to take our chances and continue onto Spokane and barely arrived at a gas station running on fumes. We visited the local fly shop and had a short chat with Swede, the owner of the shop. After lunch at a Korean diner we hit the road again for Missoula, Montana where we planned on spending the night with Kevin Griggs, an old fishing friend of mine. On the east side of Lolo Pass we ran into a massive hail storm that put a few dents in vehicles and tin roofs. Many vehicles were parked under the highway over-passes or pulled off the road to avoid damages. Chuck thought it best to just drive through and out run the storm. We got lucky and did not get any major hail damage. After dark we got lost trying to find Kevin's house so we arranged to meet him at the fly shop in Florence, Montana. His family graciously put us up for the night on their family room couch in the basement. They had to move the pet hamster to the bathroom so we would not hear it running the hamster wheel all night. Kevin made a huge breakfast for us the next morning and we were on the road again a little after 6am. It was good to have friends and we appreciated Kevin.

August 2, 2010
We picked up park fishing licenses and groceries in Bozeman. Upon entering Yellowstone Park we met the usual crowd of tourists and their cameras. Traffic thinned the closer we got to Cooke City. We were disappointed to see the Soda Butte River blown-out and muddy, where we had planned to fish most of the week. Pebble Creek was running clear, as it always does, so we pulled over for a few casts. I caught a six inch cutthroat on my second cast with a #14 Elk Hair Caddis and hooked another dozen small fish over the next two hours. Chuck also caught a few fish. Just below the foot bridge in the shade of a large spruce tree I caught a respectable fourteen inch cutthroat. Upon leaving we talked to two Swedish tourists about bears and fishing. Just past Soda Butte we encountered yellow tape for the second time. A van hit a buffalo during the night and the buffalo made it several hundred yards off the road, toward the river, before expiring. The carcass was attracting every bear and wolf within miles and the tourists were clamoring to take photos. A quarter mile of road was taped off to prevent tourists from parking and creating a traffic jam. It did not work. The river access was also restricted around the kill. Around 6pm we met the rest of our group at the motel.

Soda Butte River, Yellowstone

August 3, 2010
We met at the Log Cabin Cafe in Silver Gate, Montana for breakfast. This year we had members from Australia, Belgium, Pennsylvania, California, Utah, Idaho, Montana, and Oregon. Soda Butte had cleared up a little over night and we decided to fish it and the Lamar River. The traffic around

the bear kill was thicker than yesterday afternoon. We could see several large grizzlies in the distance jockeying for position around the buffalo. Chuck and I decided to fish about a half mile below Soda Butte. We parked his truck at the Lamar River trail head and headed about a quarter mile down river to several nice riffles and a large pool. We had to share the river with several other people, but unfortunately they arrived first and got the better positions. A PMD hatch began around 1pm and lasted for a couple of hours. The fish ascended the pool and stacked up in a short riffle where a guy just upstream hooked and landed a dozen large cutthroats. I fished a dozen different patterns, which were all inspected by fish but not inhaled. I finally caught two fish during the hatch on a #18 PMD Emerger. After the hatch Chuck and I had the run to ourselves and I fished the undercut stream bank with a #10 Foam Black Cricket and picked up seven fourteen and eighteen inch cutthroats. We also fished a long, fast riffle and noticed fish flashing on the bottom taking nymphs. I picked up two more fish on a #18 Bead Head Flash Back Pheasant Tail Nymph, behind a heavily weighted Possie Bugger. I tried a #12 Green Drake Emerger and caught another fish. The river got clearer throughout the day and was running clean by the time we left for dinner.

Cutthroat Trout, Soda Butte River, Yellowstone

August 4, 2010

We took horses nine miles to the third meadow of Slough Creek. We encountered yellow tape for the third consecutive day. In second meadow the park service posted signs in all the camping areas warning hikers that the area was frequented by bears. At third meadow a group of rangers on

horses were milling around the trees. We found out later what they were doing. The fishing was good, I fished with Dick from Utah and Bert from Belgium. We headed downstream about a mile with plans to fish back up stream to the group. I tied a #10 Black Foam Cricket to ten feet of leader and 5X tippet, on my six weight nine foot rod.

Second Meadow, Slough Creek, Yellowstone

I hooked three fish on the hike down river, sight casting to them from a high bank, and quickly released them, trying not to disturb the water for others in our group. I hooked my next fish after letting my fly drift over a gravel bar, through a riffle and into a back eddy. The cutthroat saw and followed my fly the whole way through the run. My next fish was in a small side channel about three feet wide and a foot deep. He was hiding next to an undercut bank and took my fly the second it hit the water. The next couple of fish were a little more challenging. The river made a long, wide, smooth turn in the large meadow. The river was deep and had large pockets of what looked like submerged grass-sod. I could get a forty foot drift and the fish could see everything, including my mistakes. I had three twenty inch cutthroats rise slowly to inspect my fly, follow it for about ten feet, and finally inhaled the fly. I could not hook them but only pricked them, felt a slight tug, and then nothing. I tried setting the hook immediately and letting the fish take and turn for a few seconds, nothing worked. I assume these fish tried to take the cricket by the legs to the bottom of the river before eating it. Who knows, but I was frustrated by these smart fish. Late in the afternoon, where the river ran close to the trail, I heard a dozen gun shots near where the park ranger's horses were tied to the trees. It was time for me to leave, assuming the shots had something to do with a bear. I picked up one more fish on the hike back to our horses. When he took my cricket I gave him slack and let him run until he hooked himself. Actually, I was looking behind me at the rangers coming out of the trees and not paying attention to my fly when he hooked himself. He was a strong fish and tore up and across river before I brought him to the net. The fish was 19 inches of gold cutthroat that barely fit into my net. Back with the group we saddled up quickly and headed down the trail. Others in our group also heard the gunshots and were concerned with the bear situation. The horses knew we were going home and wasted no time hustling back to the trailhead. The rangers were gone when we got to their camp, but there were a few more "Caution, bear frequented area" signs along the trail. Between the first and second meadow we ran into a large blonde grizzly bear about 200 yards off the trail. He stopped eating huckleberries long enough to crouch down and watch us pass on the trail. The wind was blowing towards the bear so the horses did not spook. We were glad not having to deal with an ornery bear. Back at the trailhead we learned from several vacated backpackers that a rogue black bear had been harassing several camps the previous few days. He would enter camp, tear up tents and try to eat their food. Earlier that morning the rangers set up a tent and left food out to lure in and test the bear. While we were fishing the bear came into the camp and tore it up. The rangers tried to scare the bear away and then fired warning shots but he bear continued to stay in camp. When the bear continued to behave aggressively, they shot him. On the drive back to Cooke City a large buffalo decided to control traffic for a half hour by walking down the middle of the road along the Lamar River canyon. We had dinner in Silver Gate and hit the sack early, tired with saddle-sore butts.

August 5, 2010

Chuck and I took it easy today, fishing a nice run on Soda Butte River several hundred yards up from the Lamar River. I caught two eighteen inch cutthroats in less than a foot of water, next to a gravel bar, before Chuck had rigged up his rod. Chuck caught a nice fat cutt and I hooked another fish before a hatch of PMDs and gray drakes floated down river. The fish exploded in the pool. I'd originally thought we'd fish through this hole in route to a better run, but we ended up staying for most of the day. It's amazing that a twenty yard section of water could hold so many fish. We sight cast to at least two dozen large fish who were focused on mayflys. We caught over a dozen fourteen to eighteen inch cutthroat on #18 Cream Parachutes, #12 Extended Body Drakes, #12 Parachute Adams, and #10 Black Foam Crickets. Mid-afternoon the hatch subsided. Only one fish kept rising, and he was the biggest of the pool. The fish was hanging below a semi-submerged willow branch, which was impossible to drift a fly through. We got to know him fairly well after spending an hour trying to put a hook in his lip. We finally gave up, had a late lunch, and hiked though a large gravel flood plain dotted with willows to the Lamar River. It was apparent the Lamar Valley experienced a large flood event not long ago. There was no vegetation within fifty yards of the water and the river was mostly wide and shallow. We fished the pocket water below log-jams and picked up a couple cutthroats, but for the most part this section of river was not fish-friendly. We hiked back to our hole on Soda Butte and saw several large fish nymphing in the middle of the run. I was convinced one was the same fish who hid below the willow all morning. I tied on a #18 Pheasant Tail Nymph behind a heavily weighted nymph, cast and hooked him on my first cast. He was the biggest fish of the run, a little over twenty inches, and I believe he was the same fish that eluded us all morning. We fished up Soda Butte until the sun went below the ridge, picking up two more fish on crickets along the grass bank.

Cutthroat Trout, Soda Butte River, Yellowstone

We called it quits and on the drive home saw five grizzlies lumbering around the buffalo kill along the road.

August 6, 2010

We packed up and headed towards West Yellowstone. After visiting a couple of tourist sites along the way, we stopped to fish the Yellowstone River, a couple of miles below Yellowstone Lake, at the Cascade Day Use Area. This area is known for large fish that migrate in and out of the lake. There was only one other guy on the water, and he had two young daughters with him, so his hands were full. Within minutes of rigging up our rods and stepping in the river we saw pods of big cutthroats cruising the shallow flats. I first tried a #12 Elk Hair Caddis, but the fish were too smart to be fooled by a standard pattern. The water was thick with insects - you name it, and it was probably floating down the river. Green drakes, grey drakes, pale dunns, three types of caddis, and occasional golden stoneflys. To further complicate the situation, spinners, duns and emergers were also on the water. Who knows what was going on sub-surface. I tried a #12 Parachute Adams, #12 Green Drake Emerger and #18 Pheasant Tail Nymph with no luck. The only logical remaining option was an ant. So on went the #16 Tri-Hackle Black Ant. I hooked and lost two large cutthroat over the next hour, after casting a twelve foot leader ten feet upstream of their rises. Out of the half dozen rising fish within casting distance I noticed a particularly large and dark fish. I thought "that would be a nice fish to catch", but quickly dismissed the idea from my mind. Several casts later he took my ant. I did not see the subtle take, but he took the slack out of my line and I quickly set the hook. He was as big as I imagined and made my reel sing while heading to the middle of the river. The shallow gravel-bottomed river gave him few options but to quickly expend energy. I had him in my net five minutes later, well mostly in my net. He was over two feet long. We took a few photos while admiring this magnificent fish before releasing him back to the river. This fish made my day. I lost a little intensity in my casting and even took a break in the shade to watch others in our group fish. The fish stopped rising late in the afternoon and the bugs all but disappeared. We headed up river and found a few rising fish in the slough water just below the lake. Bob Kloskowski and Bert waded out into water

up to their armpits and tried to cast to the fish, but were a few yards short of the rises.

Cutthroat, Yellowstone River, Yellowstone

Chuck and I called it quits, drove to West Yellowstone, visited three fly shops, picked up a bucket of fried chicken for dinner and checked into our motel at 9pm - all during an intense rain/hail storm.

August 7, 2010

On our last day fishing Yellowstone we wanted to catch big fish so we headed back to the Yellowstone River and were disappointed with the lack of insects. Something must have happened over night, maybe it was the storm, but there were few insects on the water. Chuck managed to hook two large trout on a #12 Extended Body Green Drake, but both broke off. Before noon the wind kicked up making it difficult to cast on the big river, so we packed up and headed towards the Gibbon and Madison Rivers. We saw a small creek meandering through a meadow and took a short detour along a one-way road at Virginia Cascade. Big mistake, a buffalo with a broken hind leg was blocking traffic as it lumbered up the road in the steep canyon. We were twenty cars behind the buffalo and progress was slow. I convinced Chuck to park and fish until the traffic jam subsided. I caught half dozen six inch brook trout in less than fifteen minutes on a #16 Elk Hair Caddis. There were probably bigger fish, but we did not stick around to find out. The brush and willows were thick and I assumed a large bear was following the buffalo's blood trail. When the buffalo made it to an open meadow the traffic cleared and we left the brookies and the buffalo to their fate. We followed the Gibbon River through thick woods and parked along the road and hiked to a promising looking log jam and deep run. It looked good, but we caught no fish. Our next stop was at some riffle water where the meadow entered a deep canyon. The water looked good but there were no fish. Maybe we were too close to the road and this area received a lot of fishing pressure. We drove up the lower Firehole River, but there was little access and too many tourists swimming in the river. We decided to fish the Gibbon in the large meadow above the confluence with the Madison River. Chuck and I split up. He took the upper meadow and I hiked to the middle of the meadow. The area smelled of sulfur from several hot pots leaking into the creek. I rigged up a #14 Elk Hair Caddis and immediately caught a small brown trout. I'd forgotten the Madison was full of browns. Over the next two hours I caught three foot long browns and one rainbow. If we'd caught a cutthroat today we'd have the Yellowstone grand-slam. Late afternoon we headed to the Madison River, about a half mile below the confluence with the Gibbon. The water was fast but covered with egg-laying caddis. I fished up the middle of the river and Chuck focused on the bank water.

Brown Trout, Madison River, Yellowstone

I quickly caught three browns and a rainbow in the fast pocket water, where fish would usually not be found, except during a massive caddis hatch. We fished two more spots on the Madison on the drive back to our motel. The water looked excellent and we saw a lot of rising fish but we had no hook-ups. We speculated that this water was heavily fished because of its proximity to the highway.

August 8, 2010
Chuck and I made the long fourteen hour drive home, taking a brief look at the Henry's Fork of the Snake River. The Rail-Road Ranch and Three-Dollar Bridge looked good but we were out of time. The total trip cost was a little over $400 each for eight days on the road. We've already started planning our next trip.

August 19, 2010
I was asked to give a presentation on fishing Davis Lake and the Owhyee River to the Rainlanders Fly Club, in Astoria, Oregon. They bought me an oyster burger dinner and we had a good meeting.

August 20, 2010
I hooked my first Klickitat steelhead. Chuck Cooney picked me up at 2:30pm after work, we met Tom Wideman in Troutdale and we were on the Klickitat River at 6pm. It had been hot and in the mid-ninety's all week and Mt. Adams was contributing a significant amount of glacial milk to the river the past week. Yesterday was the first day in the low 80s. It took glacial runoff about three days to reach the Columbia, so we thought the river might be in good enough shape to fish. The water temperature was in the low 60s, which is about where summer steelhead like it.

Klickitat River, Washington

I put a #4 Red Body Brown Squirrel Tail streamer on my six weight Spey rod and began casting downstream and across near Milepost 16, in a long run below some fast riffle water. I landed a small trout on my second cast. I worked down river about twenty yards when I got a tug, saw a fat tail flip out of the water and a second stronger pull on my rod. A large steelhead took my fly in the fast current in the middle of the river. After a couple of rolls, a short run and staring me in the eye she broke my seven pound leader. I was not upset but happy to enjoy what little time we had together. I wished I'd landed her. I picked up another foot long trout a few minutes later, which did not make me feel any better. I noticed two other steelhead roll mid-stream but they were not interested in my offerings. We saw a pair of large beavers working the willow-lined stream bank. As I worked my way downstream toward them they spooked and headed down stream and directly across the river. I struggled to get my line out of their way, but ended up hooking one in the back. He took out about thirty yards of line and did not seem too concerned. I had no option but to torque back on my rod. To my good fortune the hook pulled free from his fur and did not penetrate any muscle. We finished the run and headed downriver to fish another hole before it got dark. No more fish today, but maybe we'll give it another try next week.

August 26, 2010

Tom Wideman and I made a trip back to fish the Klickitat River, but only made it to the confluence with the Columbia River. The canyon was on fire. The police had the road blocked, helicopters were taking dip-buckets up the hill and the entire mouth of the canyon was covered with smoke. We decided to check out a couple other Washington rivers. We drove up the White Salmon and Wind Rivers but did not fish. It was mostly private land without public access.

September 9, 2010

Tom Wideman and I went back to the Klickitat River for a third time steelheading this year, and were disappointed. We fished a good looking run just below a bridge near milepost 16 and caught a couple of ten inch trout. The water was clear and not affected by the fire a few weeks earlier. We saw a few Chinook salmon roll in the slow water near the far bank and figured the more aggressive salmon were pushing the steelhead out of the run (which is common in small rivers). We fished two more runs and caught a few more trout but no steelhead. On our next trip I plan to bring my five weight rod and a couple of Elk Hair Caddis for the trout. They were very aggressive towards our Spey flys and should be fun and easy to catch.

September 18, 2010

We had a club trip to Coldwater Lake on Mt. St. Helens. It had been raining hard the day before and we awoke the next morning to fog and low clouds. We decided to give it a try anyway and I picked Dave Wesley up at 7am in Beaverton. We were on the lake at 10am. At 5,000 feet the morning sky was cloudless and I put on sunscreen as the sun rose over Johnson Ridge. Within an hour the clouds came in, covered the sun and it started to rain. Not a heavy rain, but enough to fog up your glasses and wet your shoulders. I didn't hook a fish the first two hours, until I got to the far south-east corner of the lake. I picked up three foot long rainbows and then hooked a big fish. I was fishing a five weight rod, intermediate sinking line and a #14 Tri-Color Damsel on a three foot five pound leader. After trolling for about a hundred yards I let the line sink for a few seconds before retrieving it to check the hook for debris. I'd been kicking my pontoon boat around a submerged fir tree that stuck up out of the water about four feet and intuitively knew there was a big fish there. As I retrieved and slowly lifted my line, a big fish took and started pulling. I knew he was big because he did not jerk, but had a steady, slow, hard pull.

Rainbow Trout, Coldwater Lake, Washington

After a couple of minutes I brought him to the surface and quickly wore him out. I measured him in my net at 19 inches, and let him go. After catching three more twelve inchers I hooked another big fish in almost the exact location. He was eighteen inches. By this time Dave noticed my luck and came to fish the same area. We caught a couple more fish while the storm was building.

When it got difficult to fight the wind and waves we headed back to fish the sheltered cove near the boat ramp. Dave picked up a fish before it began to pour buckets of rain. We quickly loaded our boats on my trailer and were home around 7pm. By now it was really raining. I dumped about a gallon of water on our garage floor while parking and unloading the trailer. It was really wet.

September 25, 2010
Dave Wesley won a club auction prize for a day of fishing on the pay-to-play Rocky Ridge Ranch, a hay and cattle ranch about seven miles southwest of Wamic, Oregon. He invited Tom Wideman, Pete Prepke, and I to fish with him. We arrived first thing in the morning and had our choice of several lakes. We chose Mullen Lake because it was supposed to have the biggest fish. Within a hundred yards of the put-in I hooked and landed a twenty eight inch rainbow that was about eight pounds. I could not get a photo because he was too strong to hold without help and the other guys were too far away. He was a chunky, healthy fish with perfect proportions and colors. I fished a six weight rod, intermediate sinking line, 5X tippet and a #6 Green and Olive Carey Bugger. The fishing was fantastic. I caught a half dozen twenty to twenty four inch rainbows and another dozen sixteen to twenty inch fish before lunch. The water was deep, cold and full of small mouth bass fry. There were a few insects, but it appeared the fish were gaining weight by eating the juvenile bass. About noon I caught what the ranch owner called a golden trout. His entire body was pastel orange with a crimson red stripe along each lateral line. It was not an albino because his eyes were not pink but black. I caught a few more regular rainbows before catching another golden trout at the put-in before lunch. We later learned they were called palomino rainbow trout, and were discovered at a fish hatchery in the eastern United States. Dave brought sandwiches and all the trimmings for lunch and we ate in the shade of the fisherman's cabin along shore. We hit the water again until dark. It was a little slower in the evening, but we each picked up a couple more sixteen and twenty two inch rainbows and a few smallmouth bass.

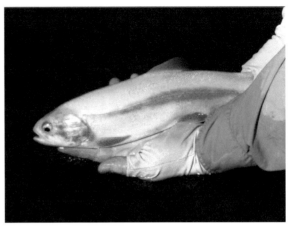

"Golden" Trout, Rocky Ridge Ranch, Oregon

The day was prefect, not a cloud in the sky, and a gentle breeze strong enough to put a faint riffle on the water. We hated to leave so we fished until dark. Finally we packed our gear in the moon light and were home just after 11pm.

October 4, 2010
The Washington County Fly Fishers had their fourth annual week-long trip to the Owhyee River, Oregon. Attendance has been on the rise since I began organizing this trip in 2007 and we went from nine people, to twelve, sixteen, and twenty four fishers this year. This trip has been a success because it is no-host, meaning all we do is pick a time and place to fish and everyone is on their own for meals, camping, and equipment. We gather each morning and evening to share meals and fishing stories. I rode with Phil Oliver in his camper again this year.

October 5, 2010
We hit the White House Hole early in the morning and it paid off handsomely. Before the day was over, I caught two dozen twelve to fourteen inch browns and one nineteen inch fish, all on a #20 Beadhead Pheasant Tail Nymph just beneath the surface. It was obvious the irrigation district was changing the river management, but it was not apparent how. The water was colder and clearer than it has ever been. We could see gravel on the bottom in three feet of water, which was unheard of in the last few years because of the silt and aquatic vegetation. The fish were more plentiful and smaller. We even hooked a couple of three inchers. I hope the big fish this river is known for were not displaced by smaller and

more plentiful fish. The nineteen inch fish I did catch was a challenge.

Brown Trout, Owhyee River, Oregon

Mid-afternoon two fish were competing for emergers in a slick between broken water. I must have cast to them fifty times before the bigger of the two rose to my fly and the fight was on. He took off to fast water and I finally landed him in the willows along the stream bank. I went back for the other fish but he wanted nothing to do with me.

October 6, 2010
Dave Wesley and I fished the rock garden run first thing in the morning. Once again the water was clear and the fish were spooky. I hooked a dozen fish at the top of a deep hole in relatively fast water. The biggest fish was a seventeen inch brown. I fished a #20 Bead Head Pheasant Tail Nymph below a #14 Elk Hair Caddis. I usually fished a #18 nymph, but the water was clear and the sun bright. All the fish we caught were sight cast to and there were a lot of fish rising to midges. When the action cooled we fished the rock garden. I was very disappointed at not seeing a single large trout where we usually see a dozen or more. At the next deep run I switched to an indicator and deep nymph and picked up three, sixteen to eighteen inch browns. It was tough going because all the fish were in deep water behind boulders and I broke off several times on sharp rocks. That evening we caught up with several others in our group and fished the White House Hole. I caught a couple of small fish and then saw a monster twenty four inch brown jump two rod lengths away in fast water. After trying for

him for a half hour, another large fish jumped in the same place. I could not raise either of them and gave up at dusk. That night the rain was heavy and it was nice to be in Phil's camper.

October 7, 2010
This morning Roger Lehman cooked me a huge six egg omelet in exchange for a dozen flys. It filled his fourteen inch frying pan and contained almost everything that could possible go into a breakfast. We fished the White House Hole again and were becoming pretty familiar with this run. We had full sun all morning and the fish were deep. I tried a new technique and tied two droppers below my Elk Hair Caddis, first a #18 Midge Pupa and below that a #20 Pheasant Tail Nymph. The pupa pulled both flys just a little deeper. Most of the two dozen twelve to sixteen inch fish I caught were on the Pheasant Tail. I caught one unlikely brown in the oddest place. Just above the pool was a fast riffle with a large boulder in the middle of the river. The water boiled and up-heaved behind the rock and I thought it would be difficult for a fish to hold in that kind of water. I took a few casts just for kicks and noticed a large fish rise to a natural. I re-focused and began casting again. Ten minutes later he took my fly and the fight was on. I played him in the hole for a few minutes, giving him slack every time he tried to leave the safety of the boulder. Finally he headed to open-fast water and I chased him downstream, hoping he would not go under a rock to hide - which he immediately did. When he was worn out I brought him to my hand and he slipped the hook in my hand.

Brown Trout, Owhyee River, Oregon

What a gorgeous fish. I caught a few more fourteen inchers before it got dark, but he was the fish of the trip.

October 7, 2010
We had breakfast, packed up and headed for the Crooked River. We arrived at the campground around 4pm and I quickly suited-up and headed to the water. I was surrounded by fisherman but no one was fishing the best, and my favorite water: the boulder field at Big Bend. Tom Wideman came down to the water to offer moral support as I waded into the fast water and held onto large rocks to keep from being washed down river. My #14 Elk Hair Caddis worked like a charm and caught two dozen Redside Rainbow Trout before it got dark. Tom caught a few fish, but was not willing to brave the fast water for more fish. Most of the fish were in the twelve inch range, but I did catch one nice sixteen incher. It seemed to get dark early and we met around Roger's campfire before hitting the sack early.

October 8, 2010
It rained last night, but let up for us to fish in the morning. A few fish were rising to midges and the fishing was slow until it started to rain again. Rain on water seems to do something to fish, and fish began rising all over the river. They were not picky. We each caught a dozen fish until we were soaking wet, cold, and tired. We called it quits early and changed into dry clothes. We stopped by the Welches Fly Shop on the way home and were with our wives before eight that evening.

Redside Trout, Crooked River, Oregon

October 19, 2010
I was asked to give a presentation on fishing for Alaska rainbows by the Clackamas Fly Fishers in Gladstone, Oregon. We met at the High Rocks restaurant and about three dozen club members showed up. Our discussion went very well, until the karaoke contest began in the bar across the hall. We got through it.

October 27, 2010
It rained an inch the last three days and Wednesday's forecast was for dry weather before it rained the rest of the week. I made a few phone calls and lined-up six guys to fish Merrill Lake, Washington. The day was clear, but the wind was terrible when we arrived at the lake about 10am. There were white caps and gusts up to thirty miles per hour. Phil Oliver put on his life vest as we rowed across the lake to a sheltered cove. Two other boats were on the water, but they left soon after lunch. I parked my pontoon boat at the mouth of a small creek and cast a #10 Carey Special on an intermediate sinking line into the current and swung my fly over some good looking water. I immediately hooked and landed a sixteen inch native cutthroat, which had beautiful markings and bronze color.

Coastal Cutthroat, Merrill Lake, Washington

A half our later I landed a seventeen inch fat rainbow. I assumed he was a triploid that Washington Fish and Wildlife had released in the lake last year. He'll be a big guy next year. The wind never did let up and the fishing slowed down so I went in search of a sheltered cove to the north, and hit the jackpot. I cast toward shore amongst some large fallen timber and started to catch fish, not a few but a bunch. Every third cast was a hook-up. All were cutthroats twelve to sixteen inches long, and one brown trout. The wind kept blowing from all directions, but it didn't matter, the bite was on. I must have caught fifty fish before it began getting dark. Chuck Cooney, Chuck Smith, Phil Oliver, and Greg Kohn also caught a lot of fish. The wind never did stop blowing and I suppose the fish were looking for shelter too. We all met at a diner in Woodland, Washington and had fried chicken and ice cream for dinner.

November 3, 2010
I gave a presentation to the Washington County Fly Fishers on *The Year in Review Fishing Trips*. I assembled a bunch of fishing-trip photos into a slide show and spoke about fishing. I was surprised to discover that I'd fished about fifty days since January, that's one day in every eight days. It's been a very good year.

November 6, 2010
This was my sixth year as fly tyer chair for the Pacific Northwest Fly Tyers Rendezvous in Troutdale, Oregon. We had great participation from thirty five tyers and from the public. We auctioned off over eighty fly boxes and assorted fly fishing gear, and earned $3,600 to donate to fishery scholarships and conservation activities.

November 12, 2010
Chuck Cooney planned a Washington County Fly Fishers trip to the Deschutes River and made reservations for us at the Deschutes Motel in Maupin. We swung bucktails for steelhead, upriver from Maupin, all day with our Spey and Switch Rods to no avail. Catching steelhead is all about timing, and we had bad timing. That night we were surprised at the condition of the motel. There were four rooms in the building, three were gutted and being re-modeled. Our room (in the middle) had not been worked on yet. The heater had been removed and the electrical wiring was being worked on. The motel had recently sold and the new owner stopped by our room to apologize for the mess, and see if our portable heater was working. We did not feel bad for wearing our wet wading boots on the carpet. The construction workers were living in the un-finished rooms next door and were polite enough, but still noisy.

November 13, 2010
We fished for steelhead downriver from Maupin all morning and saw no fish. After noon we watched a Spey fisher hook and land a beautiful nine pound buck steelhead across the river. That was it. I broke out the trout gear and caught a rainbow on my first cast.

Redside Rainbow, Deschutes River, Oregon

He was a sixteen inch Redside and took a #18 Pheasant Tail Nymph. It felt good to have a fish on after two days, even though we were after big fish. My shoulders needed a break from casting a heavy rod anyway. We fished from Wapinitia upstream to the big pool above Harpham Flats.

Deschutes River, Oregon

I caught a half dozen fourteen to sixteen inch trout just feet from the deep, grass lined bank. All the fish took the Possie Bugger, except the first fish. They must have been keying on the October caddis because the bugger was slightly brown-orange. We did pick up a few fish swinging soft

hackles in the Harpham Pool as it was getting
dark. A very large trout kept rising at the tail-out,
but we could not reach him. The club had a pot-
luck microwave dinner at the motel that night.
One of the guys brought a friend fishing on his
first fly fishing trip. What his friend did not tell us
was that he has a bad case of vertigo. Watching an
indicator bob up and down on the river all day
made him sick and he could hardly walk. We had
to help him off the river and to bed, while he kept
moaning about a migraine headache and upset
stomach. I took off after dinner for the long drive
home. The snow and ice had melted off the
mountain the previous day. I got home a little
after 9pm.

2011

January 12, 2011
Chuck Cooney and I gave a presentation to the Stonefly Maidens Fly Club about fishing Yellowstone National Park. What an interesting group of ladies. They bought us dinner at the Iron Horse Restaurant in Portland, Oregon.

January 15, 2011
Joel La Follette invited me to do a fly tying demonstration at his new Royal Treatment Fly Shop in West Linn, Oregon. I tied the "life cycle of the Blue Wing Olive". There was a good turn-out but I was not sure if it was for me or for the homemade cookies Joel's mother puts out every Saturday morning. I was able to sell three framed flys for $175 each.

January 27, 2011
I was working in Bozeman, Montana all week so I called Bob Kloskowski to see if he wanted to fish. Bob picked me up at the motel a little after noon. I purchased a fishing license at the fly shop on the outskirts of Bozeman, Montana and we high-tailed it to the Ruby River. The weather was perfect, sunny, very light wind, temperatures in the low forties and patches of snow underneath the sagebrush. The Bureau of Reclamation was doing construction on the Ruby Dam and the area was closed to the public for the last few months (which meant the river directly below the dam had not been fished in weeks).

Ruby River, Montana

We drove through the open gate, past the keep out signs and parked behind a large juniper near the construction foreman's trailer-office. I jumped out of the truck, walked to the river bank with a camera and notepad and pretended to be someone of importance. The construction crew ignored us. After a few minutes we jumped in our waders, grabbed our gear and headed down river just out of sight. The first hole was good. Bob pulled out two Browns at the tail-out on a #18 Midge Pupa. I fished a #18 Midge Pupa at the head of the hole with no luck. Bob and I switched places and he began catching rainbows at the head of the run. I added a split-shot to my line, about eighteen inches above my two midges and began catching fish, fourteen to sixteen inch Browns.

Brown Trout, Ruby River, Montana

I froze my hand the first time I put it in the water. An hour later we headed down river and fished another nice run with midge pupa, but no luck. We switched to #14 Peach Yarn Eggs and began catching fish. Bob thought the rainbows headed up river this time of year to spawn and piled up a mile or so below the dam. The browns followed the rainbows up river, taking advantage of their stray eggs. We picked our way down river over icy stream banks for about a half mile, hooking two or three fish in every hole. The fish were well fed but a little sluggish, they did not put up much of a fight in the cold water. We headed back to the truck when the sun went behind the ridge and it got cold. I was glad Bob was willing to take me to one of his favorite winter hunts and to have had such good luck.

January 28, 2011

Bob and I were back on the Ruby River in the morning, but we took too much time at the fly shop in Ennis. Someone was parked where Bob wanted to fish. We headed downstream to the Vigilante Day Use Area, suited up and walked to the river. The snow was about three inches deep in the willows and bunchgrasses. The weather was a repeat of yesterday, a little chilly but comfortable. We hoped for a midge hatch and began fishing dry flys (as indicators) with midge pupa droppers. A few fish were rising, but after an hour we switched back to indicators, split-shots, eggs and pupa. Bob picked up a few fish on a #16 Lightning Bug (silver tinsel pheasant tail) and I lost several fish. It just was not my day. I'd hook a fish and lose it seconds later, probably setting the hook too fast on cold, sluggish trout. We fished one nice long run below an irrigation diversion; I went first and hooked and lost three fish. Bob played clean-up and landed half dozen nice browns. Bob reminded me this was his home water, but I detected little sympathy in his voice. At dusk we were tired, had caught enough fish, and were ready for dinner. Dean Larson called us on our way home and invited us to dinner at the Veteran's Lodge in Bozeman. We had double cheeseburgers, salad, and sodas in the crowded hall with a bunch or Dean's war buddies, and had a great time.

February 2, 2011

The featured speaker canceled for our monthly Washington County Fly Fishers meeting, so the night before our meeting I was asked to give a presentation on our Yellowstone trip. It went well... except for the usual cat-calls from the back row. "Hey, same fish again, what do you do, keep it in the freezer?" or "Same pet fish, but you changed your shirt". The next time someone cancels these guys should give the presentation. All in all we have a pretty good club, and don't take ourselves too seriously and we're not pretentious.

February 5, 2011

I was invited to give a fly tying demonstration at the North West Fly Fishing Shop in Portland, Oregon. About a dozen people showed up. I tied traditional Spey and Dee flys, including a northwest favorite the Skagit Mist. Later the shop bought me lunch and we had a good conservation.

February 16, 2011

I was invited to teach twelve scouts how to tie flys and fly cast at our church. I lined up three other guys to help out for our first meeting, and even with their help it was total bedlam. We used the fly club's tying kits and gave each boy a bag with enough hooks and materials to tie three flys. The first fly took a half hour. Two or three boys were intent on learning a new skill, half the boys took a moderate interest and the others just went through the motions. Each boy did get through three flys, with varying degrees of success.

March 4, 2011

After a year's work my son Grady finished his Eagle Scout project. He worked with the Oregon Department of Fish and Wildlife's Trask River Fish Hatchery, and made seventy five displays showing five stages of the "Development of Coho Salmon Eggs to Fry."

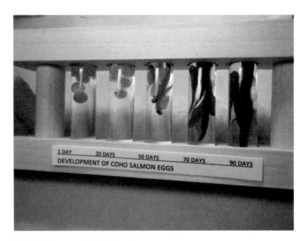

Fish Egg to Fry Display

He wrote a proposal, procured funding from fly fishing clubs, recruited volunteers, made the displays, and distributed the displays to various conservation and educational groups.

March 11, 2011

I tyed my seventh year at the Fly Tyers Expo in Albany, Oregon and demonstrated the CDC Comparadun. I met old friends, met new tyers and learned some new tricks. I won one of Henry Hoffman's signature original rooster pelts at the tyers reception and also some framed steelhead flys at the banquet. I caught a ride with Chuck Cooney both days.

March 19, 2011
Mike Frank picked me up at my motel in Columbia, South Carolina at 1pm for an afternoon's worth of fishing. He began guiding float trips in the area four years ago and was working to develop a wider audience and fly fishing clientele. In route to the river we picked up barbecue at the local soul food joint from Ernest, who made riverside sack lunches for Mike's guide business. Mike was a Yankee but appeared to have made a smooth transition to southern culture. Mike grew up fishing in New York and Washington DC but headed south for school, a girl, and fishing opportunities. We loaded the barbecue into the van and headed above town a couple of miles and parked up river from the zoo, along the frontage road parallel to the Saluda River. From the road we could see about one hundred yards of class III white water dropping about ten feet over solid rock and boulders. We put on our waders and headed to the river. There were dozens of sun-bathers, mostly college students, tanning on stream bank rocks, drinking, listening to boom-boxes, and celebrating St. Patrick's Day (apparently a three day affair in this college town). The Saluda River was about 55 degrees and considered a tail-water below Lake Murray Reservoir. The river is barely habitable for rainbow trout and several thousand fish were planted each spring. A few trout survived the fisherman, otters, stripers, bass, and grew fat on the abundant aquatic life in the river. We began targeting carry-over trout in the fast water.

Rainbow Trout, Saluda River, South Carolina

Mike tied on #6 Wooly Buggers in white-silver and brown-yellow and we swung them deep and across large pools. We waded to mid-river and stood on a submerged ridge of solid rock to reach the good water. After two hours I had a couple of chases and hits and Mike landed one slim fourteen inch rainbow. A couple of hours later we headed downriver, stepping over co-ed sunbathers and avoiding barking dogs. I was concerned with one drunken fellow in a huge sombrero, shamrock-green shorts, and an extra-large leprechaun tee shirt that wanted to talk but could not form a coherent sentence. We worked the lower end of the fast water and I hooked and lost another trout. After several kamikaze kayakers came barreling through the rapids, ricocheting off rocks without life jackets, we decided it was time to leave and look for more pleasant water. Mike pointed out old rock abutments on both sides of the river and explained how General Sherman blew up the weir here during the Civil War, and took a strategic position on the far side of the river by placing snipers on the top floor of an old grain mill. Funny how from a distance all the sun bathers scattered along the river banks on this historic site could have been Civil War causalities after a battle. We loaded our gear in the van and headed back to town and parked at Riverfront Park, less than a mile from my motel near downtown Columbia. We unloaded two kayaks off Mike's trailer, threw our gear inside and carried the boats a couple of hundred yards to the headwaters of the Congaree River. We launched our kayaks in a slough and headed up river a short distance to the main river where the Saluda and Broad Rivers came together forming the Congaree River. The Saluda is a cold tail-water, the Broad warm and shallow, together they create an interesting fishery. There were bream, crappie, smallmouth and largemouth bass in the river. The main attraction however were the large stripers migrating up stream, which grow to over fifteen pounds. We were a little early for stripers, but Mike thought we might run into a few fish. The smaller males enter the river earlier than the larger females. We tied on #4 White and Chartreuse Clousers to ten pound tippets on seven weight rods and began fishing the Broad River side of the Congaree River, because it was warmer and Mike assumed it would hold more fish this time of year. We fished several back-water spots along shore from our kayaks, just below the confluence of the rivers, with no luck. It had been sunny all day, but just before sundown the clouds came in and it was 10 degrees cooler.

We headed to the main stem of the Congaree, parked our kayaks on top of several boulders, and waded the lower end of a short stretch of riffle-water. After a half dozen casts and drifting our flys over the lip of the cobble riffles and swinging-stripping them though the deeper water Mike hooked a nice fish. The fish took line out, rolled a few times, and flipped its tail in the air before Mike brought a two pound striper to the net. Mike quickly switched our Clousers to big foam #2 Yellow Sliders and we began casting, stripping and causing a lot of commotion on the surface of the water. I had a couple of hits until finally hooking and landing a nice three pound striper.

Striper, Congraee River, South Carolina

He was strong and pulled deep, but came in easily after I got his head on the surface. We got a couple more hits but no hook-ups. As it was getting dark a large adult bald eagle flew over our heads and downstream carrying a small fish. Storm clouds began heading our way and we could see lightning in the distance. We switched to #4 Black and White Clousers and caught two smallmouth bass. Each fish was about three and a half pounds, strong and healthy. Mike said they were unusually large for this location and time of year. We fished for another half hour in the dark before the lightning starting hitting a few miles to the west and it started to rain. We made our way back to the put-in with head-lamps. Mike began seeing imaginary alligators as we paddled near shore, under the Spanish moss, near submerged boulders and wind-fall trees.

Smallmouth, Congraee River, South Carolina

He said alligators were rare in this river, but they occasionally did get this far north. Mike dropped me off at the motel a little after 10pm. I thanked him for an enjoyable day and ate my microwaved barbecue while watching the late night news.

March 21, 2011
I got a call from Mike Frank last night asking if I wanted to fish the Congaree River again, specifically help him search for new spring water. He picked me up at the motel at 4pm and we parked in the zoo parking lot. We carried a fourteen foot raft from the parking lot to the river, making three trips. There was a crowd of sun bathers at the put-in (apparently the same group of college co-eds from last weekend) who were very interested in the raft. Mike went to park his van and could not get back fast enough to rescue me from the gathering bathing suit crowd. No, we can't take you fishing with us. We finally put-in, rowed up river a hundred yards and fished for trout at the base of the whitewater for a few minutes, with no luck. It was sunny with a slight breeze and a perfect 80 degrees. We fished some deep bank water while heading down river and over a series of class II rapids at the confluence of the Broad River. The frog water of the lower Broad River looked good and from a distance we saw fish rising. They later turned out to be several large turtles cruising the surface. I did bring one large bass to my fly, but he did not take. As the sun was going down and the light conditions were getting better for fishing we parked the raft on a large boulder near some promising riffles and waded up river to fish the fast water. The fast water did not produce so we exchanged our foam

flys for #6 Chartreuse Clousers and began catching fish. My first was a three and a half pound smallmouth bass who was hanging at the lip of a long riffle.

Smallmouth Bass, Congraee River, South Carolina

He hit hard and used the fast water to swing to the far end of the pool before we landed him. The next three fish were small stripers averaging about fourteen inches. I caught three fish on four casts. Unknown to me a large otter snuck-up behind a large boulder and began eating fresh water clams three rod lengths away from where I was standing. I fished around his rock, surprised him and he jumped and slapped the water. I kept remembering the alligators Mike was talking about.

White Bass, Congraee River, South Carolina

The next fish was a White Bass, which Mike said were not common in this part of the river because the gear fishermen kept them all. The next fish was a big one. I cast to the lip on the far side of

the riffle and swung my fly through the back of the pool hoping to get my fly as deep as possible. It worked and when I began stripping my fly a large fish took and quickly stripped out thirty yards of line. I worked him half way through the pool before he slipped the hook. That was a big fish. A few minutes later I hooked his twin in the same place and fought him for ten minutes before putting him in the net. He felt bigger, but ended up being an eighteen inch, four pound striper. That was the last fish of the day. We drifted and cast to likely looking water in the dark. We passed under a couple of highway bridges in town and ran into two other fishermen in a John Boat at about 10pm.

Striper, Congraee River, South Carolina

Mike anchored below one bridge and we fished within sight of the state capitol. Next we pulled in below an old check-dam across the entire river and cast into the pitch-black air and water. Finally after a six mile float we took out at a nice boat ramp near a gravel pit below town. I got back to the motel just before midnight. It was a good day.

April 16, 2011
Paul Skelton invited Chris Roe and me to fish the Metolius River on Saturday. We met at the Fly Shop and were in Camp Sherman by 9am. It rained most of the way over the Cascades but was slightly drier on the east side, at least dry enough to pop sunflower seeds in our mouths without getting our hands wet. We bought a donut, then looked at fly-gear and tourist trinkets at the Camp store before heading down river to Allingham Bridge to fish. I tied a #6 Olive and White Dolly Lama to four feet of fifteen pound fluorocarbon

tippet and began casting my six weight Switch-Rod with a Skagit Head and ten feet of sink tip. The pool directly under the bridge was perfect Bull Trout habitat. Both sides of the river were deep-cut and full of root wads, timber, and large boulders. I cast to the far side of the river into a small, shallow cove, mended my line over the drop-off into deep water and swung my heavily weighted fly through the run and tail-out. It seemed a perfect drift, but no takers. I repeated the cast again. On my third cast, in the middle of the run, a fish hit my fly and about pulled the rod out of my hands. The battle was on. The fish took line, played the current, took cover in the under-cut bank root wads and generally did everything in its power to get away. The fifteen pound tippet and Octopus stinger hook held strong and after a five minute struggle, and several attempts with the net, we had him. The Bull Trout was over twenty inches and maybe five pounds. These guys were not pretty, they were mean looking and full of spite.

Bull Trout, Metolius River, Oregon

We admired him for a minute and slowly released him to the depths. Whew, that was fun. I kept swinging the smolt pattern through several likely looking deep holes with no luck. Mid-morning I hit smooth, two foot deep water in between two shallow riffles. It screamed trout water. I rested the run and sat on a semi-submerged island of grass and ate a sandwich. I began swinging again and hooked a fat Redside rainbow about fourteen inches long, a good fish in the Metolius. The fly was half as long as he was, but apparently he thought he could handle it. I swung several more runs until hitting a nice, deep pool that looked

very fishy. I crept up behind the willows and flipped my fly into the head of the run and dead-drifted it down river about ten feet before getting a good swing at the tail-out. I saw a fish flash and repeated the cast, except casting a little further upstream and swinging though the head of the run. He was another aggressive, fourteen inch fish. He had brilliant colors, a golden brown spine, and a deep crimson red band. He was wearing his spawning colors.

Redside Trout, Metolius River, Oregon

We skipped fishing the canyon and drove down river and parked near the fish hatchery. Three guys were fishing near Wizard Falls, but they did not appear to know what they were doing. One guy broke his rod and asked us how to fix it, we told him to get a new rod. We fished down river to the next large run, the dolly hole, without much luck. Paul took the head of the pool where it swept into a calm pool. I fished the fast, deep boulder water above the pool. I hooked and landed a foot long rainbow swinging deep though the fast water. We fished the pool hard for about an hour with no more luck. A couple of guys on the far bank hooked two rainbows on soft-hackles. That was it for the day. We headed back for one more try at Allingham Bridge, but there was a guy standing in the middle of the run, right where the fish were supposed to be. When he saw us he sat on the bank and had a cigar, signaling to us he was not leaving and this was his water. It was getting late, beginning to rain again, so we packed up our gear and waders and hit the road. We hoped to get dinner at the Camp Sherman Store, but we were five minutes late. The lady shop keeper just smiled at us through the window and pointed to the closed sign. I'm sure she's seen our types before. Dejected, we hiked into the head of the Metolius to see the entire river come out of a crack in the basalt hillside. On the way home we stopped in Salem for burgers and milkshakes.

April 21, 2011
Chuck Cooney and Tom Wideman talked me into leaving work early to fish Lost Lake in Clatsop County, Oregon. Apparently the lake had been fishing well. I finished a meeting at 9am in Portland, drove through rain in the Tualatin Valley, hail at the Coast Range Summit, snow along the Nehalem River, and arrived at the lake in full sun shine. I brushed a couple of inches of hail off the float tube in the back of Chuck's pick-up truck, put on my fins and launched into the cold water. Tom and Chuck had already caught several dozen fish. My first fish came ten minutes later, a seventeen inch rainbow. Large compared to what Oregon Fish and Wildlife usually stocks in this lake. The sunshine ended minutes later, the wind picked up, and it became colder. We happily gnawed on sunflower seeds, ducked the bad weather in the shelter of the alders along shore, and caught a bunch of fish. We were catching at least one fish every ten minutes on every pattern we threw in the water. Tom had a sore throat and I was getting cold. About 4pm I offered to give Tom a ride home. Chuck elected to fish a few more hours with Chris (another guy from our club). On the way back to the boat ramp I picked up another beautiful seventeen inch rainbow and took him home for Jean. She's always asking for fresh trout for dinner. Later I learned that Chuck caught a seven pound Steelhead after we left. Maybe we should have stayed a little longer.

April 26, 2011
I flew into Honolulu, Hawaii and walked the jetty in front of the Ala Moana Marina the first night, looking for fish. I was back on the jetty the next evening in time for low tide at 6pm. I ignored dozens of Tilapia feeding in the brackish water on the harbor side of the break-wall and focused on the reef fish. I'd heard this was a good spot for Bonefish and Trevally, but was not sure whether I should fish high or low tide. I invited Wallace Jennings, a friend of mine from Swains Island (north of Samoa) who I'd worked with in Saipan a few years ago, to go fishing. I had given Wallace an Atlantic salmon fly ten years before and during

this meeting he gave me two traditional flys he made out of mother of pearl shell, black coral, coconut fiber cord, and rooster feathers. Something the Polynesians fished with several hundred years ago. We walked the rock rip-rap until sunset, looking for fish and blind casting, but had no luck. The low tide was not low enough to wade out onto the reef; maybe fishing would be better at high tide.

April 30, 2011
Saturday I had the whole day to fish. I'd sent my Honolulu friend, Louie the Fish, a letter a few weeks earlier to see if he wanted to fish, but did not hear back from him. Yesterday morning I got a message from Louie saying he was getting too old to wade the reef but said his son could take me. I decided to call the local fly shop instead and lined up a day with saltwater guide Eddie, Nervous Waters Fly Shop owner Clay, and past owner of California's Caddis Fly Shop, Ted. Eddie picked me up at the hotel at 9am and we were on the water in an hour.

Keehi Small Boat Harbor, Hawaii

We used the boat ramp at Keehi Small Boat Harbor off of Sand Island Access Road. The tide's timing was perfect, low tide was at 8am (-.14') and high tide at 3pm (+1.64'). The depth was not ideal but doable. We dropped Clay and Ted off at Rat Island to blind-cast to bonefish in the slightly deeper channels and seams on the southwest corner of the reef. Eddie and I preceded a half mile north to Triangle Reef and anchored the motorboat directly across the channel from the concrete pill-box on Rat Island. Half a dozen other fishermen were working the middle of the flats, a couple using spinning rods. Eddie knew several of them. We began walking in a northeasterly direction on the edge of the reef, staying about one long cast away from the deep water. The theory was that bonefish would enter the shallow reef water to take crabs and shrimp and hustle back to blue water if threatened. The water was below our knees and 75 degrees. I had an eight weight, nine foot rod and fourteen feet of fifteen pound tapered fluorocarbon leader. It was a little windy and the water choppy. My bead-chain eyed Crazy Charlies were too light to sink to the bottom and stay there, so we tied on one of Eddie's #6 Bar-Bell Dark Brown Rubber-Leg Crab patterns. We could see bones in the shallow rough water when the sun was out but when a cloud passed overhead we could see no fish, which was about a third of the time. We saw a few tails and fins above the water, but most fish were feeding in a zigzag pattern and we randomly intersected them. Most casts were less than twenty five feet because of the glare on the water, but we caught our first bonefish after casting to a dozen fish. I took the first cast dropping my fly about ten feet in front of the direction he was traveling. The fish took notice and followed my fly to the end of my rod tip. I could do nothing but stand completely still while Eddie took a second cast five feet away, and after two short strips hooked the fish. The bone stripped out thirty feet of line while Eddie laughed and said "this is too easy". We landed him ten minutes later, a nice five pounder.

Bonefish, Triangle Reef, Hawaii

We worked towards the northern tip of the flat, then southwest across the channel from the

airport and finally cut across the middle of the reef back to the boat. I cast to a dozen fish, and I had half of them turn and follow my fly for several feet, but no hook-ups. They were really spooked, probably because of the on and off clouds and fishing pressure. We came within a few feet of a large puffer fish and one small sting ray. When the water was waist-deep we jumped in the boat and went searching for Clay and Ted. They had given up blind casting (probably because of the high, choppy water) and were working the flats. The reef around Rat Island appeared to be one or two feet higher than Triangle Reef, so we could still fish it at high tide. We anchored the boat in the mangroves on the northeastern tip of the reef and saw fish less than five minutes out of the boat. I hooked a bonefish on my third cast, about a four pounder.

Bonefish, Rat Island, Hawaii

I cast ten feet ahead of him, dropped my rod-tip an inch into the water surface and stripped all the lose line in to keep the line tight. When he was within sight of the fly I slowly pulled the line in six inch strips, not in jerks that would spook a fish. I hooked another bone on my very next cast. He was slightly smaller but lots of fun. Wow, a double in two casts! After the excitement we began working west along the edge of the reef, seeing lots of fish. We saw a monster bone thirty yards away heading straight at us on top of white coral sand. I dropped my crab fly well in front of him and when he was two feet away, gave my fly a slow, smooth pull to get his attention. It worked; he followed my fly about six pulls over ten feet before I ran out of room to strip anymore. Every time he would look away I'd give the fly a short pull and he would immediately be on top of it again, stare it down, look away, and I'd get his attention again with another pull. He was supposed to chase the fly during the pull and take the fly as it dropped to rest. He apparently did not know the rules and finally swam off. I began pulling what was left of my hair out. The wind and tide picked up a little more as we worked the edge of the reef towards the World War II concrete pill box. The abandoned gun turrets were manned by several white terns. Dozens of small crabs were jockeying for position along the waterline, re-adjusting after each wave of water hit the structure. At high tide we walked back to the boat on higher ground. A few bones were poking into the mangrove roots and we cast to a few more fish with no luck. There was little cover for fish and they were restless.

Rat Island, Hawaii

Back at the boat the once knee-deep water was over our waists, it was time to go. At the boat ramp we changed our clothes and washed the boat and rinsed our fishing gear with fresh water. It was a good trip, we could have caught more fish with better conditions but I'll take a day like this in paradise anytime.

May 2, 2011
I turned fifty years old and had planned to fish the Ala Moana Jetty near Honolulu, but there was a big storm and the hotel got pounded with a wall of rain. I watched two water spout tornadoes off-shore of Waikiki Beach make havoc with the tourist boats, causing them to scramble back to the marina. We had thunder, lightning, and rain

for several hours before the storm passed around midnight.

May 13, 2011
I went in to the office at 5am so Tom Wideman and I could fish the afternoon for carp on Sauvie Island. It was still a little cool in the afternoon with partly cloudy, late spring weather. The carp were moving around. We visited several small lakes before selecting one to wade and fish, in the Mud Lake unit. Several weeks earlier my cousin (who is the Oregon Department of Fish and Wildlife refuge manager of Sauvie Island) outlined on a map several likely places to fish. Each spot corresponded to where ODFW allows cattle to graze on the island. We figured if the soil could support wandering cattle, we also could walk the bank and wade the shallows without getting stuck in the mud. Our theory paid off and we were able to wade about ten acres of knee-deep water on solid ground. Carp were everywhere, but mostly in a foot of water in thick weeds. We knew where the carp were by watching the top of the grass move as a carp swam by the roots. We could also see wakes in the water made by fast moving fish and occasionally saw fish jumping out of the water. The fish were in spawning mode and showed little interested in our flys. Tom and I had a few hits, so we believed, but no solid hook-ups. We would locate a fish, determine its direction of travel, cast several feet in front of where we thought it was heading and slowly strip when the fish was within striking distance. Good theory, except for the weeds and spawning distractions of the fish. We called it quits after a couple of hours of workout with our rods. It takes a lot of work and perseverance to find good carp fishing. We had not paid our dues yet. We' decided to come back in a few weeks.

May 24, 2011
I visited Washington DC, the land of monuments, tourists, and bureaucrats. The Potomac River was running high, muddy, and not fishable. The tidal basin was a short walk from the office and I'd seen people fishing there over the years. I walked down the mall and headed east at the Washington Monument. The basin was clear and a few fish were rising in the late afternoon. This is going to be interesting. I walked past the Jefferson Memorial and spoke briefly to a couple of bait-fishing homeless guys under the bridge with surf

rods. I assumed they were fishing for Stripers or large carp. They had not caught anything. Underneath a row of cherry trees, I set up my fly rod, tying on a #14 Cary Special behind a weighted #10 Cary Bugger. A sidewalk and rock wall, descending into the water, completely encircled the basin. The water was three or four feet deep next to the wall and looked fishy. Three casts later I caught a hand-sized Bluegill. Between the Jefferson and Franklin D. Roosevelt Memorials I caught two dozen fish including, Sunfish, Bluegill, Smallmouth Bass, and Crappie.

Jefferson Memorial, Washington DC

No fish were over twelve inches, but they were all fun to catch. A few tourists stopped to chat, wondering if fishing was allowed. Of course it was, this is a National Park isn't it? The best fishing was between the Franklin D. Roosevelt and Martin Luther King Memorials. Imagine fishing in such a historic place, with people from every country in the world wandering by for friendly conversation, and you're the only person fishing within sight. I trolled along the base of the rock wall, about six feet from shore. A back cast was impossible because of the cherry trees, so I cast sideways along the walkway. Once the line was in the water I'd hold my rod over the water and slowly walk until I hooked a fish. Towards the bridge near the Washington Monument I located a couple of huge carp that must have been at least thirty pounds. I cast at them for a half hour with no success. They were more interested in scrapping algae off the rocks and eating semi-ripe mulberries falling into the water, than my flys. After at least three dozen fish I put my rod away and rode the Metro Train from the Smithsonian

back to my hotel in Rosslyn, Virginia in the dark. Never leave home without your fly rod.

Washington Memorial, Washington DC

June 4, 2011
Our son Grady graduated from high school and will attend Portland Community College this fall.

June 8, 2011
The North Fork Trask River has a three week spring trout fishing season. Tow Wideman and I blew off work for the day and went fishing mid-week. I don't know how we we're still employed and draw a paycheck, but we manage. After a quick stop at the Tillamook jerky factory and my Tillamook field office we headed up the North Fork of the Trask River. We fished a large pool at the confluence and picked up a half dozen resident cutthroats from ten to sixteen inches. Elk Hair Caddis were not working even though there were bugs all over the water. Fish were not rising. I switched to a heavily weighted #14 Possie Bugger and swung it through the deep runs. It worked like a charm. A friend of mine liked to fish eight and a half miles up the South Fork so we skipped a lot of good looking water and headed upstream. The river was in a deep canyon and full of large boulders and gravel. I picked up another dozen fish on the Possie Bugger, the biggest a beautiful sixteen incher. Fish started rising so I switched back to a #14 Elk Hair Caddis and caught a half dozen trout in a riffly-run about ten yards long. These fish had no fear and struck with abandon at my fly. Tom fished the slower gravel bars upstream and picked up a few more fish. Back at the car we shot a box of shells in our handguns and killed a couple of paper cups. I'm a

terrible shot and need more practice. We headed downriver and crossed the bridge heading towards Gold Creek. We pulled over at a nice campsite above the bridge and fished a large pool from a sandy beach. This has got to be a great place to hang-out on a hot August afternoon. I caught a fifteen inch rainbow on my caddis fly before Tom could rig up his rod.

Cutthroat, North Fork Trask River, Oregon

Not to be outdone, Tom swung a weighted chartreuse fry pattern deep and caught a sixteen cutthroat near the tail-out. It was a very nice fish. That was it for the day. We finished the remains of our lunch and headed back to the Trask River Highway, in search of a short-cut home a friend of mine had told me about a few days earlier. We turned up the hill not far below Trask River County Park and went up to the ridge and down the other side of the hill on Kansas Creek Road, saving about twenty miles and a half hour of driving. I wished I'd known about this road years ago. It would have saved a lot of rubber. The cutthroat season closed a few days later so I didn't get out again but definitely planned to fish here next year.

June 9, 2011
I was invited to give a presentation on Steelhead Fly Fishing to the Northwest Steelheaders in Aloha, Oregon. They were mostly gear and bait guys, but seemed cordial enough during the meeting. I think they were curious about fly fisherman, and not so much about fly fishing. I discussed the history of fly fishing relative to gear fishing, showed a few slides of my steelhead and ended with a short video clip of catching a steelhead on a fly line. I was embarrassed to win the club's raffle, but they gave me the raffle tickets.

June 11, 2011
We had one of the best days on the Deschutes River ever. The weather was unusually cool this spring, and with 200% plus of average snowpack in the mountains and high water, the salmon fly hatch was delayed by several weeks. I picked up Ralph Brooks at his house in Beaverton and met the rest of the club at the Deschutes Angler in Maupin at 9am. It was partly cloudy and about 70 degrees when we started fishing a short way up from town. I tied on a #8 Black Foam Salmonfly with a #18 Pheasant Tail Nymph dropper and began casting next to the grassy bank. I noticed a trout rise about twenty feet out in the faster current and flipped my fly his direction. He appeared out of nowhere, nosed the salmonfly, and turned and took the pheasant tail. He was strong and jumped a couple of times before I landed and released him. The poison ivy was abundant this year and we had to pick through thick patches to get on the water. I had a few more refusals before I hooked my next fish. He took the salmonfly under a larger alder tree's limbs and headed mid-stream. I could not hold the rod high enough to prevent it getting tangled up in a tree so I fought him sideways under the branches until Ralph came to help land him. He was a big fish, almost seventeen inches, and a jumper – he cleared the water a half dozen times. After two nice fish in the first half hour, it was a good day already. After a couple more fish I walked a half mile back to the car and picked up Ralph along the road and drove upstream to the first day-use area. Ralph immediately picked up three fish in the flat water, along shore, below a small riffle. I picked up another fish in the same riffle and had a monster fish refuse my fly twice, a rod's length away. A whitewater rafting group drove up and began unloading their gear upstream in the next riffle. I hustled up and fished the water before they disturbed the fish, landing a nice, fat twelve incher. At the next run we stumbled through yet another group of swimsuit clad, lawn chair lounging, sunbathing rafters. Ralph commented on the beautiful day we were having. We each picked up another half dozen fish before heading back to the car for lunch. Next we drove past Harpham Flats and fished a long run in the shade

of a huge cottonwood tree. I took the tail-out and caught two fish in the pocket water next to shore. Ralph had hit after hit in the deep run but could not hook them. He kept hitting his rod on the branches of the cottonwood every time he tried to set the hook. It was obvious that's where the fish were, no reason to move on. He solved the problem by swinging a soft-hackle downstream, and then he began hooking and landing fish. I headed upstream and fished my favorite type of water, the pocket water along shore. I hooked several more fish on the stonefly. I'd cast below semi-submerged rocks, got a five to ten second drift, and knew within a few casts if fish were home or not. Most fish would appear as dark shadows out of the foamy froth and hit the fly with a solid whack. If not hooked the first time, they rarely returned for a second look. I thoroughly covered this type of water for the next mile before heading back to Harpham Flats to meet Ralph and the rest of the club for dinner. When we arrived, Chuck was fixing hot dogs and chili for the group. We shot-the-bull until the shadows hit the water, hoping for a caddis hatch. We had caddis everywhere, but the wind kept them in the bushes and out of the water. We caught a few more fish before calling it a day around 8pm. It's been a good trip because we had most of the water to ourselves for several reasons. First, I suppose most fishermen assumed the river was too high because it had rained all week in Portland and the Willamette and Columbia Rivers were at flood stage. However, the water height and color were just right. Second, they thought the salmon fly hatch was over, but it was just a little late this year. Most of the big black bugs had expired, but the golden ones were all over the water. Third, no fishing license was required because it was free fishing day and most die-hard Deschutes anglers assumed the river would be crowded. It was not crowded. We could not have picked a better day to be on the water. We bought a pizza in Maupin and ate it on the way home. The pizza was bad, but we were hungry so it balanced out. I got home after midnight, just in time to give Jean her 25th wedding anniversary gift. Hard to believe we've been married half our lives. I'm still amazed I can get this much fishing in and still have a wonderful marriage.

June 19, 2011
The fly tying feather hackle market was out of control because of a women's feather hair extension fad. I sold a purple grizzly saddle hackle skin for $250 and a chartreuse grizzly saddle for $380. I only paid $19 apiece for them three years earlier. A friend of mine sold a natural grizzly saddle a week earlier for $520. I think I'll sell a few more skins before the market fades away, but keep my best stuff for fishing flys.

June 24, 2011
The drive to Barney Reservoir is always eventful, we never know if the gate on private timber land is unlocked, or locked on the return trip. A locked gate means an extra 100 mile trip to the coast and back home over the coast range. The fishing is usually good, mostly because it's a fly-only lake. The lake has not been stocked and contains native cutthroats and land-locked steelhead. We ran into the Yamhill County Sherriff a couple of miles before reaching the lake, he was looking for poachers. Apparently there were a lot of problems. He gave us his card with instructions to call him if we saw any difficulties. The first thing we saw at the lake was three guys illegally fishing with bait, we told them about the fishing regulations. They immediately left after we took their license plates. Chuck and Tom had float-tubes, I had my pontoon boat.

Barney Reservoir, Oregon

It was unusually cold for late June, but the sun was bright and the wind strong as it usually was on top of the ridge at Barney. We were hoping for a Hex hatch, but were disappointed. I crossed the reservoir and fished a sheltered stretch of shore line, dotted with submerged stumps. I picked up a half dozen cutthroats on a #12 Tri-Color Damsel Nymph in about two hours. The fish were running a little small and skinny this year, but they'll fatten up as the summer progresses. At sundown the action stopped and I trolled a fly deep, on a full-sinking line, in the middle of the lake. This method usually picks up a few fish, but not today. I next fished the shoreline near the log boom and picked up two more fourteen inch cutthroats before it was time to go home.

July 5, 2011

Paul Keefner, Matt Avila, and I got an early start and met David Eisenhower, Chuck Smith and Greg Richards in Castle Rock, Washington a little after 8am. David had two boats on a trailer and the rest of our gear scattered between two vehicles. We were off to British Columbia to fish a lake rumored to be full of trophy rainbow trout. Our car was stopped at the international border and we were escorted into customs for questioning. The border patrol was trying to scare us. They did not want us to catch too many of their fish. Back on the road we had a late lunch in Hope, BC and watched a small black bear grazing in the median between two highways. We caught up with David's group at the motel in Merritt, BC. The country music festival was coming to town this weekend, so all we could find was a lousy motel populated with tree planters for the Canadian Forest Service. The place was trashed. After buying groceries and putting them in the fridge we headed southeast of town, about twenty minutes to Kidd Lake. The lake was less than thirty acres, was surrounded by reeds to the south, and a steep pine covered hillside to the north. About two thirds of the lake was less than three feet deep and covered with aquatic vegetation. The other third was a twenty foot deep trench running the length of the lake. The lake was a perfect bug factory. Midges, mayflies, caddis, damsels and dragon flys were everywhere. I parked my pontoon boat on the edge of the trench and began casting a short-shank #10 Black Rabbit Strip Leach on a clear intermediate sinking line with three feet of eight pound tippet. An hour later I got a soft tug, a strong pull and all heck broke loose. A big fish made a sweeping arch up the channel and exploded out of the water. I must have hooked a steelhead. He stripped line, sulked on the bottom, and jumped two feet out of the

water a second time. The tug-of-war lasted another five minutes before I got him in the net, all twenty six inches of him. By now the sun had disappeared behind the ridge and the wind died down a little. There were no bugs on the water. I hooked a second fish, a seven pound twenty eight inch bruiser. He was less acrobatic, but fought deeper and longer. I must have found the spot, because I landed another twenty four and twenty seven inch fish, and lost three other fish - four fish all over six pounds from the same spot. The rest of the group was not as lucky, catching two fish. We called it quits about 11pm, as a quarter moon rose and shed just enough light to make it back through the reeds to the put-in.

Rainbow Trout, Kidd Lake, British Columbia

July 6, 2011

The day started a little slow with full sunshine and a very slight breeze. A few Callibaetis mayflys emerged at day-break, but not enough to bring the fish to the surface. Around 11am a swarm of tan damsel fly nymphs began heading to shore and fish began rising. I switched to a #14 Rabbit Hide Damsel Nymph and picked up a beautiful twenty five inch Pannask Rainbow, who jumped twice and ripped twenty yards of backing out of my reel before succumbing to my net. The rest of the afternoon was slow. I dredged a few scuds, leeches and mayfly nymphs out of the water on snagged aquatic weeds, but saw no fish. I trolled a leech the length of the lake with no success and finally headed to the north shore for a nap in the shade of several tall pine trees. David warned us of bears in the area, but we felt safe in the 80 degree weather. At 4pm we had barbeque ribs for dinner on shore and headed back to the water for more casting practice. At dark I hooked what felt like a monster rainbow, which rolled deep and cruised over an acre of water.

Rainbow Trout, Kidd Lake, British Columbia

He was darker than yesterday's fish and was probably a Frasier Valley strain of rainbow. He measured twenty eight inches and had massive shoulders. He took the black leech.

July 7, 2011

Today was a repeat of yesterday. It started slow and the damsel hatch did not start until late morning. I caught a chrome twenty seven inch rainbow on my damsel nymph around 10am. While stripping line and watching a coyote wander the far shore, I missed a fish by not paying attention. It was slow the rest of the daylight hours. We tried indicator chironomids, scuds, and damsels with no luck. At dusk the fishing picked up. The fish returned from the deep and began cruising the edge of the trench. I lost three fish in a row, all over six pounds. The first jumped three feet in the air and broke-off. The second must have been foul-hooked in the tail because he jumped ten times and took line out like a banshee and finally broke off in the reeds on the far side of the channel. The third fish was strong, taking out all my line and fifty feet of backing, twisting in the weeds, and finally throwing the hook. The others in our group were having difficulties hooking fish even though we were all side-by-side along the edge of a deep water trench. My speculation at their lack of success was they were all fishing out of row boats and kept their rods fairly high out of the water and away from the weedy lip of the channel. I was fishing low from my pontoon boat

and dredged weeds and debris with every retrieve from deep to shallow water. I literally had to clean several inches of Chara weed stems off my fly after every cast. Along with the weeds came bugs, most of which swam off disoriented into the surrounding water. The fish keyed into the bug confusion and hung around the water I was fishing, just a little longer than where my friends were fishing, allowing me to have a slight edge on catching fish. I finally landed another fish in the dark under a rising quarter moon. He was twenty seven inches long and a little on the dark side.

July 8, 2011

Our last day on the water, I went out early with David in search of the really big fish. We fished the stream channel at the far end of the lake. The lake funneled down to a narrow neck and emptied into a large marsh-wetland. We cast #12 Tan Marabou Devil Damsels for an hour before I hooked a fish. He was the biggest fish of the trip and gave my five weight rod a workout. He jumped once just to take a look at us, then did half-circles around the boat for ten minutes. He was strong and resisted the net a dozen times. We finally got him in the net along the boat but did not chance bringing him on the boat. Dave weighted him in at a tad over eight pounds. I could not get my hand around his tail section and lost him before we could get a photo. A short time later a storm front moved in and it got cold and a little rainy. I caught another twenty seven inch fish just before noon.

Rainbow Trout, Kidd Lake, British Columbia

We fished the rest of the afternoon and evening without touching a fish. The storm front put the bugs down and the fish stayed in deeper water.

We spent the next day drying out our gear, packing and driving home. Total trip cost: $350, with a 1:1 exchange rate with Canada.

July 14, 2011

I'd always wanted to float the Deschutes River from Trout Creek to Maupin and finally had a chance to with Rob Crandall and Water Time Outfitters. Relatively few people have access to this stretch of river because of several Class IV rapids and lock-gated roads. The fishing can be very good. I met Rob, his crew of three and five other guests at Harpham (upriver from Maupin, Oregon) and loaded our gear into his rigs and headed to Trout Creek. Marty was our porter and moved our gear to campsites down river. Our guides were Gill (a local from Tygh Valley), Bob (a New Jersey transplant living in Bend), and Rob (from Clackamas County, Oregon). We loaded our gear into four drift boats at Trout Creek and headed on our three day adventure. I was in Gill's boat the first day. At the boat launch I tied on my usual #16 Tan Elk Hair Caddis and #18 Pheasant Tail Nymph dropper. We headed directly across the river to fish a likely looking riffle. Without discussion Gill cut my flys off the leader and tied on a #18 Cinnamon Caddis dry fly and a #14 Tan Sparkle Caddis Emerger as a dropper. I gave him a funny look. He said try them. Fish were rising at the head of a long run and I immediately began picking up Redside trout on both flys.

Redside Trout, Deschutes River, Oregon

After the fifth fish in twenty minutes (the biggest sixteen inches) I knew it was time to stop and let Joe fish the run. Joe caught a couple more fish before it was time to head downriver, or we'd miss lunch. We fished one more run, picked up two more trout before having a barbeque chicken lunch with all the trimmings. We picked up another half dozen, foot long trout below a shallow riffle before running Whitehorse Rapids. The first 100 yards were messy. I now understood why the typical recreational floater avoids this stretch of river. It eats boats. The next mile of fast water was not so bad, but you have to pay attention to the rocks. Marty set up camp for us below Whitehorse at the 76 Hole campsite, two of us to a large tent with cots and inflatable mattresses. Dinner was baked salmon, salad, vegetables, and fresh berry pie for desert. Why have I not booked a trip sooner? After dinner we hit the water again, I picked up three small fish up river from camp along a grassy bank on a #14 Tan Elk Hair Caddis, then headed below to some good looking water. The water ran relatively slow and deep between two large piles of semi-submerged boulders. The slick water looked fishy as I pushed through the willows, poison ivy and tall grass then quietly stepped into the knee-deep water. I picked up four Redside while working upstream towards the best water below the boulders. A fish rose. I cast and connected with a large trout and immediately tried to pull him downstream away from the rocks. He wanted nothing with that and headed under the boulder pile and dislodged the hook, which promptly stuck on the bottom of a rock. I broke off hoping not to scare another fish. After the run rested for a few minutes, I cast again and had the exact results. I hooked another big fish and broke him off in the boulder pile. It was getting dark. I'd had a good day. It was time to call it quits for the evening.

July 15, 2011

I awoke late, but was ready before breakfast was served. Bacon, cinnamon rolls, and fruit, it was all good. I quickly packed my gear and went to fish the camp hole. Ten minutes later I returned to camp and emptied my waders and dried out, after having slipped in two feet of water and putting a gallon of water down my left wader leg. Today I fished with Rob and his guest Darrin. Rob prefers not to blind cast, but likes to hunt trout. We began our float by drifting slowly by shore, looking in the tree shadows for rising trout. After spotting a few fish under a group of alder trees we anchored the boat to shore and climbed over a steep rocky slope to position ourselves in the trees across from the fish. We watched a half dozen trout take midges and small caddis fifteen feet below us. Rob whispered "bow and arrow cast when the fish are pointed away from us". I strung six weight bow and let the fly go several times, missing the mark. The fish were patient with me the first couple of casts, but got bored and moved on after a while. Darrin moved up stream and almost immediately was into a big fish. When we had cast to and spooked all the fish in the area we moved down river to a large back-eddy that swirled around a grove of alders and a sheer basalt-obsidian cliff. Rob dropped me off on a rock ledge (because you can't fish from a boat on the Deschutes) and I climbed a few feet up the rock face, and peered over the edge at a large trout feeding three rod lengths below. I made a cast down river to get my line distance and made a second cast toward the fish when she was facing away from me. She ignored my fly and kept feeding while my fly drifted away. I false cast a second time to get the water spray off my line and then flung my fly toward the trout. She saw my #18 Caddis fly hit the water, slowly turned, inspected my fly and inhaled it. I lifted the rod and spooked her. As I set the hook she took a hard right and broke off. I carefully slid off the rock, glad to have had some success.

Deschutes River, Oregon

We did not see any trout for the next mile or two, but quickly pulled over below a shrubby ash tree. Darrin went up stream and fished the grass bank. Rob and I went downstream where we spied a nice fish through the thick brush. The fish was hovering in still water, a foot from shore, in several inches of water and was taking midges and

small caddis off the surface. We were less than a rod's length away and could only see him through a thick tangle of leaves and small branches. Our only hope was to side-arm cast around the tree limb, and drop the fly on top of his feeding lane. To complicate matters further, there was an algae matt to the fish's outside so if the cast was not perfect the fly would get stuck in the mire and spook the fish on the retrieve. Rob provided encouragement and I tied on a fresh tippet and a #18 Cinnamon Caddis. The first cast fell short, but the second cast was perfect and the fish inhaled and spit out the fly before I could set the hook. This happened two more times. I was going nuts. The third cast worked. He took the fly, turned slightly and I set the hook. He zipped out of his hideout and headed to the middle of the river. We both struggled with the current, but he was hooked solid. I was relieved when he was in the net, a handsome sixteen incher.

Redside Trout, Deschutes River, Oregon

We met the rest of the group for a shish-ka-bob lunch below Buckskin Mary Rapids. After lunch we made a couple of stops to fish the grassy banks and picked up a few more trout. Rob found a large rattlesnake in the grass. Camp was on the west side of the river at "Upper Doctor Dick", a couple of miles above Locked Gate. In the late afternoon a thunder storm appeared over the ridge out of blue skies. We huddled under a large canopy as the dark clouds opened up and poured. We were completely surrounded by lightning strikes and thunder rolled through the canyon. Through it all we feasted on steak, corn-on-the-cob, and berry pie. It was all good. We hit the sack late, tired, and a bit damp.

July 16, 2011

The storm lingered over night and we had a short break in the weather for breakfast. I fished with Bob and Carson. All three guides had their water preferences: Gill liked broad riffles dumping into pools. Rob put us in trout under trees and Bill liked grassy banks next to fast water. We worked an under-cut bank a couple hundred yards below camp. My shirt was soaked within minutes while walking in the tall, wet grass searching for fish. I picked up one small fish before it began sprinkling and we moved down river. The next spot looked very good. It was slow, pocket water with boulders next to fast water. The air was filled with caddis flys. I had a monster trout rise and roll to my #14 Tan Elk Hair Caddis, but missed him. That was it. Although it was such good looking water, there were no fish. The previous group must have hit this water earlier in the morning. The next water was better. I picked up four fish right where they should have been, in transition water off the main current, along the shoreline. Carson also picked up a couple of fish. Our next stop was an island that had nice riffles on both sides.

Redside Trout, Deschutes River, Oregon

A few mayflies appeared in the intermittent rain and I tied a #18 Pheasant Tail Nymph dropper to my elk hair caddis and cast into the shallow riffle water at the head of the run. I caught three small Redside in a few minutes, and missed a large trout that inspected my fly on the first pass and rolled on it the second pass. I'll let this guy rest a bit before showing him a fly again. I took a few casts in the riffle on the other side of the island, and then told Bob I had to show him something. He

was not impressed with the shallow riffle water I was fishing, but I knew a big fish was there. On my second cast the big fish took, pulled my drag, and made a nuisance of himself for a few minutes. Bob finally netted a beautiful sixteen inch trout and shook my hand. He knew I was showing off. The rain frequency increased and dark thunder clouds appeared over the canyon walls. We probably had one more run to fish before a downpour. About a mile above locked gate the west side of the river was deep, slow, and had some foam pockets that just screamed fish. I carefully walked up to a likely spot and saw a nice fish poking his nose into a matt of floating midges, a foot from shore behind a clump of Wheatgrass. I dapped my fly at him through the grass and he took the pheasant tail nymph before the elk hair caddis hit the water. This was a strong, big fish. He headed deep into a pool behind a large boulder and spooked an even larger trout that leaped completely out of the water to avoid a collision. I called Bob for some assistance and he helped me net and photograph the dark, crimson, beautiful fish.

Redside Trout, Deschutes River, Oregon

The storm caught up with us and we were forced to make a run for the takeout a couple of miles downriver. Around 3pm the sky was black. We got soaked. It hailed for about ten minutes and we were surrounded by lightning. What an unusual event for mid-July. At the Harpham take-out we exchanged business cards, said thanks, shook hands, and went home. It was another memorable fishing trip. Rob and his crew gave us an excellent experience.

August 19, 2011

The Coast Range is full of hidden creeks and waterways. I spent the afternoon investigating one of the more remote and interesting ones, Rock Creek. The Nehalem Watershed is relatively large and supports a large population of salmon, steelhead and cutthroat trout. Rock Creek is a major tributary to the Nehalem and upper Rock Creek begins near Highway 26 and dumps into the Nehalem River at Vernonia about forty miles downstream. I began my quest for residence cutthroats by studying several forest maps and finally taking McGregor Road near the Sunset Highway rest area (about milepost 30). After dodging two logging trucks, driving to the end of several closed roads, and taking two-track trails through closed canopy second-growth trees and brush I finally arrived at the end of the Rock Creek Bypass, a little over ten miles from pavement. I parked at the base of a high cliff covered with moss and dripping spring water. My little 19 year old Toyota Corolla station wagon did a pretty good job getting me to the river. I hope she'll start again and get me out or it's going to be a long walk back to the highway. The river did not look fishy. It was running low and the majority of the bottom was solid rock. I found an area with sunshine, several small plunge pools and riffles, and rigged up my two weight rod with a tan #14 Elk Hair Caddis.

Rock Creek, Oregon

I wet-waded and found the water colder than I suspected, but I got used to it. I cast for half an hour with no results and was starting to think this trip was a mistake. Finally, a three inch fry took my fly and the odds for success improved

dramatically. At the next pool I had half a dozen hits and lost two, eight inch fish before solidly hooking and landing a dark 11 inch cutthroat. Things improved at the next run catching two, eight inchers. I noticed a splashy rise above a deep slot at the tail end of a long pool and riffle. I gently cast my fly, got a good drift, and watched a large cutthroat engulf my fly. I hooked him as he submerged and enjoyed his company briefly before he flipped the hook back at me a minute later. These two weight rods were a blast, but lousy at keeping fish. I walked another half mile upstream over solid rock stream bed without seeing any good fish habitat. Finally giving up, I headed back to the car, hoping it would start again, or that I didn't have two flat tires (I had one spare tire). Everything was good. I tried to follow a couple of old logging roads down the watershed, but encountered gates, road-trenches, and down timber. I headed back the way I came to the main highway. Off to Vernonia to find fishing access to lower Rock Creek. It was a waste of time because the first fifteen miles were all private land with no public access. When I did finally make it to State and private forest land the roads were all gated and only allowed walk-in traffic. The sun was doing down and I really did not feel like hiking this late in the day. I headed home. I supposed I'd fish here again if nothing else was available. It was beautiful, remote country, but a lot of work for a couple of fish.

August 27, 2011

Matt Avila, Paul Keefner, and I did a road trip Saturday, picking the Santiam Watershed in the central Cascades as the area of our fishing assault. I'd gotten a tip from a fellow in a campground several years ago that the Middle Santiam River had excellent fishing, but no road access. Yesterday I called the Forest Service in Sweet Home, Oregon and they assured me that even though the road had been closed for the past five years because of a fire, it was now open. We showed up at the gate early in the morning. It was still closed and locked. Never trust a USFS Information Officer. We had a slight change in plans. We headed to the north side of Green Peter Reservoir and drove up Quartzville Creek. Hundreds of campers lined the highway, enjoying the first 90 degree day of the year, and the second to last weekend before public school started. We took a few casts along a good looking pool-riffle run about a mile up from the reservoir, but saw no fish. It was still too early in the morning and too cool for the caddis to be active. Several miles upstream we pulled into Yellow-Bottom Day Use Area and rigged up our three weight rods. On the river an older fellow was fishing the waterfall that spanned the entire river. I received his permission to take a few casts, and quickly landed two foot long rainbows. The gentleman did not look too pleased, so I excused myself and headed up river to fish with Paul and Matt.

Quartzville Creek, Oregon

The river was a series of pools carved into solid rock, with occasional piles of sand and gravel riffles where the river slowed. The water was more than crystal clear; we could see crayfish in six feet of water. There was no question where the fish were, there was only one place to hide: in the frothy water at the head of the pools.

Rainbow Trout, Quartzville Creek, Oregon

We caught a dozen fish as we worked up river toward a small group of gold panners (who were not finding much color) in a shallow section of the creek. It began to get hot in the late morning and we hiked back to the car for lunch before heading in a new direction. We followed Quartzville Creek to the summit and into the North Santiam Watershed. As we pulled into the Straight Creek Camp on the Santiam River, Matt's Jeep's brakes began to smoke. Paul (a school bus mechanic) checked everything out and found no damages, just a little wear-and-tear on the brake pads. We fished a section of fast water while the car cooled down, and caught half a dozen rainbows. Our next stop was Marion Creek, a swift river still running high and delivering snowmelt late in the unusually cool summer. I picked up two small, beautifully speckled native cutthroats on my #16 Elk Hair Caddis. We ate a few wild strawberries and blackberries before continuing our quest for trout. Our next and last stop was at the confluence of Pamelia Creek and the North Santiam River. The water looked good from the road, but it was tough going down the steep canyon. We held onto spruce branches and roots the last 100 feet of almost vertical riverbank. It was well worth the decent, this place was really fishy. Especially because it was only a couple of miles below the Marion Forks Fish Hatchery and with the high water year there were bound to be some escapees. We found some nice transition water between three fast runs and picked up at least two dozen foot long rainbows on Elk Hair Caddis.

Rainbow Trout, North Santiam River, Oregon

They took everything, dry, submerged, swung – it didn't matter. They were hungry and wanted to be fed. It also did not hurt that there was a fairly good caddis hatch in the canyon shadows of the late afternoon. We called it quits after putting a hook in almost every fish in the twenty yard long run and they quit biting. My arms hurt. I had a small leak in my waders and was a little sun burned. Life was good.

August 31, 2011

I was invited to tye flys at the Federation of Fly Fishers national conclave in West Yellowstone, and talked Chuck Cooney and Tom Wideman into accompanying me to share expenses. I sweetened the offer by lining them up with a friend of mine who gave them a guided fishing trip on the Madison River at twenty five percent of cost. We took Tom's car and stopped at every fly shop between Portland, Oregon and St. Anthony, Idaho the first day. From our motel in St. Anthony we watched small fish rise in a large back-eddy of the Henry's Fork of the Snake River at dusk. The next morning we drove the last hour to West Yellowstone, dropped Chuck off at the conference meetings, and Tom and I headed to the river (I did not tye the first day of conclave). Based on recommendations from a friend of mine in Bozeman, we fished the Madison River between Hebgen Reservoir and Quake Lake.

Madison River, Montana

Grasshoppers were everywhere in the full sun and caddis were in the grass waiting for cloud cover and cooler weather. It should have been a good day of fishing. It was not. We only hooked a couple of small trout, in three hours, on foam grasshoppers, elk hair caddis, and pheasant tail droppers. Something was wrong, but we could not figure out what it was. After lunch I switched to indicator nymphing and caught three plump whitefish on #14 Possie Buggers and #18 Pheasant Tail Nymphs. They were deep in a trough running next to a large boulder in the middle of the river. We headed up river searching for better trout water. Within ten minutes a guide who had been watching us from across the river took our spot and began catching more whitefish for his clients. It's pretty bad when you have to play vulture to get your paying clients fish. We ignored him and he ignored us an hour later when we past him on our way down river. The braided water entering Quake Lake looked good from a distance, and a couple of other fishermen thought so too. We all crowded into the lower half mile and staked out our pools. It was slow. No one caught fish. I took a chance and waded up to my arm-pits and crossed the river to fish the pocket-water next to the steep bank. Another earth quake would have buried me in lose talus and gravel, but we had to catch fish. I found a pool with eager trout and brought two fish to the surface with my caddis imitation before hooking and landing a foot long brown trout. Four trout later I could see Tom heading to the car, so I called it quits and waded back across the river and met him in the parking lot. We headed down river looking for more promising water. We stopped and checked out The Slide, and Rayburn, and finally fished Palisades for an hour with no luck. On the return trip we fished Three Dollar Bridge which had the best looking water, but lacked fish. Each of these areas gets hammered by fisherman, so I was not too disappointed, but we should have had at least a few lookers. On the return trip back to town we noticed heavy construction equipment on Hebgen Dam. They were diverting top water through the spillway while doing improvements to the outlet structure. All the diverted water was warm water. No wonder the fishing was lousy; the fish were put down waiting for cooler water. Back in West Yellowstone Tom and I toured the fly shops, spending too much money. We lucked out at the Yellowstone Fly Shop where they had a FFF Conclave special – half price on everything. I bought a new five weight rod. We met Chuck at the motel after dark and ate dinner at a Mexican Roach Coach a block away. The food was cheap and excellent.

September 1, 2011
I did fly tying demonstrations at the Federation of Fly Fishers national conclave in West Yellowstone. I tyed: Forked Tailed Parachutes, Pheasant Neck Nymphs, and Mini Dee-Spey Flys Thursday and Friday afternoons. It was nice to see many old friends and learn a few new techniques. Chuck and Tom fished the Madison and Gallatin Rivers for two more days, having fair success. Saturday morning we drove back to Portland, visiting a few more fly shops and spending an hour in Burley, Idaho getting a flat tire fixed. Total five day trip cost: $275 per Person.

September 10, 2011
We'd had such good luck fishing the North Santiam River a few weeks ago we decided to give it another shot. This time Paul Keefner invited Eric and Roger Lehman to come along. Not because Roger had a big four-wheel-drive Suburban, but because he's a nice guy. We hiked down the steep slope to the mouth of Pamelia Creek, rigged up caddis and nymphs and began casting. Last trip we caught over a dozen fish per hour in this run. This trip we caught three fish in two hours. It was time to move along with the fish. We worked our way up stream with less luck, catching a couple of small fish. We drove upstream a mile or so, looking for a shady run in the hot afternoon, and had lunch at the foot of a tall cottonwood. Getting desperate, I began casting into fast rip-rap water next to the highway. I began disturbing caddis along the stream bank and seeing a few rising fish.

Rainbow Trout, North Santiam River, Oregon

I put on an Elk Hair Caddis and Pheasant Tail dropper, cast to a tail fin that rose briefly above the water and immediately hooked a respectable twelve inch rainbow. Another half dozen fish followed, most taking the caddis. I could not keep a secret and invited the rest of our group to fish the run. We all began catching fish, which were holding in the deep water about three feet from shore. When our flys floated by, the fish would dart out, get hooked, and head straight for the fast water in the middle of the river. Nothing was over fourteen inches, but I'd bet we caught two dozen in the late afternoon. I did catch one small but beautiful native Coastal Cutthroat trout. After we had caught all the fish (or when they stopped biting), we headed back to the Pamelia Creek hole. The fish were not there, we only picked up three fish. One of them hit my orange and white yarn indicator on two consecutive casts. I switched to a large orange Stimulator and hooked him on the third cast. It got dark and was time to head home. Nice trip, good company, and a few fish to make it all worth the drive.

September 22, 2011
After a year, I finally made it back to Casper, Wyoming to fish the North Platte River. I made a friend in town who offered to take me into Fremont Canyon and fish some of the more isolated water. Ryan Mar had lived in Casper the past few years, but recently moved to northeast Wyoming. He was as interested in fishing the canyon as I was and we met at the base of Alcova Dam just after lunch. We headed to the water below Pathfinder Reservoir and parked near where Highway 408 passes over the river. At the bridge, the water is 500 feet straight down metamorphic rock cliffs. And when I say straight down I mean vertical. Ryan showed me a rough path over the canyon rim that descended through huge boulders and solid rock to the river floor. There was a quarter mile of flat, waist-deep water upstream, and fast, pocket water pools down river. We each picked up sixteen inch trout in the tail of the slow water pool. These trout obviously don't see many anglers. We cast our #14 Elk Hair Caddis at the middle of the river and let them drift slowly downstream, moving about twenty feet a minute. With a long, slow drift, the fish had plenty of time to inspect our offerings before inhaling.

Fremont Canyon, Platte River, Wyoming

The fish disturbed the calm water so much we'd have to wait an hour for things to calm down. The faster water was much different. Fish were everywhere and only spooked if pricked by our hooks. I was awed by the first large fish that inspected and rejected my fly. He looked like a shark on the prowl on some distant saltwater flat. He slowly cruised up in flat fast water, nosed my fly with a closed mouth, hovered for a few seconds, and slowly drifted back into turbulent water behind a large boulder. I gave him another twenty casts with no response. The next hole I caught a twenty inch pig who thrashed around every submerged boulder within twenty feet, Ryan had to help me corner him into the net.

Rainbow Trout, Fremont Canyon, Wyoming

We picked up a couple more sixteen to eighteen inch broad shouldered fish while working our way down river toward El Dorado's hole. Rather than being full of gold, it was full of rainbows. We hooked no less than three dozen trout over the

next two hours, averaging eighteen inches, and I'd guess four pounds. I caught six consecutive fish, every third cast. The caddis were doing us a favor by swarming over the hole and depositing eggs. We could not see downstream more than fifty yards because the river disappeared around a bend of sheer cliff with no shelf or gravel bar to walk on. If it were not for the excellent fishing and the knowledge we were protected from flash flooding from an upriver dam, this place would have been a little spooky. This was also the only stretch of water in the shade for at least a mile. Finally, the fishing slowed as we picked off the feeding fish. I must also admit, we were getting a little sloppy in our casting and presentations, it was just too easy. After fifteen minutes without a fish, I switched to a big foam grasshopper and began a difficult cast to the far side of the river, at the base of a sheer cliff, between two semi-submerged boulders. This water had not been touched and I was sure there had to be a trophy fish lurking in the vicinity. Sure enough he took my hopper on the second cast and exploded into a three foot arch upstream. If the fish were spooked by our previous fish, they were scattered now. He took over the entire hole, sweeping my line though shallow and deep runs. Ryan had to dodge my line several times trying to get out of the way. Finally I brought him to the back side of the hole in some deep frog water and Ryan got him half way into the net. What a handsome fish.

Rainbow Trout, Fremont Canyon, Wyoming

The hole was shot after that. We fished back to the trail up the cliff with no luck, and were back at the car before 4pm. Ryan was in no hurry to make his long trip home, and I was definitely interested in more fish, even though I did not think we could have a better day. I was wrong. We drove up river about a mile and walked a quarter mile across a sagebrush and prickly-pear cactus flat to the rim of Fremont Canyon. The canyon was perfectly square, straight down 500 feet, level across the river bottom and rising straight up the far side of the canyon. How the heck were we going to get down to the river? It'd been a while since Ryan had hiked this area, but we quickly found a solid rock gully leading to a crack fissure in the rock wall. We found toe and hand holes the first hundred feet down the cliff, which emerged onto a talus slope of huge boulders and finally reached the solid rock lined stream bed. The high water mark was at least twenty feet above our heads. I made the first cast into dead water below a riffle, mostly hoping to have a little time to catch my breath. I stood six feet above the river on a flat-topped boulder. My fly drifted about ten feet when a large rainbow savagely took my fly and did a summersault. I played with him for a few minutes before I figured how to get down to water level. He was an amazing, wonderful fish. We each caught three more fish from the hole before I headed up river to fish the pocket water and Ryan waded downstream to the flat water.

Fremont Canyon, Wyoming

I hooked another hog in a deep trough, surrounded by large boulders in fast water. He flew around the hole three times before scraping my leader and breaking off. It was time to quit fishing and enjoy the moment. I lay flat on a rock, took a short nap and watched Ryan catch a few more fish. When the canyon was completely in shadows the caddis came off the water and hid in

the rock crevices, because there was no vegetation on the canyon floor. We headed back up the rock wall to the car. Ryan wanted to get back to his girlfriend and headed down the road. What a great day of quality fish and good company in the scenic high desert.

September 23, 2011

I visited the Grey Reef Fly Shop at sun up and decided to fish the North Platte River below the dam. I'd heard that indicator nymphing the wing-wall below Grey Reef Dam spillway was productive. That was an understatement. I rigged up my six weight rod with a 9 foot leader, greased yarn indicator, heavily weighted #14 Possie Bugger and #18 Bead Head Flashback Pheasant Tail Nymph on a five pound tippet dropper and cast into the foamy water next to the concrete wall. Three casts later I was into my first fish of the day, a nice seventeen inch rainbow.

Grey Reef, North Platte River, Wyoming

Over the next couple of hours I hooked and landed at least three dozen rainbows ranging from sixteen to twenty one inches. It was phenomenal. The fish were a little skinnier than the trout we caught yesterday, but they were all tough fighters. A couple of other fishermen fished through the run with me, but only stayed long enough to hook a couple of fish before moving on. Both midges and caddis were thick in the air and fish were rising to emergers. I was surprised to see many fish rising in the fast foamy water at the base of the spillway. It was impossible to get a fly to drift properly over them for more than a couple of seconds, so I gave up after a few attempts. Around 2pm the fish quit biting. I had lunch and headed down river to fish below a couple of promising riffles. The half mile below the dam was not fishing well. The bugs took some time off in the 80 degree cloudless afternoon. I took a few casts over some submerged aquatic weeds and had a large trout attack my yarn indicator. I instinctively set the hook and was surprised to also hook a second trout on my fly. In the commotion, I lost the hooked fish. I took a few more casts at the dam without any luck and decided to head back to Fremont Canyon. I took it easy down the canyon wall. Being alone I could not afford to break any bones. The fishing was not near as good as yesterday. I hooked three seventeen to eighteen inch fish, and hooked, fought, and lost another large brute before calling it quits. By now it was 4pm and only one place left to go, the Miracle Mile. It was thirty miles away, but I had the time and a rental car with unlimited miles. About fifteen miles was washboard gravel road but the scenery made up for the dusty road. I took the turnoff downriver on the east side of the river and parked at the first large riffle. The whole area looked fishy.

Miracle Mile, North Platte River, Wyoming

I rigged up a #14 Tan Elk Hair Caddis and #18 Pheasant tail dropper and began fishing the shallow riffle from shore to the center of the river. In less than an hour I'd caught a half dozen small rainbows and one brown trout. With my renewed confidence it was time to switch tactics and go after the big fish. I put on a yarn indicator, Possie Bugger and Pheasant Tail and began casting into the deeper riffle water. By now I was standing in swift water up to my knees, about twenty yards from shore. I methodically worked every inch of

river until my indicator stopped and headed sideways. I set the hook and was into a huge rainbow. He quartered up stream through the shallow water, his back completely exposed, almost reaching the gravel bar on the far side of the river. He had all my fly line out, and about twenty yards of backing. I finally turned him into the deep water below the riffle and five minutes later had him at my feet. Having no net and in the middle of the river, it was difficult to corral him and remove the hook. I finally gave him some slack and the barbless hook fell out. What a beautiful fish. Next, I began working the downstream side of a small island, where a long stretch of shallow water poured through the gravel into the mainstream, creating a long, narrow trough with excellent holding water. I began nymphing the lower end and immediately picked up a fat sixteen inch rainbow.

Rainbow Trout, North Platte River, Wyoming

Another five yards up river I hooked a chunky eighteen inch rainbow, with unusually bright chrome and relatively few spots. He must have recently come up out of Pathfinder Reservoir. I caught one more foot-long rainbow on the pheasant tail before heading back to the car as it got dark. The sunset was amazing as I took off my waders, put my rod in its tube, and headed back to town. I enjoyed the sagebrush and juniper smell through my open car window. I almost hit a huge five point buck walking out of a bushy ravine about ten miles south of Alcova. If I was a deer hunter I'd like to hang his rack on the wall and put the rest of him in the freezer. I got back to town around 10pm, filled the car with gas, had a lousy fast-food barbecue sandwich, and watched the news at the motel. The next morning I drove to Denver and flew home. I'd give almost anything to spend every September fishing in central Wyoming.

October 3, 2011
Phil Oliver drove Tom Wideman and I to the Owhyee River for another week of fishing for Brown trout. Last spring the Owhyee had some major flooding with over 200 percent of average snowfall. The fishing reports were not favorable for the river. I stopped by the Owhyee last May and it was running high and muddy. Things had improved by mid-summer, and the latest report was that the Owhyee was back in shape and the fish were on the bite. As we drove up the canyon, we stopped at the ledge to watch a dozen fish rising. The temptation was too great and we quickly rigged-up and began casting. The fish were very selective, and after a half hour I was able to hook a eighteen incher on a #18 Pheasant Tail as it swung at the end of a long drift. The fish took to the middle of the river, had nowhere to go and after a few jumps came to my hand. We met a dozen guys from our club at the State Park Campground and shared a campfire after dinner.

October 4, 2011
We hit the White House Hole early and found the river to be running about a foot higher than previous years. There was also less moss and aquatic vegetation which made it easier to wade in the deeper water. This was Tom Wideman's first trip to the Owhyee so we gave him first-water and a little more time to figure out the lay of the land. He hooked several fish, but did not land any the first hour. He had too much slack in his line in the fast water. I was going nuts watching over his shoulder, until he finally landed a fish. My work was done and I was off to pursue my own fish, which was rising on the far side of the river. I waded to the middle of the river, with the water two inches from the top of my waders, and cast to a nose that was rising behind a half-submerged rock. He took on the second cast and exploded up, down, and across the river. He wanted nothing to do with us. Tom finally put him in the net, a nice nineteen inch brown. We picked up another half dozen browns before the pool played out and Phil delivered lunch. He had been deep nymphing the run above us and only caught a handful of ten to sixteen inch trout, small stuff for the Owhyee.

After lunch, Tom went upriver with Phil and I worked the far side of the river, alternating between the frog-water next to the bank and the fast pocket-water mid-stream. I did quite well, picking up four eighteen to twenty inchers and a half dozen fourteen to sixteen inch fish. I suppose few fishermen crossed the higher than average river flow, which made the other side of the river fishier this year.

Brown Trout, Owhyee River, Oregon

On the way back to camp we explored new water and checked out the Power Line Hole. I've fished a very small percentage of the Owhyee River because every inch is good, but I'd have to rate the Power Line Hole as excellent. It starts with a hundred yards of fast riffles, a literal bug factory. The riffles become a boulder field of slower, deeper water where fish rest behind submerged rocks. Finally the run becomes flat, slow and deep. In the early evening fish were rising throughout the entire hole.

Owhyee River, Oregon

But just because they were rising did not mean we were catching. I struggled to hook my first fish. I gave the slower water to the other guys and targeted the top of the riffle. Three big browns were working a small eddy between an overhanging willow and a fast, white-water chute of river. I cast for half an hour before getting the drift right and hooking and landing a slim eighteen inch brown. He ignored the Elk Hair Caddis and took the Pheasant Tail Nymph. More fish and competition for food meant skinnier fish. I worked my way downstream along a shallow pea-gravel bar to the rest of the group, who were casting to dozens of finicky, rising fish. We tried everything, until dark colored #18 Parachutes did the trick, just as it got too dark to see. We decided to pick up the rest of the fish the next day.

October 5, 2011

We woke up to rain. Phil fixed a huge breakfast in his camper and we did not hit the water until 10am. We had to share the Power Line Hole with a couple of other fishermen, so Tom and I hoofed it across the river at a shallow spot directly under the power lines. Before we got to the far shore, I spotted a large brown working behind a rock next to a slightly under-cut bank. I froze and waited for Tom to catch up. He had not gotten his twenty inch fish yet on this trip. He cast three times before the fish rose and took his fly. The fight was on. He ripped Tom every direction downstream and finally came to the net. Minutes later we saw another fish in the same hole and I took a shot at him. He also took my fly and surprised us by inviting two of his friends to join us in the action. All three fish swirled around the pool until I got too close and scared the two non-hooked fish away. I quickly landed another hefty twenty inch brown. Tom and I worked the bank, picking up a couple more fish in the off and on again rain. After lunch we headed below the tunnel to fish a slow, shallow stretch of water. I noticed a group of fish rising on the far bank in a small cove protected by an overhanging clump of willows. This was going to be interesting. I waded to the middle of the river, up to my knees, and made a slack line cast downstream and got a good drift over the fish. I repeated the process a dozen times until the fish thought there was a hatch and finally took my #18 Pheasant Tail Dropper. I maneuvered him downstream before he knew he was hooked and the fight was on. He had plenty

of room and I was at a disadvantage having to work him from upstream. Finally, Al helped me land him, a deep bellied, golden brown, twenty one inch brown trout. Al jumped into the same spot and a half hour later caught his twin brother. We worked the remaining two fish for the next hour with no luck. They knew we were there, but kept on feeding and ignoring our flys. I spotted a large brown working in a side channel half covered with floating algae. He kept moving in a circle in the dead-calm water. I snuck-up and sat in the tall grass next to his private bath and watched him for fifteen minutes before making my first cast. Every time he'd turn away from me I'd make a cast and place my fly a foot in front of his nose. He saw my fly each cast, even looked at it twice, but basically ignored my offering. Finally I put a cast where he could not refuse it and he was hooked.

Brown Trout, Owhyee River, Oregon

He did not fight too well, probably because he'd spent so much time in oxygen depleted dead water, but in the net he measured twenty one inches, hooked-jawed kype and all. We moved down stream and fished above the old burn in the walk up the river hole. Tom and Phil swung flys in the big pool and picked up some good fish, while Al and I fished up river, catching eight twelve to sixteen inch fish that were scattered all over the river. Back at camp, the rest of our club was gone. We invited Al to have dinner with us in Phil's camper. Al provided pickled eggs along with our spaghetti, meatballs and salad for an interesting meal.

October 6, 2011

We chose the Power Line Hole for our last full day on the Owhyee River. It was cold, cloudy and rainy and perfect for a mayfly hatch. I waded across the river and picked a spot about fifty yards below the riffles, in a calmer stretch of water. Within minutes we saw noses and whole heads poking out of the water. Blue Wing Olives, Slate Duns, Tricos and midges of all sizes were emerging, on the water and in the air. I put on a #14 Tan Elk Hair Caddis and a #20 Pheasant tail Nymph and began catching twenty inch fish on the nymph. I'd cast upstream, across and then downstream, catching fish, then rest the water. After a half dozen fish, I had no more takers. I switched nymphs to a #20 Soft Hackle Emerger, repeated the process and picked up another half dozen twenty inch fish. By 1pm the fish stopped biting, but were still rising. I changed flys and put on a #20 Bead Head Pheasant Tail on 6X tippet and started casting. I had not moved more than a foot in four hours; I stood below a knee-high boulder five feet from shore on solid gravel. I had a long pool above me with fast riffle water merging into slow deep water. To my left was faster water running over several large boulders and submerged weed beds. Below was a half-acre of slow moving flat water. Fish were rising randomly and consistently everywhere. I could not imagine better fishing conditions. The #20 Nymph was golden, I picked up at least another dozen trout over the next five hours. It was the best fly of the week and matched the drifting nymphs and emergers perfectly. I can honestly say I had a triple twenty day: Twenty twenty-inch fish on a #20 fly.

Al was fishing upstream, Phil downstream and Tom across the river by the truck. We all were catching big fish. Around 6pm we called it quits, not because the fish stopped rising, but because they all knew our flys and were not taking artificials anymore. Tom and Al went back to camp to fix dinner, Phil and I headed down river to a large back-eddy pool that seemed more like a lake than a river. Phil immediately picked up two nice browns on his Elk Hair Caddis and I hooked and lost a fish swinging a soft hackle down river over flat water. At dark we called it quits.

October 28, 2011

I made the rounds at the local flys shops and everyone was talking about catching steelhead on the lower Deschutes River. I invited Chuck Cooney and Ralph Brooks to join me for the day on the river. Ralph decided to drive, because he felt a little cramped in my small Toyota. We arrived at Mack's Canyon on the Deschutes about 9am, to a cloudy, overcast, threatening-to-rain day. The fifteen miles of gravel road was rough even though it had been graded the week before. We walked above the campground and noticed several spawned-out Chinook salmon, both swimming in the deep back-water and dead along shore. I tied on a #10 Peach Yarn Egg, below a heavily weighted #14 Possie Bugger and an indicator. At the first riffle I caught a sixteen inch trout after a dozen casts. A few minutes later I hooked another fat trout. About that time Ralph burst through the willows, holding a six pound steelhead high in the air.

Brown Trout, Owhyee River, Oregon

Steelhead Trout, Deschutes River, Oregon

He'd caught it on an egg pattern. It was a hatchery fish so I cleaned it, wrapped it in plastic and put it in the car. By this time Chuck had also caught a couple of trout and a whitefish. It already was a good day. We headed back to the river just in time to see an empty drift boat floating down the middle of the river. Someone's not going to be happy. Mack's Canyon was the end of the road and the last stop before the Columbia River, another fifty miles downstream. We yelled for help towards the campground, but no one was at the boat ramp. Half hour later a motor boat with the wayward drift boat in tow beached at the boat ramp. Some fisherman upstream got a lucky break. After the drift boat was tied to a tree we drove upstream a couple of miles to nymph another likely looking run. We spread out and fished a long, straight run, casting to deep slots, behind boulders and other likely looking runs. Chuck picked up a steelhead and lost him on a rock. Ralph also hooked another steelhead and lost him when his line got wrapped around his wading staff. I caught only whitefish. The next run was a prime, fast riffle empting out over fifty yards into a slow, deep pool. Ralph fished it first, caught a couple of trout and hooked a steelhead who broke off after several leaps into the air. I fished the run next, nothing but whitefish. Chuck followed me through the hole and hooked another steelhead. He only had five pound tippet and lost him after he got into fast water. I was being out-fished today. I headed upstream and caught more whitefish in a couple of nice runs along shore. Chuck and Ralph picked me up in the car a mile upstream and we had lunch. The next run had several spawned-out thirty pound Chinook wandering around, looking lost and confused. We were several miles below Sherar's Falls, which can be a barrier to fish passage. No wonder egg patterns were working so well. I picked up a few more Whitefish and foul-hooked an old beat-up Chinook which broke my leader after I brought him to shore a couple of times. About 5pm it started to rain, we headed to Maupin where Ralph ordered a pizza and we watched the last game of the World Series on TV. Jean was happy with Ralph's steelhead. We had fish steaks for Sunday dinner.

November 11, 2011
Paul Skelton had called a few weeks before, wanting to campout and fish the Grande Ronde

River for steelhead this weekend. It snowed in Wallowa County so we changed plans and decided to fish the John Day River. Paul also invited Gordon Zanden along, who was relatively new to fly fishing, but good for gas money. We were at the John Day - Cottonwood takeout at 8am and rigged our switch-rods in a cold wind. There was no snow, but our rod guides iced up after a few casts. We had to submerge our rods in the river to keep them ice free. I swung a purple-pink Spey fly on a sink-tip floating Skagit head line. We caught no fish. We spoke to a dozen bird hunters as we fished three riffles upstream a mile before we called it quits. The fish had either passed through this area or were still on their way.

John Day River, Oregon

We decided to fish the Deschutes River and headed cross country to South Junction, which was a bad decision because there were already four guys standing in the only riffle. Both up and down stream were private property. We hiked upriver a couple of hundred yards and fished some small pockets along a steep rock bank. It was poor water but I managed to catch a foot long rainbow on an egg pattern. Next, we drove to Maupin and headed upriver to the first take-out. I knew there were fish in a fast pool below the boat ramp and invited Gordon to tag along. I put on a #10 Peach Egg pattern as a dropper behind a heavily weighted #12 Possie Bugger, pointed to where the fish was and promptly hooked and landed a nice seventeen inch Redside trout. Gordon was impressed. I cheated a little because I'd caught a fish in this same spot the last dozen trips to the Deschutes, but he did not have to know that. I caught two more small trout at the head of the run, before hooking what I thought was a steelhead that stripped line downstream so fast I could not get a reel handle on him. He broke my leader twenty yards downstream when he made a left turn below a rock. It was fun while it lasted. I turned the hole over to Gordon and preceded to fish upstream below the overhanging alder trees.

Redside Trout, Deschutes River, Oregon

Gordon and Paul insisted on swinging their Spey rods in spite of my success with egg patterns. I hooked and lost two more trout before landing my last fish in the twilight. We drove home in a rain and wind storm, dodging fir branches that were scattered along Highway 216 on the southeast side of Mt Hood.

December 3, 2011
The rain let up this week and the river levels were dropping. I met a few guys at the fly shop and had two offers to fish, either the Deschutes or the Trask River. The odds were higher for steelhead on the Deschutes. But with the cloud failure and resulting sunny weather in central Oregon it would be below freezing most of the day. The Trask would probably have more people because of the late run of Chinook and the unusual sunny day. I opted for the coast. Paul Skelton picked me up at 7am and we met Gordon Zanden on Sunset Highway. We were eating a pancake breakfast at Alice's Restaurant on the Wilson River an hour later. Paul should marry the waitress. She always brings him the usual without him ever ordering. And he always leaves her a big tip. We suited up in our waders at the Trask River County Park and headed to the large pool a short distance below the road bridge. I put on a #8 Borden Special, a

popular sea-run cutthroat fly, and began swinging my seven weight rod with sink-tip line down river through the tail-out. After a while I shortened my leader from five to three feet to get my fly deeper. Paul headed to the head of the pool and drifted a pink rubber worm below a cork bobber with his center-pin reel. He hooked and landed a small steelhead on his third cast. This was Paul's river, he lived on the Trask for several years before moving over the Coast Range to Beaverton. He knew every hole and when the fish were there. Gordon hooked and released a sea-run cutthroat. He was also using a center-pin reel. After an hour I'd had no action. Paul showed me how to use his center-pin reel. It was nothing like anything I'd tired before. Casting was both complex and primitive. We cast a thirteen foot Spey fly rod but did not use a fly line. The monofilament line comes off the side of the reel at a ninety degree angle to the rod through your left hand thumb and pointer finger, with your palm facing down. After the cast when the fly is drifting downstream, the reel spins freely on ball bearings feeding line out with no drag. To slow or stop line feeding out you push your rod-holding hand into the side of the reel. At the end of a drift the line is put back on the reel by lifting the rod to create slack line and quickly spinning the reel to bring line in. It takes coordination, but was very effective in getting long, deep, drag-free drifts. We moved to the next hole above the bridge and I began swinging a fly at the head of the pool. I was using my own rod because I did not feel confident with the center pin system yet. My fly drifted through a boulder field that lead into deep water. I immediately got a short tug.

Steelhead Trout, Trask River, Oregon

A couple of casts later I had a steelhead on. She jumped three times and dodged around a bit before I beached her on a sandy bar. She was two feet long, about three pounds and definitely not an adult steelhead, but a jack steelhead following the Chinook salmon upriver from the estuary to feed on their eggs. She was a native fish so I quickly released her. I had another tug in the same pool a few minutes later but no hook-up. Next we fished a few miles downstream at the Upper Peninsula take-out with no luck. On the way home we took a few more casts on the Wilson River at Siskeyville where I had another strike in the middle of a wide flat below white water. After an hour of no-hits we called it a day and went home.

December 9, 2011

Tom Wideman, Chuck Cooney and I headed back to the Trask River for another try at steelhead. Even though it had not rained for several weeks, and the prospects for fish were poor, we still wanted to get out and take a few casts. It was a cold ride over the Coast Range and everything was covered with thick frozen fog. We stopped at Alice's for pancakes where Tom harassed the waitress for putting Valentine doilies under his bowl of oatmeal. She must like him. We began fishing at the Trask River County Park. We each had Spey and switch rods, sink tips, and heavy winter steelhead flys. We spread out and cast for an hour with no luck. I waded across the river and misjudged the depth and slipped a little water into my waders. I fished the far bank without a hit. Next we headed up river to fish the first hole on the North Fork Trask River. There was a small pick-up truck parked on the bridge and we heard someone yelling in the thick forest. We wandered downstream to investigate and found two high school boys, in swimming trunks, jumping off the bridge abutment into a deep hole in the river. It was below freezing, the ground was covered with two inches of hoar frost and there were two crazy kids filming each other as they jumped off the bridge into the ice cold water. These Tillamook boys were tough. Back at our fishing hole I fished the fast water at the top of the run, Tom fished the deep middle section and Chuck took the tail-out. Tom caught an eighteen inch steelhead jack and beached it on a gravel bar. Chuck and I did not have a bite. Next we fished the Upper Peninsula take-out and the new concrete put-in a couple of miles downriver with no success. We

called it quits in the early afternoon and visited the jerky factory north of Tillamook to get jerky for Tom's dog. At least that was his excuse. Next we stopped by the Tillamook Cheese Factory for ice cream. As the sun was going down we barely had time to swing flys through the Siskeyville Hole on the Wilson River. Tom picked up a fat little sea-run cutthroat using an unconventional swing. He cast his sink-tip line upstream, hoping to get it deep, before covering the water he wanted to fish. This created a large "U" in his line. It did get the line deep at the expense of losing line control during most of the drift. Because the water was slow enough, the line straightened out before swinging through the deep slot where he thought the fish were. It worked for Tom because he was catching fish. Chuck and I were skunked for the day.

December 17, 2011

I got a call from Paul Skelton the night before; he needed help cutting a fallen tree out of his favorite hole on the Trask River. I had made a lot of trips to Tillamook County the previous weeks. Paul picked me up at 7am, we had breakfast at Alice's at 8:30am and were wading in the river at 10am. After the tree was taken care of, I took a few casts with my new center-pin reel and rod that Paul made for me. He is the only guy I know that fishes a center-pin and let me try his outfit a couple of weeks ago. I practiced casting with Paul's help and figured it out after about an hour. After scaring every fish in the County Park hole, we headed upriver to fish the first hole on the North Fork Trask River. I cast my bobber, lead split-shot, and purple worm at the top of the run in fast water, fed line out and fished the entire thirty yard long hole completely drag-free. This is an amazing way to deep water nymph. If you're coordinated enough to manage a reel that feeds line out the side of the reel through your fingers and with no tension or drag that is. On my third cast I let the bobber drift through the far river seam into slack water. The line was moving about two feet per second. The bobber went down, my line went tight and a large fish flashed and rolled deep in the crystal clear water. This was a big fish. She zipped around the hole a few times, jumped once and struggled deep before I tailed her with my twelve foot six weight rod. She was a beautiful chrome, bright, twelve pound native Coho salmon. Paul quickly helped me get untangled and snapped a few photos before we released her to continue her spawning journey up river.

Coho Salmon, Trask River, Oregon

Now I'm sold on the center-pin concept for fishing difficult water. Especially for winter steelhead or salmon water where you have to put your fly on the fish's nose deep in cold water. Nothing could improve the day, that was my best fish of the year.

December 15, 2011
I completed a project I've been working on this past year - a necklace of one hundred dozen #18 Bead Head Flash Back Pheasant Tail Nymphs. Strung together they all looked like a shiny brown Hawaiian lei. Luckily when the necklace string was threaded through the down-turned hook eyes, the hook points turned inward and would not prick your skin.

One Hundred Dozen Pheasant Tail Nymphs

December 21, 2011
Chuck Cooney called and said he had Wednesday open for fishing and asked where we were going. He wanted to fish the Deschutes River. I did not want to press my luck by heading back to the Trask so I agreed to head east and picked him up at 7am. After a brief stop at the Fly Shop in Welchs, we were suited up for cold wading at Mecca Flats, below Warm Springs, Oregon. Just last week the BLM completed the upgrades to the campground and it looked very nice. There were concrete tables, gravel pads, terraces, and road improvements for every campsite. We hoped this would not significantly increase the fishing pressure, but knew it would. We rigged up indicators on our six weight rods and tied on heavily weighted nymphs and salmon-egg droppers.

Deschutes River, Oregon

We started fishing at the boat ramp. I first fished the near water and Chuck the far water with his switch rod. Chuck caught the first fish. We were both surprised to find a four pound Bull Trout on the end of the line. He took the egg pattern. Bull Trout were very common in the Metolius River, up river fifty miles through two dams, but rare in the lower Deschutes. We continued fishing upriver from the campground. I caught two foot long trout and Chuck also hooked a few small fish. Around noon the frost melted on the bunchgrasses, sagebrush and willows and we headed back to the car for lunch. Next we headed down river. Chuck fished a long, slow run and I headed down river further to fish the riffle water below a small island. A spinning gear fisherman was fishing the far side of the island, and a fly fisherman was fishing another riffle a quarter mile downstream. I slipped in between them and immediately began catching fish, three hefty whitefish in about fifteen minutes.

Bull Trout, Deschutes River, Oregon

Two took my egg pattern, the other the #14 Possie Bugger. The sun headed behind the ridge about 4pm and it was time to head back. Even though it was late December, it was a pleasant 40 degrees, sunny, and dry. I even got a little sun burned. The river was running on the low side at 4,800 cfs, there had been no rain the entire month of December.

December 30, 2011
Chuck Cooney insisted on fishing one more day before our fishing licenses expired at the end of the year. He wanted to get the most for his money. We also invited Ralph Brooks to split the cost of gas. The weather report was ominous and predicted a storm front moving through in the afternoon and two feet of snow in the Cascades. We hit the road early and had breakfast in Mill City en route to the Metolius River. The road over Sanitam Pass was icy and there was a foot of snow in the forest from the week before. Lost Lake was covered with a thin sheet of ice. Camp Sherman had no snow, but it was raining. We slipped into our waders under the protective cover of the community center building awning. I was first to swing a fly through the hole below Allingham Bridge, one of my favorite spots on the river. Ralph nymphed the far side of the hole. We had no hits. The river was running a little higher than normal and we could not get our flys very deep in the swift water. A few fish were rising to midges, but they were few and far between. We started

methodically working our way downstream, concentrating on the riffle water above the deep holes.

Metolius River, Oregon

Ralph picked up the first trout, a footlong Redside trout. I caught the second trout, a thick 17 inch beauty, but could not land him. I had cast from the top of a four-foot thick, eighty-foot long fir tree that had fallen across the river and the slipery barkless trunk did not touch the river. I gave my fly a little slack and the trout slipped off the barbless hook. It began pouring rain as we headed back to the truck to dry out and have lunch. Next we drove down to the hatchery and found the river at flood-stage and muddy. We drove back upriver and after a short hike found Canyon Creek, the source of all the silt. It started to snow pretty heavily and stick to the ground so we decided to call it quits. Sanitam Pass was engulfed in a blizzard with visability limited to about twenty yards. We got behind two dozen vehicles, and one, thirtyfive miles per hour lead car, and headed home. Our next trip will be with a new license in a new year.

2012

January 7, 2012

The weather was perfect for a day chasing coastal steelhead. It had rained hard for a couple of days at the first of the week, but was sunny and about 40 degrees in the middle of the day. Paul Skelton reported that the water color and level were perfect for a float down the upper Trask River. We drove two vehicles and shuttled our pontoon boats to the Stones Camp put-in and the Upper Peninsula take-out. Somewhere along the road Paul lost one of his pontoon frame foot rests. He went looking for it but was unsuccessful. We fished about two miles of water without success. There were a few good steelhead riffles, but most of the water was salmon water with deep, broad holes. In the early evening we headed up to the Trask County Park for one last try. We split up, Paul fished the hole next to the campground and I hiked a short distance up the North Fork. I put on a single #10 Peach Salmon Egg and nymphed it through a deep, slow run, starting with the water at my feet and working towards the far side of the river. About three-fourths across the river and mid-way through the run my indicator stopped and went under water. I gave my line a slow tug, felt resistance, and pulled a little harder. My line started to move slowly down river like I'd hooked a submerged piece of driftwood until it rolled and I saw the white belly of a large steelhead. I pulled hard enough to bring him to the surface and then the water exploded. He realized he was hooked. He fought hard enough to throw the hook before I could lead him to the gravel shoal. I sat down on a moss covered rock ledge, tied on a new fly and enjoyed the moment. I rested the hole by fishing the fast water at the top of the run. Ten minutes later I began casting to the previous fish's location and hooked another fish. This time it was a solid hook-up and the fish tore up the hole. She twisted, jumped, swam at me, then away and finally tried to swim up and over the swift riffle at the top of the run. She tested my six weight rod and eight pound tippet to their limits. After about ten minutes she started coming my way and after three attempts I had her on the pea gravel bar in three inches of water. I had never landed a steelhead as chrome bright as this twelve pound beauty.

Steelhead, Trask River, Oregon

I quickly took a few photos and gently held her by the tail while she and I recovered. With a flip of her tail she was gone. I could not cast again, it would not have been right. The best way to end a day's fishing was to release a quality fish then, sit on the bank, enjoying the moment.

February 9, 2012

Bob Kloskowski and I fished the Ruby River again this year. The weather was perfect. It was sunny, 45 degrees, and no snow was on the ground. About 1pm we parked Bob's rig below the dam and walked past the closed gate. The BLM was still renovating the dam spillway and the public did not have access to the last half-mile below the reservoir. We rigged up Elk Hair Caddis and #18 Pheasant Tail droppers and began catching fish. Bob had a nice fish on his first cast. I took a dozen casts and hooked and landed a 17 inch rainbow.

Ruby River, Montana

The water was cold, probably in the lower forties but the fish were active and a few were even feeding on top. We picked up a half dozen fish on the surface before the hatch ended and we switching to weighted nymphs and indicators. I caught fish the rest of the day on a #14 Possie Bugger. Bob skipped the next hole downriver because he'd not had much luck there the past few trips. I cannot pass up likely looking water and pulled three fish out in five casts. Bob gave me a funny look. It was the Possie Bugger, one of my favorite flys. The next hole was about thirty yards long below a fast riffle. It was fast and deep on the far side of the river and slow and shallow on our side. Bob put on his dry emerger and I continued to deep nymph. We both caught half a dozen rainbows. I took a couple of casts in the fast water at the top of the run and caught the first brown, a caramel colored 18 incher.

Brown Trout, Ruby River, Montana

Ten minutes later in the same spot I caught another slightly smaller brown. In the distance we heard a dog barking and Bob said it was time to go. A black Labrador caught up with us a couple hundred yards downstream and splashed through the water we were fishing. Bob had met this dog before and it had ruined his day. I splashed water at the dog, threw a stick to the far bank, did everything to send the dog home but he stuck with us and continued to scare fish. In desperation we sat down and had our lunch. A half hour later the dog realized we were ignoring him and headed home. We could now fish in peace. The next hole was a good one. Bob pulled several heavy trout out of the depths with his nymph. He caught one fish that had large, unusual spots on his back. We speculated it was a rainbow-brown trout cross.

Unidentified Trout, Ruby River, Montana

The action slowed and I put on a peach colored #10 Egg pattern and caught five fish in a ten foot trough behind a large boulder. In the late afternoon the sun went behind the ridge and the wind started picking up. We called it quits when it got cold, and hiked back to truck and reached Bozeman about 7pm.

February 10, 2012

A storm moved into south central Montana so Bob Kloskowski and I decided to fish someplace close to town. We chose the Madison River and parked the truck at Varney Bridge. It was lightly snowing and well below freezing. We headed down river and fished a narrow slot below a hundred yards of knee deep shallow riffles. Bob hooked three fish on a weighted nymph before I knew what was going on. He offered me the hole and I caught another three fish on my #14 Possie Bugger. We had to sink our rods in the river to de-ice them every ten minutes. The wind was blowing sleet sideways. Fish were still biting so we kept fishing. We each picked up several more fish while working our way downstream to the next big hole. The hole looked excellent. It was several casts long, the bottom was cluttered with medium sized boulders, and it gradually transitioned from shallow riffle to deep run. Bob gave me the honor of the first cast and I immediately hooked and landed a fat 18 inch rainbow. Bob next caught a similar fish on the next pass. We traded turns fishing the run in between warming our hands and feet on shore. We caught another half dozen trout. When the trout finished biting I caught a large whitefish who did not want to miss out on the fun.

Whitefish, Madison River, Montana

By mid-afternoon the blizzard hit and we decided to get back to town before the roads got too bad. Bob dropped me off at the motel and I thanked him for another great trip. The fly shops did not close until six so I took a chance on the icy roads and visited two shops. I determined it was not a good idea after sliding off the road into the gutter at two stop signs (the rental car did not have snow tires). To play it safe I picked up fast-food and tyed flys the rest of the evening.

February 17, 2012
Tom Wideman called the night before and said he'd pick me up at 6am in the morning. I had a lot of work to do but I blew it off. We fished the Trask River, starting at the county park. Tom fished his 7-weight steelhead rod and I followed him with my center-pin rod. We saw nothing at the first hole except footprints in the sand. The second hole did not look promising as the water level was a foot lower than normal. Tom fished the water thoroughly but could not get a good drift across the main current on the far bank. My center-pin system worked like a charm and I got a drag-free drift from the top of the riffle, through the deep pool to the tail-out. I had a few difficulties spinning line off the reel before casting (I was still learning) but was able to muddle through enough to hit the water. I hooked a steelhead after a couple of casts, but he threw the hook. Ten minutes later a second steelhead grabbed my lure and headed straight for me. I could see him three feet deep in the clear water. I was using circle hooks - and they only work if a fish turns and sets the hook himself in the corner of his mouth. When he did turn I had limp line and he spit out the hook and swam off. I was

dejected and took a break on a large rock. Tom smiled, shook his head and then laughed. He was not much help. I hooked and lost a third fish and could not handle the pressure anymore. We headed up the North Fork about ten miles to the steel bridge, and took a few casts at likely looking holes along the way. There were few good steelhead runs but lots of promising coastal cutthroat habitat. Mid-afternoon it started to rain. We headed back to Tillamook for a sandwich and visited the Jerky Factory on the way home.

March 7, 2012
I was invited to tye Atlantic flys with Michael Radencich for two days before the Fly Tyers Expo in Albany, Oregon.

Jock Scott, FFF Expo, Albany, Oregon

We tyed an authentic Jock Scott. Mike showed us several new techniques and made some difficult techniques seem easy.

March 10, 2012
I attended the 24th annual Fly Tyers and Fly Fishing Expo in Albany, Oregon. I tyed caddis fly emergers at three sessions and was also invited to teach two classes: "Nothing but Wings" and "Framing Fishing Flys".

March 17, 2012
The Washington County Fly Fishers fished Vernonia Pond. I invited a Boy Scout group to fish with us and we outfitted two boys with pontoon boats, rods, and reels. The day began miserably. It had rained half the night and started to snow on the drive to the coast range. At the lake I set up a canopy for the cook-stove and a place to stay dry. As soon as we got our waders on

it stopped raining. The water was dark and cold but the fishing was very good. I fished a #14 Cary Special on an intermediate line and caught a dozen foot-long stocked rainbows before noon. We had a group lunch of hot dogs and chili. After lunch we had a few brief rain showers. Paul Keefner was fishing a large black Wooly Bugger with an orange bead head, and hooked a steelhead. He yelled for a net and I headed his direction, laughing as he tried to wear-out a fourteen pound fish on a 3-weight rod. Finally he got the fish pointed in my direction and I slipped the net under his head, lifted the long net handle in the air and grabbed the fish's tail, because only half the fish fit in the net. We struggled toward shore where I handed Paul the net. It was a dark, beautiful fish with crimson red cheeks and sides.

Steelhead, Vernonia, Oregon

The rest of the day we trolled the shoreline, looking for another steelhead. We caught a few more trout and called it quits about 4pm. It rained on the drive back home.

April 12, 2012
I met Michael Frank at the motel and we headed to the Saluda River at noon, and parked just upstream from the zoo. It was good to be back in South Carolina for a few days and the weather was a perfect 70 degrees and partly cloudy. We hauled a two-man raft a hundred yards down the trail from the paved road and put-in above the falls. I took a few casts while Mike was putting the raft together and before long I was casting at the base of the falls. Mike started hauling the raft over the falls to pick me up when I hooked a monster trout. This was a big fish! I caught him on a #14 Possie Bugger and floating line, under the foamy-

riffle water at the base of a ten-foot high boulder. The rainbow jumped several times and swung completely around the hole three times before he wore out. I brought him slowly to my hand, but took too long because he caught his breath and took off again. Mike finally arrived with a net just in time to watch him throw the hook. He was at least twenty inches long and probably over three pounds – a fat little bugger. Mike had never seen a trout over sixteen inches in this river so this was a rare catch. We picked up two more trout in a slow riffle another quarter mile downstream on a #16 Tan Elk Hair Caddis. We fished the confluence of the Congaree River with no luck. Last year we caught several nice smallmouth there but this year nothing. Another half mile down on the Broad River we saw our first striper. I was casting a large yellow and white foam slider in deep water near half submerged boulders when a large fish came out of the shadows and followed my fly for about ten feet. For the second cast he did the same and took a short strike at the fly's tail feathers. By the third cast we were going nuts, but he grabbed this time and had a solid hook-up. He pulled my seven weight rod all over the river and I struggled to keep him from going down a riffle into the next large hole. Mike did not think I would land him as the fished scraped my leader across several large rocks. He finally wore out and we put a five pound, twenty-one inch striper in the net.

Striper, Broad River, South Carolina

The trip was a success as far as I was concerned. Mike said he had an interesting place to show me next. We floated down river to a knee-deep gravel bar that was in the shade. We ate our lunch and waited for the large grey drakes to appear. When they did, we saw several fish taking them off the surface, including several large stripers. When you fish for stripers, they are usually chasing shad or other baitfish. They rarely take dry flys, but in this stretch of river apparently they do. We put on #8 Yarn Drake patterns and began casting. I focused on a large striper that was rising every couple of minutes in the middle of the slow current on the far, steep-bank side of the river. He was at least a five pound fish. I hooked a couple of bream but did not get a head turn from the striper. Mike also caught several bream.

Bream, Broad River, South Carolina

We tried several other good looking spots with #10 Clousers with no luck. We should be catching smallmouth but they either had lockjaw or were not in this part of the river. At dark we pulled in behind the weir check dam and switched to black, white, and purple four inch long buck tail clousers. The moon was barely visible through the overcast sky – and Mike forgot his flashlight. I hooked the first stripper, next to the concrete wall of the old locks. He went screaming downriver and I was into my backing in ten seconds. It took another ten minutes to land him, a gorgeous twenty four inch, six pound, fish. Over the next two hours we caught fish after fish, losing track after the first dozen. We blind cast thirty feet of line slightly upstream into the dark and swing and stripped our flys down river. Usually the fish hit at the end of the swing and during the first few strips. All the fish were stripers averaging four or five pounds. My arms were about to give out when a large fish hit my fly hard, headed down river and stripped the gears of my fly reel. The reel cranked like it was full of gravel.

Striper, Broad River, South Carolina

We took out at the boat ramp near the gravel pit below town. I thanked Mike for the trip and we made arrangements to fish again the next day.

April 13, 2012
Mike Frank had to take another guy fishing but gladly offered to give me a ride to the Saluda River and arranged for another guy to give me a ride back to the motel in the afternoon. I wanted another shot at the large rainbow I missed the day before. The best hole at the base of the falls was taken first thing in the morning so I wandered downstream to a likely looking run and began casting a #14 Possie Bugger. Shad were everywhere in the river and epically liked deep, fast water at the base of large boulders. I accidently hooked a few shad dead drifting my nymph.

Saluda River, North Carolina

I tried a few casts to a large striper across the river in the shallows with no luck. He was pushing shad into the flats and fins and scales were flying everywhere. Because of the fast mid-river current I could only get a ten second drift before the current swept my fly line downstream. I moved up river to the next hole and found several trout rising to emerging caddis. I switched to a #14 Elk Hair Caddis and caught a foot-long trout on my second cast. The river was deep and the bottom strewn with cobbles and boulders. The fish held behind the boulders and rose consistently to caddis along the current seams. Because most fishermen in this area do not target trout, the fish were easy to catch. I cast to and caught just about every fish that rose. I caught about a dozen fish before they stopped rising. By now the good water was open at the base of the falls. The big fish I'd hooked the day before had to be there. I maneuvered into position in the fast shallow water among a submerged pile of rocks for a long, deep drift with my Possie Bugger. I cast a couple of feet up the falls and let the fly go deep into the foamy water next to a deep ledge. A large rainbow took my fly on the first cast and I set the hook. The fish took all my flyline and several feet of backing and headed to the center of the deep pool. He had to be the same fish from yesterday, this water does not hold many big trout. He jumped several times when I got him to the surface. He finally wore out in the less oxygenated warmer water away from the falls and I beached him on a moss covered, shallow, gravel bar. He was a beautiful rainbow slightly over twenty inches weighing a little over three pounds.

Rainbow Trout, Saluda River, South Carolina

After a photo I quickly revived and released him. He made by day. I fished several pools up the falls and hooked and lost another rainbow. By 2pm it was getting hot and humid. I thumbed a ride back

to the motel with Darren, Mike's shuttle driver. I spent the rest of the weekend in the motel tying fifteen dozen elk hair caddis.

April 27, 2012
I dropped off $500 worth of flys to a businessman in downtown Portland at noon and then hustled to meet Paul Skelton to fish the Trask River for the rest of the afternoon. Technically we were fishing for late steelhead, but tyed on searun cutthroat flys to cover both fish. Within minutes I landed a skinny searun near the Tillamook County Park in the slow tail-out water.

Searun Cutthroat Trout, Trask River, Oregon

He took a #12 Red Reverse Spider on a sink-tip line. That was the only fish of the day. We fished several more runs and gave up when the weather turned from showers to rain. We had plate-sized hamburgers at Alice's Restaurant on the drive home.

May 3, 2012
I met Tony Reeser on the Owhyee River at 9am and we began fishing the White House Hole. The river was running a little high and off-color and it was threatening to rain. There were no bugs on the water. Tony had a bad ankle and had difficulty moving around. We caught no fish. We moved up to the Power Line Hole and waded along a smooth gravel bar next to a deep, fast run. I was fishing a new bamboo rod and antique Hardy reel for the first time. I put on a yarn indicator, heavily weighted #14 Possie Bugger and #18 Pheasant Tail Nymph and began catching fish. I had to keep mending the line to keep the current from stripping the line downstream. The first brown took my Possie Bugger in the slow water on the

far side of the current, after a 10 yard drift. He was a beauty, about twenty inches.

Brown, Owhyee River, Oregon

We picked up a couple more fish on nymphs and had a late lunch of hard boiled eggs and crusty sandwiches. In the late afternoon I crossed the river and fished the slow frog water interspersed with submerged boulders. A few fish were taking emergers, but there was no hatch. I targeted and hooked a couple of fish before the run. Tony didn't have much luck so we headed down river and checked out a few of my favorite spots but they were already taken by Boise, Idaho fishermen. About 6pm we called it quits and headed to town. Tony was new to the area and was caught by a cop speeding through Nyssa, Oregon. The speed limit was twenty five, he was doing forty five, we both were pulled over. The officer told me I was only going thirty and ordered me to leave. Tony was not so lucky, he got a ticket. We made it to a Japanese restaurant in Ontario, and had Bento boxes before they closed. We split a cheap motel for the night.

May 4, 2012

Tony Reeser and I fished Upper Bridge Hole a short distance below the Owhyee Dam. The run looked good with about a hundred yards of moving water over a boulder field. It was on and-off-again rain for several hours and we did not see a fish. Next we fished the run below the White House Hole and enjoyed a mediocre Callibaetis hatch. I picked up three sixteen to twenty browns before convincing Tony to take my spot. He immediately hooked and lost a large brown. Ten minutes later he had another fish on and landed a very nice twenty inch honey colored brown. I

noticed several fish working the dead water on the far bank so I waded across until the river was three inches from the top of my waders, and began casting. I had a couple of followers but could not tempt the biters. Off in the distance a storm was building and we heard thunder on the other side of the ridge then took cover when the thunder and lightning was half mile away.

Owhyee River, Oregon

I left my rod in the willow and walked forty yards away and sat on a rock in a small ravine to wait out the storm. It was bad, the storm front brought strong wind gusts, lighting, rain, and hail. We took a beating by not heading back to the truck. The storm ended as fast as it began and we hit the river again and picked up two more browns. The lighting really got the fish hopping. We played it safe as the second storm front headed our way. We were safely in the truck before a wave of rain hit. A torrent of tan colored clay and water poured over several portions of the paved road as we drove downriver. At the Walk Up of the River Hole I talked Tony into stopping and scouting for big fish. We immediately noticed two large fish, one fish steadily rising in the middle of the river and a second fish next to shore alongside two hummocks of bunchgrass. Tony said "go for it" so I tied on a #16 Ant (assuming the rain had flooded at least one ant nest) and crept slowly down the rock rip-rap and two rod's length away from the still rising fish. The first cast was on target, the fish paid no interest. The second cast was all it took and the fish inhaled, I set the hook and the battle was on. He tired quickly and I brought him to the net, a nice twenty-two inch brown. I could see Tony's jaw drop from thirty yards away as I walked up the hill back to the truck. The moment was just to perfect to cast again.

Brown Trout, Owhyee River, Oregon

We drove down to the Ledge Hole and Tony took a few more casts at rising fish, until the wind began blowing and his ankle began to hurt. We cleaned up at the motel and had dinner at a posh Irish Restaurant in Ontario. This time we drove the speed limit through Nyssa and the cop waved us through town.

May 18, 2012

Chuck Cooney and I fished the Deschutes River. It was the salmon fly hatch and we assumed the river would be crowded, so we headed to Oak Springs and parked the truck next to the fish hatchery. We were the second car there in the morning and it was obvious the first crew was not happy to see us and they quickly headed down river. We took our time and headed up river, poking into every back-eddy and riffle. The fishing was not exceptional, but Chuck landed a couple of foot-long rainbows in one nice run on nymphs. I fished a #12 Clarks Stonefly and picked up a nice fish next to a grassy bank about a half mile up river. The water looked perfect for steelhead, but was a disappointment for trout. I picked up two more fish before calling it quits and heading downriver to find Chuck. We had lunch in the shade of a large ash tree and threw a couple dozen adult stoneflys into the hatchery raceway to ten pound brood stock. Later in the afternoon we headed to Maupin and visited the fly shops and fished the first meadow upstream from town. The fishing was excellent. I picked up four large trout in about fifteen minutes on my adult stonefly. We fished the first takeout, where there were over two

dozen campers and tents. I had a few takes but hooked no fish. This water had been heavily worked over all day. Our last stop was Harpin Flat, where we were surprised to find only three campers occupying the large campground. We fished the large pool and run upriver from the boat launch.

Deschutes River, Oregon

Chuck picked up a few trout swinging soft hackles on his switch rod. I hooked a couple of small trout and got my fly and line stuck in a tree over a pool. While retrieving my fly I slipped on a rock and got soaked. I dried out while Chuck took a few more casts and we were on the road as the sun went down. We camped at Rock Creek Reservoir near Tygh Valley and went to sleep early.

May 19, 2012

Tom Wideman picked me up at Rock Creek Reservoir and we headed back to the Deschutes River for a second day of fishing. The rest of the fly club was fishing the reservoir and not interested in the salmon fly hatch. We went back to Oak Springs and headed downriver along the railroad tracks about two miles and hit the water just above the White River Bridge. Tom hooked the first fish on his second cast on an adult stonefly. We fished the water next to the steep bank and each picked up three or four fish at each riffle. It was difficult moving around the steep bank, loose large rocks, poison ivy, and rattle snakes. I saw two snakes and played with one for a while with my rod tip. He must have enjoyed it because he sure was shaking his rattle. The fish were healthy and fat after eating salmon flys for a couple of weeks. We both were surprised by a very large trout that took a bug two rods lengths away, and rose again a few minutes later. Tom and I took turns casting towards the submerged rock where he was hiding. We did not see him a third time.

Redsides Trout, Deschutes River, Oregon

By two o'clock we each had caught a couple dozen trout and were tired. Tom headed back to the car along the railroad and I bushwhacked it up river and fished a few more holes along the many springs that emptied off Tygh Ridge.

Deschutes River, Oregon

We packed up and headed to town for a soda and a visit to the fly shop. We had a couple of hours of daylight left and fished the first take-out up river from Maupin. We had a few rises but only hooked two fish. While we were packing our gear we watched a guy break into the outhouse for his wife. Apparently the lock got jammed and the door would not open. Tom and I had oversized burgers at Calamity Jane's in Sandy on the drive home.

June 2, 2012

The Orvis Fly Shop in Tualatin set up a "carp clinic" at Sauvie Island and lined up three guides to talk about and demonstrate carp techniques. Tom Wideman and I were the only participants – so we all just fished together. Adam McNamara was the Orvis shop manager; his guides were Brian and Matt. We started fishing at Grass Lake on the northwest part of the island. We walked through several inches of water as we approached the pond and carp scattered when we were thirty feet from the pond. We could see deep V-wakes in the shallow weed filled water. We slowly and quietly waded into the pond and waited for the carp to return and resume feeding.

Grass Lake, Sauvie Island, Oregon

The conditions could not have been worse for carp fishing. It was cloudy with an occasional drop of rain and a slight wind that created ripples on the water. We'd hoped for bright sunshine and no wind to improve our changes of seeing feeding carp. It was barely 70 degrees, the lower threshold for actively feeding carp. We saw a few carp moving but none were actively feeding. We headed towards Big Martin Lake and saw a few feeding fish off in the distance, too far for us to wade to in the muddy lake. We next cut around to Round Lake and saw several feeding fish. We made a few casts without success. Then we headed back to the car and drove to the north east side of the island and parked at a wildlife viewing platform and hiked toward Gay Lake. We passed a weed choked canal and noticed several feeding carp above an irrigation weir. I crept to within casting distance and put my fly two feet from a fish's nose, and waited as the lightly weighted fly sunk into the weeds. On my second cast I put the fly six inches from his mouth and waited a couple seconds before sliding the fly toward the fish. He took the fly and the fight was on. He swam to the bottom and it was difficult to bring him back to the surface on my eight pound tippet. He began rolling in the weeds and I brought him towards an area of clear water where he wore out fighting my rod. We slipped him onto the bank and admired a handsome five pound carp.

Carp, Sauvie Island, Oregon

We cast to the remaining fish with no luck. We continued hiking along Gay Lake and Racetrack Lake, which looked really fishy, but we did not see or cast to any fish. We called it quits as the sun hit the horizon and scattered sunshine below the storm clouds. We could not see a thing on the water. We called it quits and began planning our next carp trip.

June 9, 2012
I thumbed a ride with Dave Wesley and a friend, Gary, to fish the Deschutes River. We were surprised to see freshly fallen snow on the road on Mt. Hood. We met a couple of other guys form Washington County Fly Fishers at Mecca Flat. It was unseasonably cold on the river and did not get above 60 degrees. The wind blew 30 mph all day long. My first fish was a large whitefish that was hiding in the riffle below the island. He took a #12 Possie Bugger and by sheer force broke my four pound tippet. I did not hook another fish for two hours. The second fish ignored my #18 Pheasant Tail Nymph dropper and took the Possie Bugger in the foam-line of a long, deep back eddy.

Redside Trout, Deschutes River, Oregon

Immediately after hooking the fish another fisherman slid down the bank and started asking twenty questions. It was free fishing day and the crowded river was filled with once a year fisherman. I landed the fish and politely answered his questions without giving too much information away. I kept telling him you got to put in the time before you start catching a lot of fish. I headed downstream to fish one of my favorite runs, the Big Back Eddy. Fish were rising all over. Most fish were out of reach, but occasionally the constantly changing current swept a fish within casting range. I broke off three large fish over two hours of casting. The odds were not in my favor. The strong current swept upstream, turned and headed downstream. The rising fish were congregated where the two currents converged. The fish took my #10 Orange Stimulator and turned into the cross current, doubling their resistance and torque on my line. Three fish played this trick and broke off.

Deschutes River, Oregon

I finally hooked a 17-incher in the slow current under a tree next to shore, and brought him to my feet – then he broke off on a submerged log. It was just not my day. I picked up two more foot-long trout on the hike back to the truck. There were a few leftover black and golden stoneflies along the willows but the hatch was basically over. We were home about ten o'clock.

June 18, 2012
I met Dave Wesley at his house early Monday Morning and we met Tom Wideman and Chuck Cooney at Biggs Junction for breakfast. The river looked a little high and muddy at Cottonwood Bridge.

John Day River, Oregon

After repairing a lock on Chuck's mom's house in Condon, we unloaded our gear at our rented house in Spray and headed eight miles up the John Day River to the green locked gate and set up our pontoon boats for a day of smallmouth bass fishing. The river was running about 1,600 cfs and slightly off-color. The wind was bad and we had a few short rain showers throughout the afternoon. The fishing was not so good; I only landed a dozen bass. It was difficult fighting the wind and trying to cover eight miles of river in half a day was too much. After dinner we all went to sleep exhausted.

June 19, 2012
We decided to fish a shorter stretch of the John Day today and headed up river from town, four miles to the "gravel pit". There was less wind and no rain today and we caught dozens of bass. I used a #10 Tan/Black Chernobyl Ant all day with a 5-Weight rod. I learned something new this trip.

We always float down the middle of the river and cast towards the shore, focusing on the deep water pockets between grass and sedge clumps. I caught very few fish next to the grass banks and almost all fish near sedges and rushes (grass-like but different plant species).

Smallmouth Bass, John Day River, Oregon

Upon careful observation I discovered that the grass dominated shoreline was always on deep topsoil, well above the water table, that sloughed into the river and created a muddy bottom. The bass usually did not like the muddy bottoms. The sedges and rushes grew on shallower soils, closer to the water table and almost always in rocky areas that created gravel river bottoms. The bass liked the rocky areas for both cover and food sources. On our float down the river I began ignoring the grass banks and focused on the sedge/rush areas and caught more fish – about three dozen today.

Rainbow Trout, John Day River, Oregon

There were fish in the grassy bank areas, but they were usually about two rod's lengths away from shore. In the sedge/rush areas, the bass were inches from the riverbank. I was surprised to catch a rainbow trout in fast water about a mile above town. He took my foam ant and quickly wore out in the warm water. In the same bend of the river Chuck caught the biggest bass of the trip, a dark 17-inch fish.

June 20, 2012

We chose a new stretch of the John Day River today and floated from Kimberley to the gravel pit. It grew warmer and the clouds and wind disappeared. The fishing was slow and between the three of us we probably picked up two dozen bass. At the gravel pit take out, a small army had set up a camp of half-dozen camper/trailers, tents, and pickup trucks. They were having a really good time – and it was only noon. We packed our gear and headed home. A couple of miles before Wasco, Chuck pulled over to change a bad tire. We set up lawn chairs to watch and critique Chuck. He was a good sport, and as he was an auto mechanic, he replaced the tire in minutes. We got home just before dark, sunburned, and exhausted.

June 23, 2012

Chuck Cooney and I attended the quarterly Federation of Fly Fishers Oregon Council meeting at Sherry Steele's home in Sisters, Oregon. They were recruiting new board members and I was curious about volunteering. On the drive over, there was an unusual six inches of snow on Santiam Pass. After the meeting we took a chance and headed up the mountain to fish for brook trout in Three Creeks Creek.

Three Creeks Creek, Oregon

It was partly sunny as Chuck and I each caught an eight-inch trout at the first hole. The weather proceeded to get worse and we had gale winds, rain showers, and finally a snow blizzard. Summer will be late this year. We caught a half-dozen small trout in a half-mile of meadow creek and called it quits. We had milkshakes in Detroit and stopped at the fly shop in Salem on the way home.

July 12, 2012

Tom Wideman and I went searching for carp after work. We'd been told that Johnson Creek was a good spot, where the highway crossed the creek near the pumping station north of the Scappoose Airport. We saw a couple of dozen huge carp milling inches below the surface in frog water. A guy and his girlfriend were bait fishing from shore – and they did not want to be bothered. We decided to come back another time and headed to the north-eastern corner of Sauvie Island. We found good carp water at Rentenaar Point.

Sauvie Island, Oregon

Two older gentlemen were fishing the shallow grassy bank when we arrived, but they quickly left as we set up our rods. I don't think they had fishing licenses. Tom had the first shot at several carp about ten feet from shore. They were gulping cottonwood seeds and insects below several large trees in stagnant water. The fish were not interested and slowly headed to the middle of the waterway. By the time I put my rod together Tom had moved down shore and the fish had returned. I cast to several fish and put my fly inches from open mouths. The carp were not interested and left after several bad casts. We headed to the shore of Sturgeon Lake and found carp heaven. The wind was blowing and creating riffles but several acres of the shallow lake shoreline were calm, and we could see carp nosing about and jumping out of the water. We'd left our waders in the car and could not get within casting distance without getting muddy feet. We marked the spot on the map and will return another day. On the walk back to the car I took a long cast into open water to clean the mud off my fly line. During the fast retrieve I hooked and landed a little crappie. He was as bright as a silver dollar. A couple of circling osprey swooped in close after I threw him back into the water. I think the fish got away. As the sun disappeared behind the coast range we made our last stop across from the dog kennels on Reeder Road. The bay looked very good for carp, with lots of semi-submerged grass and trees. There is just not enough time in a day to fish. We got home at ten o'clock.

July 14, 2012

Paul Skelton called late the night before asking if I wanted to fish for summer steelhead on the Wilson River at sun-up, and volunteered to pick me up at 5:30am. I don't turn many fishing invitations down, but needed to get some work done around the house. He promised to be back in town before 10am so I agreed to go. We picked up Gordon Zander en route and the three of us were on the river an hour later, at a large, deep hole less than a mile below the confluence with Elk Creek.

Wilson River, Oregon

We were fishing center-pin reels to achieve long, slow, drag-free drifts. I fished a three inch, skinny, pink worm about six feet below a small plastic pencil bobber. The weather was perfect, about 60 degrees and overcast. It had rained the night before and everything was damp and quiet in the

dense forest. On my third cast I hooked a large fish, which rolled a few times then slipped the hook. I was casting twenty feet above the hole on an overhanging rock cliff and could see the chrome fish flash ten feet below the water's surface. We took a few more casts and headed downriver. The river was relatively crowded. We passed several turn-outs with vehicles and fished a couple of holes near the new Tillamook State Park Interpretative Center. Around 8am the tourists started to show up on the river and began reserving their swimming holes. It had been 90 degrees in Portland the week before and a lot of people like to cool off in the Wilson River. We could not compete for space on the river and were home by 10am.

July 19, 2012

I was asked to give a presentation to the Rainlanders Fly Club in Astoria and made arrangements with one of their club members to fish for the day. Tom Scoggins graciously volunteered to be our guide. I also invited Tom Wideman to tag along. Tom told us the best resident coastal cutthroat fishing was after 10am when the insects woke up, and on rivers that had barriers to salmon and steelhead where the resident fish did not have to compete for limited food. We headed to the upper reach of the North Fork Klaskanine River along Highway #202. We parked the truck and bush-wacked down a steep slope, a half mile to an overgrown railroad grade that followed the river. We hiked another mile downstream before entering the river.

Coastal Cutthroat, North Fork Klaskanine River

The water was relatively low, crystal clear, and had many pools and riffles. I put on a #14 Elk Hair

Caddis Parachute and began casting my six and a half foot #2 weight rod. I caught an eight-inch cutthroat in the second hole. She was a beauty with a bright red throat and spots all over her dark green back and sides. The forest was thick and dark and everything but the river gravel was covered with thick green sphagnum moss. The coast range was cloudy and as the temperature rose from 60 to 80 degrees it got very humid. Every hole in the river produced a couple of fish ranging from six to ten inches. The fish were small, but all were adults. They were a challenge to catch on a two weight rod. After noon we hiked back to the truck and had lunch.

North Fork Klaskanine River, Oregon

We spent the rest of the day touring around the watershed, with Tom showing us his favorite fishing areas. We looked at the South Fork Klaskanine River and at Youngs River. Both rivers had locked gates but the public could hike or bicycle the gravel roads. After having dinner at the Merry Time bar in Astoria I gave my presentation about "how rainbow trout conquered the world" and talked about the history of the fish hatchery program in the United States. Tom and I got home before midnight.

July 21, 2012

Paul Skelton built me a combination "switch rod" and "center-pin rod" and offered to help test it out on the Wilson River. The river was crowded in the late, hot Saturday afternoon. There were cars parked in almost every turn-out and swimmers in every hole. We tried a few spots below the confluence with Elk Creek, the rest area, and behind the Tillamook Forestry Center. Paul caught a couple of smolts and I caught

nothing. The rod and reel cast very well and I look forward to fishing when the big fish arrive in the fall.

Wilson River, Oregon

July 28, 2012

Tom Wideman and I continued our pursuit of the elusive Willamette Valley carp. After stacking a cord of oak firewood in the backyard and tilling our raised-bed garden, I met Tom at his house and we headed to St. Paul, Oregon. Tom had seen carp in Mission Lake several years ago and we were eager to cast a few flys at them in the hot afternoon. The dam site was muddy and too deep for fly casting to carp. We headed to the top end of the long, narrow lake and parked on a side-street across the road from St. Paul's Cemetery. We could see a dozen large carp cruising in the shallow, grass lined flats. We waved to the homeowner up-slope from the lake and he came down to see what we were doing. He had recently moved from Idaho and was an avid fly fisherman – but never for carp. He was polite but I could tell he thought we were nuts. I tied a bead-chain soft hackle to my 7-weight rod, walked into the flooded pasture to just below my knees and waited for a cruising carp. It did not take long. I put a fly a foot in front of a large fish, he turned and watched my fly sink to the bottom before swimming off. This happened several more times. One fish poked at my fly, but did not inhale. I was getting frustrated. I changed to a #12 San Juan Worm with a copper bead and cast to a few more fish. Finally after about an hour a carp swam past me and then directly away from where I was standing. I put my fly about two feet ahead of him and a foot over his right shoulder, hoping the fly would sink to his level when he swam by my fly. It worked. He took my fly and spun out of control. He thrashed a little near a submerged grass island and then headed directly towards me. I kept the line tight as he slid into the submerged grass, a rod's length from my feet. The line was tight as he lay half out of the water. I'd guess he was about five pounds and twenty inches long. I did not want to submerge my knee-high boots so Tom tried to tail him but was unsuccessful. The hooked finally worked itself loose and off he sank to the silty depths. The neighbor watched the commotion from his lawn chair and came down to show us his prize bamboo rod. I kept looking for fish and casting at swirls and bubbles. A half hour later the fish disappeared and we were off looking for a new spot. We walked through the cemetery and were impressed by several headstones that dated before the Civil War. We followed a semi-hidden trail down a steep hill towards the lake and found a lake-side bench hidden in the waist-high grass. Huge carp were rolling just beyond casting distance. Tom and I agreed this spot was best fished from pontoon boats. We checked out two more spots in town before heading home. Both were off of Scholls Ferry Road near Tigard, Oregon. They were surrounded by restaurants, grocery stores and townhouses. We saw a few carp, but they were not worth the hassle.

August 8, 2012

It had been 100 degrees most of the week in Salt Lake City and I had the morning free to fish. My first choice was Farmington Canyon until I learned that the access road had washed out. My second choice was the Provo River. I got an early start and was on the river before six in the morning. The sun was just barely poking over the Wasatch Mountains when I stepped into the cold water above the water treatment plant. I did not have room in my luggage for waders so I wet waded. The first half hour I could not feel my feet because the water was so cold. Several fish were rising in the slack water on the far side of the river. A swift chute of water separated us and it was difficult to get a decent drift. I finally found a position where I could loop and mend my line upriver and get a two or three foot drag-free drift. A brown took my caddis and I landed him a short time later on my side of the river. I tried for another half hour to entice a couple of other fish but finally gave up – mostly because I could not

feel my cold feet anymore. Down river where a diversion split the river, the water piled up on the near bank and created a long, deep pool.

Provo River, Utah

It was easy to cast in several directions. There were three main currents in the pool and fish were scattered and rising everywhere. I was thankful to have the river to myself and hooked into two dozen fish before the sun was high on the water. All the fish were brown trout and they only took my #14 Tan Elk Hair Caddis. Most of the fish were about 16 inches long. After the pool was exhausted I headed back up river to explore several short trails along the river. Most of the river was too fast to hold fish, except for a few short pockets along the riverbank.

Brown Trout, Provo River, Utah

Just below the day use parking area the outside bend of the river created a deep, fast run that was littered with large rock and boulders. A long trunk of an old cottonwood tree lay parallel across the run. I put on a heavily weighted #12 Possie

Bugger and cast it at the top of the run, and directed it alongside the tree trunk. On my third drift, at the tail end of the run, a large brown took my fly and headed across the river. I stressed my line bringing him back into the run and played him out in the deep pool. I jumped down a four-foot step mud bank to land him on a grassy bank. He was another gorgeous wild trout. I was glad to have picked the "lesser traveled" willow infested lower section of river rather than the more popular open meadows in the upper section. Back at the car I changed clothes and quickly warmed up in the hot sun. I was at the airport an hour later and slept on the flight home.

August 11, 2012

We had a long, cool spring in the Pacific Northwest and the water levels from snowmelt were finally low enough to fish the Santiam River. I invited Roger Lehman and Paul Keefner fishing for the day. We fished at the confluence of Pamela Creek where we caught lots of fish the year before. The fish were not there this year and I only caught a six inch rainbow. We gave it another try a mile upriver and it was a little better. I hooked half a dozen foot long rainbows on a #16 Tan Elk Hair Caddis.

Santiam River, Oregon

I fished a Pheasant Tail dropper for several hours, but nothing took the nymph, so I took it off. After lunch it started to get hot. We headed to new territory and explored Marion Creek about two miles above the town of Marion Forks. The river flowed through dense Doug Fir forest. We could hear the river in the distance but could rarely see the water. Finally we saw a patch of sunlight in a clearing and hiked a couple hundred

yards into the woods and found a large riffle and pool, with tall grass on our side of the river and tall, thick trees and shade on the far side of the river. The fish were stacked up and rising to caddis in the shaded water. I quickly hooked and landed a dozen native cutthroats while Roger and Paul were fishing several plunge pools downstream.

Coastal Cutthroat, Marion Creek, Oregon

These fish were jewels with bright colors and perfectly shaped bodies. They were fighters and I wished I had brought along my two-weight rod. When Roger appeared out of the brush, I gave him the pool and he caught another half-dozen fish. Paul caught another dozen fish in several short runs below where we were fishing. We called it a day around three in the afternoon and had milk shakes in Detroit before driving home.

August 31, 2012

I had not fished the Deschutes River all summer so Paul Skelton and I headed to the river Friday morning. This was my first time fishing for trout with a center-pin reel. We started fishing below Sherar's Bridge at Pine Tree put-in. I put on a heavily weighted #12 Possie Bugger and #16 Caddis Pupa dropper and cast at the top of the run and immediately got a fifty-yard dead-drift. The long, smooth drifts were nothing short of phenomenal. It would have been impossible to deep-nymph the water so effectively any other way. I was still new to center-pinning and missed a few strikes while fumbling with the line and reel, but did manage to pick up a fat sixteen-inch whitefish. Our next hole was up river where a large, shallow riffle emptied into a long, deep trough. I immediately caught a nice seventeen inch redside rainbow in the shallow water at the head of the run. He jumped all over the hole and was fun to fight on my twelve foot, six weight rod. At noon we had hamburgers at the Oasis in Maupin. The afternoon was hot and got close to 90 degrees. We fished a couple more holes above Harpin Flats and I caught another nice rainbow.

Redsides Trout, Deschutes River, Oregon

Center-pinning was nice because we could stand in the shade of a tree and fish an entire run without moving. I still think a single-hand fly rod is the most fun, but center-pinning was very effective on a hot, sunny day where the trout are hugging the bottom of the river. By mid-afternoon the wind kicked up and made fishing impossible. We headed back to town for a cold drink and then went home.

September 21, 2012
I took Friday afternoon off work and headed towards Astoria, Oregon to fish Big Creek – about a two hour drive.

Big Creek, Oregon

Salmon and steelhead are restricted to the lower river by a weir at the fish hatchery and the upper river is a haven for resident coastal cutthroat and rainbow trout. Most of the watershed is private land owned by timber companies and public access is restricted to foot travel. I parked my car at the locked gate above the hatchery and hiked up river along a gravel logging road about a mile before climbing down a steep bank to the creek. The canyon was steep, narrow, and heavily timbered. A little sunlight made it through the alders, but under the canopy of fir and hemlock the creek bottom was dark. The creek was dominated by plunge-pools and separated by shallow riffles. I tyed a #14 Elk Hair Caddis to my three-weight rod, cast into a slow pool, and hooked a ten inch trout on my second cast. Caddis cases covered the rocks and mayflies were in the air. I fished about a quarter mile of water and hooked about two dozen small trout.

Rainbow Trout, Big Creek, Oregon

It was difficult to wet-wade the slick rocks but definitely worth the risk for the excellent fishing. I crawled up the steep bank and hiked up river about three miles past an old concrete bridge. The canyon flattened out and was a little easier to wade and cast. The pools were also larger and deeper and the fish bigger – up to fourteen inches. I hiked back to my car as the sun was going down, a little chilled, but happy to have found another little remote trout stream.

September 25, 2012
I had the opportunity to fish the North Platte River, Wyoming and invited Tom Wideman to join me and split expenses for the week. We flew to Denver, rented a car and drove about 250 miles

north to Saratoga, Wyoming. In town on the way to the motel we met the rest of our group: Ralph Brooks (from Oregon) and his brother Jeff, Ralph's son Brian, and Doug and Greg from Kansas (both botany professors). The next morning we had breakfast at the only restaurant open in town and headed south to the Colorado line to fish Six Mile Gap.

Six Mile Gap, Wyoming

The fall colors were beautiful. The aspens were bright yellow and the current bushes were crimson red. We hiked down a steep trail to the river and were disappointed by the river flow, which was about thirty percent of average (about 90 cfs). The water was low and clear. We were lucky to find any runs deeper than two feet.

Rainbow Trout, North Platte River, Wyoming

Fish scattered as we approached them and were spooked by our fly lines. I fished up river through a steep rock canyon, hoping the freestone water held more fish. It held fish but they were not biting. Ralph did pretty well and caught several

fish on a #20 PMD Camparadun below the canyon. I only caught one fish on a #18 Pheasant Tail Nymph. We left mid-afternoon, drove back to town and fished Saratoga Lake. We fished the east side of the lake where there was a sandy beach and easy wading. I put on an unweighted #8 Dark Brown Carey Bugger and waded up to my waist, thirty yards from shore. A few fish were rising in the choppy water and I hooked a seventeen inch fish in about a half hour. He was football fat, chrome silver with rose colored sides, and feisty. I hooked and lost several other fish, but did land a twenty inch trophy.

Rainbow Trout, Saratoga Lake, Wyoming

It started to get cold as the sun went down and the wind began to pick up. It looked like a storm was coming up the Front Range from the south. I landed a half dozen more sixteen inch fish before calling it quits. Tom and I had green chili soup at the cowboy bar.

September 26, 2012
We woke to rain on the tin motel roof before we all met for breakfast. Ralph had been fishing this area for over twenty five years and one of his favorite places was Pickaroon Campground. Our rental car took a beating on forty miles of rough gravel roads to the river between the Savage Run and North Platte Wilderness Areas, but we made good time and were fishing by mid-morning. The water was low and clear around dozens of large boulders scattered along the river. I spotted several fish rising a couple hundred yards down river on a glass smooth run. I put on a #20 PMD emerger and quietly approached them from below. After a couple of casts to get my line distance

right I drifted a fly between the two fish and pricked a large fish in the lip.

Pickaroon, North Platte River, Wyoming

Both fish scattered making large V-wakes on the water surface. It was useless to blind-cast in the shallow water so I hiked another mile up river before seeing another fish rise. The glare on the water forced me to drift a fly downstream to him and I hooked and lost another large fish. I immediately cast into a long riffle to straighten out the line on my reel, and was surprised to hook a fat little brown trout.

Brown Trout, North Platte River, Wyoming

I cast to several other fish with no luck. Tom and I called it quits after lunch and headed back to town. We got a tip from Hack's Fly Shop and fished the Encampment River upriver from Baggott Rocks, at the public access. We followed a fence line which separated us from a couple dozen buffalo. At the river we found a long, slow bend of river that had several rising fish. I tried a #20 Emerger with no luck and switched to a #18

Black Ant. On my first cast I hooked a spunky sixteen inch rainbow who headed downstream, jumping all over the water. He spooked the remaining fish and they did not start rising for another fifteen minutes. Tom caught another nice trout. Rather than waiting for the fish to settle down again we headed up river. We did not see rising fish so we swung streamers through the riffles – but hooked no fish.

Encampment River, Wyoming

On the way down stream we tried to get closer to the rising fish on the outside bend of the river, but got stuck up to our knees in the soft, saturated clay. I almost fell over trying to get out of the sticky mess. We hiked back to the car along the fence and this time the buffalo took an interest in us. The entire herd slowly walked toward us and stood twenty yards away and stared at us. We watched them for a few minutes, cleaned off our waders in an irrigation ditch and headed to town. We had fried chicken from the grocery store for dinner.

September 27, 2012
We'd had enough of the shallow water and headed north to the "Miracle Mile" of the North Platte River. There was plenty of water coming out of Seminoe Reservoir and we found a nice riffle all for ourselves – after racing there to beat a guide boat a quarter mile upstream. I put a weighted #12 Possie Bugger and #18 Pheasant Tail dropper nine feet under a yarn indicator and began fishing the riffle water. I hooked a half dozen ten inch fish in the riffle water, then moved to the deeper side channels hoping for bigger fish. They were waiting for me and I hooked, and lost at the net, a seventeen inch rainbow. The next fish was a foot

long brown trout. At the top of the run, where the water pooled and created a slight back eddy, I hooked a twenty inch rainbow. He took my Pheasant Tail in the corner of his jaw and exploded all over the run. I almost lost him several times at the tail-out as he tried to reach the fast current and head downstream. I finally beached him and rolled him into my net.

Rainbow Trout, North Platte River, Wyoming

I picked up another foot-long brown and rainbow on the trip back to the car. Tom and I headed downstream looking for another riffle to watch while eating lunch. We saw a few fish rising, but only caught a couple of small trout. At the tail of the run I hooked and lost a large Brown who was hiding below a large submerged boulder. I was not paying attention and he slipped the hook while I was trying to get the loose line on my reel. The next run was the second to last riffle before the river emptied into Pathfinder Reservoir. We worked the riffle hard for an hour, but caught no fish. Black clouds appeared to the north and we heard thunder in the distance. We quickly headed up river to fish one more hole before the storm hit. We were too late and were deluged with rain and lighting within minutes of stepping out of the car. We called it quits, headed back to Saratoga, and had hamburgers at the bar.

September 28, 2012
Our last day on the North Platte River we headed to Sanger Sportsman's Access but we turned away due to a large herd of Black Angus cattle and two cowboys who hinted we were trespassing (we were). We stopped at the Orvis Fly Shop in town and the shop help recommended we fish below Bennett Peak Campground, where there was a

nice riffle at the base of a cliff. The riffle was nice, even in low water, but there were a few fish. I had one slash and rise to my #14 Elk Hair Caddis. We gave up on the river and headed back to Saratoga Lake to cast and strip streamers. The lake did not produce as well this time and we only caught a half dozen fourteen inch rainbows. We all met at the bar for hamburgers and watched the football game.

September 29, 2012
Saturday morning we all had breakfast together, exchanged a few more flys, and said our farewells. Tom and I took the scenic route to Denver, stopping at three fly shops along the way. We saw a large moose just north of Granby, Colorado. The flight home was painful. We sat in front of a grandmother and two small children who screamed at each other in Spanish the entire flight while kicking the back of our seats. Jean graciously picked us up at the airport at midnight. I was glad to be home to peace and quiet.

October 4, 2012
The summer was coming to an end and clear skies were forecast the rest of the week. Once it starts raining in the Pacific Northwest it does not stop for eight months.

Car and Trailer, Oregon

I wanted to get one more long fishing trip in before it started raining and took the afternoon off work, packed my gear, and headed over the Cascade Mountains to Suttle Lake. The wind was blowing and there were whitecaps on the lake. I'd heard rumors of large brown trout cruising the Lake Creek inlet at the west end of the lake. I dumped my pontoon boat in the lake at dusk and started dragging a dark brown #8 Carey Bugger, on an intermediate line, along the lake bottom. I hooked and lost a fish in fifteen minutes. That was just the encouragement I needed to keep kicking my fins in the cold water and wind. I passed the inlet several times with no hits. Another fisherman unloaded his boat and started trolling a spoon on the north shore. He appeared to know what he was doing so when he left to fish the south side of the lake I started to fish the north shore. The bank was littered with large windblown fir trees protruding deep into the lake making perfect habitat for trout. I hooked a nice fourteen inch brown and lost him at the net. The next fish was his twin and was fat and healthy in my hand. It was too dark to see the third fish who threw my hook a rods length away. I followed the running lights of the trolling boat to the boat ramp and back to the campground. I was too tired to carry my gear back to the trailer so I secured it on shore, crawled onto a sleeping bag in the back of my car and went to sleep listening to the news on my transistor radio.

October 5, 2012

It was 20 degrees cold that night and Suttle Lake was calm as glass in the early morning. A few fish were rising, but not enough to entice me to stay and fish another day. It had been over ten years since I'd fished Hosmer Lake, and it was just far enough away for me to warm up by my car's heater. I arrived at Hosmer at 9am and met two other fishermen from Bend at the boat ramp.

Hosmer Lake, Oregon

We exchanged flys. They gave me a heavy bright orange chenille and marabou streamer called Kokanee Candy. I was told to cast and strip the fly

as fast as I could. I was leery but promised to give it a try. My favorite Hosmer fly was a dark green #14 Metallic Caddis, but I only had one in my fly box. I decided to save it for the late afternoon and put on a #18 Pheasant Tail Nymph. I had a hit one hundred yards off the boat ramp and nothing for the next couple of hours. Hundreds of brook trout and Atlantic salmon were gathering in the channel between the upper and lower lakes. A half dozen fisherman were competing for the fish's attention in the small channel, while sightseeing kayakers dodged around us. I had a few hits on my pheasant tail, but hooked nothing. I switched to a #18 Zebra Midge Pupa, which is not typically trolled around a lake, and I was mildly surprised to begin catching brook trout. The first fish was twelve inches and the second sixteen inches. By late afternoon the channel was choked with a group of bird watcher boats. It was time for one more pass before heading to the less crowded lower lake. I put the reserved Metallic Caddis on my tippet and headed down river. At a slight bend of the river I took the outside of the channel and my fly slowed to a crawl. A large brook trout took my fly and headed to the weed infested bottom of the channel. I knew he was big because he pulled with the strength of several of the fish I'd caught earlier in the day. I finally landed him, a nineteen inch handsome brook trout in full spawning colors. He was barely hooked by the skin of his teeth and the hook fell off in the net.

Brook Trout, Hosmer Lake, Oregon

I asked another fisherman to take a photo. If my memory is correct, that was my biggest brook trout. By the time I released him three other fisherman were casting where I'd hooked the fish. I kept on heading to the lake and made a couple of rounds before changing to the Kokanee Candy. I stripped hard and fast like I was told, and even had a few hits, but caught no fish. I switched back to my Metallic Caddis and headed towards the boat ramp, and caught a foot long Atlantic salmon. That was a good way to end a day of fishing. I loaded my gear on the trailer while chatting with another fisherman who was waiting for his buddies to come off the lake. They had the car keys and were over an hour late. He was not too happy and wanted to get his lunch out of the locked car. On the drive west I had a burger in Sisters, but was too tired to drive home and decided to camp the night on the Metolious River. I slept in my car in the group camping parking area down river from Camp Sherman.

October 6, 2012

I got up early to avoid paying camping fees and headed down the road, past the fish hatchery, to the Highway 99 Bridge on the Metolious River. The sky was clear and it was very cold, but surprisingly there was no frost. I soaked my frozen wading boots in the river to soften them before putting them on.

Metolious River, Oregon

I'd heard rumors of a very nice hole up river a mile or so and headed up the west side trail to find it. The lower river was much more fishable than the upper river. There were more long pools and riffles. I put on a weighted Possie Bugger and Pheasant Tail dropper and indicator nymphed a few good looking runs. My rod guides froze with ice after every few casts so I gave up fishing and hiked almost to the hatchery, scouting for good water. I had a Saturday evening meeting back home so I called it quits around noon and headed

back to the car. The drive home was nice in the afternoon sun. I try to take advantage of the good weather whenever I can.

October 20, 2012

I was invited to enter the "clipped fly" contest sponsored by the Royal Treatment Fly Shop in West Linn, Oregon. The premise of the contest was to tye a fly with five secret materials, we were given five minutes earlier, in front of several judges and the public. We were given twenty minutes to tye a fly. The competition lasted several weeks and fifty tyers entered the contest. Some of the secret materials included a tennis ball, potato chip bag, latex balloon, fly line and other odd items. I moved up the ranks by beating seven other tyers.

Clipped Fly Contest, West Linn, Oregon

In the final tye-off I faced ten year old George Marshall – a very good fly tyer. My last fly was a folded foam extended body parachute grasshopper. George tyed a hair-wing sheelhead pattern. I won the contest and received a $500 Winston rod and $500 Simms waders. George was a good sport and said "I'll see ya next year" with a smile as his parents took him to soccer practice. That kid has got a future in fly tying.

October 26, 2012

I made my first trip back to Las Cruces, New Mexico since graduate school to receive New Mexico State University's 2012 Outstanding Departmental Alumni Award.

November 3, 2012

We had our fourteenth Pacific Northwest Fly Tyers Rendezvous in Troutdale, Oregon. I've been the tyer chair the past seven years. We had a pretty good turn-out and had a great time.

November 8, 2012
I'd been encouraging Henry Hoffman the past few years to convert his 35mm slides to digital format. He finally made the conversion and we invited him to give a presentation to the Washington County Fly Fishers club about how he developed the modern genetic dry fly hackle. After his presentation I offered to record his presentation as an oral history and he accepted.

Hal Gordon and Henry Hoffman, Aloha, Oregon

Henry came to our home early Thursday morning. We connected a microphone to my computer and recorded Henry's voice as he gave a slideshow about how he developed the super grizzly hackle. Henry is one of the nicest and humblest men you'll ever meet. He has had a significant role in making fly tying and fishing what it is today.

November 19, 2010
I fished the Trask River with Paul Skelton. Even though it was in between spring and fall salmon runs, too early for steelhead, and closed for searun cutthroats, we decided to float the river anyway. We wanted to see how many Chinook were spawning. We borrowed Gordon's drift boat, hired a shuttle from Tillamook and put in at Stones Camp. We did not see spawning salmon the first mile. The second mile there was a run of shallow water over gravel and cobble and we began seeing fish. Several fall Chinook were in the thirty pound range and pretty beat up. There were lots of redds and it looked like a successful spawning season. We took a few casts in the

deeper holes and runs hoping for a Coho but had no luck. We took out at Upper Peninsula.

Trask River, Oregon

The shuttle guy forgot to take his fifteen dollar fee out of the windshield visor so we met and paid him in town.

November 16, 2012
Winter comes on slowly in the Pacific Northwest. In the first part of November it rains for a few days intermingled with a day or two of sunshine. When the forecast projects a full week of rain then summer is over and it's time to tye flys or wait for winter steelhead to arrive on the coastal rivers. When the weatherman predicted a couple of partly cloudy days I knew it was time to fish the Deschutes River one last time for the year. I talked Paul Skelton into paying for a half a tank of gas and we were at Mecca, near Warm Springs, a little after eight in the morning. Two other vehicles were parked at the trailhead. While we were putting on our waders, two more pick-up trucks pulled into the parking lot. I was not concerned; we were going to use our center-pin rods and fish completely different water than the Spey casters. I took a few casts at the boat launch with no luck. I was fishing a heavily weighted Possie Bugger with a #14 Peach Glo Bug egg pattern. We hiked downstream about a quarter mile and drifted several hundred yards of relatively slow, three to four feet deep, flat water. A traditional fly rod could not effectively fish this water because the fish could be anywhere and it would take hours to cover all the underwater structure to find fish. A center-pin could easily cover the water with very little effort. After a couple dozen casts my indicator went down, I set

the hook and a large fish jumped several times out of the water about thirty yards downstream. I could see he was a very large trout or a steelhead. I brought him to within a rods length and tried to beach him on a grassy bench. He broke off. It was going to be a good day. The next good run was below an island where the water ran over shallow gravel and converged into deep water near the shoreline. I fished the egg pattern deep and hooked another large fish. He was strong and pulled line out for the first minute until he headed towards the middle of the river and upstream. I had him in my hands a couple of minutes later, a large sucker.

Sucker, Deschutes River, Oregon

I released him and worked my way to the top of the run, hooking and losing two smaller fish. As I was working my way back downstream, I let my egg drift into the seam between the fast and slow current. My indicator went down and was pulled underwater towards midstream. I set the hook on another large fish. I did not get too excited, thinking it was another large sucker vacuuming up eggs. I was wrong. When I got the fish within a rods length he rolled on the surface. It was a beautiful dark crimson red steelhead. When he saw me he took off across the river. It was another five minutes before I got him close to shore. By now two other fishermen were watching me from shore, offering to help land the fish. We finally beached him on the grassy shore, took a few pictures and released him. I took a short break and savored the moment. Paul and I walked down river, fishing a couple of other runs and picked up a couple more suckers. Apparently they were near shore feeding on Chinook redds. Just above the Peter Ogden crossing I picked up another

steelhead and immediately lost him in the fast current. In front to the House Hole I hooked and landed another large sucker.

Steelhead, Deschutes River, Oregon

I'd had enough of suckers for the day and exchanged the center-pin for a Spey reel and began swinging a #6 Night Dancer though the run. A half dozen casts later I was into another big fish who swept my line to mid river. He was powerful and I struggled with him for several minutes. When I beached him I was disappointed to find a foul hooked five pound sucker. That was enough for me. I had a sandwich under a tree while I watched Paul make a few more casts before calling it quits. Large black clouds were rolling in from the southwest when we got back to my car and we took off our waders, just before the rain hit. The rain quit when we were about half way through the Warm Springs Indian Reservation. We had hamburgers at Calamity Jane's in Sandy and were home before nine o'clock.

November 23, 2012
Paul Skelton invited Tom Wideman, Gordon Zander, and I to fish Three Rivers on the Oregon coast. It was dry in Hillsboro but by the time we reached Tillamook it was like passing through a wall of water. I'd guess it was raining about half an inch an hour. We got soaked getting out of the car and while putting our rain coats on. We parked in beautiful downtown Hebo and walked downstream a couple hundred yards to fish. The river was running a little high and off color. I rigged up my center-pin rod and began casting into a good run. It was the day after Thanksgiving and a few other fishermen beat us to the prime

holes. Paul caught a nice sea-run cutthroat and the rest of us got skunked. We headed north on the highway. Both the Wilson and Trask Rivers were getting muddier by the hour so we gave the Kilchis River a try. The water was clear, but high and swift. We cast for an hour and called it quits. It was still too early for winter steelhead, and the few remaining summer steelhead and fall Chinook were not cooperating.

December 7, 2012

Today we fished the Trask River. Paul Skelton offered to drive and we were on the North Fork of the Trask at sun-up. It was a steady drizzle and the river was rising. We fished below the bridge a little over a mile up the canyon. This was not the best run, but the high water made it a good bet that fish were holding close to shore rather than mid-stream. This run had a lot of slow, deep bank water, and looked fishy. I fished the near bank with my center-pin and had a few hits from what were probably small cutthroats. Paul did well casting to the opposite side of the river and caught a beautiful eighteen inch sea run cutthroat.

Sea Run Cutthroat, Trask River, Oregon

We fished another hour and headed downstream to the Trask County Park Hole. This water was too high and we could not get a good drift. Both the lower Trask and Wilson Rivers were blown out. Next we headed to the fish hatchery on North Fork of the Nehalem River. The river was perfect, grey green and below flood stage. The only problem was the number of fisherman. They were standing about a cast apart for about a half mile. We saw three steelhead on the bank, but that was not enough to convince us to stay and fish. The rain kept coming down and waterfalls started

to form in the solid rock. A little after noon we called it a day and had lunch at Camp 18 on the drive home.

North Fork Nehalem River, Oregon

Heavy rain was forecast for the rest of the week. We were lucky to get a couple of hours of fishing in before the deluge.

December 15, 2012

Paul Skelton and I headed back to the Trask River for another shot at winter steelhead. It was snowing at the Coast Range summit and it was coming down thick. We only had a few short hours before the roads got bad. We put our center-pin rods together at the Trask County Park and headed to the river. Paul hooked and landed a chunky three-pound jack steelhead on the third cast. He drifted a purple plastic worm along the far side of the river, and the fish took it behind a large boulder along shore. Now it was my turn. I cast at the top of the run and let my rig drift about four feet deep along the current seam. Half way through the drift my indicator headed sideways underwater. I slowly lifted the rod and set the hook. A large buck steelhead felt the sting of the hook and exploded out of the water, shaking his tail two feet in the air. He headed deep into the main current and I was forced to chase him downstream. He rolled on the surface several times and clearly showed his chrome sides and dark back. With the current in his favor he stripped line off my reel and I did not get an inch of line back on my reel. He swam behind a large submerged rock and broke my leader. I sat on a rock to catch my breath, feeling a little worn-out. It started to snow. We quickly headed up the North Fork and made a few more casts before heading home. Highway Six was a disaster. Trucks and cars were piled in the foot-deep snow up along the summit. Tow trucks and the county sheriff were hauling off vehicles. Paul and I snuck through the traffic in all the commotion and were on the east side of the mountain before they shut the road down for the afternoon.

December 24, 2012

No one fishes on Christmas Eve, so we had to go. It had not rained for several days and the water level was down to fishable. Paul Skelton and I hit the road early and arrived at the Trask River County Park at first light. Paul announced that he would hook a fish within three casts, and he did. He landed a bright three pound Steelhead Jack, who was hiding behind a large boulder off the far shore.

Trask River, Oregon

We fished the park run for another hour before heading up to the first hole on the North Fork. On my first cast I hooked a sea-run cutthroat that was hanging next to a deep drop-off at my feet. We fished a couple more runs up river with no luck. On the drive home we had an early dinner at Alice's Restaurant and celebrated Christmas with the kitchen help. We were their only customers.

December 31, 2012

To celebrate New Year's Eve we fished the Trask River. A couple of other guys were poking around the river, but they did not appear to know what they were doing. They probably were trying out new gear they got for Christmas. Paul Skelton and I started at the county park and then headed one mile up the north fork. I fished downriver until I heard Paul yelling for help. He hooked a very large

Steelhead and I maneuvered down river to help him land the fish. I got within a rod's length several times before the fish broke off. He was a big chrome bright 30 inch fish with a dark blue topside. We were both disappointed. Next we fished the Gravel Pit Hole and picked up a pair of skinny foot-long sea run cutthroats. We gave up on the Trask and fished the Wilson River, near the rest area, on the drive home. We caught no more fish.

2013

January 5, 2013

Tom Wideman and I fished the usual runs on the Trask and Wilson Rivers. The water and weather were perfect, but the fish were either high in the watershed or still at sea. We spooked two dozen elk in a forested pasture about four miles up the Trask canyon. We called it quits early and were home by mid-afternoon.

February 7, 2013

Weekday mornings Dean Larson has breakfast at McDonalds in Bozeman, Montana. He didn't seem too surprised to see me when I walked through the door at 6am. Dean and his retired fishing buddies reserve the back table and hold court to solve the world's political problems and plan fishing trips. The diverse group includes a couple of retired Montana State University professors, a sheriff, a homeless guy (who sleeps in his van down the street), a few government workers and assorted businessmen – all of which like to fish. I've had breakfast with this group during the first part of February for most of the past ten years. After breakfast, I talked Dean into a road trip to visit the headquarters of the Federation of Fly Fishers in Livingston, Montana. We visited several fly shops enroute and made several purchases from the discount bins. Fritz Girtz, an acquaintance of mine from Vancouver, Washington, passed away last year, and his family donated several hundred pieces of framed fly art to FFF. Dozens of the frames were on display and Dean and I spent a couple of hours looking at the flys, taking photos and visiting the FFF special collections library. The picture frames on the walls had to be straightened every time a freight train passed behind the old second story office building and shook everything in the building. Dean and I hit several more fly shops in Bozeman on the way home.

February 8, 2013

I talked Bob Kloskowski into a day of fishing, even though he was getting over a bad cold. "The cold air will do you good" I promised as we headed through Virginia City, Montana to the Ruby River. We parked below the dam and rigged up our rods with indicators and nymphs. The sun was shining early in the morning but it was still below freezing – I'd guess about 25 degrees. The first two fish took an hour to locate and were sluggish in the cold water. Bob took them both on a weighted #18 Pheasant Tail Nymph about three feet below a small plastic indicator. My first fish was a foul-hooked whitefish. After noon the temperature improved to the low 30's and a few fish actually began rising. Bob and I both began picking up twelve to eighteen inch browns and rainbows. After every few casts we had to clean the ice out of our rod guides. The ice was a small price to pay for the fun we were having. Midafternoon I found the sweet spot of the river. Above one of Bob's favorite deep holes was a three-foot deep riffle running over large cobble stones and gravel. Large juniper trees lined the far bank and a large dead juniper laid half way in the water creating cover for fish. The entire run was less than twenty feet long. I was surprised to see a large stonefly nymph floating down stream. If the nymphs were moving, this was a perfect spot to cast my heavily weighted Possie Bugger. Before my first cast, a large trout took a midge off the surface. Everything looked perfect – and it was. I took my first cast at the tail of the run and immediately hooked a large rainbow. I worked him downstream, to avoid spooking the other fish, and landed him on a snow bank. I held in my hands a dark seventeen inch rainbow. I took another dozen casts before I hooked and landed five more fish in fifteen minutes.

Ruby River, Montana

Bob kept shaking his head, I felt a little guilty about my streak of good fortune. I invited Bob to take a few casts, but he turned down my offer and said "that's your run". That's all it took, I did not catch another fish in that run and we headed upriver toward the truck. I hooked another monster brown that would have gone twenty inches, but he broke off on the far shore in fast water. The smart fish know how to throw a hook. Bob took two more foot-long browns before the sun was off the water and a cold wind started blowing down the canyon. It started to snow on the drive back to Bozeman. Bob still had his cold, but at least he got a little sun shine and fresh air. I promised him he'd feel better tomorrow.

February 16, 2013

I invited Tom Wideman to fish the Deschutes River after looking at the favorable weather report, water levels and hearing that the fishing was fantastic last week. We picked up Vietnamese teriyaki sandwiches along the way for lunch – I don't know why, it was Tom's idea. We began fishing upriver from Maupin, above Longbend Campground. The weather was a perfect 50 degrees with scattered clouds. Tom began fishing the calm water below a long run, and I headed downstream a quarter mile to give him some room. The water was extremely clear and a few midges were in the air. I tied on a #14 Possie Bugger and a #24 CDC midge emerger. I picked up a beautiful 16 inch redsides trout within minutes. He was hugging the bank and took the midge about three feet from shore in two feet of water. Twenty yards upstream a second fish took the Possie Bugger. He was hiding behind a submerged log that created a small riffle.

Redsides Trout, Deschutes River, Oregon

I slowly worked my way up to Tom and picked up a couple more trout and whitefish at the tail of the run, most of them took the Possie Bugger. Tom also caught a few fish. Together, we picked up

another dozen fish before the hole played out. As we were leaving we met two of our other fishing buddies, Paul Keefner and Roger Lehman. We all fished the next run together and picked up a few small whitefish. Tom and I poked around up river around the locked gate will little success, while Roger and Paul headed down river. In the late afternoon the clouds began moving over the ridge and the wind picked up making it difficult to cast.

Deschutes River, Oregon

We called it quits at 4pm and met Paul and Roger for dinner. The only place open in Maupin was the Rainbow Tavern, a seedy, dark place with a couple of local rowdies playing pool. The stuffed deer, elk, and bighorn sheep heads were watching the Sci-Fi channel on cable television in the back of the bar. A couple of construction workers were getting plastered. The waitress brought us some burgers and chili – which were excellent. In the late afternoon we could see dark storm clouds engulfing Mt. Hood. A bad storm and skiers returning home dictated that we take The Dalles route home.

March 7, 2013

I volunteered to help the Oregon Council Federation of Fly Fishers put on their annual Fly Tyers Expo. It was the event's 25th anniversary. I had been attending the event for at least twenty years and tyed there the past eight years. This year I was asked by Jim Ferguson, the Fly Tyer Chair, to be his assistant. After six months of planning we had 200 tyers ready to demonstrate their tying skills. We met dozens of fellow tyers, tyed flys for two solid days and exchanged flys. I won a full brown-grizzly rooster skin from Henry Hoffman at the banquet auction. The bird was one of

Henry's original breeding stock and was mounted in a glass display case. At the end of the event, I was asked to be the Tyer Chair next year.

April 1, 2013
I became a life member of Trout Unlimited.

April 6, 2013
The International Fly Fishers Association planned a spring conclave on the Big Horn River, Montana. I invited Chuck Cooney and Paul Keefner to attend and split the travel costs. Chuck offered to drive his new truck and pull my small trailer with pontoon boats and gear. We left Portland about 5am, visited fly shops in Spokane, Washington and Coeur d'Alene, Idaho and spent the night in Missoula, Montana. It was snowing on Lolo Pass and mostly cloudy and rainy, with some hail, along the drive. The next day we drove to Ft. Smith, Montana on the Crow Indian Reservation. While driving up the river we stopped at the boat take-outs to become familiar with the river and the lay of the land. It was a nice day, partly sunny and about 50 degrees. We rented a place to stay at the Absaraka Fishing Bear Cabins near the 3 Mile take-out. We unloaded our gear, fixed dinner and visited with Bob and Judi Kloskowski from Bozeman, and Andy Killoren from Wisconsin. Several other club members had cancelled at the last minute so our group was limited to six people.

April 8, 2013
We woke up to a blizzard. There was several inches of snow on the ground, strong winds and a cold 27 degrees. We decided the weather was not going to interrupt our fishing trip. The pontoon boats were frozen solid to the trailer so we left them behind. We bundled up, drove the short two miles to the 3 Mile put-in, put our rods together and waded into the storm and began casting. We fished heavy #12 Possie Buggers and #18 Pheasant Tail droppers on 5X tippet. Our rod guides froze solid with ice after every dozen casts and we had difficulty casting. A half hour later, Chuck caught the first fish – a hefty 16 inch rainbow trout. Over the next three hours we each caught fish, mostly browns and one more rainbow. The river was easy to wade in the low winter flows and all the fish were in deep trenches along the transition water. No bugs were on the water and we saw no fish rising. After noon we headed back to the cabin to warm up and have lunch. About 3pm it had warmed up to 33 degrees.

Big Horn River, Montana

We headed back to the 3 Mile put-in and hiked up river about a half mile to fish a short run between two islands. A few fish were rising to midges and I switched to #18 Black Midge Pupa and caught four browns over the next three hours. The fish were lethargic and would not take a fly unless it was put on their nose. Late in the afternoon we had rain, snow, hail, sleet, and gusts of wind. We called it quits around 6pm and headed back to the cabin for a hot meal.

April 9, 2013
We woke to a frigid 17 degrees and freezing rain. About 10am the wind stopped blowing and we headed back to the 3 Mile put-in and hiked up the river about a mile to a long, shallow run called the "landing strip." We were excited to see a few fish rising in the calm water. It was difficult to cast on smooth water with a semi-frozen line so we searched out riffle water. I tied on a #18 Black Midge Pupa and a #22 Grey Biot Pupa dropper and began catching fish. The fish were steady and widely scattered risers. We targeted individual fish and cast ten feet upstream and tried to get a drag-free drift. Many fish were willing and we each caught over a dozen fish. The fish were a little on the skinny side in the late winter, but all were fighters, and averaged sixteen to seventeen inches. Three fourths of the fish were browns, the rest rainbows. Then, in the late afternoon, the hatch was on. We had midges, blue wing olives and a very few pale evening duns. Fish were grouping into pods and I found that slowly swinging a small fly through a pod brought at least one hit. It never

did get above freezing. We were worn out and cold by 6pm and headed back to the cabin. Andy shared goose and venison sausage and ten year aged cheese with the group, and it was very good.

April 10, 2013

We woke up at 6am to clear skies, no wind and 25 degrees below zero. It was cold even looking out the window. We hoped for the best and pulled the boat trailers out into the sun to thaw. About 10am Paul, Andy and I drove up to the Yellowtail Dam put-in and hiked a mile downstream to the "meat hole" below the first island. A small creek around the backside of the island created a deep channel and pool in the main river that held a lot of fish. We each caught a half dozen fish ranging from thirteen to eighteen inches. Andy caught a gorgeous brightly colored eighteen inch rainbow that probably weighted close to three pounds.

Rainbow Trout, Big Horn River, Montana

The fish took small pink scuds, pheasant tails and midge pupa. All flys were fished deep with indicators. At 2pm we hiked back to the put-in to meet Bob and Chuck with the boats. It was a balmy 40 degrees and most of the ice was off the pontoon boats and Bob's drift boat. Bob, Chuck, and Paul shuttled the vehicles while Judi and I set up the boats. Andy stayed behind to fish and shuttle his car back at the end of the day. About a half mile below the put-in I tied on a #18 Black Midge Pupa and a #22 CDC Biot Pupa and hooked a nice brown in two feet of deep calm water along shore. An hour later we all met at the "meat hole" and caught several more fish before floating another half mile down river to the "aquarium". At this time of day we had the river all to ourselves and only two boats passed us in

the late afternoon. The "aquarium" is a 100 yard long flat below shallow riffles with a deep fast channel on the far side. The water is only three feet deep and draws fish during a hatch. We saw dozens of noses in water as fish swam around in pods slurping up midges and mayflies. I took off the #18 pupa and slowly swung the #22 CDC Biot Pupa, targeting individual fish. The fish were willing players and over the next three hours I landed over two dozen 16 and 17 inch browns. We were told there was an unbelievable 10,000 fish per mile in the Big Horn River, I believed it. I caught many fish by letting my fly hold still at the end of a swing, sometimes for over a minute. My guess was that cautious fish would follow the fly, taking a close look in the clear slow water, and take a bite when it held still in the calm current. Other fish would slam the fly on the swing, bend the small hook or break my tippet. I only landed half the fish that took my fly. As the sun dropped toward the Big Horn Mountains it was time to head to the take-out a mile and a half down river. Andy grilled bear and venison steaks, Chuck baked a loaf of bread and Judi shared brownies for dinner.

April 11, 2013

On our last day on the Big Horn River, we awoke to 40 degree stormy weather. The wind was blowing widely scattered showers through the Big Horn Valley. We decided to do the three mile float from Yellowtail Dam to 3 Mile take-out. A half-mile down river I noticed several fish rising in the shallow flat above the first island. I cast my #22 CDC Biot Midge Pupa to several dozen wary fish, and hooked three brown trout.

Brown Trout, Big Horn River, Montana

The fish were super selective and the cast, tippet, and fly had to be perfect to elicit a strike. I headed down river when the wind picked up and I could no longer see fish rising. The rest of our group occupied the "meat hole" so I decided to fish another mile downriver at the "aquarium." A guide boat was making loops in the run, picking up fish deep-nymphing in the channel and letting the wind blow them back upstream along the shallow flat. I sat down on the bank and watched them fish while eating my lunch. When it was my turn I waded onto the flat and began casting my #22 midge. I could only see fish rising briefly between wind gusts and only caught a few fish. The rest of our group made a few casts and continued downstream. I figured the winds would calm down later in the evening and I took another break on shore. About 3pm the winds subsided and pods of fish appeared from the depths. The fishing was excellent and I had the run to myself. I hooked a dozen fish and landed a couple of them. The fish were strong and it was fun to get a tug and let the fish run before putting pressure on them. In the late afternoon I made a mad dash back to the take-out just as it was getting dark. It had been an enjoyable and productive day.

April 12, 2013
We said our good byes to Bob, Judi, and Andy and Chuck, Paul, and I headed home at 5am. We took the southern route home and visited several fly shops in Livingston, Bozeman, West Yellowstone, and Island Park, Idaho. We spent the night in Twin Falls. The next day we made it home late in the afternoon.

May 4, 2013
Our daughter Bethany graduated from Utah State University, Cum Laude, with two degrees: History and Technical Writing. She used my rough journal notes to develop this book for several of her class projects. Our son Grady is working full time at a grocery store and attending Portland Community College part-time.

May 11, 2013
I fished the Deschutes River with Paul Skelton and Chris Roe. The weather forecast was for sunny skies and high clouds in the late afternoon. We were not disappointed, the day was perfect. The salmon fly hatch was ahead of schedule with the early season warm temperatures and low water

flows. We drove downriver to Mack's Canyon and fished the "pipeline" about a mile up from the take-out. I fished a #10 Black Foam Stonefly and a #14 Softhackle dropper. I was surprised at the number of caddis on the trees, the bugs were very early this year. I caught a couple of 10 inch smolt within an hour. A few larger fish were rising twenty yards out, but the water was too fast for them to hold there, so it was a waste of time to cast at moving fish. All my fish were caught about ten feet from shore below the overhanging trees. My best fish on the day was a surprise. I was randomly casting upstream in four foot intervals, starting from the shoreline and working further out into the river. I took a short cast and my fly disappeared in a swirl. I set the hook and the fish exploded across the river into the fast current. I had four pound line and let the fish run, not wanting to test the line's breaking strength. I followed the fish downstream, ducking under several tree limbs and finally working the fish into a small back eddy. He was a fat 18 inch redsides trout, stuffed to the gills with adult stoneflies.

Redsides Trout, Deschutes River, Oregon

The hook popped out of his jaw as soon as he was in the net. I took a quick photo and released him. That fish was worth the trip. Over the next hour we caught a few more smolt before working our way up river to Beavertail Campground. Paul stayed behind to dry out his pants and Chris and I headed to the river. I immediately caught two 12 inch rainbows near the put-in. I caught up with Chris above the meadow, just as he was landing a very nice 17 inch rainbow. We fished up river until we came to poison ivy, four feet tall, which blocked the trail. We worked our way back to Maupin and ironically got a flat tire near Wreck

Rapids. After a quick tire change we had hamburgers at the Oasis Resort. On the drive home we shot a few cans with Paul's new .45 handgun in the National Forest and were home by 10pm.

May 14, 2013
I was invited by Tony Reeser to attend the Flyfishers Club of Oregon's annual auction. We had a great time and my three fly boxes in the auction got a good price. The club raised over $15,000 and made donations to fishery student scholarships, the Native Fish Society and several other conservation activities.

May 16, 2013
The Deschutes River salmon fly hatch was coming to an end. Tom Wideman and I played hooky from work and made an early trip over the mountain to the river. We chose Oak Springs as our starting point. We walked down river on the railroad tracks to the confluence of the White River. We poked our flys in a few holes along the way, but we mostly wanted to be the first to fish the run and pool near the railroad trestle. We were not disappointed. I tied on a #10 Black Foam Stonefly with a #16 Possie Bugger dropper. A few fish were rising below a large rock/gravel riffle that dropped off into a deep, slow pool. I quickly hooked a large trout that jumped three times as it headed down river into fast water. I could not stop him on my four pound tippet and he broke off. I was disappointed but pleased to have hooked into a quality fish. In a few minutes I was into another big fish. We battled for about ten minutes, fighting each other in the strong current.

Redsides Trout, Deschutes River, Oregon

I brought him to the net several times before he struggled again down river. I finally cornered him between two grass lined semi-submerged boulders and got him in the net. He was a gorgeous 18 inch redsides trout. My third and last fish came ten minutes later. He was a bit smaller and put up less of a fight. Tom also hooked and lost a large fish as it ran towards the middle of the river. After a break for lunch we headed back to Oak Springs. We wanted to fish the "outflow" of the hatchery but a few novices were working through the area. I chatted with them briefly and suggested they cast into the foam line that surrounded a deep slot below some fast riffles. They made a few casts, ignored me and left, not taking our generous advice. We watched them fish upstream covering a good half mile in an hour. It was obvious they were not taking the time to read the water and look for bugs and rises. Tom and I thoroughly fished the "outlet" slot and picked up another dozen foot-long trout over the next half hour. Next we headed to Maupin for ice and a snack. We drove up river from town with hopes of taking a few more casts, but the wind began blowing and made it difficult to cast. We headed back towards Portland. We spent an hour scouting Still Creek near ZigZag, but were disappointed with the number of cabins along the river and the lack of access.

May 18, 2013
The Washington County Fly Fishers had a club trip to Rock Creek Reservoir, on the east side of Mt. Hood. The fish were stocked weeks before and the fish came easy. I fished an intermediate line and a #12 Cary Special. I caught three dozen foot-long rainbows before getting bored and headed to the northeast bay to catch hold-over trout from last year. I was not disappointed and began catching 17 inch fish. I cast in between the tall water weeds in the old stream channel running down the middle of the bay. I saw two 5 pound trout jump out of the water chasing large Callibaetis mayflys, but gave up on them after an hour. We called it quits as the sun was going down. Chuck and I had hamburgers at Calamity Janes, in Gresham, on the drive home.

June 1, 2013
I had a chance to fish with John "Montana" Bartlett and Teri Beatty (from the Flyfishing Club of Oregon). We fished for carp on the Columbia

River. John runs a blog called "Carp on the Fly" and is a serious and very successful carp fisherman – in fact he excessively fishes for carp. We met at 8:30am in Hood River, Oregon and crossed the Columbia River and suited-up at the first pond, heading east, in Washington state. We could see a few fish, but they were not feeding. We proceeded to the next back-water lake. We parked high up on the highway grade and below saw a few feeding fish and dozens of cruising carp. Some of the fish were over twenty pounds. John recommended we wait a little longer for the water to warm up (carp prefer 65 degree water) and we continued east to a flat on the Columbia River. We parked and crossed the rail road tracks and hiked a short distance down a steep rocky slope to the river. The sky was mostly high clouds with sun breaks. The wind was blowing about 5-10 mph and causing slight riffles on the water. Both clouds and wind are not good for carp fishing. As we walked the silt and gravel flats we saw few fish. John said we would find the most fish on shallow silt flats and the bigger fish on gravel flats. We spooked a couple of fish not seeing them before they saw us. The river bottom was littered with broken clam shells and small round disturbed areas in the mud where carp had been feeding. John said this was a good place in May and June to fish a "berry" fly, under the overhanging brush along shore. We waded in water up to our thighs and gave up after a fruitless hour. We returned back to the second lake and walked down the rail road tracks. As we headed to the far end of the lake we saw large fish were everywhere and we restrained ourselves from stopping and taking a few casts. We were surprised by a west bound train and forced to crouch down a few feet off the tracks on the steep rocky slope. The train blew dust and gravel on us as the engineer expressed his displeasure by wailing on the trail horn. We survived and continued down the tracks, paying more attention to our surroundings. We finally reached a wade-able flat and broke a path through the thick blackberry bushes that covered the steep grade to the lake. We waded through soft mud to a small peninsula called "carp alley". Fish were everywhere. We rigged up our rods and began casting at feeding carp. I was fishing a 8-weight, nine foot rod with floating line. I used a nine foot, ten pound, tapered leader. I fished two flys, the first a #8 Beaded Magenta San Juan Worm and second a #8 Hybrid olive barbell worm/soft

hackle dropper. The flys were about 20 inches apart, allowing them to be cast in front of a fish where they could be seen on both sides of the fish. John gave us the three rules of carp fishing: 1) Do not cast until you can identify the head of a feeding fish, 2) Your fly must be presented 6 to 8 inches slightly in front of the fish. You may have to "drag and drop" the fly if your cast is off target. Carp prefer a falling fly inches from their noses and will not chase a stripped fly, and 3) Target and cast to individual fish. If you apply all three rules and a carp makes a short pause, slight head turn or drops its head – set the hook. I applied John's rules and after a few failures at a dozen fish, hooked my first carp. I saw the carp 30 yards away, in two feet of water. She was heading directly toward me. As she got close I made a short cast, maybe 15 feet, and put the fly two feet in from of her. The fly fell right on her nose and I set the hook as she sucked it in. John said a carp can suck food in ten inches away and expel non-food in less than one second. The hook up was solid and the fish made my reel sing as she peeled out twenty yards of line in less than five seconds. Anything less than a seven-weight rod would not have stopped this fish. It was a challenge to keep her out of the thick weeds a hundred feet from shore, but I was successful. After a ten minute tug-a-war I brought her to John's net and we brought her to shore.

Carp, Columbia River, Oregon

She was just short of ten pounds and bronze-gold in color. A beautiful fish. While landing the fish I lost the interchangeable soles of my wading boots, and found them later stuck in the muck after the water cleared. A few clouds began rolling in making it difficult to see fish. It is absolutely essential to have full sun when carp fishing. In the Pacific Northwest, sunny days and 65 degree water can only be found from May to September, with the best months being July and August. Take away the wind and there is excellent carp fishing in the Columbia Gorge. John said the carp get bigger, but less abundant, the further you go down the Columbia. He also mentioned excellent carp fishing in the Tri-Cities, Washington and Boardman, Oregon areas, but thought the Hood River to The Dalles was a good stretch of water. We continued to look for feeding fish, with their heads down, as a storm cloud rained on us for a few minutes. We resumed fishing during the preceding sun break and I was into another large carp. He weighted eight pounds (which John said was average) and took the San Juan worm. Over the next three hours Terri and I hooked almost a dozen carp.

Carp, Columbia River, Oregon

Terri got the biggest fish just shy of 12 pounds. We kept John busy slogging through the muck netting our fish. We saw over 200 fish and could have caught more if there were fewer clouds and less wind. On the hike back to the car we stopped on the Columbia side of the rail road tracks and spotted a huge carp feeding ten yards out from the rip-rap, in three feet of water. John claimed the fish and quickly slid down the steep slope to the river. Teri and I watched from above as John stocked, cast, pricked and lost the fish. The fish would have gone over twenty pounds. At the car we had an excellent lunch that Teri had prepared. Teri left after lunch to attend a wedding in Portland. John and I headed back up the river to the flat we had fished earlier, but opted not to fish it because the wind was blowing and creating

white-caps. We headed back to the Oregon side of the river and fished a sheltered bay west of Hood River. We fished for about an hour and cast to a couple dozen large fish. They were not feeding. Finally, John found a solitary willing fish and after a struggle landed a massive 15 pound carp. John said the Columbia River was full of carp, you just had to find shallow flats or a shelf next to a steep slope or rip-rap. Shoreline trees and brush were also good indicators of quality carp habitat. The difficult part of Columbia carp fishing was finding easy river access to good fishing areas without walking miles of stream bank. John was fairly secretive about his fishing locations and asked that we not take photos where our locations could be identified by others. He was not guarded because he did not want others to fish, but because he did not want the archery carp hunters to find his favorite spots and shoot the biggest carp. He put it best by saying "I will *show* you my best places to fish, but not *tell* you about them". I thanked John for an excellent trip and education, and we went our separate ways. I believe I'll be chasing more Columbia carp in the future.

Last Entry
A journal is never finished, only abandoned. This concludes my first fifty years of journal entries. However, I fully expect to have many more opportunities to fish and write. The biggest problem with keeping a journal is that it is difficult to write the last entry. To avoid this dilemma, here is the last entry in advance: My life has been blessed with a beautiful wife, honorable children, and great friends. I was able to acquire a good education and meaningful employment throughout my life. I've been able to fish in some of the most beautiful, well cared for parts of the world. Have hope for the future, learn from the past and fish each water like it was your last. I thank God for my life and its many blessings and trials.

Fly List

Adams Parachute *
Beadhead Soft Hackle
Black Gnat Parachute
Blow Fly
Blue Wing Olive, Parachute
Borden Special
Brassie
Caddis Pupa
Carey Special *
Carey Bugger
CDC Comparadun
CDC Biot Emerger
Chernobyl Ant
Cinnamon Caddis
Clark's Stonefly *
Coffin Fly
Comparadun
Copper and Hare
Copper John *
Crazy Charley
Damsel Nymph
Deer Hair Mouse
Deer Hair Parachute Drake
Devil Damsel
Disco Midge
Dolly Lama
Egg, Globug
Egg Sucking Leech
Elk Hair Caddis *
Emerger, BWO
Emerger, PMD
Extended-Body Parachute Drake
Foam Ant
Flash Fly
Flashback Scud, Orange
Foam Beetle
Foam Cricket
Foam Hopper
Foam Popper
Foam Stonefly
Freight Train
Glo Bug
Green Butt Skunk
Green Rock Worm
Grey Ghost
Griffiths Gnat
Hares Ear
Hex Emerger, Yellow Foam and Deer Hair

Krystal Flash Streamer
Latex Caddis Nymph
Madam X
March Brown Emerger
Metallic Caddis Nymph
Mickey Finn
Midge Pupa
Midge Pupa, Bead Head *
MOAL Leech
Mohair Leech
Muddler Minnow
Orange Spinner
Parachute Ant
Pheasant Tail Damsel Nymph
Pheasant Tail Nymph, Bead-Head Flash-Back *
Possie Bugger *
Purple Peril
Purple Spey
Rabbit Leech
Ray Charles
Renegade *
Renegade, Double
Reverse Spider
Rickards Callibaetis Nymph
Royal Coachman Bucktail
Royal Wulff
RS2
San Juan Worm
Scud
Soft Hackle
Sparkle Pupa
Spruce
Stimulator
Stonefly Nymph, Kauffman's
Stonefly, Parachute
Streetwalker
Sulfur Dun
Tom Thumb
Tyrant Bunny Leech
Tri-Color Damsel Nymph
Wilted Spinach Soft Hackle
Wooly Bugger
Wooly Worm *

* Top ten recommended patterns

Index